ENVIRONMENT, COGNITION, AND ACTION

ENVIRONMENT, COGNITION, AND ACTION

An Integrated Approach

Edited by

Tommy Gärling
University of Umeå, Sweden

Gary W. Evans
University of California, Irvine

New York   Oxford
OXFORD UNIVERSITY PRESS
1991

Oxford University Press

Oxford   New York   Toronto
Delhi   Bombay   Calcutta   Madras   Karachi
Petaling Jaya   Singapore   Hong Kong   Tokyo
Nairobi   Dar es Salaam   Cape Town
Melbourne   Auckland

and associated companies in
Berlin   Ibadan

Copyright © 1991 by Oxford University Press, Inc.

Published by Oxford University Press, Inc.,
200 Madison Avenue, New York, New York 10016

Library of Congress Cataloging-in-Publication Data
Environment, cognition, and action : an integrated approach
edited by Tommy Gärling, Gary W. Evans.
p. cm.   Includes bibliographical references and index.
ISBN 0-19-506220-5
1. Environmental psychology.
I. Gärling, Tommy, 1941–   .
II. Evans, Gary W. (Gary William), 1948–   .
BF353.E489   1991   155.9'1—dc20   90-20046

1 2 3 4 5 6 7 8 9

Printed in the United States of America
on acid-free paper

Preface

Consider the physical surroundings you are in at this moment. Your relations to these surroundings can be characterized from multiple perspectives. For example, you probably have certain affective, emotionally laden responses—I like this room, it's okay, etc.—that are often summarized in the form of a preference.

Another way to conceive of your interface with the physical environment is to focus on how much you know about the environment you are occupying. What objects are on the wall behind you, how many windows does the room have, could you reconstruct from memory the floorplan of the room you are in, the building?

Yet another perspective is to consider your actions in and plans for using the environment. What behaviors are encouraged or inhibited by the setting? What were your goals on entering the place where you are now? To what extent have those plans been accommodated by the environment?

Assessing, knowing, and acting (plus making action plans) are the basic building blocks of an epistemology of place. Within the fields of psychology, geography, architecture, and planning, scholars have begun to investigate how these three processes function in real-world environments.

In the spring of 1988 a small, international conference of psychologists, geographers, planners, and architects was held in Umeå, Sweden. The agenda for that conference was to address the problem of how to understand and research further the integration of assessment, cognition, and action in real-world enviroments. We believe that a fuller, more complete understanding of how human beings interrelate with their physical surroundings necessitates a more integrated analysis of these three basic building blocks of the relationships between humans and their environment. We hope that readers of this volume will take away one or both of the following: (1) a sense of what the current major critical theoretical issues are in each of the three areas of environmental assessment, environmental cognition, and action/decision making; and (2) some ideas about the potential value and direction of a research agenda for the study of the integration of these three processes.

The Umeå conference would not have been possible without the generous financial support of the Swedish Council for Building Research, the United States National Science Foundation (INT-87 12090), the J. C. Kempes Minne Foundation of Sweden, and the University of Umeå. In addition, we are indebted to a number of individuals who made the conference and this volume possible. We especially thank the invited conference participants who worked very hard throughout the various phases of this project. Among other things this group, in the interest of promoting intellectual integration across disparate areas of scholarship, allowed us to take them in a small rubber raft down several large whitewater rapids in a wilderness area outside of Umeå.

We also thank the following individuals for helping us with the organization of the conference: Jan-Åke Åkerlund, Manuel Carreiras, Anita Gärling, Stig Lindquist, Eva Mauritzson-Sandberg, Åke Olofsson, Lennart Sandberg, and last but not least, the late Margareta Json Lindberg, who served as conference secretary. We are also most grateful to Lars-Göran Nilsson, Chair of the Department of Psychology, University of Umeå, for his encouragement and support. Preparation of this volume was facilitated by the work of Stephen J. Lepore on the indexes and the expert, professional assistance of Joan Bossert and the staff at Oxford University Press.

Umeå, Sweden   T.G.
Irvine, Calif.   G.E.
September, 1990

Contributors

Giovanna Axia
Dipartimento di Psicologia dello Sviluppo e
    della Socializzazaione
Università di Padova
I-35137 Padova
Italia

Maria Rosa Baroni
Dipartimento di Psicologia Generale
Università di Padova
I-35137 Padova
Italia

Anders Böök
Department of Psychology
University of Umeå
S-90187 Umeå
Sweden

David Canter
Department of Psychology
University of Surrey
Guildford
Surrey GU2 5XH
United Kingdom

Michael K. Conn
Program in Environmental Psychology
Graduate School and University Center
City University of New York
33 West 42nd Street
New York, New York 10036

Gary Evans
Program in Social Ecology
University of California
Irvine, California 92717

Tommy Gärling
Department of Psychology
University of Umeå
S-90187 Umeå
Sweden

Reginald G. Golledge
Department of Geography
University of California
Santa Barbara, California 93106

Mark Gross
College of Environmental Design
University of Colorado
Bolder, Colorado 80309

Roger A. Hart
Program in Environmental Psychology
Graduate School and University Center
City University of New York
33 West 42nd Street
New York, New York 10036

Rachel Kaplan
School of Natural Resources
University of Michigan
Ann Arbor, Michigan 48109

Stephen Kaplan
Department of Psychology
University of Michigan
Ann Arbor, Michigan 48109

Rikard Küller
Environmental Psychology Unit
School of Architecture
Lund Institute of Technology
S-22100 Lund
Sweden

Lynn S. Liben
Department of Psychology
Pennsylvania State University
University Park, Pennsylvania 16802

Erik Lindberg
Department of Psychology
University of Umeå
S-90187 Umeå
Sweden

Gary T. Moore
School of Architecture and Urban Planning
University of Wisconsin–Milwaukee
Milwaukee, Wisconsin 53201

Erminielda Mainardi Peron
Departimento di Psicologia Generale
Università di Padova
I-35137 Padova
Italia

Christopher Spencer
Department of Psychology
University of Sheffield
Sheffield, S10 2TN
United Kingdom

Harry Timmermans
Department of Architecture
Building and Planning
University of Technology
5600 MB Eindhoven
The Netherlands

Gunilla Torrell
Department of Psychology
University of Göteborg
P.O. Box 14158
S-400 20 Göteborg
Sweden

Gerald D. Weisman
School of Architecture and
Urban Planning
University of Wisconsin–Milwaukee
Milwaukee, Wisconsin 53201

Craig Zimring
College of Architecture
Georgia Institute of Technology
Atlanta, Georgia 30322

Ervin H. Zube
Department of Geography and
Regional Development
University of Arizona
Tucson, Arizona 85721

Contents

ENVIRONMENT, COGNITION, AND ACTION

Environment, Cognition, and Action: The Need for Integration

GARY W. EVANS AND TOMMY GÄRLING

What we know and understand about our surroundings influences our evaluations of and behaviors in the physical environment. In addition, our reasons for using places, our goals and personal plans, bias the manner in which we acquire and store knowledge of places. The extent to which places afford the goals and plans we bring to them also affects environmental assessments. How much we like a place is colored by how well it meets certain functional objectives. Yet scholarly analysis of each of these topics has proceeded largely in isolation.

The principal objective of this volume is to promote more thinking and analysis about the integration of these three, heretofore largely distinct areas of scholarly inquiry—namely environmental cognition, environmental assessment, and decision making and action in real-world situations. We are not attempting a broad theoretical integration across the many realms of human-environment studies as outlined for example in *The Handbook of Environmental Psychology* (Stokols & Altman, 1987).

Throughout the present volume there is a distinctly cognitive bias, emphasizing the role of cognition as it influences assessment and action rather than studying how action or assessment might impact cognition. This cognitive perspective reflects the editors' own intellectual training (experimental psychology) and also mirrors the current predominant view within each of the three areas of inquiry we investigate. However, as we discuss throughout this volume, this cognitive perspective may detract from a fuller understanding of how and in what way people interrelate with their physical surroundings (see also Saegert & Winkel, 1990, for a sociocultural critique of the cognitive perspective in environmental psychology). Furthermore, we focus our analysis of cognition, assessment, and action at the individual level rather than aggregating responses intended to characterize the environment at a societal or group level.

Given that the principal objective of this volume is to promote integration across three areas of scholarship that have operated largely in isolation from one another, we begin by first describing each of these three main areas of inquiry. This is followed by a brief analysis of some preliminary attempts at integration. We conclude with a description of how the present volume is organized.

ENVIRONMENTAL COGNITION

Environmental cognition encompasses the cognitive processes involved in the acquisition and representation of predominantly spatial information in real-world settings (Evans, 1980; Golledge, 1987; Moore, 1979). Real-world settings differ from the stimuli used in most psychological investigations. Real-world stimuli occur in some spatial and temporal context, typically surround the observer, and involve a user who is interacting with the space in a dynamic way (Ittelson, 1973). Moreover, the person trying to develop or utilize a cognitive representation of a real-world space usually is doing so in concert with one or more plans that involve actions in the setting. Information from the environment is selected and processed in the context of purposeful actions (Gärling & Golledge, 1989; Miller, Galanter, & Pribram, 1960).

Most research on environmental cognition has examined one of three major issues. The first issue is: What is the nature of people's cognitive representations of physical space in actual environments? Propositional models of representation have emphasized schematic aspects of spatial representations that provide organizational frameworks and general rules for storing information about spatial relations in actual environments. Most people have general rules about spatial knowledge that they apply to real-world spaces. For example, most of us expect city blocks to be parallel and for street intersections to occur at 90 degree angles. Confusion results when the schematic expectations are violated. Moreover, when people recall spatial information, it is typically distorted in the direction of the general prototype—intersections are made perpendicular, gradual curves become straight roads, and so on (Evans, 1980). We are also influenced by superordinate categories such as districts, or countries. Distance judgments within a superordinate category, for example, tend to be underestimated relative to judgments across the boundaries of two superordinate categories (Evans, 1980).

People also have schematic representations for familiar, well-used environments. They develop cognitive maps that include information about important features of the geographic environment such as landmarks, path systems, and subareas or districts (Appleyard, 1976; Lynch 1960). These maps are indispensable for facilitating planning and actions but reveal various distortions.

Cognitive representations of real-world settings also include analogue or second-order isomorphic qualities. For example, comparative judgments about distances or relative positions in space are made in forms that reflect some rough correspondence to actual spatial arrays in the environment (Evans & Pezdek, 1980).

The second major topic of research in environmental cognition has been individual differences in the formation and accuracy of cognitive maps. To date, considerable research has examined the effects of experience or familiarity, gender, age, and, to a lesser extent, culture on environmental cognition. As we discuss later, the effects of age and experience in particular seem critical to the development and maintenance of cognitive representations of real-world environments.

The final topic of interest has been how physical elements in the environment affect environmental cognition. Environmental features such as landmarks or pathway configurations affect the acquisition and storage of spatial information in the environment. Moreover, design guidelines have begun to emerge on how best to locate and configure landmarks, streets, and interior spaces to facilitate wayfinding (Evans, Smith, & Pezdek, 1982; Gärling, Böök, & Lindberg, 1986).

ENVIRONMENTAL ASSESSMENT

Most research on environmental assessment has focused on individuals' evaluations and descriptions of the quality of the ambient environment (Craik & Zube, 1976; Kaplan & Kaplan, 1982). This research has converged on two and possibly three underlying dimensions of environmental assessments. These dimensions are pleasure (e.g., like–dislike, approach–avoid), arousal, (e.g., boring–interesting), and potency (e.g., spacious–cramped) (Canter, 1977; Ward & Russell, 1981). Some researchers have examined individual differences in such assessments and descriptions of settings. Among other topics, important differences have been uncovered in the environmental assessments of trained design professionals and the public, respectively.

Another major research topic has focused on comparisons of various simulation techniques with in situ presentations (Smardon, Palmer, & Felleman, 1986). Generally, simulations work well although limitations have been uncovered when working with children and for static, nondynamic simulations for certain types of situations. Simulation research is limited by some methodological problems. For example, there is a notable absence of results on divergent validity. Furthermore, nearly all of the simulation validation research suffers from monomethod bias, depending solely on pencil-and-paper measures.

Finally, the physical characteristics of settings can influence environmental assessments. Among some of the more important physical variables are complexity, coherence, naturalness, mystery, and enclosure (Kaplan & Kaplan, 1989; Craik & Feimer, 1987). Complexity refers to the number and variety of different elements in a scene, whereas coherence describes the degree of underlying structure or organization of those elements. Naturalness is defined as the amount of natural elements present in a setting. Good vistas, the degree of partially visible areas and spaces (mystery), and enclosed or small, well-defined, and bounded spaces are all associated with more positive assessments of real-world settings.

ACTION

In research on environmental cognition and environmental assessment, investigators assume that the individual receives information from the external environment that results in a psychological response. On the basis of this response, some output, termed action, occurs. The existence of motives, goals, and attitudes toward action alternatives is taken for granted, and the psychological responses or processes mediating between external environment and action are made a primary focus of research.

Outside of environmental psychology there is a fairly extensive literature on how individuals make decisions about how to choose and act in real-world environments (Golledge & Timmermans, 1988; Timmermans & Golledge, 1990). Such actions have been conceptualized as a process in which an individual perceives and forms preferences for different action alternatives (e.g., destinations for travel). He or she then decides which alternative to choose according to some decision rule that takes into account preferences for the alternatives as well as constraining factors (e.g., budget). Finally, the individual implements the choice in overt action. Cognitive factors such as previous experience, perceptual and representational abilities, hierarchically organized goals, and decision rules are assumed to affect the representation of the environment as well as individual choices and their implementation. Because actions in the environment are viewed as the implementation of decisions, the decision-making process, rather than action itself, has been the primary area of investigation. The formation of plans and their influence on actions in the environment is one topic of increasing interest.

One question several investigators have been interested in is how individual goals and objectives influence travel plans and decisions. For example, if an individual needs to reach X destinations and purchase Y goods, how does one solve this problem and how is the solution influenced by time constraints, geographic layout, available transportation modes, and so forth (Gärling, 1989; Gärling, Böök, & Lindberg, 1984)? Some salient environmental characteristics that influence route selection are distance, amount of goods to be carried, price and produce quality, and ease of access to target goods and services.

INTEGRATION OF COGNITION, ASSESSMENT, AND ACTION

Investigators in environmental cognition and in environmental assessment have not by and large integrated work on decision making and action with the respective processes they have studied. Moreover, there has been very little direct exchange between investigators focusing on environmental cognition and environmental assessments, respectively. The major task of this book is to promote integration among these three areas of research. We also propose to layout a research agenda, highlighting important topics that warrant further work and, where possible, make preliminary attempts to discuss how such research might be executed.

Probably the most important rationale for integration is that understanding each of these important psychological processes of environmental cognition, environmental assessment, and decision making and action will increase if we can fathom the actual contexts in which they normally operate. If one accepts the initial arguments presented in this chapter about how these processes might interrelate, then it is unrealistic to consider each of these processes strictly in isolation from the others. It is difficult if not impossible to imagine human functioning in the real world devoid of goals or purposes, without knowledge of the immediate physical surroundings, or with no affective response. What we know, how we feel, and how we plan and execute our actions in the world may be better understood by thinking more about how these activities and processes interrelate.

Integration may also be valuable because it forces a more synthetic analysis that may reveal points of convergence and divergence among the three topics of scholarly inquiry. Thought about these points of intersection may help illuminate correct and incorrect models and hypotheses.

An integrative framework may also enable researchers to analyze dominant issues from a fresh perspective and thus increase the opportunity to shed paradigmatic constraints that are overly constraining or perhaps even incorrect. It is also likely that greater methodological variety will occur when problems in one area are addressed from a different perspective.

Integration may also serve certain pedagogical objectives, better enabling students to understand the topics of a subject like environmental psychology. Practitioners may also benefit since they are often interested in questions of a broader scale, such as what makes an environment good or bad for people.

The remainder of this chapter presents a brief overview of some preliminary attempts to integrate across more than one of the three research areas. Both the paucity of integrative research plus the near total restriction of such research to two of the three areas are noteworthy.

Cognition and Assessment

Kaplan and Kaplan's (1982, 1989) model of assessment rests upon human motivations to make sense out of one's surroundings and involvement, or interest, in the environment. Environments that facilitate these two motivational properties are highly preferred by observers. Making sense is determined primarily by coherence and legibility. Coherence is the amount of information presently available in a setting that conveys organization, or underlying structure. The utilization of greater inference to comprehend distinctiveness and develop rich imagery, termed legibility, also augments preference.

Involvement, or the extent to which people are interested in a setting, is the other major dimension underlying environmental assessment in the Kaplan's model. Complexity, the amount of diversity and variety, is a major determinant of involvement. Moderate levels of complexity are associated with more positive environmental assessments (Berlyne, 1971; Wohlwill, 1974). Some settings also elicit exploration by promising further information. Mystery is a powerful variable in predicting evaluative judgments of real-world scenes. Concrete examples of mystery might include a bend in a road or a partially occluded clearing. In each case the viewer perceives that there is more to the scene that can only be discovered by gathering further information (Kaplan & Kaplan, 1982, 1989).

The balance between making sense and involvement largely determines environmental assessments. Human beings like settings where predictions are possible but not trivial (Kaplan & Kaplan, 1982). When all the information about the contents and meaning of a setting is immediately available, the setting is boring. People like to solve problems, to make inferences. Coherence and legibility foster comprehension making prediction possible. Complexity and mystery introduce sufficient uncertainty and challenge to make the situation interesting, to allow for meaningful prediction.

Although it seems reasonable that the schematic, representational structures that individuals have for particular types of spaces or classes of objects should influence environmental assessments, there is surprisingly little empirical or theoretical research on this topic. Purcell (1986) has begun to investigate this topic. In one analysis he found that individual assessments of churches were a function of the discrepancy between a particular exemplar of that category of buildings and the person's prototypic model of what a church should look like. Church designs representing slight deviations from the prototype were rated more positively than were church designs of greater discrepancy from the prototype.

Another instance in which cognition and assessment are linked is when environments do not provide adequate structure and distinctiveness to achieve well-formulated cognitive maps (Zimring, 1982). Orientation and wayfinding are important factors in postoccupancy evaluations of settings. Getting lost or being disoriented is aversive for most people and colors their affective evaluations of settings. For example, a major complaint of visitors to hospital patients is their inability to find their way in the hospital (Shumaker & Reizenstein, 1982). Users of mass transportation systems frequently report displeasure with maps and other orientation aids as well (Bronzaft, Dobrow, & O'Hanlon, 1976).

Both positive and negative affect influence approach and avoidance of places, which in turn may impact environmental cognition. Fear of crime in the elderly restricts mobility and exploration, which in turn is negatively associated with size and complexity of cognitive maps (Carp, 1987; Lawton, 1980). Children are more likely to visit places they like (e.g., candy store, playgrounds), and such elements are recalled more often on children's drawings of their neighborhoods (Hart, 1979).

Cognition and Action

The connections between cognition and action have received only scant attention. In one preliminary study Walsh and his colleagues (Walsh, Krauss, & Regnier, 1981) uncovered linkages between elderly urban residents' knowledge of their neighborhoods and their patterns of neighborhood use. The frequent underutilization of local services and resources by the elderly was associated with poor cognitive maps. Both levels of detail and specific, systematic distortions of path systems and cardinal directions can be partially explained by individual vectors of movement through the environment. Predominant patterns of use can frame an orientation perspective, positioning a cognitive map in a certain spatial plane (Evans & Pezdek, 1980). Transportation system routes can also strongly influence knowledge about place (Appleyard, 1976; Canter, 1977; Gärling, Böök, & Ergezen, 1982).

Assessment and Action

When people enter a setting, they usually do so for a reason. How well a particular setting facilitates the execution of plans to meet various goals is an important component of assessment. Theoretical models of underlying functional dimensions in places include access and convenience, comfort and security, social interaction, exploration, and rest. Environmental assessments can be explained in part by knowing the relative salience of these factors to the individual using a specific place and how well the space provides for these needs (Canter, 1977; 1983; Genereux, Ward, & Russell, 1983; Ward & Russell, 1981).

Cognition, Assessment, and Action

To our knowledge there is only one preliminary study of the interrelations among cognition, assessment, and action. Ward, Snodgrass, Chew, and Russell (1988) manipulated subjects' plans for using an unfamiliar office space and measured individuals' affective and cognitive responses. Individuals were given instructions emphasizing one of four possible uses of the space: wait, explore, spy, or redecorate. In the wait condition, subjects were asked to wait briefly while the experimenter prepared another room for the experiment. In the explore condition subjects were asked to learn as much as possible about the setting. Participants in the spy condition were asked to imagine that they had to hide sensitive materials while in the space, and finally those in the redecorate condition were instructed to imagine that the office space was their own and they could redecorate it.

Persons in the redecorate condition found the room significantly less pleasant and relaxing than the other groups did. On measures of recall and recognition memory for objects in the room, the explore group performed significantly better in comparison to the other groups. Although the study utilized a setting for a short duration of time (subjects were told they would be in the room for five minutes) and relied on some plans of questionable ecological validity, the results are nonetheless very important. What people expect to do in a space can substantially influence their assessment and cognition of that space.

ORGANIZATION OF THE BOOK

Table 1.1 provides a schematic diagram of the organization of the book. Across the top of the table are the three major research topics of interest: environmental cognition, environmental assessment, and action in real-world settings. Down the side are three perspectives or approaches that have often been employed in research on the three research topics.

The three perspectives we have employed to organize the material in this volume reflect an underlying paradigm in the field of environmental psychology. This paradigm assumes that the physical environment is an important variable that affects human behavior and wellbeing. These effects are mediated by underlying intraindividual processes. Finally, according to this paradigm, individual differences help shape the manner in which these mediating processes function. This paradigm is reflected in the organization of the three perspectives used throughout to examine each of the major research areas of cognition, assessment, and decision making and action.

Table 1.1 Organization of the Book

Part	Environmental cognition	Environmental assessment	Action	Integration and application
Physical environment	Chapter 2	Chapter 3	Chapter 4	Chapters 5 and 6
Psychological processes	Chapter 7	Chapter 8	Chapter 9	Chapters 10 and 11
Life-span development	Chapter 12	Chapter 13	Chapter 14	Chapters 15 and 16

The first perspective, *physical environment,* focuses primarily on how aspects of the physical environment impact cognition, assessment, and action. The physical parameters of objects, their arrangements in space, and the overall organization of features in settings influence assessment, cognition, and decision making and action in real-world environments. Examples of physical properties discussed in the chapters include complexity, landmarks, route configurations, land-use compatibility, size, mystery, thematic structures, and sociocultural and symbolic elements.

Authors of each chapter in the three main topic areas of interest were asked to describe the major conceptual issues within one of these three respective topics as they relate to the physical environment. The authors were not asked to integrate material across the three research domains but rather to identify and discuss key issues and questions that might assist in promoting such integration. In addition to highlighting conceptual issues, each of these three authors was asked to discuss what kinds of research should be given priority in the future. Thus critical analysis and discussion make up the bulk of these chapters. It is important to state clearly, therefore, that complete or even representative literature reviews are not part of this volume. Instead, we have encouraged the presentation of issues and ideas within each chapter that the author believes might provide the foundation for integration across the three domains of cognition, assessment, and decision making and action in real-world settings.

Following the three chapters focusing on how the physical properties of settings influence cognition, assessment, and action, respectively, there are two integrative chapters. The first of these provides a summary of the major conceptual issues raised in the three preceding chapters, includes some critical commentary on these issues, and explicitly addresses integration across cognition, assessment, and action. The second integrative chapter discusses how the issues raised by the preceding authors can be applied to environmental design, planning, and public policy. In addition, this second author points out what kinds of knowledge and research issues should be given priority in future work in light of application needs and problems. Thus in each major section of the book, integration across the three research areas is most directly addressed in the two discussion chapters, particularly the conceptual one.

The second and third parts of the book are organized in the same way, with three chapters, each devoted to one of the three research topics of cognition, assessment, and action, followed by a conceptual integration and an applications and policy chapter. The second part focuses on *psychological processes* mediating between the environment and behavior. What are the psychological processes involved in perceiving and knowing, assessing, and acting in real-world settings? A central component of this perspective has been how cognitive, emotional/motivational, and physiological processes work and what the implications of their modes of operation are for knowing, evaluating, and acting in real-world environments. Information processing models, transactional perspectives, and functional/evolutionary views are reflected in this second section of the book.

Part III emphasizes a *life-span developmental* perspective on cognition, assessment, and action. This perspective on individual differences is the most developed theoretically within the field of environmental psychology. As we shall see below, it also represents a particular approach to understanding the nature of the human–physical environment interaction. What we perceive, what we like, and how we act are determined in part by underlying biological and cognitive changes that occur as a function of time but also in the organism's constructive engagements with his or her physical and psychosocial world. Thus a life-span perspective emphasizes processes of behavior that are dynamic and interactive, with multiple and reciprocal causal factors.

The last section of the book provides a summary and conclusion. Major issues raised within each of the three subareas of research are summarized, followed by some integrative discussion. Salient issues in application are reviewed as well. Finally, this last chapter concludes with a research agenda.

REFERENCES

Appleyard, D. (1976). *Planning a pluralistic city*. Cambridge, Mass: MIT Press.

Berlyne, D.E. (1971). *Aesthetics and psychobiology*. New York: Appleton-Century-Crofts.

Bronzaft, A., Dobrow, S., & O'Hanlon, T. (1976). Spatial orientation in a subway system. *Environment and Behavior, 8,* 575–594.

Canter, D. (1977). *The psychology of place*. London: Architectural Press.

Canter, D. (1983). The purposive evaluation of places. *Environment and Behavior, 15,* 659–698.

Carp, F.M. (1987). Environment and aging. In D. Stokols & I. Altman (Eds.), *Handbook of environmental psychology* (pp. 330–360). New York: Wiley.

Craik, K., & Feimer, N. (1987). Environmental assessment. In D. Stokols & I. Altman (Eds.), *Handbook of environmental psychology* (pp. 851–918). New York: Wiley.

Craik, K., & Zube, E. (1976). *Perceiving environmental quality*. New York: Plenum.

Evans, G.W. (1980). Environmental cognition. *Psychological Bulletin, 88,* 259–287.

Evans, G.W., & Pezdek, K. (1980). Cognitive mapping: Knowledge of real world distance and location information. *Journal of Experimental Psychology: Human Learning and Memory, 6,* 13–24.

Evans, G.W., Smith, C., & Pezdek, K. (1982). Cognitive maps and urban form. *Journal of the American Planning Association, 48,* 232–244.

Gärling, T. (1989). The role of cognitive maps in spatial decisions. *Journal of Environmental Psychology, 9,* 269–278.

Gärling, T., Böök, A., & Ergezen, N. (1982). Memory for spatial layout of the everyday physical environment: Differential rates of acquisition of different types of information. *Scandinavian Journal of Psychology, 23,* 23–35.

Gärling, T., Böök, A., & Lindberg, E. (1984). Cognitive mapping of large-scale environments: The interrelations of action plans, acquisition, and orientation. *Environment and Behavior, 16,* 3–34.

Gärling, T., Böök, A., & Lindberg, E. (1986). Spatial orientation and wayfinding in the designed environment: A conceptual analysis and some suggestions for postoccupancy evaluation. *Journal of Architectural and Planning Research, 3,* 55–64.

Gärling, T., & Golledge, R. (1989). Environmental perception and cognition. In

E.H. Zube & G.T. Moore (Eds.), *Advances in environment, behavior, and design* (pp. 203–236). New York: Plenum.

Genereux, R., Ward, L.M., & Russell, J.A. (1983). The behavioral component of the meaning of places. *Journal of Environmental Psychology, 3,* 43–55.

Golledge, R. (1987). Environmental cognition. In D. Stokols & I. Altman (Eds.), *Handbook of environmental psychology* (pp. 131–174). New York: Wiley.

Golledge, R., & Timmermans, H. (1988). *Behavioral modeling in geography and planning.* London: Croom Helm.

Hart, R. (1979). *Children's experience of place.* New York: Irvington.

Ittleson, W. (1973). Environmental perception and contemporary perceptual theory. In W. Ittelson (Ed.), *Environment and cognition* (pp. 1–20). New York: Seminar.

Kaplan, R., & Kaplan, S. (1989). *The experience of nature.* New York: Cambridge University Press.

Kaplan, S., & Kaplan, R. (1982). *Cognition and environment.* New York: Praeger.

Lawton, M.P. (1980). *Environment and aging.* Monterey, Calif.: Brooks/Cole.

Lynch, K. (1960). *The image of the city.* Cambridge, Mass.: MIT Press.

Miller, G.A., Galanter, E., & Pribram, K. (1960). *Plans and the structure of behavior.* New York: Holt, Reinhart, & Winston.

Moore, G.T. (1979). Knowing about environmental knowing: The current state of theory and research on environmental cognition. *Environment and Behavior, 11,* 33–70.

Purcell, A. (1986). Environmental perception and affect: A schema discrepancy model. *Environment and Behavior, 18,* 3–30.

Saegert, S., & Winkel, G. (1990). Environmental psychology. *Annual Review of Psychology, 41,* 441–477.

Shumaker, S.A., & Reizenstein, J. (1982). Environmental factors affecting inpatient stress in acute care hospitals. In G.W. Evans (Ed.), *Environmental stress* (pp. 179–233). New York: Cambridge University Press.

Smardon, R.C., Palmer, J. E., & Felleman, J. (1986). *Foundations for visual project analysis.* New York: Wiley.

Stokols, D., & Altman, I. (1987). *Handbook of enrvironmental psychology.* New York: Wiley.

Timmermans, H., & Golledge, R.G. (1990). Application of behavioral research on spatial problems: II. Preference and choice. *Progress in Human Geography, 14,* 311–359.

Walsh, D., Krauss, I., & Regnier, V. (1981). Spatial ability, environmental knowledge, and environmental use: The elderly. In L. Liben, A. Patterson, & N. Newcombe (Eds.), *Spatial representation and behavior across the life span* (pp. 321–360). New York: Academic.

Ward, L.M., & Russell, J.A. (1981). The psychological representation of molar physical environments. *Journal of Experimental Psychology: General, 110,* 121–152.

Ward, L.M., Snodgrass, J., Chew, B., & Russell, J.A. (1988). The role of plans in cognitive and affective response to place. *Journal of Environmental Psychology, 8,* 1–8.

Wohlwill, J.F. (1974). Human adaptation to environmental levels of stimulation. *Human Ecology, 2,* 127–147.

Zimring, C.M. (1982). The built environment as a source of psychological stress: Impacts of buildings and cities on satisfaction and behavior. In G.W. Evans (Ed.), *Environmental stress* (pp. 151–178). New York: Cambridge University Press.

I

THE IMPACT OF THE PHYSICAL ENVIRONMENT

The authors in this section were asked to write about how the physical environment impacts assessment, cognition, and action, respectively. Some researchers in each of these subfields have framed their research questions in this way. For instance, Craik and Feimer (1987, p. 891) state that "establishing dependable predictive relations between descriptive attributes of places and how they are evaluated and used provides the ground for advancing our understanding of environment-behavior transactions and affords the basis for improving the planning, design, and management of our environment." These authors view knowledge of the relations between environmental assessments and descriptive attributes of places as valuable both for addressing practical questions and for advancing our understanding of the processes engaged in assessments. This view certainly extends to the subfields of cognition and action.

We have elicited three initial chapters from researchers whose own work has examined the impact of the physical environment on assessment, cognition, and action, respectively. All three of these contributors appear to hold views similar to Craik and Feimer's. Perhaps, partly for this reason, none of them was prepared to fully accept the usefulness of our simple view that there exists a physical environment with measurable properties that can be shown to affect some measurable psychological response. More of the discussions than we had expected are devoted to mediating, psychological processes. As a consequence, there is considerable overlap in the foci of Parts I and II. We note this overlap not as a criticism, however. It may in fact reflect an important, underlying dilemma within environmental psychology: What is the appropriate stimulus (or set of stimuli) to consider? Each author acknowledges the importance of investigating how psychological processes are linked to environmental stimuli. Nevertheless, perhaps because consensus may be low about what these stimuli are, the authors continue to examine the mediating processes.

In Chapter 2 Rachel Kaplan notes the difficulty in separating physical features of environments from perceptual or conceptual features. The problem would perhaps be less if the physical environment was defined as molecular, consisting of well-defined stimuli impinging on the individual. The environment of interest to environmental psychology is, however, the molar physical environment (Proshansky & O'Hanlon, 1977; Russell & Snodgrass, 1987; Ward & Russell, 1981). Thus, it becomes nearly impossible for R. Kaplan to discuss the impact of the physical environment on assessment without reference to mediating psychological processes. Much of her discussion is consequently focused on the process of how people conceptually categorize their environments. The differences between experts' and laypeople's categorizations are also discussed, and an interesting parallel is drawn between such differences, on the one hand, and differences between assessments of physical and psychological attributes of the environment on the other hand. Furthermore, the evaluative component of assessment, as distinct from what may be termed descriptive assessment, is discussed and through the key concepts of purpose and prediction is related to descriptive assessment.

In a similar vein, Reginald G. Golledge in Chapter 3 finds it difficult to treat the theme in the simple way in which we conceived it. As noted earlier in our introductory chapter, a main focus of research on environmental cognition is how spatial properties of the environment are cognized. Physical features of the environment clearly influence the accuracy of cognitive representations of real-world spatial information, as demonstrated by, for instance, Appleyard (1969, 1977), Evans, Smith, and Pezdek (1982), and Lynch (1960). After a review of the complexities entailed in conceptualizing the molar physical environment, Golledge takes a broader view on the relationship between the physical environment and environmental cognition. He asks three critical questions: (1) How do concepts used to conceptualize the physical environment enter into people's constructions of this environment? (2) Are people's constructions isomorphic with those concepts from which they evolve? (3) Are the concepts a sufficient basis for answering questions concerning how people encode, store, recall, and use environmental information? It is clear from Golledge's subsequent review that these questions are addressed in varying degrees in all research on environmental cognition.

Action is not a well-defined subfield of research in environmental psychology. In Chapter 4 Harry Timmermans reviews the conceptual underpinnings of the current, rather extensive research on spatial choices in physical environments. Examples of such everyday spatial choices are the choice of a new residential location, the choice of shopping locations to patronize, and the choice of locations for leisure activities. This particular area of research is largely outside environmental psychology and is more closely connected to cognitive research on decision making (Slovic, Lichtenstein, & Fischhoff, 1988). Because action or choice is viewed as the implementation of decisions, the decision-making process rather than actions themselves becomes the primary focus. The paradigms and models developed in this area make possible an analysis of actions in terms of the cognitive—and to some extent, affective—processes entailed by decisions preceding actions. Because this analysis is typically detailed and precise, it is perhaps inevitable that it appears somewhat narrow. This approach can be contrasted to other approaches to action in Parts II and III (Chapters 9 and 14).

A salient goal of research on spatial choice is to provide data that can be used at the planning stage for predicting the impact of changes in the physical environment on people's choices. Naturally, the variables that can be controlled in planning are those whose impact one would like to predict. These variables tend to be spatial–physical features such as distance and layout rather than specific physical elements such as form, light, color, and texture, which are of more immediate interest in assessments research within environmental psychology. Like the other chapter authors, Timmermans notes that, even though the practical goal may be to predict choices from manipulable physical features of environments, the main interest of research is to find out what factors (in the physical environment or not) people take into account in the decision-making process underlying spatial choices. Both research problems and methodological issues discussed by Timmermans naturally reflect this interest. The question of how to reconcile it with the practical prospect of relating spatial choices to variables in the physical environment becomes, however, very salient throughout the discussion. For instance, whether expressed preferences for different alternatives truly reflect actual, revealed preferences is for this reason an interesting methodological issue.

Even though none of the chapter authors were prepared to discuss the more narrow question of the impact of the molar physical environment on assessment, cognition, and action, they have nevertheless illuminated the important role of the physical environment for psychological adjustment. Our efforts in environmental psychology of trying to reveal this role is clearly worthwhile. Views on what directions we should take were also expressed, thereby providing valuable input to the chapters by Craig Zimring and Mark Gross (Chapter 5) and Ervin H. Zube (Chapter 6).

REFERENCES

Appleyard, D. (1969). Why buildings are known. *Environment and Behavior, 1,* 131–156.

Appleyard, D. (1977). *Planning a pluralistic city.* Cambridge, Mass.: MIT Press.

Craik, K.H., & Feimer, N.R. (1987). Environmental assessment. In D. Stokols & I. Altman (Eds.), *Handbook of environmental psychology* (Vol. 2, pp. 891–918). New York: Wiley.

Evans, G.W., Smith, C., & Pezdek, K. (1982). Cognitive maps and urban form. *Journal of the American Planning Association, 48,* 232–244.

Lynch, K. (1960). *The image of the city.* Cambridge, Mass.: MIT Press.

Proshansky, H., & O'Hanlon, T. (1977). Environmental psychology: Origins and development. In D. Stokols (Ed.), *Perspectives on environment and behavior* (pp. 101–129). New York: Plenum.

Russell, J.A., & Snodgrass, J. (1987). Emotion and the environment. In D. Stokols & I. Altman (Eds.), *Handbook of environmental psychology* (Vol. 1, pp. 245–280). New York: Wiley.

Slovic, P., Lichtenstein, S., & Fischhoff, B. (1988). Decision making. In R.C. Atkinson, R.J. Herrnstein, G. Lindzey, & R.D. Luce (Eds.), *Stevens' handbook of experimental psychology* (Vol. 2, pp. 673–738). New York: Wiley.

Ward, L.M., & Russell, J.A. (1981). The psychological representation of molar physical environments. *Journal of Experimental Psychology: General, 110,* 121–152.

2

Environmental Description and Prediction: A Conceptual Analysis

RACHEL KAPLAN

Environmental assessment is a basic tool in numerous professions and occupations. Anyone whose business it is to modify an existing situation must necessarily take into account what is already there. The existing situation might be a region, a site, a building, a room, or even a bookshelf: in any event, it constitutes a physical setting that must be understood in terms of what is there. The assessment of the physical environment is equally central to occupations that require movement through space. Pilots, navigators, and taxi drivers depend on such spatial considerations, as do individuals whose livelihood stems from sports, both team and individual.

The centrality of environmental assessment, however, is not limited to such occupational contexts. Assessment of the physical environment is a pervasive process. It is an ongoing, usually nonconscious, ingredient of wakefulness. Only when the opportunity for sensory input is removed is this activity temporarily halted. In fact, impairment to any single sense modality leads to the realization of how much one depended on that source of input to assess the physical world. The good things as well as the bad, the interesting and the mundane, the important and the trivial, and even the neutral ones all rely on an assessment of the environment.

Given the broad range of issues that this topic encompasses it is not surprising that there is a considerable literature focusing on different kinds of settings, on legal mandates, on methods, and on application. This chapter does not attempt to do justice to all these concerns. In very general terms, I have chosen to explore the following domains: (1) what is important, (2) what is valued, (3) by whom, and (4) for what? These questions, however, are so interrelated that they do not lend themselves to a systematic discussion. Instead, the chapter is organized into two major topics: Description and Prediction.

The section on *description* examines the perception or experience of the environment. Two key concepts discussed in that section are categorization and the question of what is important, both inherent aspects of description. The section on *prediction*, by contrast, brings in the issue of "assessment for what?" The two key concepts in that section are, therefore, the purpose of the assessment and the question of what is valued, both inherent in the predictive process. Central to both description and prediction are the questions of who decides what to include in the assessment and how the decision is made. This necessarily brings in the central role of expertise in environmental assessment.

The concluding section of the chapter explores three domains that require further attention: (1) Both description and prediction are guided—and possibly misguided—by unexamined assumptions. (2) The selection of attributes for the assessment can be strengthened by theory. (3) The role of experts in the assessment process is necessary but not sufficient.

Although description and prediction are concepts that apply to any environmental context, and I will use examples from a variety of settings, the chapter draws most heavily on the literature in landscape assessment. The notion of the visual resource and the importance of its management have become accepted in many parts of the world.[1]

The landscape assessment context is also useful for examining the degree to which one can clearly distinguish between assessment that concerns the ''physical'' as opposed to the ''psychological'' environment. It turns out that ''physical environment'' is a far fuzzier concept than first appears. It can be discussed at many levels and proponents of the different levels are likely to disagree. For example, in much of the landscape literature form, line, color, and texture are taken to be the essential elements of the physical environment. On the other hand, one could focus on bricks and leaves, or streams and waterfalls, trees and telephone poles. It would be equally appropriate to assess the landscape at yet another level in terms of forests and parks, farmland, and parking lots. These all entail different levels of organization, but they nonetheless focus on specifiable objects, that is, on the physical. The environment, however, is also often examined in terms of the juxtaposition of such physical objects. Thus concepts such as Complexity or Harmony or Edge Contrast do not refer to specific objects but to their combination. That there are many perspectives on physical measures of the environment need not, however, be a problem or source of concern. As with any natural category (Rosch, 1978), it is far more useful to depend on common usage to acknowledge what we mean by the physical environment than is likely to be achieved by a definition.

ENVIRONMENTAL DESCRIPTION

To describe a place inherently calls for an environmental assessment. The same place can be described in many ways and on many levels, depending on the reason for doing it, the assumed audience, the knowledge of the narrator, communication skills, and so forth. Much of our knowledge is acquired through such environmental description. Newspapers, magazines, literatures, and conversation, as well as professional judgment, all entail such assessments.

Basic to any description is categorization. Both the perceptual process, which provides the basis for description, and the communication process, which provides the format for transferring information, depend on classification. Much of the time none of us is aware of performing such categorization and the choice of categories is not conscious. When misunderstandings occur, or when learning new ways to "see" an environment, the importance of categories is more evident.

Although there are many approaches to environmental description, for present purposes I would like to contrast two that have been useful in environmental analysis. The first is the most prevalent and direct: an inventory of "what is there." Here the classification or categorization process (though not necessarily its rationale) is explicit. The second approach is indirect, permitting the classification to emerge, rather than establishing it at the outset.

Inventory of Environmental Condition

If asked to describe one's present surrounding it is likely that the description will highlight specific elements or objects. The room I am in contains file cabinets, bookshelves filled with books arranged vertically and stacks of files that are horizontal, a large desk barely visible beneath the array of paper, books, and colorful notes. There are two lamps and a telephone on the desk as well as small canisters filled with colored pens. The view from the room to one side is to the dining room and living room and through the window to the grassy area across the street. In the other direction the view through a large window is to the garden. The description could be quite lengthy as there are many specific objects that might be enumerated and these could be described in varying degrees of detail (e.g., the content, size, and color of the books, as opposed to mention of books as a category). The description could also be quite abbreviated: one might simply classify the room as a "study."

A carpenter's description of the same room is likely to be totally different, though elements and objects would still be the basis for the description. The type of window, the wood paneling, the wooden door into the room, the inset bookcases and cabinets with no visible hardware, the narrow folding door into the adjacent bathroom, the style of trim around the doors and windows might all be included in this context.

Environmental decision making generally requires an assessment of "existing conditions" before recommendations are made for modification. This too entails an inventory of the objects and elements in the setting. What is included in the inventory can be expected to be influenced by professional training. The need for such inventories arises in so many contexts that procedures become accepted and standardized. Numerous examples of such procedures for describing a region are included in *Foundations for Visual Project Analysis* (Smardon, Palmer, & Felleman, 1986). In the United States several federal agencies (e.g., U.S. Forest Service, Bureau of Land Management, Soil Conservation Service, Federal Highway Administration, Army Corps of Engineers) have developed detailed procedures for recording the visual resource. Each has a somewhat different format, as do comparable systems used in parts of Australia, Canada, and Great Britain.

Despite their differences, however, these various systems all identify specific features in the environment that are coded for their presence. Features that might be included in such landscape assessments include landform, vegetation, water, and land uses, among many others. Depending on the scale of the project, numbers of trees and their diameter and canopy type might also be recorded. In some cases, the inventory is not only of the myriad "things" in the environment, but also describes these in terms of other considerations. For example, the "Visual Environmental Assessment Form,'' used by the State of New York in its Environmental Quality Review, codes the various land uses, landforms, featured attractions, and even featureless aspects in terms of their distance from the viewer, seasonal variation, context of likely visibility, and compatibility with adjacent environment (Smardon, 1986).

The reason for providing this much detail here is twofold. First, it provides some imagery of the magnitude of the task. To do justice to the description of the physical environment is an arduous, extensive, and ever-expanding task. Proliferation of categories is likely to occur as there are so many justifiable items to include in the assessment. Second, the decision about *what* to include in the assessment has important consequences. Implicit in such decisions is a theory of ''what matters.'' Before one permits modification to the environment, one must know what will be impacted. The decision to assess landform or soil type or architectural diversity all involve categories that are selected because of their presumed importance. In other words, inherent in these procedures are experts' models of human values.

Although inventories that are based on such expert-generated systems generally emphasize physical aspects of the environment, the approach does not dictate that decision. Descriptive assessments can also include more psychological features of an environment in addition to the physical characteristics. The inclusion of ''scarcity'' or ''uniqueness'' in the U.S. BLM (1980) system, for example, can be viewed as not purely physical.

Küller's (1988) demonstration of the role of furnishings in the well-being of institutionalized dementia patients is most instructive in this context. A considerable number of properties in this setting could be inventoried without a useful outcome. One could count how many chairs, dressers, and tables are present in the room, how many pieces of furniture there are, how many are made of wood, how many are plastic, how much the room is ''soft'' or ''hard,'' and so on. Küller's work, however, had a psychological dimension: The familiarity of the type of furnishing was hypothesized to be the aspect of the environment that would matter to these aged individuals. The furniture inventory could easily have omitted categorization in terms of the period of the furnishings. In other words, a notion of what might be important to these patients led to a different approach to furnishing the rooms, and to remarkable changes in their ability to function.

The work of Christopher Alexander (Alexander, Ishikawa, & Silverstein, 1977) also provides a particularly intriguing example of environmental description that goes well beyond the enumeration of ''things'' in the environment. At one level it is an inventory of elements—253 ''patterns''—that describes physical entities (''A garden seat,'' ''Road crossing,'' ''Traveller's inn''). But the patterns describe human values on multiple levels. Even in their names one can appreciate that they identify much more than the physical place itself (''Windows overlooking life,'' ''Work community,'' ''A room of one's own''). As Seamon (1987) points out, ''the significant fact about *Pattern Language* is its provision of reasoned descriptive structures which help to draw a link between human dwelling and the built environment'' (p. 15).

Emergent Categorization

The work of Alexander and his colleagues (1977) provides a useful bridge between the expert-based inventories of the environment and procedures in which the basis for categorization is derived rather than asserted. Although Alexander's own expertise has much to do with the language he has proposed, at the same time the patterns are derived from considerable observation and interaction. The categories that emerged from this process are multifaceted and psychologically rich. They capture a diversity of human values that is difficult to articulate.

The patterns also attempt to capture a way of seeing. It is difficult to appreciate that "seeing" is so much a function of experience. The expert-derived inventories are the outcome of learning particular ways to "see" or categorize. Combinations of elements that for the untutored have no relationship to one another are given a name that shares importance for a professional group. For example, particular window treatments, roof lines, and materials are designated as comprising a distinctive architectural style. Similarly, in other areas of expertise, combinations of "things" become classified in terms of settlement patterns, forest practices, or styles of painting. During the period when one is acquiring such new information and learning to identify the combinations of elements in terms of their new appellation, one may be sensitive to the fact that a new way of seeing is indeed developing. Before long, however, the new terminology is a part of one's vocabulary and what had been a new way of seeing seems no different than the way one had seen things all along. In fact, it may be difficult to see the previously separate, individual components.

All animals have expertise in "seeing" the environment. If expertise is gained by practice and experience, one cannot help become an expert about the environment with which one has continuous involvement. As is true with other areas of expertise, here too one is not aware that one has acquired a way of seeing. The fact that one is not aware of one's perceptions much of the time, and does not even have labels for much that is experienced, makes environmental description more difficult.

How, then, can one find out how people "see" the environment if the process is not accessible to consciousness? This question has been central to our research program for the last 20 years. We have found that a convenient path to learning about environmental perception is through environmental preference. Rather than asking people to describe the environment or to provide them with potential descriptors (e.g., adjective check list), the approach we have used generates categories empirically. Category-identifying methodology (CIM) refers to statistical procedures that extract common patterns or groupings or themes based on empirical data (in this case, preference ratings). These categories, then, give one insight into the perceptual process.

We have written extensively about this approach and by now it has been used in dozens of studies (R. Kaplan & S. Kaplan, 1989). I will, therefore, provide only a brief sketch of the methodology common to these studies, and concentrate on some of the major findings.

In the context of landscape assessment, the CIM paradigm entails a series of "items" (e.g., scenes presented as slides or photographs), preference ratings for each scene provided by a relatively large number of individuals, and the statistical procedures (generally nonmetric factor analysis, often in conjunction with other approaches) to extract categories. Scene selection requires a great deal of attention as the adequacy of *environmental* sampling is a key element to finding common patterns. At one level, the selection of scenes in itself constitutes an assessment of the environment. They are, after all, defined in terms of a priori visual categories (e.g., landcover types). Specifying the domain of the study and ensuring adequate representation of that domain do not, however, prejudge the categories that are *empirically derived* from the preference ratings. Such emergent categories may be based on any number of implicit criteria, such as use, style, or meaning, which may or may not match one's a priori notions.

This may seem to be a risky approach to learning about environmental description. After all, each set of pictures and each new group of raters might lead to new sets of categories (as is likely to be the case with approaches that are based on interviewing individuals about the meaning a particular place holds for them). In fact, the results show strong consistencies, despite the great diversity of visual material that has been studied. The studies have included individuals in several countries, in many regions of the United States, of varying backgrounds, ages, and so on. They have included scenes of many kinds, urban, rural, wilderness, roadside, common and novel.

Examination of the empirically generated categories that have emerged from some 40 studies could be an awesome challenge. As it turns out, however, the categories can be described in terms of two major types. One of these can be described as based on *content* and the other focuses on *spatial configuration*.

The *content-based categories* have as their theme or common characteristic that they deal with classes or types of objects. Any example of such categories is necessarily specific to the domain of a particular study. In Anderson's (1978) study of forest practices, for example, one category that emerged consisted of scenes of Red Pine Forest. Hammitt's (1978) study of visitors to a boardwalk trail in a bog environment generated four categories, one of which consisted of the scenes that included the boardwalk itself. The boardwalk example is consistent with many cases of these content-based categories in that it reflects a balance between human influence and natural aspects. In studies that focus on natural areas (such as Hammitt's), the scenes that have clearer human influence emerge as a common content theme. Conversely, in studies emphasizing built aspects, the more natural scenes emerge as a category. In some instances land use is the clear basis for a category. This is most evident in the case of industrial settings, which often form a single category despite being visually and functionally different (Hudspeth, 1986; Miller, 1984).

In certain respects the content-based categories are akin to the expert-based "items" in environmental inventories, except that many kinds of issues that would be included in inventories have not emerged in these empirically derived categories. For example, even though roads are easily identified, they have generally not been the basis for grouping. Residential settings have also not formed single distinct categories. Although these may reflect a common land use, and a clear human influence, people make many subtle distinctions among residential settings—perhaps a reflection of fine-tuned expertise even on the part of the layperson.

The *spatial configuration categories* are based on the way the elements are arranged in the implied space of the scene. The fact that categories emerge in study after study that have as their theme not the content but the arrangement of the space suggests that individuals are imagining themselves in the depicted area when they produce their preference rating. These categories suggest that an underlying criterion in making a preference judgment (completed in a matter of milliseconds) is an evaluation of the scene in terms of both the presumed possibilities for effective function-ing as well as the potential limitations.

The spatial configuration categories can be grouped along two major dimensions: the degree of openness and the spatial definition. Consistently, scenes that are wide open and lack any particular differentiating aspects emerge as a category. At the other end of the continuum, scenes that are relatively blocked or impenetrable also form distinct categories. Both these extremes have clear implications for wayfinding, for a sense of security, and for effective functioning.

The categories that reflect a high spatial definition, by contrast, include distinctive features, have a greater sense of depth, and make it more likely that one could find one's way there and back. In relatively open settings, spatial definition might be provided by a row of trees. In more forested settings, spatial definition is enhanced by openness or transparency through the canopy.

Even from this hasty summary of the results of the CIM approach it is evident that the implied environmental description is in many respects different from the assessment based on an inventorying approach. The categories are based on charac-teristics of the physical environment, yet they reflect more than the physical setting, providing one with some insight into psychological dimensions of environmental as-sessment.

It thus becomes clear that any approach to description implicitly provides infor-mation about what is considered important. One would presumably not assess build-ing density and style or forest practice or adjacent land uses if these were not salient to some decision. Similarly, implicit importance is evident from the empirically de-rived categories. The fact that settings that are wide open as well as those that are dense and difficult to penetrate consistently emerge as distinct perceptual categories informs one about psychological dimensions that are important to functioning.

PREDICTION

In the preceding section the focus was on description. Much environmental assess-ment concerns such description—whether explicitly (as in expert-based inventory ap-proaches) or implicitly (as in the underlying bases for perceptual categories). In either instance, description reflects what is assumed to be important, within a particular context. Importance implies that one needs to pay attention, but it does not necessar-ily assign value to the implicit categories. The presence of animals in a scene may be important, but whether to consider such a state of affairs to be good or bad depends on the reason for the assessment. Thus the *purpose* of the assessment and the question of assigning value, or evaluation, are closely linked.

It is probably reasonable to assert that most environmental assessment is carried out for a purpose, although the purpose is often not explicit. A colleague wrote recently that the Australian aborigenes describe the landscape in terms of its "inher-ent good resources—good 'tucker' (food) country versus bad tucker country" (E.J. Herbert, personal communication, 1988). A current phenomenon on our campus shows a similar basis, though with a slight variation. Individuals whose survival is based on foraging, urban foraging, make their way across town pushing a shopping cart and collecting bottles and cans that can be turned in at the supermarket for a rebate. College students who are affluent enough to toss these away, rather than "bothering" to collect a dime for each emptied bottle, come in sufficient numbers to provide a niche for the urban foragers. On the first warm day of spring one such individual was pushing his cart across the central campus lawn among the sunning students. His environmental assessment was motivated by the sight of empty soda cans; the need to avoid stepping on people or their belongings was also instrumental in his assessment.

A child's assessment of a somewhat novel setting is presumably also motivated by personal objectives. The location of places where one can hide may be one basis for such assessment while discerning the availability of interesting play objects may also guide the overview. There is no assumption here that these purposes are conscious or even likely to be verbalized. In fact, any response to a request to describe the setting may include neither hiding places nor play objects.

What these examples show is that the reason for assessing the physical environment is likely to affect the choice of attributes. In many cases there is an implicit prediction that certain characteristics will be salient in the context of the given purpose and these, then, are the target of the assessment. Such steps are basic to much human action/decision making (column 3 of the framework undergirding this volume). Human actions and decisions are generally guided by purposes, and assessment is implicit in such plans and actions.

Even though purposes are essential to evaluation, they are frequently multidimensional and difficult to articulate. To determine the adequacy of an evaluation, however, requires being relatively explicit about these purposes or desired outcomes. Those that are relatively easiest to stipulate involve economic or other tangible domains, such as safety. With less tangible purposes the issue of values is often more readily recognized. In fact, purposes necessarily assume values, and values are not always shared by those involved in an assessment. An example that is repeated worldwide on a daily basis involves the stated purpose for land development projects: to increase local economic viability. This may seem tangible and is often accompanied by large numbers. Needless to say, it subsumes values not only with respect to who will gain from these riches, but also with respect to the land that had previously been used for other purposes.

Not only is the purpose or outcome subject to differing views, so also are the proposed indicators that are used to substantiate the assessment. It is useful to look at the question of environmental prediction in terms of these two components: the *predictors* and the *outcome*. The predictors are the attributes that are considered (by someone) to be important factors, singly or in combination, to produce an outcome. The outcome (e.g., scenic quality, preference, satisfaction, viability) reflects the valued end state or purpose. In any environmental assessment both of these components play a role, though often they are not explicitly articulated. Outcomes are often assumed to involve a common perspective, such as safety, maintenance, or scenic quality. The attributes that lead to such results, the "predictors," are also often assumed to be given.

Both components, predictors and outcomes, raise the question of "who decides"? Who designates the standard: who establishes what constitutes a "quality" environment? Just as in the case of decisions about what to include in the inventory of the physical environment, in the case of prediction, in many instances, it is professional judgment that guides decisions both with respect to the outcome (''quality'') and what makes it so. The frequent clashes between citizens and bureaucrats over proposed changes to the environment reflect conflicting notions with respect to desired outcomes and the factors that affect them.

The role of experts is thus central to a discussion of environmental prediction. Here again it is meaningful to examine two approaches: procedures that rely on expert judgment with respect to the selection of these components and those that attempt to determine empirically what is valued. With respect to prediction, however, there is the added dimension of whether any verification is sought with respect to the expert's judgment. These issues are addressed in this section in terms of three models of expert input. First, a view of the expert or professional as knowledgeable and confident about what is valued. In this approach, no verification is sought with respect to either the choice of predictors or outcome. Second, an orientation that invites verification of the attributes that are presumed to be valued. Here experts may select predictors as well as outcome variables, but check to see whether the selections were appropriate. Finally, an approach that attempts to determine empirically what is valued. Although such an approach is implicitly oriented to verification, it nonetheless requires professional judgment both in the initial selection of environmental material and in the interpretation of the results.

Expert Judgment

In many domains one would not question experts' authority and confidence. These individuals have special skills, training, and experience that certify their appropriateness to make judgments. In fact, an expert is often hired precisely because of this knowledge base. When the ''existing situation'' is a tooth and the dentist declares that it needs repair, there is the implicit prediction of dire consequences if such action is not taken and, generally, no discussion about the diagnosis. Although the tooth's owner may have signs of problems, the dentist's standard of a healthy tooth is much better developed.

As we all know experts are not always to be trusted. One would not seek a ''second opinion'' if there were not doubt of its equivalence with the first. Each of the individuals offering the expert opinion, however, may be quite confident of the judgment rendered. They considered the likely factors (predictors) and had some notion of a desired outcome. In a medical context this might entail assessment of symptoms (predictors) and assumptions about a desire for longevity. In a planning context, the predictors may have to do with available facilities and services, and the implicit standard may be some notion of a community's economic viability.

Experts are individuals who have ''know how.'' They know what is relevant and needed, assess the situation, and act on their findings. Whether the basis of their deliberation is articulated varies widely. In many cases, elaborate calculations document the contribution of specific factors in the explicitly stated outcome. In other cases, the ''predictor'' side may be carefully assessed but the outcome or purpose is less clearly stipulated. The opposite pattern also occurs, where the purpose is well defined, but the basis for the judgment is far more intuitive. To a large extent these variations are a function of the field of expertise. An engineer and a music critic, both experts, are likely to approach the issue of "outcome" and "predictors" quite differently.

Explicit Verification

Underlying much expert judgment is knowledge about what is needed and helpful for human well-being. This includes health, safety, accessibility, productivity, aesthetics, and satisfaction (Zube, 1980). Not only do experts trust their judgments with respect to these goals, they often assume that they are more knowledgeable about them than are the humans on whose behalf they deliver these services. Every now and then, however, challenges arise and questions are asked about the experts' accuracy of prediction.

The practice of medicine has changed considerably as a result of such challenges. There was a time when surgery was not a likely procedure because of the lack of expertise with respect to the salient factors (even though the desired outcome was quite clear). Then surgery became routine practice (in certain situations) as experts were quite confident of its success. Still later, some efforts at verification have cast doubt about the appropriateness of the procedures. Such challenges can arise both from unanticipated empirical findings or from a revised perspective of desired outcomes (e.g., survival vs. quality of life).

Let us look at verification in the context of environmental decision making. Although some professionally based assessments are largely systems of inventorying the environmental features deemed to be essential, others are more clearly evaluative (Taylor, Zube, & Sell, 1987, provide several useful examples). In other words, such systems go beyond enumeration of environmental characteristics to a rating system that assigns a value to different levels or amounts of the characteristics.

The approach to Visual Resource Management used by the U.S. Bureau of Land Management provides a good example of such an evaluative system. Scenery is classified in terms of seven aspects (Landform, Vegetation, Water, Color, Adjacent Scenery, Scarcity, and Cultural Modifications). For each of these, a score is assigned, ranging between 0 and 5 in some cases, between 1 and either 5 or 6 in other cases, and between -4 and $+2$ in the case of Cultural Modification (U.S. BLM, 1980). Such numeric ratings constitute predictions of what is likely to be valued in the landscape. The assignment of "0" to the absence of water and "5" to "clear and clean appearing, still, or cascading white water, any of which are a dominant factor in the landscape," is an implicit indication that water is highly valued. Similarly, the decision to assign a maximum of 6 points to "one of a kind, or unusually memorable, or very rare within region" implies that scarcity is greatly valued over commonness.

Much research has concerned verification of such systems and assessment of the role of specific environmental factors in the prediction of scenic quality. Such research has two basic components, corresponding to the "predictor" and "outcome" issues we have been discussing. For the predictors, such studies rely on the experts' judgments. If amount of land, size of trees, or volume of grasses has been identified as a potential predictor, it is professionally assessed and entered into the equation. The "outcome" side generally does not rely on experts. Rather, individuals without specific training in environmental assessment are asked to judge settings (either visually presented or in situ) with respect to the underlying purpose of the assessment (i.e., visual quality or preference). Shafer and Mietz's (1969) study offers an early version of such research; Daniel and Vining (1983) mention numerous other psychophysical studies that have also contributed in important ways.

As was true with respect to environmental description, such studies often rely on physical characteristics of the environment. There is nothing implicit in the methods used in such studies, however, that specifies the nature of the "predictors." The fact that more psychological dimensions of the physical environment are generally not included in these scenic quality predictions is presumably a reflection of the judgments of the experts doing this work as to what is worthy of assessment.

Emergent Criteria

The literature on expertise has amply demonstrated that experts "see" differently. The famous work by de Groot (1965) with chess players, for example, shows that the assessment of the environment (here a chess board) is strongly affected by extensive experience—if the environmental display is meaningful with respect to the area of expertise. In other words, the result of a great deal of experience is a different way of perceiving (here seeing the board in terms of such abstract dimensions as "areas of strength" and "areas of weakness").

Not surprisingly, several studies have found that experts in environmental professions also react differently than nonexperts. Groat (1982), for example, found "strong differences between architects and non-architects in their evaluations of buildings" (p. 17). Architecture students, in contrast to those lacking design training, were also found to have significantly different assessments of the role of site characteristics in the anticipated comfort and livability of simulated residential settings (R. Kaplan, 1987).

Without realizing it, their basis for judging what is important as well as what is valued depends on the experts' specialization. Thus, "good" architectural style may affect judgment of quality of a residential setting for those who are particularly sensitive to this dimension. Adequacy of management of a forest may affect scenic preference for a forester, while a nonexpert would have no way to judge such adequacy (Anderson, 1978).

Given that expertise necessarily affects both perception and evaluation, some experts have opted for an approach that permits them to ascertain what factors predict "outcome," rather than to depend entirely on their own expertise. Implictly, that is how Alexander et al. (1977) developed their pattern language, which incorporates a considerable amount of empirical input and keen observation. Although postoccupancy evaluation studies have often approached the assessment of satisfaction (or livability or effectiveness) of a facility from the perspective of expert panels (Bechtel, 1988), there are examples here too in which the task was approached without prior commitment as to what factors are the most pertinent (Gifford, 1987).

The CIM paradigm has also been instructive in this respect. As we have seen, the empirically derived categories consistently show that nonexperts view scenes in terms of how well one might function in the depicted space.[2] One would expect then that categories that facilitate such functioning would be more preferred, and, indeed they are. Categories depicting blocked settings generally receive much lower ratings than do those where visual and locomotor access seems unhampered (R. Kaplan,

1985). It may not be surprising that notions of comfort, security, and likelihood of wayfinding would be useful predictors of scenic quality. Perhaps it is more surprising that these factors are not evident in the expert-based systems.

Prediction is for a purpose and the purposes, in many situations, relate to human needs and values. Yet the relationship between the predictors and the purpose is often obscure, or insufficiently examined. Verification and exploration of a full range of predictors are, thus, of utmost importance.

CONCLUDING COMMENTS

A bibliography on environmental assessment would be lengthy, even if limited to the more social scientific aspects. It could be organized in terms of environments (e.g., forest, agricultural, dams, urban, residential), legislative mandates, or different professional perspectives (e.g., engineering, design, public health). It could also be arranged in terms of topics addressed in the research literature: How the environment is represented, what kinds of descriptors/predictors are used, what "outcome" variables are specified (e.g., aesthetics, satisfaction, quality), and how assessment is affected by familiarity, knowledge, age, and so on. In fact, a bibliography that addressed only methodological approaches to environmental assessment would in itself be vast. Many of these topics have not been addressed in this chapter. (However, Chapters 5, 6, 10, and 12 address some of them.)

Staying at a more conceptual level, however, has been useful. For me the analysis has highlighted three domains that have both practical implications and potential research thrusts. First, many hidden assumptions guide environmental assessment. Second, environmental assessment leans heavily on the physical aspects of the environment. Third, the role of experts in environmental assessment needs to be viewed with some caution.

Hidden Assumptions

Environmental assessment is fraught with hidden assumptions of many kinds. Description is based on categories, yet the choice of categories is often not explicit. As we have seen, categorization can be studied more directly and the results of such analysis can lead to inclusion of other domains of categorization—generally ones that reflect easily ignored psychological dimensions. Prediction implies purpose, and these purposes are also often insufficiently specified.

Assessment is often guided by what is countable and assumes that if you can count it, it is likely to be important. Even in a regression model, where both the predictors and the outcome are clearly stated, there often are many unstated aspects. The decision to include certain "predictors" often stems from how easily the information can be obtained rather than from an analysis of "what matters." A grid overlaid on a picture makes counting easy. Once one is counting, one may as well include all kinds of things. Computerized data bases, such as geographic information systems, also invite such blindfolded assessments. Neither are the underlying categories examined, nor is the choice of predictors a necessarily reasoned process.

Assessment procedures often make assumptions about what is valued and to what degree. Numeric rating systems may be convenient, but their implicit assumptions about the magnitude of the value of an attribute are rarely validated. Assigning equal values to form, line, color, and texture (Yeomans, 1986) entails such a decision just as much as does the BLM's (1980) procedure of assigning the values of 4, 3, 2, and 1, respectively, to these visual elements. The total score computed in such assessments takes on a life of its own. Decisions about environmental impacts, about hazards of facilities, and about quality of air or water are frequently based on such scores that are constructed of a series of assumptions about the relative value of the attributes assumed to be important.

Purposes themselves are often selected without sufficient attention to the complex and highly interrelated sets of assumptions that underlie them. Economic development frequently serves as an unquestioned purpose for change to the physical environment. Although assessment in terms of visual quality is desirable, it is inappropriate to consider visual quality as a unidimensional desideratum, even if one could agree on a standard. The difficulty of reaching such agreement, however, is an excellent indication of the multifaceted nature of the ''purpose.'' A mall that is ''beautiful,'' but where customers cannot find one's shop, loses some of its charm.

The Psychophysical Environment

There are many good reasons to measure attributes of the physical environment. Even a long list of these, however, is likely to exclude many environmental features that are psychologically pertinent. Despite considerable research on cognitive and psychological aspects, both in the landscape assessment domain and in studies on built environments, there seems to me to be a major gap between what is often assessed and what is important and valued in terms of human functioning. Perhaps more work needs to be done that permits discovery or emergence, as opposed to stipulating what is salient. Such empirical procedures permit new insights and can inform the intuition of professionals.

It is difficult to determine what needs to be included in environmental assessment without theoretical insight into how humans function in the environment. Inviting such theory, however, may be foolish or even dangerous. After all, psychologists have studied humans for a long time and there have been plenty of psychological theories. Researchers in the environment–behavior area have also proposed theories that bring humans and the environment into a common context. In terms of the needs of environmental assessment, however, many of these theoretical efforts have been either too global or too limited. Approaches that identify broad, general categories (e.g., ''behavior,'' ''environment'') and stipulate that the interactions among these must be recognized are far too vague for present purposes. On the other hand, specifying a single aspect of psychological process is too restrictive to do justice to the complexity of the task. To be useful for environmental assessment, a framework must fit somewhere between such extremes; it must, in other words, provide understanding of how different environmental patterns have their diverse effects on human experience, effectiveness, and well-being.

The review process for research involving nonhuman animals, at least in the United States, has clear guidelines for environmental conditions that must be met for animal welfare. I have long found it ironic that we know more about the requirements for maintaining healthy animals in the laboratory than we do about environments that support human well-being. Clearly, the environments many humans live in fail to meet "minimum standards." It is also clear that what is missing in these environments, as well as in those where the more fortunate dwell, goes well beyond physical description.

Expertise and the Guidance of Intuition

All of us are experts, both in the sense that all people have enormous knowledge and experience acquired in the course of their lifetime, and in the more usual sense that we are endowed with professional wisdom. Wisdom comes at a cost. In gaining expertise we also become blinded. We "see" differently *and* we are not aware of the differences. Although this may not have been included among the themes of the Greek tragedies, it is, in fact, a significant shortcoming of human functioning that must be acknowledged.

The way around this source of potential tragedy is not to sideline all experts! There is little doubt that expertise is helpful, even essential. Instead, the solution lies in recognizing that confidence in one's judgment must be balanced by other perspectives. Environmental assessment must include mechanisms for expanding how one "reads" the environment; there must be ways to permit new insights to surface. To blindly repeat the same procedures, despite differing settings and differing circumstances, is to invite disaster, and with increasing frequency, the wrath of affected publics. For the same reasons, efforts to standardize environmental quality indicators are likely to nurture the experts' blindness rather than encourage adjustment as conditions change.

Determining when emergent characteristics are useful and when standard operating procedures are appropriate is a challenge in itself. It is not impossible to have the best of both in many assessment situations. Permitting the public a role in the assessment need not be at the expense of inventorying whatever else is considered important. The inclusion of public input, however, greatly strengthens the likelihood of discovery, which in turn can improve one's theory and thereby lead to better assessments the next time around.

ACKNOWLEDGMENT

I gratefully acknowledge the support of the U.S. Forest Service, North Central Forest Experiment Station, Urban Forestry Project, through several cooperative agreements.

NOTES

1. There is by now a sizable literature related to the assessment of the landscape. In fact, there have been several efforts to partition this research literature into meaningful subsets (or models or paradigms). The most comprehensive of these efforts were by Daniel and Vining (1983) and by Zube and his colleagues in various combinations (Zube, Sell, & Taylor, 1982; Sell, Taylor, & Zube, 1984; Taylor, Zube,

& Sell, 1987; Pitt & Zube, 1987). Although those familiar with this literature might find the distinctions I will draw to be somewhat different from those previously identified, my intention here is neither to dwell on methodology nor to focus on these oft-cited paradigms. Rather, this domain offers a rich and useful context for looking at the questions of description and prediction.

2. The decision as to what scenes to include requires expert judgment; much as the researcher's expertise always enters into decisions regarding the conduct of the study. Similarly, the interpretation of the categories that result from the CIM statistical procedures are not free of expert influence. This is no different, of course, from any other research; "results" necessarily depend on many decisions about forms of analysis as well as interpretation. In the case of the CIM procedure, our experience has been that others are invariably involved in the interpretation of the category names. When a study is a part of a dissertation, such interpretation is never the student's alone. In other studies as well there is always a community of interested individuals who participate in the identification of the emergent categories.

REFERENCES

Alexander, C., Ishikawa, S., & Silverstein, M. (1977). *A pattern language.* New York: Oxford University Press.

Anderson, E. (1978). *Visual resource assessment: Local perceptions of familiar natural environments.* Doctoral Dissertation. University of Michigan.

Bechtel, R.B. (1988). Advances in POE methods. In *Looking back to the future* (Proceedings of IAPS 10). Holland: Delft University Press.

Daniel, T.C. & Vining, J. (1983). Methodological issues in the assessment of landscape quality. In I. Altman & J.F. Wohlwill (Eds)., *Behavior and the natural environment.* New York: Plenum.

de Groot, A.D. (1965). *Thought and choice in chess.* The Hague: Mouton.

Gifford, R. (1987). *Environmental psychology: Principles and practices.* Boston: Allyn & Bacon.

Groat, L. (1982). Meaning in post-modern architecture: An examination using the multiple sorting task. *Journal of Environmental Psychology, 2,* 3–22.

Hammitt, W.E. (1978). *Visual and user preference for a bog environment.* Doctoral Dissertation. University of Mighigan.

Hudspeth, T.R. (1986). Visual preference as a tool for facilitating citizen participation in urban waterfront revitalization. *Journal of Environmental Management, 23,* 373–385.

Kaplan, R. (1985). The analysis of perception via preference: A strategy for studying how the environment is experienced. *Landscape Planning, 12,* 161–176.

Kaplan, R. (1987). Simulation models and participation: Designers and "clients." In J. Harvey & D. Henning (Eds.), *Public environments.* Washington, DC: EDRA.

Kaplan, R. & Kaplan, S. (1989). *The experience of nature: A psychological perspective.* New York: Cambridge University Press.

Küler, R. (1988). Environmental activation of old persons suffering from senile dementia. In *Looking back to the future* (Proceedings of IAPS 10). Holland: Delft University Press.

Miller, P.A. (1984). *Visual preference and implications for coastal management: A perceptual study of the British Columbia shoreline.* Doctoral Dissertation. University of Michigan.

Pitt, D.G. & Zube, E.H. (1987). Management of natural environments. In D. Stokols & I. Altman (Eds.). *Handbook of environmental psychology* (Vol. 2). New York: Wiley.

Rosch, E.H. (1978). Principles of categorization. In E. Rosch & B.B. Lloyd (Eds.), *Cognition and categorization.* Hillsdale, N.J.: Erlbaum.

Seamon, D. (1987). Phenomenology and environment-behavior research. In E.H. Zube & G.T. Moore (Eds.), *Advances in environment, behavior, and design* (Vol. 1). New York: Plenum.

Sell, J.L., Taylor, J.G., & Zube, E.H. (1984). Toward a theoretical framework for landscape perception. In T.F. Saarinen, D. Seamon, & J.L. Sell (Eds.), *Environmental perception: Inventory and prospects.* Chicago: University of Chicago, Department of Geography.

Shafer, E.L. & Mietz, J. (1969). Aesthetic and emotional experiences rate high with northeast wilderness hikers. *Environment and Behavior, 1,* 187–197.

Smardon, R.C. (1986). Review of agency methodology for visual project analysis. In R.C. Smardon, J.F. Palmer, & J.P. Felleman (Eds.), *Foundations for visual project analysis.* New York: Wiley.

Smardon, R.C., Palmer, J.F., & Felleman, J.P. (Eds.) (1986). *Foundations for visual project analysis.* New York: Wiley.

Taylor, J.G., Zube, E.H., & Sell, J.L. (1987). Landscape assessment and perception research methods. In R.B. Bechtel, R. Marans, & W. Michelson (Eds.). *Methods in environmental and behavioral research.* New York: Van Nostrand Reinhold.

U.S. Bureau of Land Management (1980). *Visual resources management program.* Washington, D.C.: Department of Interior.

Yeomans, W.C. (1986) Visual impact assessment: Changes in natural and rural environments. In R.C. Smardon, J.F. Palmer, & J.P. Felleman (Eds.). *Foundations for visual project analysis.* New York: Wiley.

Zube, E.H. (1980). *Environmental evaluation: Perception and public policy.* Monterey, Calif.: Brooks/Cole.

Zube, E.H., Sell, J.L., & Taylor, J.G. (1982). Landscape perception: Research, application and theory. *Landscape Planning, 9,* 1–33.

3

Cognition of Physical and Built Environments

REGINALD G. GOLLEDGE

Environmental knowledge is acquired by interacting with, or experiencing, different environments. The interaction may be direct and active, as would be the case when a person lives in, travels through, or otherwise physically experiences a particular environment. Interaction may also take place, however, by accessing different sources of information including such things as photos, slides, movies, videos, paintings, or other visual representations, as well as haptically perceived information such as might be acquired from tactual maps, table models, or different types of sensing devices. Information abstracted from these many sources is stored in long-term memory as part of a general knowledge structure. As the need arises, such information is processed to provide knowledge of location, distribution, pattern, dispersion, connectivity, configuration, and other properties, which assist in preparing travel plans and activating movement.

There are of course many "environments," and it makes little sense to refer to "the environment." Even the "physical" environment encompasses the markedly dissimilar worlds of landforms, marine, surface and groundwater domains, vegetation, atmosphere, weather, and climate. Add to that the complexities of other external realities such as the built and transformed landscapes of human occupance, and it makes even less sense to regard them as one. Often these domains compete with each other via invasion and succession procedures (e.g., the invasion of agricultural land by urban uses; the successful invasion of inner city residential areas by expansion of commerce, business, and industry; the invasion of natural grasslands by domestic plants and animals), while at other times they exist in harmony. Perhaps the one common feature is that they are assumed to exist independently of mind—that is, they are "external" to mind. Assuming this to be so, the concept of "environmental cognition" can be examined. In this chapter, we will first discuss the basic spatial elements or components that allow both differentiation and clustering of phenomena found in large- and small-scale environments. This is followed by discussion of the components of an environmental knowledge structure, highlighting both individual and integrated components of knowledge, and emphasizing spatial characteristics. The final sections of the chapter discuss the process of assessing or evaluating environments, and the relation between cognized environment, the making of decisions and choices, and the tie between such activities and human spatial behavior.

BASIC COMPONENTS OF THE ENVIRONMENT

Occurrences, Distribution, and Process

Elements *in* an environment include inanimate objects, behaving life forms, and structural and behavioral processes. The processes of space generally include the ongoing actions of energies and forces that hold all parts of a space together and prevent its instantaneous destruction and or reincarnation (i.e., what we might loosely understand as the life force of the environment). Elements *in* a space exist within its boundaries, and represent the features that can differentiate one place from another.

Let us call the most fundamental unit in space an *occurrence*. Thus, we can speak of the occurrence of a phenomenon, the occurrence being the primary unit of the phenomenon, however so defined. By definition, an occurrence occurs *in* space. To have such an existence each occurrence has a minimal set of characteristics of identity, location, magnitude, and temporal existence.

Identity is a name or label that can be attached to an occurrence. Throughout the history of civilization, humanity has pursued a confusing course even at this fundamental level by allowing any given occurrence to be labeled with different identities depending on the language being used or the location at which it occurs. Languages may use symbolic, iconic, analog, or spoken modes of articulation. As long as an isomorphism occurs between the language unit chosen and the occurrence, identity can be established.

In the language of environmental cognition research, identified or labeled occurrences can be called ''environmental cues.'' This term covers occurrences that have a unique physical existence (e.g., a tree, a house, a sign, a mountain, a freeway segment, or a river), regardless of whether it is part of the natural or built environment. It also includes less tangible occurrences epitomizing the spatial existence of some affective or emotional state (e.g., a beautiful scene, a noisy place, a high crime area, or the occurrence of heavy pollution).

To comprehend the enormous variety of environmental cues, classification and categorization principles must be used. Thus we speak of cue ''classes'' that allow occurrences of phenomena with similar sets of features or characteristics to be grouped. For many years, geographers in particular have undertaken inventories of both natural and built environments. Numerous classifications of natural environmental features resulted, including soil or vegetation classifications (e.g., Ivanova & Rozov, 1967; Soil Survey Staff, 1975; United Nations F.A.O., 1974; U.S. Forest Service, 1977), landform features (Klingebeil & Montgomery, 1961; Varnes, 1958), and climates (Bach, 1972; Thornthwaite, 1948). Cognitive interpretations of natural environments often draw on established procedures and codes to identify components of settings (R. Kaplan, this volume). The built environment has been similarly generalized by classification and categorization procedures including (among many others) types of cities (Berry, 1972; Harris & Ullman, 1945), road systems (U.S. Department of Transportation, 1969), and types of land uses (Countryside Commission for Scotland, 1971; Wales, 1981). Much of this work was undertaken so that map summaries of different occurrences could be produced at a scale that permitted discovery of patterns, shapes, orders, frequencies, and areal associations of phenomena (Cliff & Ord,

1981; McCarthy, Hook, & Knos, 1956). Although much of the earlier work on environmental cue classifications was undertaken by laborious and time-consuming field work, classifications today can be produced from aerial photographs or remotely sensed data from satellites (Campbell, 1983; Holz, 1973). Given this volume of work, there is little need for the researcher in environmental cognition to invent their own classification schema unless the phenomena being examined have only recently come into existence. In the built environment cue classes such as residential, industrial, recreational, educational, open space, business, commercial, entertainment, transportation, and other types of land use classes are also commonly recognized. Obviously not all residential areas are the same, but all are different from, say, open space areas. They can be readily differentiated using simple decision rules or heuristics (e.g., based on type of land cover), and their occurrence can be summarized in some conceptually tractable form (e.g., a map or photograph).

Occurrences need, in addition to a label or name, a statement of existence. Here we use the term *"location"* as an indicator of existence. The language of location is as troublesome as the languages of identity. Precise multidimensional coordinates tied to arbitrary or absolute measurement systems lie at one end of a set of locational descriptors, whereas universally defined two-valued binary systems (such as "in" or "out") epitomize the other end of such a spectrum. As we move among realities, different location descriptors may become necessary.

All environmental cues are associated with some location. Thus members of the general cue classes discussed in previous paragraphs are made *place specific* by attaching locational descriptors to their identity. For example, members of one class of commercial establishments (supermarkets) found in Goleta (California) are designated by adding a street or shopping center location to their identifying label (e.g., Smith's Supermarket in Calle Real Shopping Center; Smith's Supermarket in University Village Shopping Center).

Some locational identifiers are imprecise, however, resulting in mismatches between location in external physical reality and location in a knowledge structure. Stevens and Coupe (1978) pointed out the anomaly that Reno (Nevada) was usually cognized as being east of San Diego (California) when in reality it is to the northwest of it. They hypothesize that since the State of Nevada is generally conceived as being east of the State of California, this relationship among superordinate categories is assumed for all cues located in each state. Similar inaccuracies exist when comparing the "northness" of places in western and eastern United States and Canada. Imprecision in specifying the location of a cue can produce distortions in cognitive mappings of environmental cues and help account for some of the incompleteness, foldings, tearings, fuzziness, or other characteristics of such mappings.

Even single units of phenomena may come in different sizes. Thus, *magnitude* becomes another essential descriptor of occurrences. Once again, even this primitive can be expressed in a variety of ways depending on the language being used. Specifying the most appropriate measure of magnitude to summarize the quantity of occurrence of physical phenomena has its problems. For example, how is a city defined? The definition of an urban or a metropolitan area, city, town, village, or hamlet, varies from country to country and from one time period to another within countries (King & Golledge, 1978). Questions concerning the most appropriate indicators of the occurrence of phenomena become more complex when we leave the physical environment (where counting is the most frequently used device to measure magnitude) and enter the domain of the altered or built environment. Here "use-measures" sometimes replace "occurrence" measures, as might be the case when differentiating between the amount of wilderness as opposed to the amount of lightly used open space (which might be intermittently used in animal transhumance practices, where animals graze at high elevations at selected times of the year, and are moved to lower elevations at other times). Similar problems might occur when attempting to assess the amount of usable open space in a built-up area that also encompasses otherwise vacant land. And what proportion of the floor space in a high-rise building needs to be "commerical" to identify it as such from other mixed-use buildings? Perhaps more important for the environmenal cognition researcher, how much of an attribute is required before an occurrence is perceived to be a member of a common cue class and categorized as such (Kosslyn, Murphy, Demesdeer, & Feinstein, 1977)? We shall explore this question later in the discussion of regionalization.

Quite obviously it matters whether we describe something by one measure or another (e.g., area vs. population size), for individual, local, regional, national, and cross-cultural differences occur when interpreting such measures. A "high-density residential environment" does not mean the same thing to a Hong Kong resident as it does to a resident of Des Moines, Iowa. Thus allocating magnitude measures to environmental cues, while being a necessary adjunct to identity and location, carries with it equally as many sources of confusion, misunderstanding, and error as do these other descriptors.

Finally, each occurrence exists in *time* as well as space. Temporal existence can be identified in an absolute sense (relating to the actual or possible life cycle of existence) or it can be related to an arbitrary measurement system that allows existence expectancy to be set into a base of defined intervals of elements of the space itself (e.g., arbitrarily defined time intervals).

The *temporal life* of an occurrence also plays an important role in its recognition and categorization. Development, growth, and change are essential parts of the life span of all matter, whether sentient or not. Landforms erode or are changed by human intervention; components of the biosphere grow, die, and decay; humans develop physically and mentally; land uses undergo constant change and modification. When we return to a location not visited for a long time, it may be different physically *and* perceptually.

We accept the dynamics of existence. Although some changes occur we may regard phenomena either as being relatively invariant or stable and unchanged over a "sufficiently long" time period, or as a permanent object or occurrence. Permanence becomes a major factor in deciding what features "anchor" our cognitive maps. Occurrences with unambiguous identities, well-specified locations, reliable and acceptable measures of magnitude, and permanence in the temporal domain appear to have the greatest capacity for anchoring spatial knowledge structures.

Even with a strong dose of the physically observable elements of identity, location, magnitude, and temporal existence, an occurrence may not be the same to all persons. Individuals add salience to the things and events they experience. Weights or saliences may be attached because of functional characteristics. Thus a blind pedestrian may give high salience to permanently fixed waste baskets while the sighted pedestrian ignores them and instead gives weight to architectural design or color. A member of a religious sect may give high salience to his/her place of worship; to others that occurrence may be just another building. Symbols painted on a wall or fence may to some inner city residents clearly demarcate gang turf; to others it is just more urban graffiti. Thus, although the existence of phenomena in complex physical reality may not be in doubt, their existence characteristics may become subordinate to sets of social, cultural, economic, political, religious, historical, or psychological characteristics that add distinction, uniqueness, importance, familiarity, or other critical attributes. These identifiers or saliences may become the key to categorization and classification of phenomena that is experienced, stored in memory, recalled, and used in day-to-day living and planning. It appears that a combination of cognition and affect provides many of the rule and procedures for environmental cognition.

On a slightly higher level of organization we can postulate that the occurrences discussed above may be *categorized and grouped* if they conform to well-specified criteria. Occurrences with the same identity may be grouped even though they are distinguished one from the other by the unique characteristic of location. Similarly, another grouping may occur by examining what occurrences occupy a single location at different points in the temporal existence of the universe of discourse. For our purposes, we will consider a collection of occurrences to be defined as a *distribution*. In particular, a spatial distribution is defined as that collection of occurrences identified and grouped by well-specified criteria such that each occurrence retains its unique locational property. Collections of occurrences can be regarded as having their own sets of properties. These include density (or the ratio of the number of occurrences in the distribution to a defined subset of the host space), arrangement (or the pattern or shape of the internal structure of the distribution), and spatial variance (the degree of spatial concentration, clustering, or dispersion of the occurrences in the distribution).

Occurrences, and the distributions they form, are inherently static. In some ways these can be considered the *facts of existence*. Complexity is introduced into this picture by adding processes. Processes are responsible for chaining occurrences and their distributions into events, activities, and behaviors.

Both elements in an environment and elements of an environment are held together in a matrix of processes. The generic term "process" implies temporal change, along some definable path or course of action, initiated and perpetuated by some natural, voluntary, or involuntary operation. Thus, a process may be considered a mechanism or instrument for inducing change. A spatial process thus becomes a procedure or mechanism for inducing a change that does not act simultaneously and in the same way at every location in a spatial system. Spatial processes involve spread over space, given that space is a barrier that must be overcome as a course of action spreads throughout a system. Evidence that the process is in operation appears at different places at different points in time. Processes are continuing courses of action that in theory have infinite life spans.

In practice the birth and death of a process may not be observable. When processes are continuous and on-going, however, it is generally found convenient to conceptually halt the process by taking a cross section through it and examining the nature of the state of existence along that cross section. Taking a series of such cross sections can simulate the temporal unfolding of a process. A process that illustrates at each cut through time that the state of the system varies from place to place is thus by definition spatial. Not all processes need be spatial but in the course of this chapter we shall try to provide spatial interpretations of processes that may not inherently be spatial.

Spatial Concepts

Associated with occurrence, distribution, and process are sets of spatial concepts and properties. A fundamental axiom in geography, for example, is that no two discreet things can occupy the same point in space at the same moment in time (Tobler, 1976). A fundamental spatial concept deduced from this axiom is spatial separation. The elemental term used to describe separation is distance. Understanding, measuring, interpreting, and explaining distances are critical concerns to any theory of spatial knowledge. Distance, one of the earliest and most popular spatial concepts examined in environmental cognition research, has become a standard measurement concept at all scales of operation.

Another spatial concept related to separation is that of contiguity. This is an expression of closeness, and together with its antithesis, dispersion, gives meaning to the concept "degree" of separation. Other terms that are freely used to elaborate this concept include proximity, spatial similarity or dissimilarity, clustering, nearest neighbor, spatial variation, and spatial heterogeneity (Anselin, 1988). In geography, contiguity is considered a fundamental axiom—for example, the more contiguous things are the more alike they will be. Such a concept is central to the geographic measure of contiguity called spatial autocorrelation (Cliff & Ord, 1981).

Another fundamental spatial concept is that of linkage or connectivity. Connectivity refers to a linkage pattern among discrete locations. Degrees of connectivity range from complete to null. Intervening between the extremes by inference are concepts of concatenation, spatial sequence, and spatial order. The linkage concept is well represented in the broader literature of most social and behavioral sciences. Of recent importance is the notion of semantic networks, which has led cognitive scientists to theorize about activation spread, production strings, and quad tree structures (Smith, Pellegrino, & Golledge, 1982). Such concepts are organizing principles of hypotheses as to how information from large-scale environments is sensed, stored, accessed, recalled, and used.

Many connectivities and linkages are readily observable in both physical and built environments. Soils and vegetation types form an example of natural link, as does elevation and vegetation type. Linked land uses are a common feature of economic or planning environments—for example, corn growing and hog farming, or high income residential districts and good school systems. At a more reduced scale, linkages occur among specific functions in cities or even within single stores, for example accessory stores near shoe stores, restaurants and bars near business offices, and medical, dental, and pharmaceutical functions concentrated in a single "professional" building.

Connectivities are expressed in many ways. Some places are directly connected by a single mode of transportation; others require mixed modes and transfer points and are less directly connected. The daily journey to work consists of linked route segments using some combination of local streets, arterial roads, and highways or freeways (Pailhous, 1970; Golledge & Zannaras, 1973). It may also require transfer among different modes of transportation. As might be expected, the more segments requiring connection, the more time consuming, difficult, or stressful the journey (Hall, 1983); the same appears true the more modes of transport are used. More connectivities or linkages along a route require more decisions to be made, more forced choices to be considered, and may be responsible for introducing fuzziness, distortion, or error into cognitive mapping processes (Allen, 1981; Evans, Skorpanich, Gärling, Bryant, & Bresolin, 1984; Golledge, Briggs, & Demko 1969; Sadalla & Magel, 1980; Sadalla & Staplin, 1980a,b).

Since both conceptually and practically it is undesirable to imagine a space consisting of an infinite series of discrete locations, a third spatial concept is region. A region is an area or segment of space in which the elements contained therein are more closely allied or identified with each other, than they are with any other elements outside the designated area or segment. Appropriately related terms are inclusion, exclusion, spatial grouping, spatial set, spatial class or category, and so on. Couclelis, Golledge, Gale, and Tobler (1987) and Hirtle and Jonides (1985) have discussed how regionalization processes manifest themselves in cognitive mapping and environmental knowledge structures.

Since each of the above spatial concepts imply that there can be spatial variation in magnitude, number, size, or other identifiable characteristics, a fourth one may be spatial stratification or spatial leveling. This implies dominance, superiority, and order, and is expressed in concepts such as spatial hierarchies, or ordered levels in spatial structures. Concepts of leveling or hierarchy are firmly entrenched in language. "Mountains" are larger than "hills," which are higher than "foothills," which are higher than "plains." "Metropolitan areas" are bigger than "cities," which are bigger than "towns," "villages," and "hamlets" (in that order) (King & Golledge, 1978). Distances between points or places can be monotonically ordered and described richly by varying adjectives (e.g., a "long" way; a "short" walk). Stratification concepts abound in our attempts to make sense of all environments, natural or built. Such concepts are important to include in theories of environmental cognition and in general discussions of the nature of environmental cognition. Although noticeably missing from early conceptualizations of spatial knowledge (including developmental theories), this organizing concept is so fundamentally part of all environments that it can no longer be ignored.

A fifth spatial concept becomes a more general overarching concept, spatial structure. Such structures consist of combinations of locations, connections, and regions, which may also have identifiable internal stratification, and be produced by unique processes. The observable structure in an environment is often summarized in model form. The arrangement of cities in a region may be modeled as a Central Place System (Christaller, 1966); the internal structure of a city may conform to a model based on social classes (Burgess, 1923), economic activity (Hoyt, 1939), or multifunctional regions (Harris & Ullman, 1945). Urban populations may be modeled as a density gradient decreasing exponentially from the inner city (Clark, 1967). The pattern of health and other emergency services often is dictated by minimum or maximum travel constraints (Revelle, 1987). Even the spatial structure of common phenomena such as gas stations, dry cleaners, hairdressers, and grocery stores is conditioned by principles of threshold (minimal market area size) and maximum range (i.e., distance people are prepared to travel to purchase the good or obtain the service) (King & Golledge, 1978). Some of these spatial structures are widely recognized and may enter into daily travel plans (Gärling, Böök, & Lindberg, 1985) or daily time budgets (Hägerstrand, 1970; Lenntorp, 1976). Other structures are less known, perhaps because they exist at a macroscale that is not readily observable until highlighted and summarized in some comprehensible form. Knowing such structures exist influences decision making and choice behavior opportunities and helps define sets of feasible alternatives. These may be locations (e.g., if selecting a shopping place), route segments (e.g., if choosing a path to work), or areas (e.g., if choosing a neighborhood in which to live).

RELATIONS BETWEEN KNOWLEDGE STRUCTURES AND ENVIRONMENTS

With these primitives before us it is now possible to ask critical questions, including (1) How do these concepts enter into human constructions of environment? (2) Are human constructions of environment isomorphic with the conditions from which they evolve? (3) Are these primitives and their derivatives a sufficient basis for exploration of questions concerning how humans experience, filter, code, store, recall, and use environmental information?

Investigating phenomena for the purpose of answering such questions involves creating a knowledge base, which contains within it the rules for attaching meaning to an experience. These rules are generally embodied in a language and contain rationalizations for recognizing, categorizing, connecting, associating, rejecting, and remembering experiential data. A knowledge system, therefore, consists of a structure enhanced by a net of meaning. Environmental knowledge consists of information obtained by a process of experiencing elements of and in space to which meaning can be given. An individual's knowledge structure depends on the unique way the net of meaning filters experience, and on what meanings are consequently attached to information that passes through for storage in mind.

In a given knowledge structure, each bit of information can be envisaged as existing in its own multidimensional space. In its essence each bit is unique. Out of necessity unique individual multidimensional existences overlap or coincide, thus reducing the overall dimensionality of their contact or joint space. As more and more of these multidimensional bits attach to each other their common dimensionality becomes smaller and smaller, but more capable of comprehension, understanding, recognition, and labeling. Thus, to have environmental knowledge is to have realized how a bit of information becomes embedded in a multidimensional concept space that is of substantially fewer dimensions than the original bit contains. The reduction of multidimensionality allows both simplification and generalization to occur, and for a language label to be attached to the join of overlapping sets. This is the first step in giving meaning to a bit of information and the first step in the creation of environmental knowledge.

The question now arises as to how space and spatial concepts enter into this whole process of sensing, absorbing, and using bits of information. Initially it was argued that space by itself provides an axiom for existence. At least part of our comprehension of the elements of space is tied to identifiable properties of space and to the meaning that we give to those properties.

Knowledge is individual or personal; however, we accept that knowledge components can be shared or commonly agreed on and the context in which this sharing takes place is generally referred to as culture. Thus, culture consists of shared knowledge, meanings, images, and habits of a group. For different cultures distinctiveness is made obvious by variations among any of these categories of phenomena.

Mental models are also unique to the extent that our own senses experience and extract information from the universe outside of mind. Variations in the human sensory modalities provide the uniqueness for mental models. As culture provides the conceptual matrix that encompasses experienced information, a sharing or commonality of meaning emerges that describes a given knowledge base. Both uniqueness and commonality are added by cognitive activities, which, while relying on genetically coded physiological and mental abilities, rely perhaps as much on internal processes of remembering and recall to become effective contributors to a useful and usable knowledge structure. In such a context meaning becomes a primitive of the knowledge structure, and is obtained in two ways: (1) obtaining understanding through definition; and (2) obtaining understanding by attaching significance. Information passing through the sensory filters to be stored in some way in mind becomes the mental "map" or "model" of an external universe. Thus the information itself (however stored in mind) becomes the knowledge base. Cognitive processes work on that knowledge base to provide context, meaning, and information combinations. This process facilitates interaction between an organism and an environment in which mind is the mediator. A model of existence then would be one in which an organism is constantly and inexorably bombarded with infinite bits of information all of which have the capacity for passing through sensory filters. Some of these may become entangled in nets of awareness, meaning, comprehension, understanding, and so on, and then stored in long-term memory. Alternatively an unanchored bit may float in and out of short-term memory until some later thought process allows an attachment to be made. The content of awareness is in dynamic flux.

Given this conceptual base, it is now possible to further elaborate the nature of an environmental knowledge structure and how the different components found in complex external environments become embedded in such a knowledge structure.

THE STRUCTURE OF ENVIRONMENTAL KNOWLEDGE

Environmental cognition has become an increasingly important area of study since it represents a major type of human knowledge with considerable theoretical and practical significance. The development of a tie between theories of environmental cognition and the computer modeling of it, for example, has focused attention on questions relating to the optimal procedures for storing and accessing such knowledge. In particular, concepts such as pattern matching and activation spread have been emphasized, particularly in a hierarchically structured context (Gopal, 1988; Smith & Gopal, 1990; Smith et al., 1982). Pattern matching processes determine the similarity of two or more symbol structures and are responsible for matching and identifying information received through the sense with a lexicon of stored potential interpreters.

Activation spread refers to the state of excitation that determines which part of a basic knowledge structure are available for access and use.

In recent decades, research on environmental cognition has focused on topics ranging from search strategies through map-reading skills to memory for spatial layouts at different scales and in many different environmental contexts. In environmental psychology, many of these studies have concentrated on preoperational and concrete operational stages of development (i.e., the ages from 3 to 14); in geography and other disciplines, normal adults have been the focus of attention. In general, Piaget's developmental theories have provided a common framework for much of this work, but since most of the empirical research has used adult subjects, the original developmental theories have proven to be of limited use. Now other embryonic life-span theories that are powerful in their own right and that, with continued modification and refinement could conceivably provide a more comprehensive theoretical base for adult environmental cognition, do exist (Golledge, 1978a; Shemyakin, 1962; Siegel & White, 1975). Each of these has developmental consequences and suggests that the acquisition of spatial knowledge progresses through different levels. Levels change from egocentric orientation of space, to relative spaces having critical elements of sequence, directionality and spatial relational and order concepts, to absolute space independent of self and specific objects. In each theory, the understanding of how places are linked together to form a coherent whole and the development of understanding of how to proceed between places previously unconnected represent important components of understanding.

Research and theory in cognitive science have also focused on how to represent a spatial knowledge structure and the processes that underlie human behavior in a wide variety of complex domains. The general assumption is that an individual's permanent knowledge structures provide the basis for interpreting objects, actions, and events in the external environment. It guides the decisions and actions of the individual in response to perceptions and interpretations of self and environment. Critical issues within this approach address the types of knowledge that exist, how such knowledge is represented and organized, the mechanisms by which it is activated, and the elementary and higher level cognitive processes that operate on the knowledge base to produce new knowledge, inferences, evaluations, and external behaviors.

A major problem area is the representation of processes by which knowledge structures change and grow. This is the fundamental problem of explaining learning and development. Computational Process Models (CPMs) are one way of addressing this issue directly (Kuipers, 1978). CPMs develop adaptive systems that have the capability to produce new knowledge structures in response both to specific input and to feedback generated in response to that input (Smith et al., 1982).

A question now arises concerning how different knowledge structures (i.e., declarative or landmark, procedural or route, and configurational or survey) are integrated to produce a single comprehensive and abstract knowledge structure. Although it is common in the recent cognitive science literature to acknowledge only the existence of declarative and procedural knowledge structures, much research provides a strong indication that a level of abstract, associational, relational, or configurational knowledge exists that is more than the sum of the declarative and procedural components. The existence of this type of spatial knowledge structure was postulated by

Shemyakin (1962) and Piaget and Inhelder (1975) and Golledge (1978b). Piaget and Inhelder, for example, proposed that, from infancy to adulthood, there is a progressive change in human ability to comprehend space and spatial relationships. These abilities combine with actual experience in large-scale space to produce varying types of knowledge with different levels of detail and integration. Most researchers accept this developmental hypothesis as a guiding principle but modify it to suit situations (e.g., neophyte learning in new environments), or specific populations (e.g., the aged, the retarded, the blind).

Declarative (Landmark) Knowledge

At the simplest level an individual has knowledge of what is in an environment. This is called declarative knowledge and consists of lists of objects, persons, things, events, and places. The general term "environmental cue" can be used to describe the elements in such a knowledge structure. When a cue is identified with a specific place, it can be referred to as a "location cue," and is sometimes defined in the literature as a "landmark." This term, originating in the pioneering work of Lynch (1960), was initially used to define dominant landscape features that would readily impress themselves on the senses and have a high probability of being retained as an organizing element of a cognitive map. Its use degraded, however, and now usually refers to any object or element in an external environment regardless of its significance.

Declarative knowledge requires an ability to state with certainty that an object or place exists, an ability to recognize it when it is within a sensory field, and an ability to communicate with others about cue properties (including its location and composition). The elements of a declarative knowledge structure are characterized by identity, location, magnitude, and temporal existence. Specific elements can be recognized as belonging to general cue classes and as being uniquely identified by a label that includes location. Since it is axiomatic that no two or more objects can occupy the same point in space at the same time, location becomes an essential distinguishing component in the declarative knowledge base. Topological characteristics such as proximity, inclusion, or exclusion, and metric information such as interpoint distance relations and orientation with respect to a selected frame of reference, allow the development of heuristics that can classify and coordinate elements in such a knowledge structure.

Declarative knowledge structures of a given environment differ among different people. They also vary depending on the nature of the man-environment interface (i.e., the experiential purpose). Thus Carr and Schissler (1969) used head-mounted cameras with devices to determine viewing angle and point of focus of drivers and passengers traveling a segment of urban freeway. Although they showed that passengers noticed and remembered more things than drivers, there was a great overlap in terms of the things noticed and remembered by both groups. The composition of a declarative structure might, however, differ significantly for some populations. For the vision impaired, the degree of resonance of a building's walls may be more important than its size, shape, color, or area covered. It can usually be assumed that a limited number of environmental features will occur in the cognitive maps of most people. Table 3.1 shows the most commonly recognized features of Paris (France) according to the classic study by Milgram and Jodelet (1976), along with sets of

Table 3.1 Most Frequently Mentioned Cues

Paris[a] (1970)	Columbus[b] (1974)	Santa Barbara[a] (1978)
1. Etoile	1. Graceland Shopping Center	1. La Cumbre Plaza, 140 S. Hope Avenue, Santa Barbara
2. Notre Dame	2. Eastland Shopping Center	2. Santa Barbara Airport, 500 Fowler Road, Goleta
3. Tour Eiffel	3. Westland Shopping Center	3. County Court House, E. Anapamu Street, Santa Barbara
4. Seine	4. Lazarus, downtown	4. Mission Santa Barbara, Upper Laguna Street, Santa Barbara
5. Bois de Boulogne	5. Port Columbus	5. UCEN Building at UCSB
6. Champs Elysees	6. I-71 N and I-270 intersection	6. Goleta Beach
7. Concorde	7. Veterans Memorial Auditorium	7. FEDMART, 500 S. Fairview Avenue, Goleta
8. Louvre	8. Ohio State Fairgrounds Coliseum	8. Santa Barbara Harbor
9. Chaillot	9. Western Electric, East Industrial Plant	9. Botanical Gardens, 1212 Mission Canyon Road, Santa Barbara
10. Cite	10. I-71 S. and I-270 intersection	10. Robinson's Department Store, 3805 State Street, Santa Barbara
11. Luxembourg	11. Northland Shopping Center	11. Dos Pueblos High School, Alameda, Goleta
12. Montmartre	12. N. High Street and I-161 intersection	12. Arlington Theatre, 131 State Street, Santa Barbara
13. Montparnasse	13. Columbus State Hospital	13. Santa Barbara Museum of Art, 1130 State Street, Santa Barbara
14. St. Germain	14. Anheiser Busch Brewery	14. Magic Lantern Theatre, 960 Embarcadero Del Norte, Isla Vista
15. St. Louis	15. Morse Road and N. High Street intersection	15. Picadilly Square, 813 State Street, Santa Barbara
16. St. Michel	16. Lane Avenue and N. High Street intersection	16. Bank of America, 935 Embarcadero Del Norte, Isla Vista
17. Tuilleries	17. Capital University	17. YMCA, 36 Hitchcock Way, Santa Barbara
18. Bastille	18. Ohio Historical Society	18. Rob Gym at UCSB
19. Buttes Chaumont	19. Riverside Hospital	19. Greyhound Bus Station, Carillo and Chapala, Santa Barbara

[a]Ranked by importance. Data from Milgram and Jodelet (1976).

[b]Not ranked by importance. Unpublished data from surveys conducted by Golledge.

features for Columbus (Ohio) and Santa Barbara (California). The fact that it is possible to make such lists gives importance to both the concept of a declarative knowledge structure for a given environment, and to Lynch-type hypotheses that environments can be decomposed into significant components. Combinations of unique individual information sets (e.g., including an individual's home, work place, and favorite recreational places) make up personalized knowledge structures of an environment. The uniqueness or commonality of components is instrumental in communication about an environment and interaction with it.

Procedural (Route) Knowledge

It is generally assumed that, apart from some early sensorimotor experimentation, human movement is purposive. Spatial movement can be defined as the processes of changing location over time. Human spatial movement usually takes place for some particular purpose, is deliberate, and is often associated with solving a problem. Such movement involves traversing distances between origins and destinations, and making any directional changes required to successfully reach a destination. This process is referred to as "route" or "procedural" knowledge utilization. The more general term, "procedural knowledge," embodies within it the knowledge of specific paths through complex environments, an ability to preview and preprocess information to help in developing a travel plan, a propositional structure for organizing travel plans, and heuristics to translate plans into spatial activity (Gärling et al., 1985; Moar & Carleton, 1982). Route knowledge requires an ability to order or sequence information about location cues and distance segments connecting those cues, an ability to evaluate the temporal dimension of navigation, an ability to determine direction and orientation with respect to previous and consequent route segments and to a general frame of reference, and an ability to estimate the nature and severity of barriers that might occur along any given route. This latter characteristic also implies an ability to modify a travel plan to circumvent a barrier even when it requires traversing unknown and unexperienced segments of space. Procedural knowledge therefore builds on a declarative knowledge base, and adds to that base new and more complex abilities for linking information and translating such information into movement.

Like declarative knowledge, route or procedural knowledge appears to be hierarchical. Pailhous (1970) studied the ability of Parisian cab drivers to navigate in Paris. He differentiated the city into its inner and outer components and suggested that the two were connected by primary and secondary networks. The primary or basic network provides a skeleton-like structure of major roads and highways from which any subarea can be readily reached in a reasonable time frame. This basic network provides the anchoring route segments for the cab drivers' cognitive map of the city. This basic network is extremely well known and drivers were able to select route segments that provided near optimal shortest path connections between end points in the basic structure for any given trip. The secondary network represents the sum total of lower order information about local neighborhoods. Precise information is often obtained only by reference to a street guide or by detailed instructions from a passenger. Connections between points in the secondary network were usually made by finding the nearest connector to the basic network, using the basic network to traverse the city, and existing into a neighborhood from the most conveniently located node on this basic network. Although the study used only cab drivers as subjects, it can reasonably be inferred that most individuals will develop a basic network consisting of a web of efficient routes linking major anchor points in their local environment. The combination of primary node or landmark sets and primary route or basic network route segments provides an important organizing structure for information contained in a mental map. This structure also appears to be significant when estimating either the location of places, and their distances apart or other spatial characteristics.

One shortcoming of much of the research on landmarks (or place-specific environmental cues) is that the cues are considered in isolation. Their distinctive properties are itemized in terms of perceptual characteristics such as dominance of visual form, angularity, size, shape, and color, as well as their experiential importance (including their social or historical significance or even their behavioral importance to the perceiving individual) (Appleyard, 1969; Carr & Schissler, 1969; Lynch, 1960). Rarely has this research focused on environmental cues as significant components of routes, or as instruments for segmenting routes that are important in the recall of segment order or sequencing. Exceptions to this can be found in the work of Golledge, Smith, Pellegrino, Doherty, and Marshall, (1985). In the latter research, which concentrated on children learning a route through a neighborhood, environmental features were characterized as discrete objects ("plots" such as houses) and grouped objects ("scenes" such as views down a road segment). Differentiation among the plots was made on the basis of characteristics and their salience to each decision maker. Both field and laboratory testing was undertaken to determine the significance of specific plots and scenes, and errors of recognition, location, or sequencing were recorded. The research found clear differentiation among the plots (or landmarks) such that those where complex decisions were required (e.g., stop, select a new direction, cross a street, proceed in a new direction) became signficantly better known and less error prone than other plots. Similarly, scenes that were anchored at choice points were significantly better recognized, recalled, and less error prone in terms of identification and recognition than those scenes that had little importance in the decision-making process. The research indicated that both declarative and procedural knowledge structures were probably hierarchically organized around multiple anchor points. Errors were fewest in the vicinity of anchor points and increased with distance from such anchor points. The research also indicated that declarative knowledge was integrated with procedural rules to facilitate movement behavior. On repetitive trials, choice point and key segment differentiation became much clearer until a fully integrated route, anchored by choice points and key route segments, was learned.

At a minimum, route knowledge is a series of procedural descriptions involving a sequential record of the starting point or anchor point (e.g., one's home), subsequent landmarks, distances between them, and the destination for each route (Kuipers, 1978; Leiser, 1987; Stern & Leiser, 1988). The procedural knowledge representation must contain productions associated with decision points (e.g., where things such as a change in direction take place), along with a knowledge and description of the appropriate actions to perform at those choice points. More detailed route knowledge includes information about secondary and tertiary landmarks along a route, distances between landmarks, and relation of landmarks and route segments to a larger frame of reference. Routes of equivalent physical distance may differ substantially in the amount of stored information necessary to traverse them (e.g., the number of landmarks, intersections, or other locations where critical information about the route is stored). The distance between two points along a route may be a function of the amount of information stored in memory that must be processed to mentally traverse that section of the route between them. According to this hypothesis, an individual's estimate of the distance between two points is based on information pertaining to the effort involved in traversing the route. Effort can refer to directional changes, travel time, or physical distance. Empirical evidence supports such conjectures (Mac-Eachren, 1980; Sadalla & Staplin, 1980a,b). Distance and orientation estimates also appear to be dependent on whether a person has actively or passively experienced an environment (i.e., moved through it or learned from maps) (Thorndyke & Hayes-Roth, 1982).

Configurational (Survey) Knowledge

As knowledge accumulates about an environment and as distance information becomes more precise, notions of angularity, direction, continuity, and relation emerge. The exact nature of how the transition from route knowledge to survey or configurational knowledge occurs is largely unknown, however. There is a volume of literature that argues for the importance of attention processes in selecting the spatial sensory information for further processing. Of critical importance appears to be information such as whether a reference point is visible from the origin, destination, or some intermediate decision point. It has been hypothesized that the acquisition of information about nonvisible points requires central information processing or deliberate attention processes (Gärling et al., 1985). Interfering with deliberate attention processes reduces the probability that information about reference points could be integrated in an overall frame of reference system.

Kuipers (1979) has categorized much of our knowledge of environment by the term "common sense knowledge." This is knowledge about the structure of the external world that is acquired and applied without concentrated effort by any normal human. It allows him or her to meet the every day demands of the physical, spatial, and temporal environment with a reasonable degree of success. In this common sense context, it is feasible to assume a hierarchical ordering of knowledge. Elements of the environment that have relevance for everyday use have salience attached to them that make their recognition or identification and use much more simple. In general, signs and symbols are used to make environmental elements place specific and function specific such that potential interaction with them is made as simple and easy as possible. Note that even though environmental elements may be closely spatially linked with others, they need not share the same salience. Examples of configurations tied to specific anchor points can be seen in the work of Couclelis et al. (1987), Hirtle and Jonides (1985), Spector (1978), and Stevens and Coupe (1978).

Configurational knowledge adds associational and relational components to the declarative and procedural knowledge bases. Experiments with 9- to 12-year-old children (Golledge et al., 1985) have shown their inability to solve associational and relational problems even among well-known cues along well-known routes. This implies the lack of a type of spatial understanding that is more abstract and metric than can be found in declarative or procedural structures. The knowledge gained to allow successful wayfinding along separate routes was insufficient to solve configurational problems concerned with the relative location of cues. This lack of ability is consistent with the development hypotheses of Piaget and Inhelder (1967), Shemyakin (1962), Hart and Moore (1973), and Siegel and White (1975). However, when a small selection of adults was tested on this same problem, performance improved only slightly. Ongoing experiments with a larger adult sample should clarify whether or not this configurational knowledge is part of "natural" or "common sense" knowledge or whether it is an abstract form of reasoning that appears rarely. Evidence from other experiments using mapboards for cue location, or requiring proximity judgments between all pairs of places in a spatial distribution (Golledge & Rayner, 1976; Golledge & Spector, 1978), *have* shown that mature adults can reproduce real-world cue configurations with good accuracy. However, knowledge of the way that declarative and procedural bases are integrated to produce configurational structures is still uncertain.

Regions and Hierarchies in Knowledge Structures

Stevens and Coupe (1978) discussed experiments in which they identified systematic errors occurring when subjects made large-scale directional judgments (e.g., is Reno, Nevada east or west of San Diego, California?). They suggested that some decisions appear to be made with respect to a superordinate locational system and that errors in part may be due to relating such judgment tasks to a general knowledge framework (e.g., California has a Pacific coastline and Nevada does not, therefore, San Diego on the coast must be further west than Reno). Judgmental tasks similar to this can be found in many introductory cartography texts. The critical idea expressed in the Stevens and Coupe experiments is an important one; it appears highly likely that there is a close interdependence between phenomena such as landmarks and the area in which those landmarks are located, and that landmarks may take on some of the general informational characteristics (correct or incorrect) about the area in which they are located. Maki (1981) and Wilton (1979) separately found that the response times involved in making directional and other judgments was faster across clusters of phenomena than was the case with respect to equally distant phenomena occurring within a cluster. Stevens (1976) and Shute (1984) showed the importance of spatial priming, with Shute's experiments looking at intraurban scales and Steven's examining inter-state scales. Their results parallel the findings of Sadalla, Burroughs, and Staplin (1980) and other researchers (Cadwallader, 1979) regarding the asymmetric nature of many interpoint distance judgments, while Allen (1981) found that across-cluster distances were judged to be consistently longer than identical length within-cluster distances. Allen also pointed out that the presence of boundaries altered distance judgments. This supports the contention that some type of *regionalization* process takes place in association with spatial judgments, even when the judgments may refer to pairs of points.

As pointed out by Hirtle and Jonides (1985), the acquisition of information about an environment builds a multilevel structure, and this structure includes hierarchies, reference points, distance knowledge, and semantic information about elements in the space. Adding hierarchy to regions raises questions about the appropriateness of representing the latent spatial structure of very well-known places (e.g., primary and secondary nodes) on a two- or three-dimensional Euclidean surface (Golledge & Rushton, 1973; Golledge & Spector, 1978; Golledge, Rayner, & Rivizzigno, 1982;

Golledge & Zannaras, 1973; Richardson, 1979, 1982; Spector, 1978). In other words, spatial information about the best known places in each of a set of hierarchies appears to be able to be captured and represented on a simple two-dimensional surface. Such a representation has been termed by Golledge (1987) a "cognitive configuration." However, as one attempts to recover information about places lower down a single hierarchy or at lower levels generally within a set of regions or hierarchies, simple Euclidean relations may no longer hold, and indeed, as Baird, Wagner, and Noma (1982) and Golledge and Hubert (1982) suggest, the resulting information set may be "impossible" to represent in a single two-dimensional Minkowskian space. It may even prove difficult to represent it in more complex hyperbolic or elliptical spaces. For example, part of a knowledge structure (e.g., at the highest levels of a cluster) may be adequately represented by simple Euclidean measurements or transformations, while other internal and between-cluster relations may, at best, have a topological relationship, or even just a cluster identity attached to them. It is feasible to suggest, therefore, that distance relationships between points, either within a single cluster or between clusters, may most feasibly be measured in terms of some edge or link characteristics that passes upward and downward through cluster substructures, or may be directed through the dominant anchor points if between-cluster relationships are desired.

ASSESSING THE ENVIRONMENT

Given the preceding conceptualization of environmental cognition, it is reasonable to accept that a given physical or built environment means many different things to the people who view it, experience it, or use it. One cannot assume that the same environment means the same to all people. There is a need therefore to find out if there are "common" perceptions of different environments, particularly if interventions such as planning for new uses or planning to preserve old uses, is imminent. Even in the absence of planning needs, however, there is incentive to know if similar encoding of environmental information takes place, and if different saliences are attached to the same components of such environments. Differential weighting of features may result in designation of different anchors and thus result in different distortions in cognitive mappings. As pointed out by Amedeo and York (1984), R. Kaplan (1976, and this volume), S. Kaplan and R. Kaplan (1983), Nasar (1983), Ward and Russell (1981), and others, affective responses to an environment may differ significantly among sociocultural groups and among geographic regions. To the inner city dweller, an urban street scene may be perceived as safe and stimulating, while a wilderness scene may be perceived as dangerous and threatening. Suburban or rural dwellers may give reverse evaluations.

The formal procedure of describing or assessing a particular environment is usually (but not always) carried out by professionals. A typical reason for engaging in such an activity might be the preparation of an environmental impact report, preparation of a land use or development plan, or the designation of places for preservation. This formal process has three components: (1) identification of *what is there* in physical reality; (2) specification and definition of the appropriate *attributes* that allow description or assessment of the environment to take place; and (3) selection of *indicators* of the quantity of attributes so that some measure of magnitude of occurrence can be made. To describe what is there, recourse is often made to established descriptive or classification systems that have a potential for being used at any scale from local area to national scale. Scotland and Wales, for example, have descriptive systems for classifying land uses and landscapes on a national scale (Countryside Commission for Scotland, 1971, Wales, 1981; Linton, 1968), while in the United States the Bureau of Land Resource Management (BLM, 1980a,b) and many other classificatory schemes exist. These schemes allow an inventory to be taken of what is there that allows both detailed listing of all the principal identifiable components of the environment as well as facilitating a holistic description of that environment. Such schemes can provide the base of physical reality against which cognitive or perceptual evaluations can be made. Although it is true that once identified, many attributes of the physical environment can be defined and measured (e.g., the number of trees; the area devoted to natural vegetation; areas of crops; magnitude of the built-up area; building heights, shapes, and other characteristics), it is often the case that attributes of critical importance are not directly measurable in physical quantities but rather reflect an aesthetic evaluation by a viewing person or population. A typical attribute might then be the level of enjoyment or pleasure experienced by people exposed to an environment. To obtain such attributes, it is usually necessary to view an environment in its natural state or to experience an adequate simulation, such as might be found in slides, photographs, videos or movies, and perhaps maps or remotely sensed images. Lists of landuse types and quantities rarely evoke the type of aesthetic response sought as part of many assessments, nor are they likely to allow assessment of the cultural, folkloric, religious, or other significant properties of the given environment.

Even if a set of important attributes can be determined, there remains the additional problem of specifying and defining indicators of the occurrence of such attributes. This is the well-known measurement problem. In assessing physical or built environments, it is mandatory to include both objectively and subjectively derived indicators. Thus, both an indication of the quantity of vegetation in a scene and an indication of the amount of beauty, enjoyment, or satisfaction the vegetation in a scene and an indication of the amount of beauty, enjoyment, or satisfaction the vegetation generates in a viewer, should be accountable. If the three tasks of identification, attribute selection, and indicator definition can be achieved, then a given environment can be adequately described or represented. This is usually the first step in a process by which specific environments are then evaluated by nonprofessionals (e.g., the general public) in circumstances such as the evaluation of management or landuse plans, public hearings on environmental impact statements or development projects, and so on. This facilitates the evaluation process at large by allowing collection and analyses of data extracted from individuals or participating parties, which may include citizen judgments of preference, satisfaction, enjoyment, or even use.

Once description and evaluation have been made feasible, explanation is also possible. Although evaluation provides evidence of how much of any given attribute is perceived as being present and to what extent various emotions and beliefs or values are embodied in the task environment, explanatory processes go beyond this by attempting to determine the degree to which changes in specific attributes or qualities contribute to changes in the holistic image and to the types of judgments likely to be made about the task environment. The explanatory phase may concentrate on physical properties or combinations of physical and perceived qualities (e.g., R. Kaplan, this volume; S. Kaplan, 1979; Zube, Pitt, & Anderson, 1975).

Most environmental assessments involve some combination of the following characteristics or attributes: (1) Physical attributes (e.g., landforms, land covers, atmospheric quality, light, ruggedness, height, slope); (2) landscape attributes (e.g., land uses, color, texture, form, line, uniformity, variability, shape); (3) subjective attributes (e.g., perceived complexity or diversity of elements, perceived harmony or coherence, dominance of visible form, uniqueness or distinctiveness, mystery, beauty, enjoyment, satisfaction, aesthetic value, traditional life-style value, historical significance); and (4) man–environment interaction attributes (e.g., familiarity, travel frequency, actual or expected use, observer location, scale, distance to key attributes).

The assessment of an environment involves description, evaluation, and explanation. What must be regarded as being of paramount importance for all environmental cognition researchers (regardless of discipline) is that the first phase (i.e., description of physical reality) is not the whole picture. Ability to describe what is there can draw from long traditions of descriptive research in disciplines such as geography, planning, forestry, biology, geology, and the other environmental, hydrologic, atmospheric, and natural sciences. Most governments, regardless of country of origin, have well-defined procedures for inventorying their country's resources and specifying what exists in their physical environments. There is no need to duplicate these or reinvent the wheel to find what is out there. Vast quantities of remotely sensed and image-processed data from satellites exist and can provide mapped or visual images of virtually any given environment on earth (and its satellites). Although it is essential to know what is there in physical reality, however, the researcher in environmental cognition must place the greatest part of his or her attention on the interface between human and environment. Thus, perceptions, memories, and otherwise cognized information must be regarded as at least as important as physical descriptors of an environment. And it is quite feasible to expect that attributes may be generated that have no existence in physical reality. Although in physical reality one may not be able to tell one pool in a stream from another, the people to whom a particular pool has religious significance for baptism purposes can readily tell them apart. They add attributes to the environment that are not readily observable, by any physical means. The environmental cognition researcher must assess not only the quantities of attributes as defined by presence in physical reality but also those sets of attributes that provide hidden dimensions and attributes of environments, that give meaning and significance to them, and facilitate identification, recognition, storage, recall, and use of environmental information. Thus assessment must be conscious both of physical reality and transformations of that reality that are stored in mind by our cognitive mapping process. As pointed out in other chapters in this volume (R. Kaplan, Zube, and Zimring), perhaps the most important task facing those interested in assessment of environments is not to inventory what *is* there in physical reality, but to develop the appropriate procedures for identifying and measuring attributes via sets of commonly recognized and accepted indicators, that in turn allow evaluations of environments to be undertaken with a great degree of confidence. Only by achieving this degree of confidence will moves to the explanatory and predictive phases of environmental assessment be possible.

In the assessment or evaluation phase of environmental cognition then, significance is attached to the brute facts of physical existence. This provides a matrix of meaning that helps select relevant bits of information for storage in memory and later use. In the process of adding meaning, the full impact of culture-specific beliefs and values can be seen. Stereotyped "views" of environments have for years dictated public and private attitudes toward environments, labeling them severally as exploitable, endangered, risky, mysterious, safe, beautiful, and so on. The question arises, however, as to what environmental components represent the "core" of such designated areas? Further, how can environmental image be appropriately evaluated? And how can this evaluation be incorporated into private and public decision-making processes? These and other related questions have been more fully examined elsewhere in this book (see chapters by R. Kaplan, Zube, and Zimring); no further attention will therefore be paid to them in this chapter, except to suggest how images and imagery can be incorporated into various decision-making processes.

ENVIRONMENTAL COGNITION, DECISION MAKING, AND CHOICE BEHAVIOR

The building of a knowledge structure consisting of environmental information is a first and necessary antecedent for human spatial behavior. While developing an understanding of the declarative base has occupied most researchers to date, ever more attention is now turning to the procedures required to access and use that base. Decision rules and choice heuristics must be fed with declarative substance to make enlightened and purposive decisions and choices.

The tie between a knowledge base and a decision process applied to it has been summarized graphically by Amedeo and Golledge (1975) (Figure 3.1). This model starts with a quiescent or unmotivated population whose members have both unique and shared components in their knowledge base. The environment in which the population exists is partly known and understood, but it includes all the concepts and primitives discussed earlier. The external environment in which the population exists can be described and modeled with much precision using image-processing technology, and can be stored in a large geographic information system (either in a computer or in a person's mind). Summaries and abstractions of the total knowledge set can be represented in a variety of ways, including maps. The geography of the environment can be explored either in its external form or in its cognitive form.

Now assume members of the population are exposed to some motivating force (e.g., physiological or psychological drive or cue). The first motivated act requires a search of the knowledge base for information about the consequent task situation (e.g., "obtain food"). This search initiative activates anchoring nodes in the knowledge structure. Information may be gathered introspectively as well as by tapping external sources such as acquaintances or mass media. A subset of the general task environment might then be constructed by activating relevant segments of a cognitive map. Such segments would include the origin area, a destination area (if spatial behavior is involved), and connecting pathways. Alternative places at which satisfactory solutions to a given task might be examined, are evaluated in light of

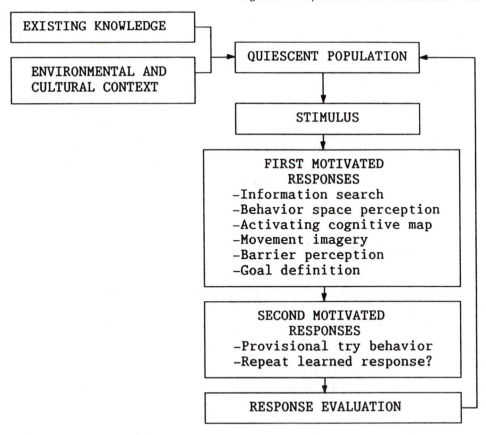

Figure 3.1. Structure of a decision process. (After Amedeo & Golledge, 1975.)

stored information and prior experience. Thus some "feasible opportunity" set is defined.

A next step involves creation of movement imagery or a travel plan (Gärling et al., 1985). At this stage of the decision process barriers to movement may be envisaged. Barriers include distance (or separation of self from solution place), or they may involve nonphysical factors such as cost, preference, attitude, compatibility, and so on. (For a discussion of constrained decision making see Desbarats, 1983; Eagle, 1988; and Timmermans, this volume). Movement itself must be imaged, requiring selection of a transportation mode. This particular problem has been researched extensively in recent years (Golledge & Timmermans, 1988). Individuals must also rationalize travel plans with household requirements, resolving any consequent conflicts (Recker, McNally, & Root, 1986).

After selection of a solution path and a suitable destination, travel plans are implemented and the problem solved. This usually involves an overt act—movement through space. Reward or satisfaction is then experienced and assessed against expectations. The result then feeds back into the knowledge base, perhaps altering saliences or weights attached to various bits of information. This feedback may create new anchors, resolve fuzziness, correct errors, or otherwise impinge on the nature and structure of the original knowledge base. This dynamic is usually described as "learning" and is the critical concept tying together all components from the original task environment to the evaluation of achievement.

This simple conceptualization links objective environment, resident population, individual decision maker, decision process, and ultimate choice behavior in a single loop. Practically, the loop is much more complicated than shown here, and vast quantities of research energy continue to be allocated to understanding all segments— the nature of the declarative base, the procedural rules, the imaged structure or configurational knowledge on which decision rules operate, the role of experience in changing the salience of bits of information, and the most appropriate models to link environment and human behavior through decision making and choice procedures.

CONCLUDING REMARKS

Although research is ongoing on many aspects of environmental cognition, assessment, and decision making, many questions remain unresolved. We know much of *what* is likely to be contained in a declarative knowledge base; however, we still know little about how it is arranged, stored, or accessed. Are hierarchical theories the best or are complex variations of the various network theories (e.g., of trees, semantic nets, and quad trees) more appropriate? What are the rules or heuristics used in decision-making situations? Can choice of a transport mode be modeled the same way as the choice of a shopping center? And how does one assess which of several environments is the more beautiful, or the more likely to satisfy some problem-solving activity? Exactly how are declarative and procedural knowledge bases integrated? Are there developmental constraints on the likelihood that integration can occur? And of what does configurational knowledge really consist? Is it images (Kosslyn, 1975) or propositional strings (Pylyshyn, 1981); is it really map-like or only metaphorically map-like (Downs, 1981; Kuipers, 1983)?

Undoubtedly some answers to such questions will result from experimentation with computational process or parallel distributive process models typical of current work in cognitive science, artificial intelligence, and now environmental cognition (Gärling & Golledge, 1989; Golledge et al., 1985; Leiser, 1987; Smith et al., 1982). Other chapters in this volume will develop some of these themes further. Other problems await future research attention.

Although it is possible to agree with Wohlwill's oft-quoted comment that "the environment in NOT in the head," it must also be realized that there is not likely to be a perfect one-to-one mapping of elements of an environment and its symbolic representation in mind. The world is too complex for us to comprehend without sets of culture-specific concepts that serve to categorize, order, and manage environmental information. Our systems for managing information are imperfect. Hence, differences occur between knowledge structures and the environmental elements they represent. This explains why the definition of a cognitive map emphasizes that our mental models are abstractions, or summaries, are partial or incomplete, and may have gaps or holes.

ACKNOWLEDGMENTS

This research was partially sponsored by Grant PHS EY07022-01 from the National Eye Institute, National Institute of Health, by NSF Grant SEA-87-20597, and by the John Simon Guggenheim Foundation.

REFERENCES

Allen, G.L. (1981). A developmental perspective on the effects of 'subdividing' macrospatial experience. *Journal of Experimental Psychology: Human Learning and Memory, 7,* 120–132.

Amedeo, D., & Golledge, R.G. (1975). *An introduction to scientific reasoning in geography.* New York: Wiley.

Amedeo, D., & York, R. (1984). Grouping in affective responses to environments: Indications of emotional norm influence in person environment relations. *EDRA Proceedings,* 193–205.

Anselin, L. (1988). *Spatial econometrics: Methods and models.* Dordrecht: Martinus Nijhoff.

Appleyard, D. (1969). Why buildings are known. *Environment and Behavior,* 1, 131–159.

Bach, W. (1972). *Atmospheric pollution.* New York: Prentice Hall.

Baird, J., Wagner, M., & Noma, E. (1982). Impossible cognitive spaces. *Geographical Analysis, 14,* 204–226.

Berry, B. (ed.) (1972). *City classification handbook.* New York: Wiley Interscience.

Bureau of Land Resource Management (1980a). *Visual resource management program.* Washington, DC: U.S. Department of the Interior.

Bureau of Land Resource Management (1980b). *Visual simulation techniques.* Washington, DC: U.S. Department of the Interior.

Burgess, E. (1923). The growth of the city. *Proceedings American Sociological Society, 18,* 85–89.

Cadwallader, M. (1979). Problems in cognitive distance: Implications for cognitive mapping. *Environment and Behavior, 11,* 559–576.

Campbell, J. (1983). Mapping the land. *AAG Research Monograph.* Washington, DC.

Carr, S., & Schissler, D. (1969)). The city as a trip: Perceptual selection and memory in the view from the road. *Environment and Behavior, 1,* 7–35.

Christaller, W. (1966). *Central places in S. Germany* (C. Baskin, Trans.). Englewood Cliffs, N.J.: Prentice Hall.

Clark, C. (1967). *Population growth and land use.* New York: St. Martins Press.

Cliff, A., & Ord, J. (1981). *Spatial processes: Models and applications.* London: Pion.

Couclelis, H., Golledge, R.G., Gale, N., & Tobler, W. (1987). Exploring the anchor point hypothesis of spatial cognition. *Journal of Environmental Psychology, 7,* 99–122.

Country Side Commission For Scotland (1971). *A planning classification of Scottish landscape resources.* Perth, Scotland.

Desbarats, J. (1983). Spatial choice and constraints on behavior. *Annals of the Association of American Geographers, 73,* 340–357.

Downs, R. (1981). Maps and metaphors. *The Professional Geographer, 33,* 287–293.

Eagle, T. (1988). Context effects in consumer spatial behavior. In R.G. Golledge & H. Timmermans (Eds.), *Behavioural modelling in geography and planning* (pp. 299–324). London: Croom Helm.

Evans, G.W., Skorpanich, M.A., Gärling, T., Bryant, K.J., & Bresolin, B. (1984). The effects of pathway configuration, landmarks, and stress on environmental cognition. *Journal of Environmental Psychology, 4,* 323–335.

Gärling, T., Böök, A. & Lindberg, E. (1985). Adult's memory representation of their everyday physical environment. In R. Cohen (Ed.), *The development of cognition* (pp. 141–184). Hillsdale, N.J.: Erlbaum.

Gärling, T., & Golledge, R.G. (1989). Environmental perception and cognition. In E.H. Zube, & G.T. Moore (Eds.), *Advances in environmental behavior and design,* (Vol. 2, pp. 203–236). New York: Plenum.

Golledge, R.G. (1978a). Environmental cues, cognitive mapping, spatial behavior. In D. Burke et al. (Eds.), *Behavior-environment research methods* (pp. 35–46). Institute for Environmental Studies, University of Wisconsin.

Golledge, R.G. (1978b). Learning about urban environments. In T. Carlstein, D. Parkes, & N. Thrift (Eds.), *Timing space and spacing time: Making sense of time* (pp. 76–98). London: Edward Arnold.

Golledge, R.G. (1987). Environmental cognition. In D. Stokols & I. Altman (Eds.), *Handbook of environmental psychology,* Vol. 1 (pp. 131–174). New York: Wiley.

Golledge, R.G., Briggs, R., & Demko, D. (1969). The configuration of distances in intra-urban space. *Proceedings of the Association of American Geographers, 1,* 60–65.

Golledge, R.G. & Hubert, L.J. (1982). Some comments on non-euclidean mental maps. *Environment and Planning A, 14,* 107–118.

Golledge, R.G., & Rayner, J.N. (1976). *Cognitive configurations of a city: 2.* Columbus: The Ohio State University Research Foundation.

Golledge, R.G. & Rayner, J.N. (1982). *Proximity and preference: Problems in the multidimensional analysis of large data sets.* Minneapolis: University of Minnesota Press.

Golledge, R.G., Rayner, J.N., & Rivizzigno, V.L. (1982). Comparing objective and cognitive representations of environmental cues. In R.G. Golledge & J.N. Rayner (Eds.), *Proximity and preference* (pp. 233–266). Minneapolis: University of Minnesota Press.

Golledge, R.G., & Rushton, G. (1973). Multidimensional scaling: Review and geographic applications. *AAG Technical Report No. 10,* Washington, D.C.

Golledge, R.G., Smith, T.R., Pellegrino, J.W., Doherty, S., & Marshall, S.P. (1985). A conceptual model and empirical analysis of children's acquisition of spatial knowledge. *Journal of Environmental Psychology, 5,* 125–152.

Golledge, R.G., & Spector, A.N. (1978). Comprehending the urban environment: theory and practice. *Geographical Analysis, 10,* 403–426.

Golledge, R.G. & Timmermans, H. (eds.) (1988). *Behavioural modelling in geography and planning.* London: Croom Helm.

Golledge, R.G., & Zannaras, G. (1973). Cognitive approaches to the analysis of human spatial behavior. In W.H. Ittelson (Ed.), *Environmental Cognition.* (pp. 59–94). New York: Seminar Press.

Gopal, S. (1988). *A computational model of spatial navigation.* Unpublished Ph.D. dissertation. Department of Geography, University of California at Santa Barbara.

Gopal, S., & Smith, T.R. (1990). Navigator: An AI-based model of human wayfinding in an urban environment. In M. Fischer, P. Nijkamp, & Y. Papageorgiou (Eds.), *Spatial choices and processes* (pp. 169–202). Amsterdam: Elsevier.

Hägerstrand, T. (1970). What about people in regional science? *North American Regional Science Association, 24,* 7–21.

Hall, R.W. (1983). Traveller route choice: travel time implications of improved information and adaptive decisions. *Transportation Research A, 17,* 201–214.

Harris, C., & Ullman, E. (1945). The nature of cities. *Annals, American Academy of Political and Social Sciences, 242,* 7–17.

Hart, R.A., & Moore, G.T. (1973). The development of spatial cognition: a review. In R. Downs & D. Stea (Eds.), *Image and environment* (pp. 246–288). Chicago: Aldine.

Hirtle, S.C., & Jonides, J. (1985). Evidence of hierarchies in cognitive maps. *Memory and Cognition, 13,* 208–217.

Holz, R. (1973). *The surveillant science.* New York: Houghton-Mifflin.

Hoyt, H. (1939). *The structure and growth of residential neighborhoods in American cities.* Washington, D.C.: Government Printing Office.

Ivanoa, E., & Rozov, N. (1967). *Classification and determination of soil types. No. 1–5* (p. 271). (Translated from Russian, 1970). Jerusalem: Israel Program Science Translation.

Kaplan, R. (1976). Wayfinding in the natural environment. In G. Moore & R.G. Golledge (Eds.), *Environmental knowing* (pp. 46–58). Stroudsburg, Penn: Dowden, Hutchinson and Ross.

Kaplan, S. (1979). Perception and landscape: conceptions and misconceptions. In *U.S. Forest Service General Technical Report PSW-35,* Proceedings of Our National Landscape Conference. Washington, D.C.: Department of Agriculture.

Kaplan, S., & Kaplan, R. (1983). *Cognition and environment: functioning in an uncertain world.* New York: Praeger.

King, L., & Golledge, R.G. (1978). *Cities, space and behavior.* Englewood Cliffs, N.J.: Prentice Hall.

Klingebeil, A., & Montgomery, P. (1961). Land capability classification. *USDA Soil Conservation Service Agricultural Handbook No. 210* (p. 21). Washington, D.C.: U.S. Government Printing Office.

Kosslyn, S. (1975). Information representation in visual images. *Cognitive Psychology, 7,* 341–370.

Kosslyn, S.M., Murphy, G.L., Demesdeer, M.E., & Feinstein, K.J. (1977). Category and continuum in mental comparisons. *Journal of Experimental Psychology: General, 106,* 341–376.

Kuipers, B. (1978). Modelling spatial knowledge. *Cognitive Science, 2,* 129–153.

Kuipers, B. (1979). On representing common sense knowledge. In N.V. Findler (Ed.), *Associative networks: The representation of knowledge by computers* (pp. 393–408). New York: Academic Press.

Kuipers, B. (1983). The cognitive map: could it have been any other way? In L. Acredolo & H. Pick (Eds.), *Spatial orientation theory research and applications* (pp. 345–359). New York: Plenum.

Leiser, D. (1987). The changing relations between representations and cognitive structures in the development of a cognitive map. *New Ideas in Psychology, 5,* 95–110.

Lenntorp, B. (1976). A time-structured study of the travel possibilities of the public transport passenger. *Rapporter och Notiser, 24.* Department of Geography, University of Lund.

Linton, D. (1968). The assessment of scenery as a natural resource. *Scottish Geographical Magazine, 84*(3), 219–238.

Lynch, K. (1960). *Image of the city.* Cambridge, Mass: MIT Press.

MacEachren, A. (1980). Travel time as the basis of cognitive distance. *Professional Geographer, 32,* 30–36.

Maki, R.H. (1981). Categorization and distance effects with spatial linear orders. *Journal of Experimental Psychology: Human Learning and Memory, 7,* 15–32.

McCarthy, H., Hook, J., & Knos, D. (1956). *The measurement of association in industrial geography.* University of Iowa, Department of Geography.

Milgram, S., & Jodelet, D. (1976). Psychological maps of Paris. In H. Proshansky, W. Ittelson, & L. Rivlin (Eds.), *Readings in environmental psychology* (pp. 104–124). New York: Holt, Rinehart & Winston.

Moar, I., & Carlton, L. (1982). Memory for routes. *Quarterly Journal of Experimental Psychology, 34A,* 381–394.

Nasar, J. (1983). Environmental aesthetics in public spaces: applications in decision making. *EDRA Proceedings,* pp. 141–143.

Pailhous, J. (1970). *La representation de l'espace urbain: d'exemple du chauffeur de taxi.* Paris: Presses Universitaires de France.

Piaget, J., & Inhelder, B. (1967). *The child's conception of space.* New York: W.W. Norton.

Pylyshyn, Z. (1981). The imagery debate: Analogue media versus tacit knowledge. *Psychological Review, 88,* 16–45.

Recker, W., McNally, M., & Root, G. (1986). A model of complex travel behavior: part 1. Theoretical development. *Transportation Research A, 20,* 307–318.

Revelle, C. (1987). Urban public facility location. In E. Mills (Ed.), *Handbook of urban and regional economics, Volume II—Urban economics* (pp. 1053–1096). Amsterdam: North-Holland.

Richardson, G. (1979). *The appropriateness of using various Minkowskian metrics for representing cognitive maps produced by nonmetric multidimensional scaling.* Unpublished MA thesis. Department of Geography, University of California, Santa Barbara.

Richardson, G. (1982). *Spatial cognition.* Ph.D. dissertation. University of California, Santa Barbara.

Sadalla, E., Burroughs, W., & Staplin, L. (1980). Reference points in spatial cognition. *Journal of Experimental Psychology: Human Learning and Memory, 5,* 516–528.

Sadalla, E., & Magel, S. (1980). The perception of travelled distance. *Environment - and Behavior, 12,* 65–79.

Sadalla, E. & Staplin, L. (1980a). An information storage model for distance cognition. *Environment and Behavior, 12,* 183–193.

Sadalla, E., & Staplin, L. (1980b). The perceptions of traversed distance cognition. *Environment and Behavior, 12,* 167–182.

Shemyakin, F.N. (1962). General problems of orientation in space and space representations. In B.G. Ananyev (Ed.), *Psychological science in the USSR, Vol. 1.* (NTIS NO. TT62–11083). Washington, D.C.: U.S. Office of Technical Reports.

Shute, V. (1984). *Characteristics of cognitive cartography.* Unpublished Ph.D. dissertation. Graduate School of Education, University of California, Santa Barbara.

Siegel, A., & White, S. (1975). The development of spatial representation of large scale environments. In H. Reese (Ed.), *Advances in child development and behavior* (pp. 9–55). New York: Academic Press.

Smith, T.R., Pellegrino, J., & Golledge, R.G. (1982). Computational process modelling of spatial cognition and behavior. *Geographical Analysis, 14,* 305–325.

Soil Survey Staff (1975). Soil taxonomy. A basic system of soil classification for making and interpreting soil surveys. *USDA Soil Conservation Service agricultural handbook No. 436* (p. 754). Washington, D.C.: U.S. Government Printing Office.

Spector, A.N. (1978). *An analysis of urban spatial imagery.* Unpublished Ph.D. dissertation. Department of Geography, Columbus, Ohio, Ohio State University.

Stevens, A. (1976). *The role of inference and internal structure in representation of spatial information.* Unpublished Ph.D. dissertation. Department of Psychology, University of California, San Diego.

Stevens, A., & Coupe, E.P. (1978). Distortions in judged spatial relations. *Cognitive Psychology, 10,* 422–437.

Stern, E., & Leiser, D. (1988). Levels of spatial knowledge and urban travel modeling. *Geographical Analysis, 20*(2), 140–155.

Thorndyke, P., & Hayes-Roth, B. (1982). Differences in spatial knowledge acquired from maps and navigation. *Cognitive Psychology, 14,* 560–589.

Thornthwaite, C. (1948). An approach toward a rational classification of climate. *Geographical Review, 38*(1), 55–94.

Tobler, W.R. (1976). The geometry of mental maps. In R.G. Golledge & G. Rushton (Eds.), *Spatial choice and spatial behavior* (pp. 69–81). Columbus: Ohio State University Press.

United Nations Food and Agricultural Organization and United Nations Economic and Social Council (1974). *FAO-UNESCO soils map of the world.* Unesco, Paris.

U.S. Department of Transportation (1969). *Standard land use coding manual.* Federal Highway Administration, Bureau of Public Roads.

U.S. Forest Service (1977). Landscape management visual display techniques. *Handbook Chapter 1—Simulation FSH6/77.* Washington, D.C.: U.S. Department of the Interior.

Varnes, D. (1958). Landslide types and processes. In E. Eckel (Ed.), *Landslides and engineering practice (Chapter 3).* Highway Research Board Special Report 29, National Academy of Sciences, Washington, D.C.

Wales (1981). *A landscape classification.* Planning Services, Welsh Office, Crown Building, Cardiff CF13NQ.

Ward, L., & Russell, J. (1981). The psychological representation of molar physical environments. *Journal of Experimental Psychology: General, 110,* 121–152.

Wilton, R. (1979). Knowledge of spatial relations. A specification from the information used in making inferences. *Quarterly Journal of Experimental Psychology, 31,* 133–146.

Zube, E., Pitt, D., & Anderson, T. (1975). Perception and prediction of scenic resource values of the northeast. In E. Zube, R. Brush, & J. Fabos (Eds.), *Landscape assessment.* Stroudsburg, Penn: Dowden, Hutchinson and Ross.

4

Decison-Making Processes, Choice Behavior, and Environmental Design: Conceptual Issues and Problems of Application

HARRY TIMMERMANS

Environmental design is a conscious process in which the environment is shaped to meet certain objectives. In manipulating physical attributes of the environment, the environmental designer influences the aesthetic, functional, economic, and social dimensions of the built environment. Designs will either directly or indirectly exert impacts on the spatial and social behavior of individuals. The architect or urban planner may therefore wish to assess the likely effects of design alternatives on human behaviors when addressing the problem of ex ante evaluation of different design options.

Traditional designers employed rules of thumb and did not spend much time explicitly analyzing and predicting human behavior. However, especially in the field of urban planning, the development of public demands for higher environmental standards, the ever-increasing complexity of urban planning problems, and the process of democratization have all stimulated application of models for predicting the consequences of design alternatives on human behavior. This tendency has perhaps been most strong in the context of spatial behavior. In the Netherlands, for example, it has become common practice, especially in such problem contexts as transportation, retailing, recreation, public facilities, and housing, to base design decisions in part on analyses of human behavior.

The present chapter focuses exclusively on a particular type of decision making and action, namely spatial choice behavior. The extensive research on this type of decision making is not well known to environmental psychologists but there may be a great potential for integrating it with the more traditional research on environmental cognition and assessment. The chapter is organized as follows. First, the problem context is sketched in more depth. A characteristic of research on spatial choice is the development of mathematical–statistical models for predicting choice behavior. The following section outlines a general conceptual framework for the different modeling approaches, which are then briefly explained. A separate section is then devoted to a discussion of the role of the physical environment in spatial choice behavior. The chapter concludes with a discussion of a number of problems research on spatial choice faces. It is contended that the solution to some of these problems may benefit from a broader psychological approach similar to the one taken in environmental psychology.

PROBLEM CONTEXT

As an essential component of environmental design, urban planning is concerned with the location, intensity, and amount of land development for various space-demanding activities. Land use plans are the result of more general planning processes that fulfill certain objectives of economic and social well-being. Research is used to generate the information required to make decisions in the planning process or simply to justify certain policy decisions. Important information in this respect relates to the spatial behavior of individuals. In many cases the design or plan attempts to attract certain groups of individuals, implying insight into the likely reactions of individuals to the plan. Sometimes predictions of the future spatial behavior of individuals are required to assess the feasibility of a project or to assess possible negative external effects of a plan. Finally, predictions of spatial behavior are sometimes required as a necessary link to other evaluation criteria. For example, if design alternatives are to be assessed in terms of the degree of noise that will be created by vehicles as a function of design parameters, the future spatial behavior of individuals needs to be predicted and linked to a model of noise production.

The central problem thus is to predict the spatial choice behavior of individuals: What is the probability that a randomly selected individual will choose a particular choice alternative located at a certain point in space, given its physical attributes, the personal characteristics of the individual, and the location of the individual vis-à-vis the locational pattern of the choice alternatives? This problem was first tackled by developing aggregate models, formulated in analogy to models of physical processes. Models such as the gravity model and the entropy-maximizing model (Wilson, 1974) were not primarily concerned with individual choices but rather with interzonal orientation or interaction patterns, which result by aggregating individual choices across zones. Implicitly these models assumed the existence of perfect information, homogeneity among individuals, identical choice sets, and so on. Surrogate variables were used to define the attractiveness of the choice alternatives. Consequently, the parameters of these models were highly influenced by the chosen zoning system and did not generate much insight into the actual preference structure and decision-making process of individuals. It was this very property that generated considerable criticisms of these aggregate models (Rushton, 1969). The aggregate spatial interaction models merely describe observable interaction patterns rather than producing satisfactory explanations of such patterns. There was a clear need for a cognitive–behavioral approach that seeks to understand the decision-making process of individuals with respect to their environment.

CONCEPTUAL FRAMEWORK

From the 1970s and onward, different types of behavioral choice models have been advanced. All of these models are based on variants of a conceptual model that explicitly relates choice behavior to the environment through consideration of perceptions, cognition, preference formation, and decision making. It is assumed that individuals develop some cognitive representation of the real world. That is, in each decision-making task only a limited number of environmental characteristics are considered because individuals may not perceive or may not remember all of the attributes. These characteristics are implicitly or explicitly evaluated and yield subjective impressions of the different choice alternatives in an individual's choice set. The choice set may include only a subset of the available choice alternatives because individuals may not know all the available choice alternatives. Choices are assumed to be made on the basis of this cognitive representation rather than on characteristics of the environment itself. Individuals are assumed to attach some subjective utility to the attributes defining such a cognitive representation, and combine these utilities into some overall utility according to some combination rule or decision heuristic. This results in a preference structure, which defines the positioning of the choice alternatives in terms of overall utility or preference. Finally, it is assumed that such a preference structure is functionally related to choice behavior. That is, the probability of choosing some alternative is assumed to be systematically related to the overall utilities of the choice alternatives included in an individual's choice set.

Given this conceptual framework, the central problem can be divided into a set of research questions: What are the most important factors influencing the kind of spatial choice behavior under investigation? How do individuals perceive objective attributes of the environment? Are their perceptions related to personal characteristics? What is the functional relationship between the individuals' perceptions and their objective counterparts? How do individuals integrate their part-worth utilities to arrive at some preference structure/choice behavior? What is the functional relationship between individuals' preference structures and subsequent choice behavior?

MODELING APPROACHES

The different approaches used to predict the likely impacts of planning measures may be distinguished into two separate groups. The first set of models is explicitly based on observed behavior. Individuals' behavior in the real world is recorded and *interpreted* in terms of some underlying theory. Choice behavior is seen as the result of some decision-making process by which individuals maximize their utility, choose the alternative with their highest preference, and so on, depending on the theoretical structure that is used by the researcher. Thus, no attempt is made to measure the psychological agents that drive the decision-making process and subsequent choice behavior; revealed behavior is interpreted only in terms of such concepts. In contrast, the second set of models is based on explicit measures of individuals' satisfaction, judgments, or preferences. Space does not allow me to summarize the overwhelming amount of different model structures and advances made with respect to the most popular models (for more information, see, e.g., Timmermans & Borgers, 1986). Rather, a brief summary of the most popular models will be given.

Models Based on Revealed Preferences

These models typically relate observed behavior directly to a set of environmental characteristics. The most popular are the discrete choice models. These models are based on random utility theory and assume stochastic preferences. That is, an individual's utility for a choice alternative is assumed to consist of a deterministic utility component and a random utility component. The deterministic component relates environmental characteristics to behavior, while the random component accounts for heterogeneity, random fluctuations, measurement errors, and so on. In addition, random utility theory assumes a utility-maximizing decision rule. According to such a rule, the probability of choosing some alternative is equal to the probability that the utility associated with that particular choice alternative exceeds that of all other choice alternatives included in the choice set. The actual choice model then depends on the assumptions regarding the distributions of the random utility components. If it is assumed that the random utility components are independently and identically normal distributed with zero mean, the *independent multivariate probit model* results (see Daganzo, 1979). On the other hand, if it is assumed that these random components are independently, identically Type I extreme value distributed, the *multinomial logit model* results (Domencich & McFadden, 1975).

In recent years, various alternative models have been developed that attempt to relax one or more of the rigorous assumptions underlying conventional discrete choice models. The Independence from Irrelevant Alternatives (IIA) assumption imposes the constraint that the ratio of choice probabilities for any two alternatives is invariant with respect to the existence or nonexistence of other choice alternatives. It implies that a new choice alternative will obtain a share by drawing from the existing alternatives in direct proportion to their utilities. This assumption is unrealistic since similar choice alternatives probably compete for their joint market shares. A number of models avoid the IIA property by relaxing the assumption of identically and independently distributed random utility components. Some models allow for different variances of the error terms, others allow for positive correlations between error terms, and still others allow for both (see Borgers & Timmermans, 1988).

Another subclass of non-IIA models circumvents the IIA property by extending the utility specification to account explicitly for similarity between choice alternatives. Finally, a third group of non-IIA models may be distinguished that assumes a hierarchical or sequential decision-making process. Perhaps the best known of these is the nested logit model, in which the alternatives that are supposed to be correlated are grouped together into nests. Each nest is represented by an aggregate alternative with a composite utility consisting of the so-called inclusive value and a parameter to be estimated. To be correctly specified, the inclusive values should lie in the range between 0 and 1, and the values of the parameters should decline from lower levels to higher levels of the hierarchy (McFadden, 1978).

Another approach that avoids the IIA property by assuming a sequential decision structure has been suggested by Tversky (1972a,b). Each choice alternative is assumed to consist of a set of aspects. At each stage of the supposed sequential elimination process, an individual selects one aspect with a probability proportional to the importance of that aspect and eliminates all choice alternatives that do not possess that aspect. This process continues until a single choice alternative remains. Attempts to parameterize this elimination by aspects models include Young, Richardson, Ogden, and Rattray (1982), Young and Ogden (1983), Young and Brown (1983), Young (1984), and Smith and Slater (1981).

Conventional choice models also typically assume that the parameters of the model are invariant with changes in the variation in attribute levels of the choice set. Considerable experimental work has, however, demonstrated that the degree of variability existing among choice alternatives for a particular attribute influences the choice process. The larger the degree of variability, the more important the attribute becomes in the choice process (Eagle, 1984, 1988), implying that the weight attached to a particular attribute shifts to those attributes with the higher degrees of variability. Meyer and Eagle (1982) developed a model that can account for such weight-shifting effects.

Discrete choice models exhibit the regularity property. The introduction of new alternatives in a choice set will never increase the choice probability of any old choice alternative. Yet the introduction of new alternatives might cause an existing choice alternative to become more prominent, implying that the choice probability for this alternative may actually increase. Yu (1978) and Smith and Yu (1982) developed a series of prominence models to account for such effects. The regularity property may also be violated by attraction effects. An attraction effect is the tendency of a new choice alternative to draw choices to alternatives similar to itself (Huber, Payne, & Puto, 1982; Huber & Puto, 1983). Huber (1982) proposed a model that captures such effects.

Almost all spatial choice models are based on the assumption of independence of the spatial structure. The parameters of these models are not influenced by the arrangement of the alternatives in the study area. The models fail to account for competition effects and agglomeration effects. Recently, Fotheringham (1983a,b, 1984, 1985) suggested modifications in traditional spatial interaction models to correct this type of misspecification. Basically, he includes an extra variable, which represents the accessibility of a destination to all other possible destinations. If this parameter is positive, then agglomeration effects are dominant. If the parameter for the accessibility variable is negative, then competition forces between destinations are dominant. Following Fotheringham's general ideas, Borgers and Timmermans (1988) have shown that agglomeration and competition effects can also be included in discrete choice models.

Hanson (1980) criticized discrete choice theory by exploring assumptions that are particularly relevant in modeling destination choice in intraurban travel behavior. Basically, she criticizes conventional choice theory in that no explicit consideration of multistop–multipurpose behavior is given. Conventional disaggregate choice models assume that individuals choose only one alternative within any functional class, and only one at a time. In addition, his or her choices are assumed to be independent, while the utility associated with a choice alternative is not affected by the utility of any other choice alternative. Finally, any systematic variation in utility is denied. In recent years, this type of criticism has led to the development of models of trip chaining and activity patterns.

Finally, considerable progress has been made in extending conventional discrete choice models to the case of dynamic choice behavior. Past behaviors may influence future behaviors. Some authors have shown how the available models may be used to explain certain cases of dynamic choice behavior. Perhaps the most interesting development is the introduction of the beta logistic model, which incorporates the multinomial logit model into a dynamic framework that retains the heterogeneity among individuals (see Dunn & Wrigley, 1985).

There are only a few examples that demonstrate the tendency to incorporate different psychological mechanisms in a discrete choice type of approach to improve the theoretical underpinnings of the model. Undoubtedly, these developments are exciting from a theoretical perspective in that one attempts to integrate more ideas and concepts into some unified modeling framework. Future comparative work should learn whether these more sophisticated models also lead to better predictions of human behaviors. Results obtained in the area of including spatial structure have shown that the improvement in prediction is only minor (Borgers & Timmermans, 1987).

Models Based on Expressed Preferences

Many researchers have argued that overt choice behavior should not be considered as the result of an utility-maximizing decision-making process because overt behavior is also influenced by the constraints imposed by the environment on individual choice behavior. To fully understand individual decision-making and choice processes, one should explicitly measure individual's perceptions and preferences. Several different modeling approaches may be distinguished, but only the decompositional multiattribute preference models will be discussed.

Decompositional multiattribute preference models have in common with the discrete choice models the assumption that individuals cognitively integrate their evaluations of a choice alternative's attributes to derive the utility for a choice alternative. Individuals then arrive at a choice by choosing the alternative with the highest utility. However, unlike discrete choice models, the parameters of the decompositional multiattribute preference models are not derived from real-world data but from contrived experiments.

First, the attributes influencing the choice behavior of interest are categorized. Next, these categories are combined according to an experimental design (full factorial, fractional factorial, or trade-off designs) to yield a set of hypothetical choice alternatives. An individual is then requested to express some measure of preference for each choice alternative. These preference measures are decomposed into the contributions of the categories of the attributes given some prespecified combination rule. Finally, the preference structure is linked to overt choice behavior by specifying some decision rule. A more detailed account of the approach is provided in Timmermans (1984).

Although decompositional multiattribute preference models are not explicitly derived from some formal theory, both strict and random utility theory may be linked with the approach. In addition, Anderson's information integration theory (Anderson, 1974) is associated with this approach. The theory asserts that a response is the result of the integration of information according to simple algebraic rules such as adding, averaging, subtracting, and multiplying.

Whereas the nature of the combination rule has received relatively little attention in the context of discrete choice models, the testing of the most appropriate specification is an important step in decompositional multiattribute preference models. Conjoint measurement and functional measurement have been used to test for the functional form of the utility expression.

Since decompositional multiattribute preference models primarily focus on the formation of preferences, most of these models have assumed a deterministic utility-maximizing decision rule that assumes that the choice alternative with the highest preference score will be selected. More recently, however, different assumptions have led to more complicated specifications involving probabilistic decision rules (Louviere & Meyer, 1979; Timmermans & van der Heijden, 1984).

Although decompositional models have been used in many studies, their practical application has been hindered by a number of unresolved problems and limitations. These models lack an integrated theoretical framework linking preferences to choice behavior, and the form or the parameters of utility or decision functions may vary with differences in choice set composition and may therefore not be context independent. Finally, task demands for individual respondents become more and more onerous as the number of attributes and/or the number of levels of attributes increase. Recently, progress has been made in providing possible solutions to these problems (see Louviere & Timmermans, 1987, for a more extensive discussion).

THE ROLE OF THE PHYSICAL ENVIRONMENT

The general aim of the modeling approaches outlined in the previous discussion is to predict the probability that an individual will choose a particular alternative (shopping center, transport mode, recreation area, residential environment, etc.) from among a set of alternatives. They offer a set of related underlying theoretical considerations that might be applied to many choice situations. The operationalization of the models in terms of the attributes that are assumed to influence the choice behavior of interest will thus be dependent on the field of application.

In the case of urban planning though, most of the attributes refer to aspects of the physical environment. For example, spatial shopping choice behavior is influenced by attributes such as the location of the shopping center, the amount of floorspace or size of the center, its layout, the types of available shops, the presence or absence of magnet or department stores, price levels, atmosphere, and parking facilities. Likewise, residential choice behavior is typically assumed to be a function of attributes such as price/mortgage, number of rooms, tenure, size of the backyard, type of house, greenery in the neighbourhood, and facilities. Recreational choice behavior is modeled in terms of variables such as distance, type of terrain, activities that can be performed, and maintenance.

Hence, the role one assigns to the physical environment depends on the definition of this construct. In physical planning, one tends to use the concept to differentiate it from, for instance, the cognitive environment. It refers to different aspects that can be attached to objects or areas located in space. In this sense, one ensures that choice behavior bears some systematic relationship with aspects of the physical environment. Often, as, for example, in the context of spatial shopping behavior, the model is fully operationalized in terms of aspects of the physical environment. In other fields of application, such as residential choice behavior, aspects of the social environment may be incorporated into the model.

If one adopts a more restricted interpretation of the construct of the physical environment in that it refers to strictly physical features, such as light, color, wind, texture, distance, and size, it should be evident that the role of the physical environment in influencing individuals choice behavior is far less important. In the kind of studies referred to in this chapter variables such as color, light, wind, and texture are hardly ever incorporated in the choice model. Moreover, studies that attempt to elicit the factors influencing the choice of shopping centers, residential environments, and so on suggest that such variables are not important in these contexts. Thus, some compound physical features of the environment are often used as predictors in models of spatial choice, partly because the development of such models is so responsive to the practical concerns of urban planning. At the same time there is a realization that basic research is needed to reveal the nature of the decision-making processes intervening between physical features of the environment and choice behavior. What role the physical environment will play in conceptualizations of the decision-making process is a question for the future.

DISCUSSION

As is evident from the preceding review, there is considerable interest in developing models that represent actual decision-making processes. In this respect, a number of interrelated problems deserve closer critical examination. These will be considered now.

Revealed versus Expressed Preferences

Most models of spatial choice behavior, that is, the discrete choice models discussed in this chapter, are based on observed behavior. Apparently, many researchers believe that it is only in the act of choice that individuals can express their preferences. Others seem to think that one can ask subjects almost anything. Perhaps the truth is somewhere in between.

A fundamental problem with observed behavior is that it may not be the result either only or mainly of individual preferences. For example, patterns of housing market choice are likely to be influenced by constraints deriving from personal, environmental, and social factors. The effect of these factors on observed choice patterns cannot be readily determined. It is also very unlikely that these antecedent conditions will remain stable in time, implying that under such circumstances the predictive validity of models based on observed behavior is probably rather low.

Models relying on revealed preferences also have the clear disadvantage of restricting themselves to the domain of experience. Revealed preferences, by definition, concern the choice of actual alternatives. Since this set of alternatives is only one subset from among all possible sets of spatial alternatives, these models extrapolate beyond the actual types of alternatives. Even if the new alternatives lie within the range, the validity of the model may be relatively low because certain data points may exert a strong influence on the final results.

In contrast, experimental designs permit varying the attribute levels in every possible way, implying that subjects' responses to novel choice alternatives can be measured. Choice alternatives can be specified beyond the domain of experience. Therefore, in theory at least, the results of laboratory experiments can be transferred to real-world situations that previously did not exist. The problem, however, is that one has to demonstrate that subjects view hypothetical choice alternatives in a manner similar to how they consider real-world choice alternatives. Thus, one needs to demonstrate that the experimental measurements bear some systematic relationship with overt choice behavior. Over the years, a large amount of empirical evidence supporting this assertion has been accumulated in a variety of spatial choice contexts (see Timmermans, 1984, for a review). However, most of these studies have used alternatives with which subjects were familiar. If individual responses in experiments are based on the experiences individuals have had in the real world, as is commonly believed, there is also a limit to the validity. For example, individual choice behavior related to teleshopping cannot be predicted with discrete choice models, simply because data on observed choice behavior are not yet available. A decompositional preference model could be used, but since respondents have never had any experience with this kind of shopping, the validity of their responses could be seriously questioned.

Some respondents have great difficulty in understanding the experimental task that follows from the use of decompositional preference models. Others may adopt patterned responses to simplify the task. These problems already occur with simple designs. Many recent developments involve more sophisticated and hence more difficult experimental tasks, implying that the reliability and validity of such measurements may be in doubt for an even larger number of sample respondents. However, one should not conclude from these statements that the reliability and validity of measurements necessarily deteriorate (e.g., Akaah & Korgaonkar, 1983; Timmermans, 1987). Apparently, it is not only the difficulty of the measurement task that counts, but also whether the cognitive processes that are tapped by measurements show some similarity with those used in actual real-world decision-making processes.

The Theoretical Underpinnings of the Approaches

Discrete choice models can be derived from a number of theories. Basically, these models relate observed choice patterns directly to sets of influential variables. In contrast, decompositional multiattribute preference models represent more closely the actual decision-making process underlying spatial choice behavior. In a separate modeling step, the factors influencing the choice process of interest are elicited by methods such as factor listing and repertory grids. In addition, the cognitive representations of reality are gauged. Moreover, the way in which individuals combine their separate evaluations of environmental attributes into some overall preference is investigated. Finally, the correspondence between preference and choice is subject to explicit modeling.

The question is how much theory and what kind of theory is required to improve the usefulness of models to environmental design. It is well known that simple extrapolation procedures sometimes provide as good a prediction as very complicated models. Also, many practitioners advocate the development of simple models to maximize the chances that policymakers understand the theory underlying the models and therefore will actually use them. On the other hand, models may become too simple to be of any use, or mask some of the essential characteristics of the phenomenon under investigation. Hence, simple models should be advocated only if they produce the same kind of information and if their predictive success is not substantially less than that associated with a more complex model, given the role of the model in the design process.

It is evident that decompositional models produce more information than discrete-choice models. In addition to predictions of spatial choice patterns, they also yield information regarding the attributes considered important by the respondents, their cognitive representations of reality, and their perceptions. If this information is also important in the design or planning process, the decompositional models should clearly be preferred. However, the decompositional models arrive at this information by concentrating on the outcome of the psychological process. The process itself, not psychological dispositions, states of mind, or human needs, are explicitly considered. The question is whether a more detailed modeling of psychological processes would be necessary to improve its usefulness to urban planning. Again, the answer to this question depends on the kinds of information required in the urban planning process. In my own experience, policymakers are not specifically interested in such psychological phenomena. This implies that one could concentrate on the outcomes of the process as long as the predictive validity of the models is sufficient given the objectives of the planning process.

The Link between Preferences and Choice

Many researchers are against measuring preferences explicitly because they doubt individuals can validly express their preferences. Preferences are believed to be an artifact of the measurement procedure. At the very least, they are seldom related to subsequent choice behavior. Such arguments are usually substantiated by reference to studies demonstrating that factors such as social desirability strongly influence respondents' answers to preference questions. Although there may be some truth to this criticism, in the end it is an empirical question. If expressed preferences are used, it is important to show that they bear some systematic relationship to overt behavior. For many fields of application, such systematic relationships have been demonstrated (Timmermans, 1984).

Thus, empirical evidence suggests that in many spatial choice contexts, preferences are systematically related to overt behavior. This relationship is, however, not deterministic. Thus, probabilistic choice rules rather than simple deterministic ones should be used. This is an area that has received relatively minor attention so far. Explicit attention should also be given to the composition of the choice set, partly as a result of the constraints an individual faces and partly as a result of the imperfections of the perception and cognition of the environment.

Algebraic Rules versus Choice Heuristics

Discrete choice and decompositional models have in common the assumption that simple algebraic rules can be used to describe how individuals integrate their part-worth utilities to arrive at some overall preference or choice. In practice, a linear specification is typically used. Here the researcher implicitly assumes some compensatory decision-making process in which low evaluations of some attribute can be compensated for by high evaluation scores on one or more of the remaining attributes. Much research, especially in the field of process-tracing studies, has however indicated that individuals tend to use simple heuristic choice strategies. This is particularly common whenever the number of attributes or the complexity of the decision making task increases (Payne, 1982). There is a need therefore to assess more fully the potential contribution of computational process models, decision nets, and simple qualitative models, based on such choice heuristics, to the prediction of spatial-choice behavior. This constitutes an exciting new area of research. Nonetheless, the problems inherent in such an approach should not be underestimated. This is especially true if one fully acknowledges in the model-building process that the choice strategies individuals use are contingent on many factors.

A Typology of Decision-Making Processes

It is somewhat surprising to see the same theories being applied over and over again to a wide variety of spatial choice problems, such as shopping behavior, route choice behavior, housing market choice behavior, and recreational choice behavior. These various types of spatial behavior have some clearly distinctive characteristics. Spatial shopping behavior is repetitive, perhaps habitual; the choice set is relatively small and although individuals usually are not aware of all opportunities, they often have a rather good image of at least a few choice alternatives; most of the environmental attributes of the choice alternatives change only slowly, if at all, and there is relatively little risk involved in the decision that will usually also have little impact if wrong. In contrast, the housing choice decision is much more isolated; only a few of these decisions will be made during a lifetime, individuals will know only a few of the choice alternatives, and will probably have to acquire the information used in the decision-making process; the choice set may change rapidly and the impact of possible wrong decisions may be dramatic. Likewise, recreational choice behavior may be more influenced by a drive for variety rather than by habit (Timmermans, 1985).

Hence, it might be worthwhile to think in terms of a typology of decision-making processes and develop models that are tailored to some of the basic characteristics of the choice behavior of interest. Moreover, comparative analyses should be conducted to examine the superiority of some approach over the others. For example, van der Heijden and Timmermans (1987) have formulated a model of variety seeking behavior in the context of recreational choice behavior. This model captures many of the essentials of this kind of behavior better as indicated by a statistically significant improvement of the predictive success of the model compared to that of a conventional choice model.

Manipulable Variables

Spatial choice models are used to predict the likely impacts of urban planning decisions or environmental designs on choice behavior. This goal can be established only if the planning decisions or the design are defined in terms of a set of variables that is used as independent (explanatory) variables in the model. By definition, these are attributes of the environment that can be manipulated.

Many of the discrete choice models use only surrogate planning variables. This raises the problem that one does not know the form of the relationship between these surrogate variables and the variables actually influencing spatial choice behavior. If these relationships are nonlinear, as might be expected, a fundamental problem is that it is unclear how one can assume that manipulating the surrogate variables will have the desired policy effect on spatial choice behavior. In theory at least, this problem is avoided in expressed preferences because one explicitly examines the relationships between preferences and objective attribute levels. One way to proceed is to identify the variables individuals use in choosing from among spatial alternatives. These subjective variables are then compared to their objective counterparts. Alternatively, the manipulable variables are included in the experimental design, implying one can estimate individuals preferences and/or choices as a function of these planning variables.

Hence, from an applied perspective one wishes to include manipulable variables because this provides a direct prediction of the effect of planning decisions on choices. However, in terms of construct validity, one wishes to include those variables in the models that are really used in an individual's decision-making process. Often, these variables are different, implying the need for a model that links the manipulable variables to the variables individuals use in choosing among alternatives.

Situational Variables

A closely related problem concerns the inclusion of situational variables. Both discrete choice and decompositional preference models typically assume stable utility or preference functions. Discrete choice models usually do not include situational variables. Likewise, decompositional preference models attempt to uncover individual preferences or choice for a well-defined decision-making task, but again, situational factors are neither varied in the task description nor included in the definition of the experimental treatments. Yet there are many examples of the influence of situational factors: Interest levels and the overall economic prospects may influence housing market processes, income levels and last year's profits/losses may have an impact on entrepreneural decision-making processes, and weather conditions may exert an effect on recreational choice behavior. Hence, more research effort should be devoted to the analyses of situational variables on decision-making and choice processes. This might prove to be a very difficult task in the context of discrete choice models, but should be rather straightforward in the context of decompositional models. In a discrete choice framework, one needs time-series data, which are difficult to obtain. On the other hand, the situational variables can possibly be varied in experiments and individuals preferences and choices under such varying conditions observed and analyzed.

CONCLUDING REMARKS

The present chapter has sought to clarify a conceptual framework, modeling approaches, and problems that are prevalent in the study of the relationship between the physical environment, decision-making processes, and spatial choice. Available space did not allow the review at any depth of all the different approaches and issues worthy of discussion. Nevertheless, it is hoped that this chapter will contribute to a discussion of new directions in the modeling of human spatial decision-making and choice processes.

REFERENCES

Akaah, I., & Korgaonkar, P.K. (1983). An empirical comparison of the predictive validity of self-explicated, Huber-hybrid, traditional conjoint and hybrid conjoint models. *Journal of Marketing Research, 20,* 187–198.

Anderson, N.H. (1974). Information integration theory: A survey. In D.H. Krantz, R.C. Atkinson, & R.D. Luce (Eds.), *Contemporary developments in mathematical psychology* (pp. 236–305). San Francisco: Freeman.

Borgers, A.W.J., & Timmermans, H.J.P. (1987). Choice model specification, substitution and spatial structure effects: A simulation experiment. *Regional Science and Urban Economics, 17,* 29–47.

Borgers, A.W.J., & Timmermans, H.J.P. (1988). A context-sensitive model of spatial choice behavior. In R.G. Golledge & H.J.P. Timmermans (Eds.), *Behavioral modelling in geography and planning* (pp. 159–178). Kent: Croom Helm.

Daganzo, C.F. (1979). *Multinomical probit: The theory and its application to demand forecasting.* New York: Academic Press.

Domencich, T.A., & McFadden, D. (1975). *Urban travel demand: a behavioral analysis.* Amsterdam: North Holland.

Dunn, R., & Wrigley, N. (1985) Beta-logistic models of urban shopping center choice. *Geographical Analysis, 17,* 95–113.

Eagle, T.C. (1984). Parameter stability in disaggregate retail choice models: Experimental evidence. *Journal of Retailing, 60,* 101–123.

Eagle, T.C. (1988). Context effects in consumer spatial behaviour. In R.G. Golledge & H.J.P. Timmermans (Eds.), *Behavioral modelling in geography and planning* (pp. 299–324). Kent: Croom Helm.

Fotheringham, A.S. (1983a). A new set of spatial interaction models: the theory of competing destinations. *Environment and Planning A, 15,* 15–36.

Fotheringham, A.S. (1983b). Some theoretical aspects of destination choice and their relevance to production-constrained gravity models. *Environment and Planning A, 15,* 1121–1132.

Fotheringham, A.S. (1984). Spatial structure and the parameters of spatial interaction models. *Geographical Analysis, 12,* 33–46.

Fotheringham, A.S. (1985). Spatial competition and agglomeration in urban modelling. *Environment and Planning A, 17,* 213–230.

Hanson, S. (1980). Spatial diversification and multipurpose travel: Implications for choice theory. *Geographical Analysis, 12,* 245–257.

Huber, J. (1982). *The effect of set composition on item choice: separating attraction, edge aversion and substitution effects.* Unpublished manuscript.

Huber, J., Payne, J., & Puto, C. (1982). Adding asymmetrically dominated alternatives: Violations of regularity and the similarity hypothesis. *Journal of Consumer Research, 9,* 90–98.

Huber, J., & Puto, C. (1983). Market boundaries and product choice: Illustrating attraction and substitution effects. *Journal of Consumer Research, 10,* 31–44.

Louviere, J.J., & Meyer, R.J. (1979). *Behavioral analysis of destination choice.* (Tech. Rep. No. 112.) Iowa City: University of Iowa, Department of Geography.

Louviere, J.J., & Timmermans, H.J.P. (1987). *A review of some recent developments in decompositional preference and choice modelling.* Paper presented at the 5th European Colloquium on Theoretical and Quantitative Geography, Bardonnecchia, Italy.

Louviere, J.J., & Woodworth, G. (1983). Design and analysis of simulated consumer choice and allocation experiments: An approach based on aggregate data. *Journal of Marketing Research, 20,* 350–367.

McFadden, D. (1978). Modelling the choice of residential location. In A. Karlqvist, L. Lundqvist, F. Snickars, and J.W. Weibull (Eds.), *Spatial interaction theory and planning models* (pp. 75–96). Amsterdam: North-Holland.

Meyer, R.J., & Eagle, T.C. (1982). Context-induced parameter instability in a disaggregate stochastic model of store choice. *Journal of Marketing Research, 19,* 62–71.

Payne, J.W. (1982). Contingent decision behavior. *Psychological Bulletin, 92,* 382–402.

Rushton, G. (1969). Analysis of spatial behavior by revealed space preference. *Annals of the Association of American Geographers, 59,* 391–400.

Smith, T.R., & Slater, P.B. (1981). A family of spatial interaction models incorporating information flows and choice set constraints applied to U.S. interstate labour flows. *International Regional Science Review, 6,* 15–31.

Smith, T.E., & Yu, W. (1982). A prominence theory of context-sensitive choice behavior. *Journal of Mathematical Sociology, 8,* 225–249.

Timmermans, H.J.P. (1984). Decompositional multiattribute preference models in spatial choice analysis: A review of some recent developments. *Progress in Human Geography, 8,* 189–221.

Timmermans, H.J.P. (1985). *Variety-seeking models and recreational choice behavior.* Paper presented at the Pacific Regional Science Conference, Molokai, Hawaii.

Timmermans, H.J.P. (1987). Hybrid and non-hybrid evaluation models for predicting outdoor recreation behavior: A test of predictive ability. *Leisure Sciences, 9,* 67–76.

Timmermans, H.J.P., & Borgers, A.W.J. (1986). *Spatial choice models: fundamentals, trends and prospects.* Paper prepared for the 4th European Colloquium in Theoretical and Quantitative Geography, Veldhoven.

Timmermans, H.J.P., & van der Heijden, R.E.C.M. (1984). The predictive ability of alternative decision rules in decompositional multiattribute preference models. *Sistemi Urbani, 5,* 89–101.

Tversky, A. (1972a). Elimination-by-aspects: A theory of choice. *Psychological Review, 79,* 281–299.

Tversky, A. (1972b). Choice by elimination. *Journal of Mathematical Psychology, 9*, 341–367.

van der Heijden, R. & Timmermans, H.J.P. (1987). *Variety-seeking outdoor recreational choice behavior: empirical evidence and model development.* Paper presented at the NRPA Leisure Research Symposium, New Orleans.

Wilson, A. (1974). *Urban and regional models in geography and planning.* New York: Wiley.

Young, W. (1984). A non-trade-off decision-making model of residential location choice. *Transportation Research A, 18*, 1–12.

Young, W., & Brown, H.P. (1983). *A revealed importance elimination-by-aspects model of mode choice.* Paper presented at the PTRC Summer Conference, Sussex.

Young, W., & Ogden, K.W. (1983). Analysis of freight-facility location choice using an elimination-by-aspects model. *Proceedings of the 8th, Australian Transport Research Forum, 3*, 265–281.

Young, W., Richardson, A.J., Ogden, K.W., & Rattray, A.L. (1982). Road and rail freight mode choice: The application of an elimination-by-aspects model. *Transportation Research Record, 838*, 38–44.

Yu, W. (1978). *Contributions to applications of linear logit models in transportation research.* Unpublished doctoral dissertation. University of Pennsylvania, Philadelphia.

5

Searching for the Environment in Environmental Cognition Research

CRAIG ZIMRING AND MARK GROSS

Research in environmental cognition has been fragmented into at least three related but separate areas that reflect different purposes, viewpoints, and disciplinary conventions (Evans and Gärling, this volume). One tradition has focused on predicting spatial choices such as choosing shops or modes of transportation (Timmermans, this volume). A second tradition, driven in part by the necessity to make value judgments about settings to be spared or modified in development, has focused on the assessment of environments, and particularly on the visual quality of natural settings (R. Kaplan, this volume). Finally, a third tradition, coming principally from psychology and geography, has focused on exploring the content and structure of mental representations of the environment (Golledge, this volume).

In this chapter we discuss these three approaches to environmental cognition and examine how they can contribute to each other and to a more general view of action, evaluation, and cognition. We focus specifically on the linkages between the physical environment, cognitive mediators, and outcomes such as wayfinding, decision making, and other actions. We pay particular attention to how the environment and mediators are represented.

This chapter is organized into several sections. After the introduction, we review the chapters in this volume by Timmermans, R. Kaplan, and Golledge. Unlike much previous work in evaluation and in spatial decision making, all three authors discuss the cognitive processes that mediate between environment and behavior. The following section considers alternative approaches to cognitive mediators such as mental models and schemas. Following this, we briefly examine how the physical setting has been represented in environmental cognition. We then turn to computational models that attempt to provide rigorous definitions of both environment and mediator. Next, we propose our own preliminary schema-based model of wayfinding. Finally, we suggest some questions for further research.

THE SCRUFFIES AND THE NEATS

In artificial intelligence research a distinction is made between two alternative approaches to theory: "scruffy" and "neat" (Luger & Stubblefield, 1989). Whereas researchers following both traditions are interested in simulating human cognitive behavior, the scruffies primarily focus on producing a computational system where the *outcomes* mimic human behavior. Neats are interested in reproducing human outcomes, but adopt cognitive science approaches that attempt to accurately model people's mental *processes* as well. For example, a scruffy approach to medical diagnosis might be primarily concerned with producing a system that provides diagnoses similar to those an actual physician might provide, even if it uses information or steps the doctor might not use. Whereas a neat approach would attempt to mimic human outcomes, it would also attempt to specify the processes the doctor goes through in arriving at a diagnosis. In terms of a general model, the scruffies may be said to be searching for direct links between the environment and behavior, whereas the neats are using a mediational model. Neither of these approaches is intrinsically better; they simply provide different emphases.

COMMENTS ON THE CHAPTERS BY
R. KAPLAN, TIMMERMANS, AND GOLLEDGE

The chapters in this volume by Timmermans, R. Kaplan, and Golledge come from different fields and perspectives yet have significant commonalities. Timmermans is primarily concerned with developing methods to help architects and planners make decisions, such as about the siting and design of shopping centers. Kaplan is concerned with developing a psychological theory of landscape assessment that focuses on how and why observers categorize landscapes. Golledge provides a basic description of the elements and processes of cognitive maps. However, all three authors discuss their own neat approaches to fields dominated by scruffy strategies. In summarizing previous approaches, for example, Kaplan describes numerous methods for categorizing landscape attributes developed by the U.S. Bureau of Land Management and other agencies. These methods attempt to predict experts' or laypersons' evaluation of a scene based on attributes such as the amount of water visible or the depth of views. No special theoretical claims are made for links between attribute and assessment nor do they attempt to describe the intermediate steps between environmental features and outcomes such as evaluative judgments. Similarly, Timmermans describes several earlier discrete models of spatial choice behavior that are based on predicting "revealed" outcome behavior and that seek to relate environmental characteristics directly to observed behavior. Once again, these are scruffy models because they do not attempt to account for the cognitive processes mediating environmental characteristics and behavior. Kaplan, Timmermans, and Golledge are neats: All explicitly explore links between the environment and behavior. All attempt to understand cognitive representations of the environment that mediate between the physical environment and human behavior.

In his chapter, Timmermans discusses models of human spatial choice behavior. In his own words Timmermans seeks to model the likely effects of design alternatives on human behaviors when addressing the problem of *ex ante* evaluation of design alternatives. He is interested in helping architects and planners predict the outcome of different design alternatives.

For example, a planner may be faced with the questions: What attributes of a shopping center best predict the likelihood of a shopper coming to it? What attributes of shoppers or of location affect shopping behavior? What is the relative impact of these attributes?

Timmermans' model has several steps:

1. A choice set of possible alternatives is established. This is based on the assumption that the physical environment is encoded by the individual as a cognitive representation that includes some subset of all possible choice alternatives. In deciding which shopping center to patronize, for instance, because of lack of familiarity with some choices a shopper will probably not include all possible shopping centers in his or her choice set.

2. This choice set is represented by operationalized attributes. For shopping centers, this might include choice and convenience, operationalized as number of stores, length of time necessary to find a parking spot, and distance from home. In Timmermans' decompositional approach these attributes are derived directly from responses of potential shoppers, using methods such as the Kelly repertory grid or other interview procedures.

3. "Part-worth" utilities are assigned to each attribute that reflects their subjective evaluation. In a recent study by Timmermans (this volume), part-worth utilities were derived by having people rate hypothetical shopping centers that reflect all possible combinations of three levels of the three attributes (number of stores, distance from home, and length of time to find parking). Given the part-worth utilities, weights are assigned to the attributes.

4. A decision rule is established that is typically, though not necessarily, a linear combination of the part-worth evaluations of the attributes.

5. Behavior is predicted based on a (usually deterministic) application of the decision rule.

Unlike earlier decision models, Timmermans' approach is neat: it explicitly posits a specific psychological model with orderly steps of identifying and operationalizing attributes, establishing part-worth utilities, and defining a decision rule. Timmermans collects data at the several steps in the mental process he postulates people go through while making decisions.

Timmermans decompositional model incorporates some common-sense assumptions that were not part of earlier discrete choice models. For instance, earlier models did not allow the spatial structure of choice alternatives to affect decision making: Two choices near each other were not seen as interacting. In Timmermans' approach, spatial patterns are seen as having an effect on decisions. In addition, unlike previous discrete approaches, in Timmermans' decompositional model new alternatives can affect similar alternatives more than dissimilar ones.

Timmermans' model assumes that people respond to a cognitive representation of the environment rather than the setting itself and represents the environment as an operationalization of attributes. However, the experimental methods he uses (having people rate hypothetical combinations of levels of attributes) limits him to a small number of attributes and relatively few levels of each attribute.

In her chapter in this volume, R. Kaplan proposes that the concept of "assessment" be used broadly: In her terms it is the equivalent of taking account of what's there, or reading the environment. She suggests that assessment depends on two processes: description and prediction. Description is based on categorization, where the individual parses the environment at different levels and in different ways depending on experience and expertise. For instance, it has been demonstrated that environmental professionals attend to different environmental categories than lay people and evaluate them differently.

Rachel Kaplan, Steve Kaplan, and their co-workers have found that they can derive ''emergent'' categories by analyzing patterns of preference that people have for visual scenes. Subjects rate their preference for scenes using slides or photographs and categories are derived using multidimensional scaling techniques. The Kaplans and their co-workers theorize that these categories have considerable significance based on humans' evolutionary past as decision makers. Across a large number of studies, people tend to prefer scenes that appear to enhance possibilities for further action or decision making, such as scenes with distinctive identifiable features, or where openness makes it easier to find one's way.

R. Kaplan's model suggests that after the individual mentally describes what is there, he or she assigns value to a setting based on its ability to support a given purpose, such as wayfinding, and that this value determines preference for a visual scene. Moreover, although people with different background and experience assess scenes differently, Kaplan argues that everyone generally uses two types of categories: *content* such as presence of human intervention and *spatial configuration* such as openness and coherence.

Although coming from radically different research traditions in planning and environmental psychology, Timmermans' and R. Kaplan's approaches have several similarities. Both assume that environmental assessment can best be understood using a mediational cognitive model, where environmental behavior is mediated by people's assessments of perceived categories or attributes. Both authors focus on responses by lay users rather than experts and both attempt to discover emergent categories using analyses of preferences among simulated alternatives such as photographs or hypothetical choices.

Categories emerge at somewhat different stages in the two methodologies. Timmermans establishes categories such as choice and convenience before he provides his subjects a choice between alternative settings. As a consequence, he provides his subjects with a simplified hypothetical choice, and includes information only about the attributes he is testing. By contrast, R. Kaplan shows her subjects photographs of complex real scenes that she then clusters based on preference responses, and derives categories such as openness.

In addition, the two authors take different approaches to the physical setting. Whereas both Timmermans and R. Kaplan derive categories from subjects, Timmermans argues that the physical setting can be measured independently of human evaluation such as by counting stores or travel distance. Kaplan makes no claim that the environment can be measured separately from the responses people make to it.

The approaches also differ in their attitude toward theory. Although R. Kaplan allows categories to emerge, her analysis is based on a functional perspective that posits a central role for preference in evolution. She argues that the preference for scenes that afford wayfinding and understanding of the environment is a reflection of evolutionary pressure: people who liked to understand the environment survived. As a result, preference is a theoretically significant dependent measure and predictions are possible about what people will prefer.

Timmermans takes an empirical approach, allowing attributes, part-worth utilities, and decision rules to emerge from the data without specifying any theory that might predict them. Hence, although he posits that it is possible to measure the physical setting, he has no theory that predicts a priori what aspects of the setting will be significant. It seems to us, however, that Timmermans' inductive approach requires that implicit theories operate. He pares down interviews to arrive at a few attributes, operationalizes attributes, and comes up with a few levels of the attribute to actually test. However, it seems impossible for the researcher not to insert plausible or expected categories, even if they are general beliefs such as the importance of convenience in decision making or even the metatheoretical notion that people make decisions rationally. If the researcher is using one or more implicit theories, it is important to explicitly state and test these theories.

Kaplan's theoretical perspective can inform Timmermans' approach. Broadly, her perspective argues that *purpose* is an important issue in understanding what attributes will be chosen in a given decision framework and that what might be called "cognitive utility"—the degree to which a choice alternative affords wayfinding or understanding—will often be significant. Furthermore, Kaplan's view suggests that preference is an important and useful judgment: It may be a good measure for judging hypothetical choice alternatives. However, it is not immediately apparent how the general categories that Kaplan derives—openness, legibility, and so on—apply to the specific problems Timmermans is attempting to solve, such as the appropriate number of stores in a shopping center or maximum distance shoppers will travel to it. Timmermans' model provides categories of the physical world that are familiar to decision makers: distance, size, number. We wonder whether a linkage can be made between these descriptors and the "intermediate level" environmental descriptors that Kaplan uses.

In his chapter, Golledge provides a detailed discussion of possible links between environmental description and cognitive representation. He argues that the basic elements in a setting are life forms, objects, and behavioral processes. Elements or phenomena have identity, locality, magnitude, and temporal existence. Using a category system similar to Piaget's discussion of the child's development of spatial concepts (see, for example, Piaget & Inhelder, 1967; Robinson & Petchnik, 1976), entities in the environment can be grouped as categories or distributions and can be related by separation, connection, placement in a region, spatial stratification, and spatial structure, which may combine the previous characteristics.

Golledge is concerned with how different kinds of knowledge, such as of landmarks, routes, and overall configuration, become integrated into a common knowledge structure that in turn guides recognition and evaluation of objects and situations in everyday life. He states that this structure is developmental in that it goes through an orderly and predictable set of transformations from topological to geometric as people gain familiarity with places.

The structure is also hierarchical. There is some evidence that people often organize their planning of routes by attempting to get near their destination using a well-understood major route system, then use a secondary system, even if this plan does not result in the shortest route (Pailhous, 1970). This process is like giving directions to one's home using an expressway; one may give quite sketchy directions ("it's the next exit after the blue building") to the expressway exit then provide more detailed directions from the exit. Golledge argues that this may be a quite general process even in situations where major routes are not well defined. Also, Golledge cites evidence that people organize their mental maps by region: People can respond more quickly to judgments about distance or similarity to points in different regions than to ones in the same region (Wilton, 1979; Maki, 1981). If these hierarchical relationships do exist, they may require highly complex characterizations of the structure of mental maps. For example, points within clusters may be geometrically organized but regions may be topologically organized around "anchor points" that serve in some way to represent an entire region.

Like Timmermans and R. Kaplan, Golledge is arguing that the cognitive representation of the environment is an important mediator of the relationship between the environment and everyday behavior. He is more explicit in suggesting the nature and structure of this representation as being hierarchical and dependent on specific features such as regions and anchor points.

In sum, we can contrast the three approaches as to whether they consider the physical setting as something that is knowable separately from the response people make to it, whether any general theory is proposed that links environment to representation to behavior and how mental representation is described. Timmermans proposes that the environment is measurable but provides no theory of why some environmental attributes are significant; R. Kaplan provides a functionalist model that predicts the general categories with which people respond to scenes but provides no independent way of measuring scenes; Golledge describes cognitive mediators in detail and the role of individual environmental experience in developing representations but only hints at links to physical form.

In terms of linking environment and mediator to action, an important question about the approaches by R. Kaplan, Timmermans, and Golledge is how *existing* generic and specific environmental information directs learning and action. All three suggest that people base action on intervening cognitive mediators that provide simplified and distorted views of the world. Timmermans suggest that people use a small set of attributes to judge a limited choice set; Kaplan argues that people use a limited mental model to decide how to categorize, evaluate, and act on what they experience; Golledge suggests that cognitive maps are highly dependent on individual experience.

One way to approach these differences is through the concept of *expertise* that runs through all three chapters. All three authors argue that people's expertise is critical in understanding their evaluation and use of the physical setting and that experts and laypersons may use different psychological categories. Put most simply, expertise involves developing a facility for categorizing the world in ways that are useful for professional or other well-rehearsed purposes that may not be accessible to laypersons. Hence, different kinds or levels of expertise may result in different mental representations, different assessments, and different action.

In the next section we explore some recent proposals for the mental representation of molar knowledge.

PSYCHOLOGICAL MEDIATORS IN
ENVIRONMENTAL COGNITION RESEARCH

A number of constructs have been proposed recently to explain the mental representation of space, place, situation, and other complex phenomena: cognitive maps (Kaplan & Kaplan, 1982), plans (Gärling & Golledge, 1989), frames (Minsky, 1975), scripts (Schank & Abelson, 1977), schemata (Brewer, 1987; Mandler, 1984), and mental models (Johnson-Laird, 1980, 1983; Getnner & Stevens, 1983; de Kleer & Brown, 1981). These various approaches use a large number of terms and concepts that are seldom used precisely or with any common agreement. In this section we attempt to sort through some of these ideas.

All of these constructs attempt to explain how the memory or experience of a specific episode is dependent on some generic or long-term component of memory. In a recent review of the literature addressing frames, scripts, stories, schemas, mental models, causal mental models, and situation models, Brewer proposed two distinctions that organize the various concepts: (1) whether researchers were studying underlying generic knowledge structures or the episodic representations formed from these structures; (2) whether representations are assumed to be derived from old generic knowledge or are created at the time of use (Brewer, 1987). He argues, for example, that it is a different memory problem to remember *that* you ordered in a restaurant than that you ordered a *specific dish*. Brewer calls the first situation an "instantiated schema." In remembering a general act such as "ordering" one is taking advantage of his or her generic "global schema" of restaurants: the schema "restaurant" has "ordering" as an integral part. In the second situation, one is using an "episodic model" derived from a "local schema" of a particular experience in a specific restaurant. Hence, one's memory may derive from a generic prototype of similar events or situations or places or from specific episodic knowledge.

Although Brewer does not address the question of the development of prototypes, they can presumably be generalized from direct experience or from some kind of simulation or summary (education often attempts to provide summaries or surrogate experience to shortcut this process of developing prototypes). In addition, memory can come from specifics of the local schema, the information that one has developed about a specific place or incident. In all of these uses, rather than being composed of mental categories of objects or experiences, memory is seen as being connected in real-world units: in either the global schema of "office" or the local schema of "your office" one has a set of objects, spatial relationships, behaviors, and so on that belong together. One does not simply have mental categories such as "desk" or "chair"; these categories also fit together in a natural way.

These concepts are also differentiated by the arenas and behaviors they have been developed to explain. Several distinctions are important: (1) Are the constructs seen as merely ways to organize memory or are they seen as directing behavior? (2) Have they been applied to the issues of spatial choice or evaluation or can they reasonably be applied to such concepts? "Scripts," for example, have been used to explain routinized and predictable streams of behavior such as ordering in restaurants (Schank & Abelson, 1977). Scripts have proven useful in developing computational models of intelligence that are able to respond to context in certain situations. "Scenes" have been used to explain the role of context in visual memory. For instance, scenes that are organized understandably are better remembered; one can more accurately remember a scene with people under trees than a scene with trees under people (Mandler & Parker, 1976). "Causal models" have been developed to explain people's knowledge of simple physical systems such as the internal combustion engine (Clement, 1983). Whereas scenes and schemata have been primarily discussed as memory structures, mental models carry the implication that one can "run them" and use them to simulate or predict the outcomes of new alternatives. As Kaplan discusses in her chapter, evaluation is often dependent on this function: Settings or scenes are often evaluated with respect to the future opportunities they afford.

Early models of cognitive maps shared many of these passive qualities and were seen as descriptions of the cognitive structure of environmental information (see, for example, Lynch, 1960). Important early questions were issues such as "is a cognitive map like a cartographic map?" and "how do differences in cognitive maps result from different experiences or from different placement of urban features or landmarks?" (Evans, 1980). However, Timmermans, R. Kaplan, and Golledge all see the internal representation as something that directs action, even if "action" is seen as assessment. In addition, some theorists have argued that the travel plans that people make are critical in forming maps and in responding to maps (Gärling & Golledge, 1989).

Schemas in Environmental Cognition

Schemas in particular have gained popularity as a way to understand some aspects of environmental cognition. Although there appears to be no clear and commonly accepted definition of schema, it has been seen as a useful concept because it appears to define memory in ways that approximate how the world is organized: Schemas include associated aspects of real world scenes and situations. Conceptualizing mediators as schemas also appears to help explain memory of and response to physical settings.

Schemas are based on the notion that people have limited abilities to process the perceptual world: There is simply too much information to make sense of and people have limited attentional capacity. People must devote their limited processing capacity to critical tasks and automate as much as possible. Neisser (1976) proposed the concept of schema as a mental construct that mediates perception: Schemas accept some pieces of perceptual information and focus attention on other aspects. Once a schema is engaged it automates much memory and functioning. For example, when entering a place a person activates a schema, then looks for schema-expected elements. Once the schema is accepted as correct other aspects of a schema may be supplied even if they are not present: someone may remember that an office had a desk even if it did not because the desk is supplied by an office schema.

In their chapter in this volume, Axia, Peron, and Baroni discuss their own work with schemas. As have other researchers, they have found that schema-expected items are better remembered than schema-incompatible ones. They have also found that purpose plays a significant role in what people remember about a situation. When told in advance that they would be asked about the contents of a room, subjects tended to remember furniture; when told that they were only passing through a room they tended to remember only general information about the form and structure of the space. The authors interpret this finding as evidence of the role of schema as directing attention for a specific purpose. In the condition where subjects were told to remember the room, labeled "intentional," subjects not only had to choose a schema but focused on providing detail and identifying a subschema; in the incidental condition subjects were content to establish a general schema and move on. The elements remembered in the incidental condition were seen as the minimal schema-critical elements necessary to establish the schema. These results seem to support R. Kaplan's contention about the central role of purpose in environmental cognition. In addition, Axia and her colleagues have looked extensively at the development of schemas and at the role of schema in establishing emotional response to settings.

Purcell (1986) suggested that affective response to settings is related to the discrepancy between the environmental setting and people's schemas. He had subjects rate photographs of exteriors of churches on several dimensions and found that subjects (university students) were able to agree which churches were most "churchy," that is, most closely fit their mental prototype of a church. Furthermore he found that churches rated furthest from the prototype were judged either most or least interesting. Purcell interpreted this to mean that affective reactions to buildings result from discrepancies from prototypes. It was not clear from Purcell's work, however, what defines a schema or why schemas should be organized by functional building types such as "churches."

In sum, schemas seem to provide an explanation of why people remember some aspects of scenes in a specific circumstance and why they sometimes remember elements that were not present. They seem to provide a construct that both responds to the setting and directs action in it and provide a possible explanation for affective response to settings. However, although several authors have attempted to describe schemas—Axia and her colleagues argue that they include inventories of elements, spatial relationships, descriptive and emotional information—it is not clear how general schemas are or how they are linked to general properties of the built environment. As such, the idea of "place schema" provides a possible environmental mediator but is limited by its lack of precision and ideosyncratic nature.

ATTEMPTS TO DEFINE THE PHYSICAL SETTING

In a classic article entitled "The environment is not in the head," Wohlwill (1973) took environmental cognition researchers to task for not directly measuring the physical setting. He argued that cognitive mediators should be posited only when they increase predictability rather than assumed to exist a priori. Despite Wohlwill's admonitions nearly 20 years ago, it is still difficult to find clear descriptions of the physical environment in environmental cognition research. For example, the work by R. Kaplan and Golledge in this volume focuses on psychological constructs rather than on separately measurable environmental qualities.

Even frequently discussed "environmental features" such as landmarks are often defined in psychological terms. For example, in an attempt to explore Appleyard's (1969) findings about why some buildings are known, Evans et al. (1982) found that the ability of people to remember buildings is related to both physical factors, such as distinctiveness of shape, number of people around them, height, quality of maintenance, and social factors such as cultural importance. Even these physical factors are hard to measure and generalize. (See Peponis, Zimring, & Choi, 1990, for a further discussion of these issues.)

ATTEMPTS AT INTEGRATION

Computational Models of Cognitive Maps and Wayfinding

Recently, considerable progress has been made in understanding mental representations by experiments in computational process modeling. These represent an attempt to specify the physical setting, cognitive mediator, and action such as wayfinding. A good introduction to the application of computational process modeling in environmental cognition is provided in an article by Smith, Pellegrino, and Golledge (1982). Lately, the number of new papers in this field has risen sharply, indicating a surge of interest in computation and cognitive maps. The brief survey that follows gives an overview of some of the approaches that are being explored. In general, these models attempt to produce a simulated wayfinder that learns paths and landmarks in fairly large scale space such as a region or city, then can navigate through the space it knows. The models can be distinguished in terms of how the environment is represented, such as in terms of paths and places or geometrically placed landmarks or natural language descriptions, and the extent to which knowledge is seen as procedural, topological, or metric.

Most efforts to build wayfinding and cognitive mapping programs focus on exploring, representing, and route planning in one particular (simulated) environment. A real environment is first translated into a coded map or plan: a "world model." Then, a wayfinding program explores the world model, constructing an internal representation or "cognitive map." After constructing a cognitive map, the wayfinder "knows its way around" and can solve route-planning tasks in that environment.

A recent article by Kuipers and Levitt (1988) presents three models they have developed individually: Tour, NX-Robot, and Qualnav. Kuipers and Levitt, attempting to generalize their results, propose a "four-level semantic hierarchy" to order representations of large-scale space. Their semantic hierarchy distinguishes sensorimotor, procedural, topological, and metric levels of representation, and they use these levels to explain their three models.

The Tour model (Kuipers, 1978) was one of the earliest efforts to model cognitive maps and wayfinding using computers. The Tour model simulated a wayfinder moving about the city and built a cognitive map based on the order of places on a path and the geometry of local intersections. As the wayfinder became more familiar with the city it built a richer understanding based on Lynch's (1960) dimensions of regions, paths, boundaries, and places. It solves wayfinding tasks with incomplete information. The cognitive map is composed of frames that represent places and paths in the city. The more recent NX Robot model (Kuipers & Levitt, 1988) extends and generalizes the Tour model so that it identifies paths and places when exploring a building plan. It labels places when it finds extremes of sensorimotor input. For example, a maximum widening of a corridor is labeled as a place. The NX Robot also has the ability to follow paths. After labeling a place, the NX Robot model adds the place to its Tour-like representation of the environment as a network of places and paths. Following the work of Kuipers, researchers at Tokyo University have collected protocols and built a frame-based computer model of wayfinding at the urban scale (Hiro, 1990).

The Qualnav (qualitative navigation) model (Levitt et al., 1987,1988) explores a different representation of large-scale space, viewing the environment as a terrain with landmarks. It uses a sort of rough triangulation. By constructing imaginary lines through visible landmarks and reasoning geometrically about relative positions of landmarks on the horizon, the Qualnav wayfinder determines its location within a polygonal region bounded by the imaginary lines. The "world" is the metrically placed and identified landmarks; the cognitive mediator accomplishes route planning by identifying the current polygonal region and the direction to the next region.

A different approach is pursued by McDermott and Davis (1984; McDermott, 1980; Davis, 1983), who propose a structure they call a "fuzzy map" for representing large-scale built environments. (The word "fuzzy" reflects this structure's ability to represent partial and vague information about distances and orientations.) They show how a fuzzy map can be constructed from a world that is a natural language description of spatial relations ("Boston Common is South of Government Center"). The "world" is the natural language descriptions provided the wayfinder and the cognitive mediator is an approximate map that includes general metric information as well as topological information such as adjacencies and barriers. The wayfinder plans routes based on this map.

Other efforts related to computational modeling of wayfinding and cognitive maps include Elliot and Lesk's studies and computer simulations of route preferences by human subjects (1982), Streeter's work on automated verbal direction giving (Streeter et al., 1985), and Furugori's program for drawing maps from verbal wayfinding directions (1981). Recent work by W.K. Yeap models the acquisition and representation of room shape and connectivity information by a simulated robot exploring a building floorplan (Yeap, 1988). Leiser and Zilbershatz (1989) represent the environment in terms of a spatial network of points and paths and have developed a traveler that builds up a general network by learning connections between individual points. By designating some points as "centroids" they are able to show that their traveler can decompose the task into three subtasks of going from the origin to an adjacent centroid, going from the nearby centroid to a centroid near the destination, and going from that centroid to the destination. This strategy is very similar to the "anchor point" hypothesis proposed by Golledge in his chapter in this volume.

AN INTEGRATED APPROACH TO ENVIRONMENT, COGNITION, AND ACTION

In this section we propose a modest attempt to achieve the integration we called for in our discussion. Our approach differs from the previous work discussed in several ways. First, we are primarily concerned with wayfinding within a single building, whereas most models we reviewed focus on large-scale, urban space. Second (and more important) none of the models we reviewed addresses the role that old information plays in supporting wayfinding in new but typical situations. We use a schema-based approach and by "schema" we mean knowledge about a type of building or place distinct from particular instances. For example, a schema might represent general knowledge about airports, department stores, or college quadrangles.

The idea of schema is found in some of the earliest work on cognitive mapping (Lynch, 1960). Lynch observed, "an object seen for the first time may be identified and related not because it is individually familiar but because it conforms to a stereotype already constructed by the observer." For instance, the shape of the Boston Common was a common source of confusion among subjects Lynch interviewed. People who do not know the true shape of the five-sided Common assume that it is a rectangle, presumably because their schema for "urban park" has the item "shape: rectangle."

We posit that schemata, or knowledge about building *types,* makes it easier to recognize places and to find one's way in unfamiliar buildings. For example, most city-dwellers know that in a large traditional department store the coffee shop is typically located on the top floor. Escalators are typically located in the center of the building, while elevators will be located on one wall, most likely toward the rear of the building. Restrooms for women and men will be located close together, often with public telephones nearby. Often restrooms can be found in or near the restaurant. This kind of knowledge enables first-time visitors to find their way around a building with confidence.

Whereas the computational navigation and wayfinding models we reviewed suggest that a cognitive map is constructed de novo for each place based on exploration, our approach suggests that a cognitive map of a particular place begins with a "generic" schema for the place-type based both on topological and descriptive knowledge. For example, the cognitive map for a particular hotel begins with a generic schema for "hotel," which provides default assumptions about what features and spatial relationships to expect. Exploring the particular hotel results in a more specific cognitive map that replaces the original generic hotel schema. In our model, generic information in the form of environment schemas is used in constructing a cognitive map from a world model.

There is some evidence that people have schemas of buildings that direct their wayfinding behavior. Through introspection and in some small studies we have found that laypeople (that is, not professional designers) are quite willing to predict where key features will be located in buildings they have never visited. When shown a picture of the facade of a high-rise office building, for example, most people are willing to draw a rough floorplan showing the location of the elevators and stairs, and many are willing to locate features such as pay telephones and restrooms. Placement of these features seem to follow some rules. For instance, our participants tend to locate elevators centrally and to organize buildings symmetrically. Many people seem to be able to make similar predictions when given a verbal label only ("high-rise office building") rather than a photo of a building. Although these data are mostly anecdotal, they suggest that people have fairly well-established prototypes of at least some buildings, such as office buildings.

Similarly, we have found that when entering an unfamiliar building many way-finders take immediate and predictable action to find their goal. For instance, when looking for the restrooms in a fast food restaurant, they go to the back of the dining area toward the right. This is presumably because their existing generic knowledge of fast food restaurants leads them there. This sort of experience suggests to us that schemas *can* direct wayfinding strategies.

A recent study provides some additional evidence for this contention (Peponis, Zimring, & Choi, 1990). We asked our participants to explore a small hospital for up to 15 minutes, then to find several locations in the building. In tracking the participants we found that most people chose paths with certain topological characteristics. When engaged in an "open search" of the building to familiarize themselves with it, or when they took inefficient routes, they chose hallways that were "more integrated" or shallower with respect to all other rooms in the building. (Integration was measured using "space syntax" methods developed by Hillier, Hanson, Peponis, and their colleagues; Hillier & Hanson, 1984. It was measured by counting the number of turns required to go from a space to all others in the building.) For example, we found that people would search for locations along integrated corridors that required longer paths. This is presumably because people develop global schemas even more general than "high-rise office building." People seem to at least partially direct their spatial choice based on generic topological knowledge about how buildings are organized.

A Proposal about the Organization of Memory

In our model, a database of schemas ("schema memory") stores knowledge about types of places and generic topological organizations. Each schema describes a place-type such as "hotel," "bank," "stadium," "high-rise office-building." A hierarchic organization of schemas allows for storage efficiencies and also offers a convenient way to nest default knowledge. Thus, the "hotel" schema may have several more specific subschemas: "business hotel," "resort hotel," "motel." In every hotel, the reservation desk is in the lobby; this information can be stored in the schema for hotel. Items particular to specific hotel types (for example, the spatial relation between parking space and private room in a motel) can be stored in the appropriate subschema.

In our work we have found at least three kinds of information structures that might be called "schemas." Some buildings such as restaurants in fast-food chains are essentially mass produced. In this case, a wayfinder may have a very detailed and accurate mental representation that he or she brings to a new setting. However, a wayfinder may also have an "outline schema" that includes elements and relationships that characterize the building type, as described above. In addition, a wayfinder may have "deep structures," very general information about how buildings are organized that are much less specific, such as "most public functions are located shallow to the entry." We are primarily focusing on the second and third of these kinds of information structures and are asking the questions: "How do we recognize a building as an instance of a schema? What features of a place allow us to recognize it as an instance of a schema? For instance, do we recognize a building schema based on its use type, such as airport, hotel, office building, its architectural style, geometric aspects of layout, such as shape, or by other features? How is our memory of building types indexed?"

Each schema contains feature items that represent smaller places that are to be found within the larger place (a hotel contains a lobby), or environmental features that are not contained places but that act as clues in recognition or navigation (a hotel has a reservation desk). Additional relation items in each schema represent spatial (topological, geometric, and metric) relations between feature items. At least two kinds of spatial information can be conveyed by a schema: local relations among items (telephones near restrooms) and overall building layout (double-loaded corridor). Finally each feature item may have one or more associated actions.

We are interested in how environment schemas can be used to solve specific wayfinding tasks such as "find room 508," "find a telephone," "find a fire exit." To find a place in an unfamiliar building, the wayfinder must (1) recognize the building as belonging to a known type, (2) retrieve the schema for the building type, (3) locate the general location of the desired place in the schema, and (4) plan a route to the desired place, using the schema as a guide.

Recognizing a building as belonging to a type or class can be modeled as a process of matching a small set of environmental clues or observations with the clues associated with a building type schema. The presence of schema-necessary features (a reservation desk for a hotel) and the absence of contradicting evidence can be used to rank schemas and arrive at a best match. Once the best-match schema has been identified it can be retrieved.

Once a schema has been identified for the building at hand, it remains to locate the goal, or desired place in the schema. If the goal is labeled explicitly in the schema, then this step consists of searching the schema to find the match. Otherwise an inference must be made to identify a feature of the schema that is likely to contain the goal. For example, if the goal is to "find a soft-drink," it is unlikely that the schema will contain a place labeled "soft-drinks." However, common sense reasoning says that soft-drinks are often found in the cafeteria, which is more likely to appear as a feature in the schema.

Finally, planning a route to the desired place can be carried out by following feature links in the schema. Since the schema will omit much metric information, the route-planning process cannot produce a guaranteed path, but must be conducted simultaneously with moving through the world model.

Consider the problem of finding the "dairy case" in a supermarket. A schema may locate the dairy case along one of the perimeter walls. This schema suggests a procedure for finding the dairy case: walk in the front door, walk past the checkout lines, turn, and skirt the edge until you find the dairy case. But this procedure leaves out information that will be filled in at the time exploration actually begins. It does not say, for example, how far past the checkout lines to walk, or which direction to turn. These decisions must be made in the context of a particular environment; they do not belong to the schema.

Thus route planning may present considerable difficulties, and schemas may not be sufficient for route planning. Local clues also play an important role. For effective wayfinding, topological information from the schema must be augmented with metric information from the actual place.

We propose that schemata include slots for actions that are at different levels: overall strategies for achieving goals in a given situation and specific skillful routines. For example, a fast-food restaurant scheme includes strategies for wayfinding and general rules of behavior but also specific routines for queuing and ordering that are probably so automatic that they are hard to verbalize. This proposition seems quite similar to the concept of script (and more recently of ''mops'') proposed by Schank, Abelson, and their colleagues (Schank & Abelson, 1977).

However, it leads to a new set of questions: How direct is the linkage between place schema and script? Do some schemas have well-established scripts and others require more invention or inference? Does the clarity of schema or script-schema linkages affect evaluation? For example, the Kaplans' work suggests that settings that afford clear action options (scenes that are open, for instance) are evaluated more positively.

A major question for our model is at what level of generality schemas operate. As a point of departure we have used common definitions of building types as an initial typology of schemas. However, the hospital study described above suggests that at least some aspects of schemas may be more general than specific building types.

An additional major issue is how the physical environment is represented. We have operationalized schemas in terms of the list of elements, local topological relationships, and global relationships. We are currently struggling with how to define these in general ways.

Our model suggests that a broadened view of schema provides one alternative for further cognitive integration of evaluation and decision-making. However, introducing the concept of schema raises a question about how schemas are integrated into the mediational (recognition–assessment–action) model described above. In particular, how does a specific cognitive map of a place come to replace the generic schema of a place-type? Is the generic schema gradually transformed into a specific map in a process of modification and accretion? Or does the process of exploration simply result in a new structure wholly independent from the schema, which gradually takes precedence as a basis for route planning and wayfinding?

CONCLUSIONS

Action or decision making is dependent on the mental categories that an individual uses to make sense of a situation and on the theories of action and strategies that an individual uses to cope with the world (see Argyris, Putnam, & Smith, 1985, for a further discussion of theories of action). This link between mental representation and action appears well accepted by the authors we have discussed in this chapter. However, except for Timmermans' work, the work discussed in this chapter does not lend itself to operationalization of the physical setting in ways that laypersons or environmental professionals can readily manipulate. However, the concepts of preference, purpose, and expertise do have important methodological implications in that they suggest that self-report measures that directly ask individuals to describe the categories they are using may be invalid, and that it may often be inappropriate to use experts' judgments as proxies for laypersons'. Nonetheless, it remains an important question: How may physical attributes that are psychologically relevant be measured in ways useful to decision makers?

REFERENCES

Appleyard, D. (1969). Why buildings are known. *Environment & Behavior, 1*, 131–159.

Argyris, C., Putnam, R., & Smith, D.M. (1985). *Action science*. San Francisco: Jossey-Bass.

Brewer, W.F. (1987). Schemas versus mental models in human memory. In P. Morris (Ed.), *Modeling cognition*. New York: Wiley.

Clement, J. (1983). A conceptual model developed by Galileo and used intuitively by physics students. In D. Gentner & A.L. Stevens (Eds.) *Mental models*. Hillsdale, N.J.: Erlbaum.

Davis, E. (1983). The Mercator representation of spatial knowledge. *Proceedings Eighth International Joint Conference on Artificial Intelligence* (IJCAI 83), Karlsruhe, W. Germany, pp. 295–301.

de Kleer, J., & Brown, J.S. (1981). Mental models of physical mechanisms and their acquisition. In J.R. Anderson (Ed.), *Cognitive skills and their acquisition*. Hillsdale, N.J.: Erlbaum.

Elliot, R.J., & Lesk, M.E. (1982). Route-finding in street maps by computers and people. *Proceedings American Association of Artificial Intelligence National Conference* 1982 (AAAI-1982), Pittsburgh, Pennsylvania, pp. 258–261.

Evans, G.W. (1980). Environmental cognition. *Psychological Bulletin, 88*, 259–260.

Evans, G.W., Smith, C., & Pezdek, K. (1982). Cognitive maps and urban form. *Journal of the American Planning Association, 48*, 232–244.

Furugori, T. (1981). Computing a map from Michi-Annai-Bun or written directions. *Proceedings Seventh International Joint Conference on Artificial Intelligence* (IJCAI 81), Vancouver, British Columbia, Canada, pp. 426–428.

Gärling, T., & Golledge, R. (1989). Environmental perception and cognition. In E.H. Zube & G.T. Moore (Eds.), *Advances in environment, behavior and design* (Vol 2). New York: Plenum.

Getner, D., & Stevens, A.L. (Eds.) (1983). *Mental models*. Hillsdale, N.J.: Erlbaum.

Hillier, B., & Hanson, J. (1984). *Social logic of space*. London: Cambridge University Press.

Hiro, W.M. (1990). Presentation in workshop: "Wayfinding behavior and environmental design." Twenty-first Annual Conference of the Environmental Design Research Association, Champaign, Ill.

Johnson-Laird, P.N. (1980). Mental models in cognitive science. *Cognitive Science, 4*, 71–115.

Johnson-Laird, P.N. (1983). *Mental models*. Cambridge, Mass: Harvard University Press.

Kaplan, S., & Kaplan, R. (1982). *Cognition and environment*. New York: Praeger.

Kuipers, B. (1977). *Representing knowledge of large-scale space*. M.I.T. Ph.D. Dissertation also published as M.I.T. AI Lab Technical Report Tr-418.

Kuipers, B. (1978). Modeling spatial knowledge. *Cognitive Science, 2*, 129–153.

Kuipers, B. (1985). The map-learning critter. *Artificial Intelligence Laboratory Technical Report AITR85-17*. University of Texas at Austin.

Kuipers, B. (1987). A qualitative approach to robot exploration and map-learning. *Proceedings AAAI Workshop on Spatial Reasoning and Multi-Sensor Fusion,* October 5–7, 1987.

Kuipers, B., & Levitt, T. (1988). Navigation and mapping in large-scale space. *AI Magazine, 9*(2), 25–46.

Leiser, D., & Zilbershatz, A. (1989). The traveller: A computational model of spatial network learning. *Environment & Behavior, 21*(4), 435–464.

Levitt, T.S., Lawton, D.T., Chelberg, D.M., Koitzsch, K., & Dye, J.W. (1988). Qualitative Navigation 2. *Proceedings of the DARPA Image Understanding Workshop,* pp. 319–326. Los Altos, California: Morgan Kaufman.

Levitt, T.S., Lawton, D.T., Chelberg, D.M., & Nelson, P.C. (1987). Qualitative landmark-based path planning and following. *Proceedings American Association of Artificial Intelligence National Conference* (AAAI-1987), pp. 689–694.

Luger, G.F., & Stubblefield, W.A. (1989). *Artificial intelligence and the design of expert systems.* Redwood City, Calif.: Benjamin/Cummings.

Lynch, K. (1960). *The image of the city.* Cambridge, Mass.: M.I.T. Press.

Maki, R.H. (1981). Categorization and distance effects with spatial linear orders. *Journal of Experimental Psychology: Human Learning and Memory, 7,* 15–32.

Mandler, J.M. (1984). *Scripts, stories and schemas.* Hillsdale, N.J.: Erlbaum.

Mandler, J.M., & Parker, R.E. (1976). Memory for descriptive and spatial information in complex pictures. *Journal of Experimental Psychology: Human Learning and Memory, 2,* 38–48.

McDermott, D. (1980). A theory of metric spatial inference. *Proceedings American Associations of Artificial Intelligence National Conference* 1980, pp. 246–248.

McDermott, D., & Davis, E. (1984). Planning routes through uncertain Territory. *Artificial Intelligence, 22,* 107–156.

Minsky, M. (1975). A framework for representing knowledge. In P.H. Winston (Ed.), *The psychology of computer vision.* New York: McGraw-Hill.

Neisser, R.V. (1976). *Cognition and reality.* San Francisco: Freeman.

Pailhous, J. (1970). *La representation de l'espace urbain: l'exemple de chauffeur de taxi.* Paris: Presses Universitaires de Paris.

Peponis, J., Zimring, C.M. & Choi, Y.K. (1990). Finding the building in wayfinding, *Environment and Behavior, 22*:5, 555–590.

Piaget, J., & Inhelder, B. (1967). *The child's conception of space.* New York: Norton.

Purcell, A.T. (1986). Environmental perception and affect: A schema discrepancy model. *Environment & Behavior, 18*(1), 3–30.

Robinson, A.H., & Petchnik, B.B. (1976). *The nature of maps.* Chicago: University of Chicago Press.

Schank, R.C., & Abelson, R.P. (1977). *Scripts, plans, goals and understanding.* Hillsdale, N.J.: Erlbaum.

Smith, T.R., Pellegrino, J.W., & Golledge, R.G. (1982). Computational process modeling of spatial cognition and behavior. *Geographical Analysis, 14*(4), 305–324.

Streeter, L.A., Vitello, D., & Wonsiewicz, S. (1985). How to tell people where to go: comparing navigational aids. *International Journal of Man-Machine Systems, 22*(5), 549–562.

Wohlwill, J. (1973). The environment is not in the head! In W.F.E. Preiser (Ed.), *Environmental design research* (Vol 2). Stroudsberg, Penn.: Dowden, Hutchinson and Ross.

Wilton, R. (1979). Knowledge of spatial relations: A specification from the information used in making inferences. *Quarterly Journal of Experimental Psychology, 31,* 133–146.

Yeap, W.K. (1988). Towards a computational theory of cognitive maps. *Artificial Intelligence, 34*(3), 297–360.

6

Environmental Assessment, Cognition, and Action: Research Applications

ERVIN H. ZUBE

Environmental assessment has been defined as ''a general conceptual and method-ological framework for describing and predicting how attributes of places relate to a wide range of cognitive, affective, and behavioral responses'' (Craik & Feimer, 1987). A primary purpose for assessing environments is to provide valid and reliable infor-mation that has utility in environmental planning, design, and management decision making. Implicit in the assessment activity is the assumption of identifiable relation-ships of physical environmental factors with descriptive and evaluative assessments, and with predictions of responses to places conceptualized in plans and designs, but not yet built.

This chapter addresses the utility of research findings. Three primary questions are posed. Why are some environmental assessment and cognition research findings used successfully in decision making while others are not? What factors contribute to these outcomes? And how important are physical environmental factors in plan-ning, design, and management decision making? The preceding chapters by Rachel Kaplan, Reginald Golledge, and Harry Timmermans provide the background for the following discussion.

The first section of this chapter presents a brief review of similarities and differ-ences among the three preceding chapters, with specific attention directed to interpre-tations or definitions of the concepts of assessment and preference, the use of physi-cal environmental variables in the assessment process, and the roles of laypersons and experts in assessment.

Potential uses for and applications of environmental assessment research are de-scribed in the second section. This is followed by a discussion of the differences between instrumental and conceptual applications and of factors that have been iden-tified as influencing applications, factors such as communications between research-ers and users, responsibilities for problem definition, and the context within which the research is conducted. This chapter concludes with a discussion of the opportu-nities for and probable limitations on applications of the preceding chapters by R. Kaplan, Golledge, and Timmermans.

SIMILARITIES AND DIFFERENCES

Four concepts and elements that are addressed in the three chapters have been selected for purposes of structuring a comparison among them. These concepts and elements—assessment, preference, roles of laypersons and experts, and physical environmental factors—are particularly salient to the issue of research applications. The definitions of assessment and preference address varying degrees of specificity and of levels of analysis. The identification of physical factors relates directly to the utility of the research for applications. Defining the roles of laypersons and experts in the design and conduct of the research qualifies the potential generalizability and utility of the findings.

The authors of the three chapters, which address widely diverse topics, are a psychologist, a geographer, and an urban planner. These disciplinary differences are reflected in varying degrees in both the substantive content of the chapters and in the scientific-professional vocabularies employed. The topics range from a broad and general discussion of landscape assessment, to an examination of the concept of cognition including spatial components and the process of environmental assessment, and to an analysis of planning models developed for purposes of evaluating and making decisions about the spatial distribution of various urban land use activities. Each involves assessment, but the definition of the term varies among them in subtle and less than subtle ways.

Definitions

Assessment entails measurement. The traditional definition is measurement of values—the process of evaluation. However, in the area of environmental assessment the term has been defined as encompassing descriptive, evaluative, and predictive dimensions (Craik & Feimer, 1987). Each of the preceding chapters addresses the evaluative and predictive dimensions. They differ, however, in the extent to which they explicitly address environmental description.

R. Kaplan defines assessment as a basic tool for understanding what is important and what is valued in the landscape. She includes both description and evaluation within the concept. Golledge defines assessment as the evaluation phase of environmental cognition, with primary attention directed to "the interface between human and environment . . . which includes perceptions, memories and otherwise cognized information" (p. 53). Timmerman's use of assessment is within a more specific context than either Kaplan's or Golledge's. He is interested in the effects that design alternatives might have on human behaviors. Assessment in this context relates to the evaluation of alternatives to identify what is preferred.

Both Kaplan and Timmerman use preference as a primary concept in the assessment process and, as with the term assessment, it is employed at different levels of specificity. Kaplan uses preference as a generic evaluative term and as a means of both describing and categorizing landscapes that range from built to natural. Timmerman's use of the term carries with it an implicit utility orientation. He relates preferences to choices for specific urban land use activities in specific geographic locations within the city. His interest is in how preferences are used as a means of

addressing the locations of various land use activities, the amounts of land they require, and the intensity of the developments. Within this definition, preference is
specific to a particular environmental decision or set of decisions.

Roles of Laypersons and Experts

Laypersons figure prominently in the research discussed in each of the chapters.
Laypersons are the basic source of preference data for both Kaplan and Timmermans.
Golledge implies the necessity for studying laypersons when he acknowledges that
"affective responses to an environment may differ significantly among sociocultural
groups and among geographic regions" (p. 51). The role of the expert, however, is
treated differently in several of the chapters. Kaplan contrasts experts and laypersons
and suggests that they "see differently." She notes that the experts have usually
been the ones who have determined what should be assessed in the environment and
advises that their judgment should be balanced by others perspectives.

Golledge suggests that the normal role of the expert is that of describing environments for applied planning or management purposes. He lists three components of
this process: identifying the physical reality, specifying and defining descriptive attributes, and selecting quantitative and qualitative indicators of those attributes. He
also notes the limitations of such expert-defined descriptions for assessing meanings
imbedded in cultural, folkloric, religious, and other associations with the environment.

Timmermans describes two roles for laypersons in the development of planning
models—as sources of behavioral information in one set of models and as sources of
preference information related to spatial decision making in another. In the first example there is no attempt to understand cognitive processes, while in the second there
is. In both examples these data are used by experts (planners) to develop models that
are intended for use by political decision makers. Timmermans also notes that the
decision makers play important roles in the design of the research, in which they are
involved from the beginning.

Physical Environmental Factors

Each author addresses the topic of physical environmental factors differently. They
are all similar, however, in treating it in a very general way that provides little
detailed information about what physical factors, if any, are considered most important. For example, geographic scales under consideration are not explicit in any of
the chapters. Nevertheless, consideration of scale is important in defining the appropriate level of analysis and for identifying meaningful physical environmental factors.
For example, how might the identification of physical factors vary in three studies of
the same land use category, but at three different scales? For example, how might
they vary in a study of the scenic beauty of three open spaces, the first a one square
city block, the second a 500 hectare area along a small river running through a
suburb, and the third a 150 square kilometer regional park? Are the same physical
factors appropriate for each of these assessments?

R. Kaplan questions the validity of physical factors such as land form and vegetative cover that are frequently used in landscape assessment studies by experts. She

asks whether those factors represent the best predictors for sought-after outcomes such as scenic quality, preference, or satisfaction, and advocates the use of cognitively derived factors such as landscape content and spatial configuration.

Golledge notes that "assessment must be conscious of physical reality and transformations of that reality that are stored in mind by our cognitive mapping process" (p. 53). He suggests that the long tradition of descriptive research in a wide range of professional fields and scientific disciplines provides an ample inventory of physical descriptions, but he also warns that some "attributes of critical importance are not directly measurable in physical quantities" (p. 52).

Timmermans suggests that physical factors are important to policy makers when he notes that from his experience these individuals are not interested in psychological phenomena. One set of spatial planning models that he reviews relates observed behavior directly to a set of environmental characteristics while a second set is based on explicit measures of individuals' satisfactions, judgments or preferences that presumably are related to physical environmental factors as construed in different geographical locations and land use activities.

USES OF ENVIRONMENTAL ASSESSMENT AND COGNITION RESEARCH

A number of uses are suggested, both explicitly and implicitly, for the findings from the research discussed in the chapters. They include public policy decisions, landscape or resource management programs, evaluation of planning and design alternatives, design of specialized facilities, and as the foundation for future research. Another important and frequently overlooked use is confirming decisions that have already been made.

Public Policy

Public policy in the United States, and probably in many other countries, addresses primarily issues of public health, safety, and welfare. For purposes of this discussion, it is useful to conceptualize such policies on at least two levels, legislative and administrative (Ventre, 1989; Zube, 1984a). Legislative policy tends to express normative social values and to address questions of "what ought to be." Thus, values information derived from cognitive research can be relevant to the development of legislative policy. Administrative policy tends to address how legislative policy will be implemented, what methods, procedures, rules, and standards will be followed. Legislative policy related to environment and behavior interests in the United States, however, has frequently been the stimulus for research rather than having been promulgated as the result of research. Nevertheless, research that it has stimulated and that has been supported by agencies responsible for implementation tends to be that which is related to applications within the context of expert systems and which requires manipulation of physical environmental factors.

Administrative policies—codes, ordinances, and the like—are usually more specific than legislative policy. For example, Williams, Kellog, and Lavigne (1987) note that general terms such as harmony and compatibility are insufficient as criteria for describing aesthetic values to be protected within a community. They suggest that such terms present problems of administration being based on whim and that what is needed for a legally defendable townscape ordinance is a level of detail that removes as much ambiguity as possible. Such an ordinance would require specifying physical environmental factors such as building height limits, set back distances from the street, height-to-width facade proportions, building materials, architectural style, and the slope of the roof. These are tangible, measurable, physical elements that can be addressed in a court of law.

Chenoweth (1988) has suggested that environmental assessment and cognition research can influence policy decisions in several ways other than simply serving as an information base for policy makers. Assessment research that involves laypersons can serve as an effective mechanism for redefining issues, for citizen participation, and also to alter communications networks among interested groups and to attract the media. For example, reporters for the media like facts and provocative quotes. Such assessments can also provide factual information for citizen groups working to counteract experts opinions or self-serving motives of special interest groups. An interesting concomitant of this role for the researcher is that she or he becomes the expert.

Landscape Resource Assessment

A notable example of research following legislative policy is the substantial volume of landscape or visual resource assessment research that has been undertaken during the past two decades (Zube, Sell, & Taylor, 1982). A primary stimulus for this research in the United States was the National Environmental Policy Act of 1969 (NEPA). NEPA called for the consideration of aesthetic values and the utilization of the environmental design arts in the assessment of the environmental impacts of major construction and management projects. Much of the research that followed was undertaken in response to agency concerns with developing methods and procedures for inventorying and evaluating scenic landscape values.

Design Programming and Evaluation

Other uses for assessment research include design programming for site-specific facilities (Sanoff, 1989; Spreckelmeyer, 1987; Wineman, 1982a,b), evaluation of design, planning, and management alternatives (Zube 1984a), and postconstruction or postoccupancy evaluations (POEs) (Kantrowitz & Seidel, 1985; Moore, 1982; Wener, Frazier, & Farbstein, 1985; Zimring, 1987). These uses represent three critical points in the design, planning, and/or management process.

Programming has been defined as "an activity that precedes environmental design and provides the designer with the functional, technical, and behavioral requirements of design" (Spreckelmeyer, 1987, p. 247). Evaluation of alternatives is an important step in the midst of the process in which alternative solutions are evaluated in terms of their congruence with the design program and client/user objectives. This evaluation typically leads to the selection of a final design solution. POEs are conducted following construction and occupance of facilities to assess the congruence of the built environment with the design program and with user satisfaction. They can also provide valuable information for future designs of similar facilities and for similar user groups. POEs can also be used to generate design guidelines for general classes of built environments such as multifamily housing or community parks (Rutledge, 1981), where the guidelines are derived from multiple evaluations of similar facilities.

Other Uses

Among this sample of potential uses or applications of environmental assessment and cognition research there are two others that merit mention because they are perhaps the most common and, also, the most commonly overlooked. The first is the use of research information to confirm decisions that have already been made, and the second is as building blocks for theory development and for additional applied research.

The Institute for Social Research at the University of Michigan interviewed 204 upper-level decision makers in Washington, D.C., to learn about their uses of social science research (Caplan, Morrison, & Stambaugh, 1975). The interviews confirmed the use of such research findings, but also discovered that "Political implications of research findings appeared to override any other consideration in determining utilizations" (p. 59). Furthermore, intuitive feelings about what was right were found to influence utilization. The political arena is an unlikely place for the use of research information that runs counter to agency or individual positions on important issues, or that might support opposing points of view.

Perhaps the second use referred to above, as building blocks for additional research, should be obvious. Nevertheless, it is frequently overlooked and merits mention. The work of theoretically oriented research should serve as building blocks for those working in applied areas. Such is not always the case, however, because much applied work tends toward the atheoretical. Boulding (1980) has written about the unique characteristics of science and noted that the placing of confidence in the records of others is one of those characteristics. He is describing the process by which one individual's findings serve as the building blocks for another. This presupposes, however, that the information in question is available in suitable form and in an accessible medium for potential users.

Instrumental and Conceptual Applications

Several writers on the subject of research applications have described two modes of applications that help to categorize and generalize the preceding discussion: instrumental and conceptual (Seidel, 1985; Weiss, 1980). Instrumental applications are described as one-to-one applications of research findings to problem solving and decision making. Such applications are probably most likely to be found in design programming, the development of administrative policies, and the evaluation of design, planning, and management alternatives. Conceptual applications are described as indirect applications of a general understanding and are most likely to be found in the development of legislative policies, as foundations for future research, and in the development of design concepts.

FACTORS THAT INFLUENCE RESEARCH APPLICATIONS

What influences whether research findings are used, ignored, or unknown to potential users? A number of factors have been identified that appear to be of particular significance for instrumental applications. Several have been suggested previously including the potential users' intuitive feelings about the research and the availability of the information in forms and media appropriate and accessible to potential users. The literature on the use of social science research in environmental management decision making suggests several additional factors including differences in the ways in which researchers, environmental designers, and managers conceptualize and operationalize problems and solutions, communications between users and researchers, and the context within which research is conducted.

Altman (1975) provided a useful categorization of some differences in the ways researchers and designers address problems and their solutions. He identifies as important differences: the unit of study, an analysis versus synthesis orientation, and a doing versus knowing focus. In addition, mode of communications can be added to these dimensions.

Table 6.1 summarizes these differences. It illustrates significant differences on objectives, areas of fundamental interest, modes of behavior, and modes of communications. Designers focus on places and objects such as an urban plaza or a specific building while behavioral scientists may focus on cognitive processes or concepts such as privacy or stress. The act of design or planning involves synthesizing information from many areas that cut across disciplines including the arts as well as the social and physical sciences. In contrast, behavioral science research, like most scientific research, tends to take things apart, to analyze and investigate why phenomena behave the way they do. Altman does note, however, that these differences are less extreme when the comparison is made between designers and researchers working in applied fields. Finally, there are significant differences in primary modes of communications with designers relying strongly on graphic modes and behavioral scientists relying on the verbal mode.

Johnson and Field (1981), McCool and Schreyer (1977), and Schweitzer and Randall (1974) all note that instrumental applications are greatly facilitated by direct face-to-face communications between researchers and potential users. Spencer (1983) confirms this observation and notes that frequent contact with policy makers was "a most important means" for maintaining credibility with them in reference to research on drug use in Malaysia. Caplan et al. (1975) add another dimension to the communications issue, noting that 53% of the reported use of social science information by Washington, D.C., decision makers came from in-house research and another

Table 6.1 Designer–Researcher Differences

	Designers	Researchers
Unit of analysis	Place or object	Behavioral process
Approach to problem	Synthesis	Analysis
	Doing, implementing	Knowing, understanding
Communication	Graphic	Verbal

35% came from extramural research funded by their agencies. These observations strongly suggest that applications are enhanced when there are close working relationships between researchers and users.

Johnson and Field (1981) note another important characteristic. They suggest that research leading to instrumental applications focuses on the resolution of specific problems rather than topics pursued because of intellectual curiosity, and that the problem is usually defined by the client, or in collaboration with the researcher. This is the nature of design programming, evaluation of alternatives, POEs, and environmental management.

A final characteristic of this kind of research is the context within which it occurs (Johnson & Field, 1981). Research that gets applied is frequently time dependent, that is, there are deadlines to be met that coincide with the needs and schedules of users such as designers, planners, and managers. In addition, the variables that are used to describe and explain phenomena must be variables that are subject to manipulation and alteration by the users of the research. And, as noted previously, the products of the research must be in forms that are understandable and usable by the users.

The growing interest in "action research" among environmental designers in the United States (Francis, 1987; Schneekloth, 1987) tends to confirm the observations of Johnson and Field (1981), McCool and Schreyer (1977), and Schweitzer and Randall (1974) about a close link between researcher and user. However, action research represents a major departure from the discrete roles these two interests have traditionally represented. Action research embraces the concept of the researcher serving as an active agent of interventions in environmental modifications as well as serving as the collector of the research data that support such interventions. The researcher may also serve as the designer or as the facilitator of user participation in the design process. Questions of research goals, critical variables, timing of the research, and the utility of the research products may all be subject to negotiations between these active participants. Coupled with this approach to environmental assessment research, however, are important questions of researcher objectivity and bias.

A primary factor influencing conceptual applications is communications, both formal and informal. Formal avenues include those that most researchers normally employ—papers at scientific meetings and publications in journals. They may or may not involve face-to-face contacts. These are the avenues, however, that lead to conceptual applications in the form of future research. This form of communications is less likely to lead to conceptual applications by designers, planners, or managers, it represents scientists talking to scientists. However, to the extent that research proves newsworthy, it may have some instrumental effects. Caplan et al. (1975) reported that the most frequent sources of research information used by their 204 interviewees were newspapers, government reports, and staff papers. This use of newspapers confirms Chenoweth's (1988) notion of how research can influence public policy. Thus, serendipity should not be overlooked as a factor influencing research applications.

In summary, there appear to be three general models of researcher–user relationships that emerge from this review of factors that influence applications. As illustrated in Figure 6.1, they are direct, discontinuous, and overlapping. The first is the direct relationship identified as highly efficacious for instrumental applications. The second represents a common relationship in conceptual applications but certainly is

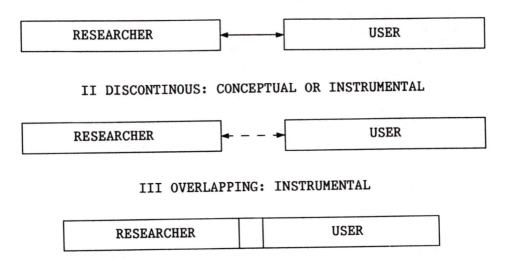

Figure 6.1.   Researcher–user relationships.

not restricted to that mode. It is possible for direct applications to be initiated on the basis of journal articles or other published materials. Whether conceptual or instrumental, the communication process is not direct face to face, but rather accomplished through some intervening medium. The third model is clearly instrumental and represents action research.

OPPORTUNITIES AND LIMITATIONS

This chapter was introduced with three questions. Why are some environmental assessment and cognition research findings used successfully in decision making while others are not? What factors contribute to these outcomes? How important are physical environmental factors in planning, design, and management decision making? The preceding review of literature addressing factors that influence research applications identified the following as important facilitating factors: face-to-face contacts between researcher and user; a focus on specific problems and the involvement of the user in the definition of the problem; temporal coincidence of research schedule with design, planning, or management schedule; the use of descriptive and explanatory variables that relate directly to the manipulation and alteration of the physical environments for which the users have responsibility; and communications in forms and media suitable for and available to the intended users.

What are the opportunities for and constraints on actual applications of the research discussed in the chapters by R. Kaplan, Golledge, and Timmermans? They span the range of opportunities represented within the instrumental and conceptual categories. As Seidel (1985) suggested, these are not discrete categories, but rather two points on a continuum of applications possibilities. However, because the three chapters deal in different levels of specificity and breadth of coverage of the fields, many of the opportunities and constraints discussed in the following paragraphs are conjectural. R. Kaplan's and Golledge's chapters fall closer to the conceptual end of the continuum, while Timmerman's falls closer to the instrumental end.

A major emphasis of the work that both Rachel and Stephen Kaplan have collaborated on for more than two decades has been understanding the cognitive processes associated with comprehending and functioning in the environment (Kaplan & Kaplan, 1982). Assessment of environmental preferences has been central to this research. Preference has been related to informational needs, to making sense and involvement in both the present and the future. Dimensions of this informational model of preference include environmental mystery, complexity, coherence, and legibility.

Their work has not employed the categories of physical factors that have become commonplace in the practice of landscape assessment and in the applied landscape assessment literature. This has certainly been an impediment to the adoption of their model by agencies having responsibility for landscape assessment and management. Another probable limiting factor to the adoption of their approach by landscape management agencies may be the emphasis on preference. The major body of research in landscape assessment has not focused on preference. Instead, the focus has been on the concept specified in both legislative and administrative policies, a concept that is expressed as aesthetic or scenic quality, scenic value, or beauty. Although there is an implicit relationship between the concepts of preference and aesthetic or scenic quality, the latter is implicitly more specific and directly related to the public policies that stimulated this area of research. Nevertheless, the Kaplans' students and other researchers have begun to explore potentials for applications (Gimblett, Itami, & Fitzgibbons, 1985). Clearly, this work has also stimulated a number of theses and dissertations that have contributed to the understanding of human–landscape relationships.

Golledge suggests an approach that merits serious consideration and that encompasses both physical and psychological factors. Based on a cognitive research perspective he conceptualizes the assessment process as including three components: a description of physical reality, identification of appropriate attributes that facilitate description, and selection of appropriate indicators of the quantity or quality of the attributes. He states that, "In assessing physical or built environments, it is mandatory to include both objectively and subjectively derived indicators" (p. 52). Understanding the diverse cultural meanings and values associated with places, as well as identifying related physical factors, can provide the planner, designer, or manager with a more sensitive and useful information base for decision making. An important point of concern and a currently unresolved issue related to this and similar concepts—if they are to provide results that have utility for decision makers—is the identification of objective attributes and indicators that are relevant to applications and that can be validly and reliably related to the subjective attributes and indicators (Zube, 1984b).

Of the three chapters considered here, Timmermans is clearly the most applications oriented. Although the models he describes draw upon behavioral and cognitive theories, they are targeted on a specific problem—decision making related to the spatial distribution of urban land uses. He notes that for his personal research, objectives as well as the desired outcomes are the product of continuing discussions and negotiations with the intended users, the responsible decision makers (1988). However, he also raises several important questions about this research: What is the link between preference and behavior? How accurately does the simplification required for the models reflect reality? Of particular significance to the topic of this chapter is his question about the form of the relationships of preferences and behavior with physical environmental factors or attributes, the same question that was posed in reference to Golledge's conceptual framework for environmental assessment.

CONCLUSION

The chapters by R. Kaplan, Golledge, and Timmermans aptly illustrate the applications opportunities and limitations for environmental assessment, cognition, and decision-making research. They vary in process versus place or object orientation and in specificity of topical or problem definition. An underlying theme of the three chapters and of this chapter is the definition and utility of physical environmental factors. From the perspective of the potential user of the research, and as Timmermans notes, "By definition, these are attributes of the environment that can be manipulated" (p. 74). They are also attributes that can be influential in establishing the legal basis of environmental decisions.

The problem as noted above is defining the nature of the relationships between those physical factors and affective and behavioral responses. This is not a simple task. It can be compounded by variable sociocultural and geographic values and meanings associated with places. Nevertheless, if there is genuine concern for research applications in environmental assessment, cognition, and decision making, future research must consider the values, perceptions, and behaviors of planners, designers, and managers as well as laypersons, and the prevailing research theories and values of the researchers.

REFERENCES

Altman, I. (1975). *The environment and social behavior*. Monterey, Calif.: Brooks/ Cole.

Boulding, K. (1980). Science: Our common heritage. *Science, 207,* 831–836.

Caplan, N., Morrison, A., & Stambaugh, R.J. (1975). *The use of social science knowledge in policy decisions at the national level*. Ann Arbor: University of Michigan, Institute for Social Research.

Chenoweth, R. (1988, June). *Functions of research in policy making*. Paper presented at the Second Symposium on Social Sciences in Natural Resources. Urbana: University of Illinois.

Craik, K.H., & Feimer, N.R. (1987). Environmental assessment. In D. Stokols & I. Altman (Eds.), *Handbook of environmental psychology* (Vol. 2, pp. 891– 918). New York: Wiley.

Francis, M. (1987). Urban open spaces. In E.H. Zube & G.T. Moore (Eds.), *Ad-*

vances in environment, behavior and design (Vol. 1, pp. 71–106). New York: Plenum.

Golledge, R. (1988). Personal communication.

Gimblett, H.R., Itami, R.I., & Fitzgibbons, J.I. (1985). Mystery in an information processing model of landscape preference. *Landscape Journal, 4,* 87–95.

Johnson, D., & Field, D.R. (1981). Applied and basic research: A difference in social context. *Leisure Sciences, 4,* 269–279.

Kantrowitz, M., & Seidel, A.D., (Eds.). (1985). Applications of E&B research. (Special issue). *Environment and Behavior, 17,* 3–144.

Kaplan, S., & Kaplan, R. (1982). *Cognition and environment.* New York: Praeger.

McCool, S.F., & Schreyer, R.M. (1977). Research utilization in wildland recreation management: A preliminary analysis. *Journal of Leisure Research, 9,* 98–109.

Moore, G.T., (Ed.). (1982). Applied architectural research: post-occupancy evaluation of buildings. (Special mini-issue). *Environment and Behavior, 14,* 643–724.

Rutledge, A.J. (1981). *A visual approach to park design.* New York: Garland STPM Press.

Sanoff, H. (1989). Advances in facility programming. In E.H. Zube & G.T. Moore (Eds.). (1989). *Advances in environment, behavior and design* (Vol. 2, pp. 239–286). New York: Plenum.

Schneekloth, L.H. (1987). Advances in practice in environment, behavior, and design. In E.H. Zube & G.T. Moore, (Eds.), *Advances in environment, behavior, and design* (Vol. 1, pp. 308–334). New York: Plenum.

Schweitzer, D.L., & Randall, R.M. (1974). The key to getting research applied Manager-Researcher Cooperation. *Journal of Forestry, 72,* 418–419.

Seidel, A.D. (1985). What is success in E&B research utilization? *Environment and Behavior, 17,* 47–70.

Spencer, C. (1983). Social scientists' and policy makers' expectations of research on drug abuse. In F. Blackler (Ed.), *Social psychology and developing countries* (pp. 245–289). London: Wiley.

Spreckelmeyer, K. (1987). Environmental programming. In R.B. Bechtel, R.W. Marans, & W. Michelson (Eds.), *Methods in environmental and behavioral research* (pp. 247–269). New York: Van Nostrand Reinhold.

Timmermans, H. (1988). Personal communication.

Ventre, F.T. (1989). The policy environment for environment and behavior research. In E.H. Zube & G.T. Moore (Eds.), *Advances in environment, behavior, and design* (Vol. 2, pp. 317–342). New York: Plenum.

Weiss, C.H. with Bucuvalas, M.J. (1980). *Social science research and decision making.* New York: Columbia University Press.

Wener, R., Frazier, F.W., & Farbstein, J. (1985). Three generations of evaluation and design of correction facilities. *Environment and Behavior, 17,* 71–95.

Williams, N., Jr., Kellog, E.H., & Lavigne, P.M. (1987). *Vermont townscape.* New Jersey: Rutgers University, Center for Urban Policy Research.

Wineman, J.D. (Ed.) (1982a). Office design and evaluation. (Special issue, Part 1). *Environment and Behavior, 14,* 267–392.

Wineman, J.D. (Ed.) (1982b). Office design and evaluation. (Special issue, Part II). *Environment and Behavior, 14,* 515–610.

Zimring, C.M. (1987). Evaluation of designed environments: Methods for post-occupancy evaluation. In R.B. Bechtel, R.W. Marans, & W. Michelson (Eds.), *Methods in environmental and behavioral research* (pp. 270–300). New York: Van Nostrand Reinhold.

Zube, E.H. (1984a). *Environmental evaluation: Perception and public policy.* New York: Cambridge University Press.

Zube, E.H. (1984b). Themes in landscape assessment theory. *Landscape Journal, 3,* 104–110.

Zube, E.H., Sell, J.L., & Taylor, J.G. (1982). Landscape perception: Research, application and theory. *Landscape Planning, 9,* 1–33.

II

PSYCHOLOGICAL PROCESSES

Understanding the psychological impact of the molar physical environment requires knowledge of the mechanisms and processes by which this impact is mediated. What are these mechanisms and processes, and how should they be conceptualized? Are they the same in assessment, cognition, and action? Are they conceptualized in the same way in these different areas of research?

We have partial answers to these questions because they were to some extent addressed in the preceding part on the impact of the physical environment. In this part, in which our main focus is on the psychological processes mediating between the physical environment and psychological responses, these partial answers will be commented and elaborated on. In their own work, Rikard Küller, Anders Böök, and Stephen Kaplan have had experience in theorizing about psychological processes.

One way of learning more about the mediating psychological processes that link people to their physical environments is to examine their physiological underpinnings. In Chapter 7 Küller discusses his own research, which ranges from the assessment of environments with conventional techniques, such as the semantic differential (Bechtel, 1987), through laboratory and field studies employing physiological measurements. The analysis is organized around his theory of how emotions are affected by different aspects of the physical, social, and task environments, and how emotions in turn affect and are affected by the individual's actions. This theory is of particular interest in this book because it illustrates an attempt to provide an example of an integrative, theoretical framework that encompasses cognition, assessment, and action.

In Chapter 8 Böök sets himself the difficult task of analyzing spatial cognition research in real-world physical environments from a new perspective. He is discontent with the nearly exclusive reliance on the information-processing analytic approach that attempts to specify hypothetical, underlying component processes and their interrelationship (Gärling, Böök, & Lindberg, 1984, 1986). Böök rightly asks what more can or should environmental psychology research on spatial cognition contribute? His answer draws on the notion of "cognition events." If such meaningful and important events can be identified in people's everyday interactions with physical environments, then they should be analyzable in terms of the compound psychological processes they entail. Such analyses may provide a testing ground for theories in cognitive psychology of how cognitive processes are interrelated under real-life conditions. Conversely, Böök's analysis may contribute a more specific level of analysis to environmental psychology by integrating basic, more developed theories in research on perception and cognition. By way of several examples, Böök attempts to demonstrate the usefulness of his approach. Of particular interest in this context is that it may be extended to encompass assessment, cognition, and action.

In Chapter 9 S. Kaplan takes a psychologically much broader approach to action than does Timmermans in Part I. Initially, he notes with some disappointment that despite its close connection to environmental cognition, research on spatial choice takes its point of departure from the normative models of decision making (Slovic, Lichtenstein, & Fischhoff, 1988) that have been the target of much well-grounded criticism. S. Kaplan then develops the embryo of an alternative theoretical framework based on the key concept of cognitive clarity. The role of knowledge or cognitive structures in people's decision making is thereby highlighted; at the same time, a connection is drawn between cognitive clarity and affect. The theoretical framework that S. Kaplan develops thus seems to go several steps in the direction of integrating cognition, assessment or affect, and choice or action.

By their nature, the contributions in this part represent progress toward our goal of a theoretical framework integrating assessment, cognition, and action in environmental psychology. However, they are not all-encompassing; thus leaving something for David Canter in Chapter 10 and Gerald D. Weisman in Chapter 11 to add to the commentary.

REFERENCES

Bechtel, R.B. (1987). The ubiquitous world of paper and pencil tests. In R.B. Bechtel, R.W. Marans, & W. Michelson (Eds.), *Methods in environmental and behavioral research* (pp. 82–119). New York: Van Nostrand Reinhold.

Gärling, T., Böök, A., & Lindberg, E. (1984). Cognitive mapping of large-scale environments: The interrelations of action plans, acquisition, and orientation. *Environment and Behavior, 16,* 3–34.

Gärling, T., Böök, A., & Lindberg, E. (1986). Spatial orientation and wayfinding in the designed environment: A conceptual analysis and some suggestions for postoccupancy evaluation. *Journal of Architectural and Planning Research, 3,* 55–64.

Slovic, P., Lichtenstein, S., & Fischhoff, B. (1988). Decision making. In R.C. Atkinson, R.J. Herrnstein, G. Lindzey, & R.D. Luce (Eds.), *Stevens' handbook of experimental psychology* (Vol. 2, pp. 673–738). New York: Wiley.

7

Environmental Assessment from a Neuropsychological Perspective

RIKARD KÜLLER

Environmental assessment is closely related to the impact environments make on people. Places that induce anxiety and stress in childhood may be regarded with dismay later in life. The relationship between people and their environments may be conceived in physiological, psychological, or ethnological terms, or, which is often the case, by concepts borrowed from these three fields simultaneously. The description of the relationship can be kept either at a molecular or a molar level. The former may be exemplified by the effect of noise on blood pressure, while the latter may be the home's impact on the developing child. The present chapter constitutes an attempt to formulate a model at the molar level of human–environment interaction, largely based on knowledge from the neuropsychological discipline. For the sake of clarity I will first discuss some of the basic concepts employed in contemporary model building in neuropsychology. I will then suggest that these concepts may be brought together into what I have called the basic emotional process. I will support this construct by results from previous research on emotion, and also demonstrate the remarkable congruence between the physiological and semantic branches of this research. Using the emotional process as a focus, a model of human–environment interaction will be proposed, which describes how the person may feel and act under the influence of the physical and social environment, mediated by his or her individual reaction tendencies. The presentation will be illustrated by reference to field studies and experiments carried out by our group since the mid-1960s. Ample use will also be made of studies carried out elsewhere. However, the chapter does not, in the conventional sense, constitute a review of the existing literature on environmental assessment. Instead, it presents one view on assessment, which naturally leads to a specific organization of the existing evidence. One advantage of the proposed model is that it has the capacity to incorporate recent findings of the neurosciences in a detailed and precise way. The model may also be developed and tested further in this direction. Another advantage is that the model has proven to be a useful tool in the environmental design process.

111

BASIC NEUROPSYCHOLOGICAL CONCEPTS
IN ENVIRONMENTAL ASSESSMENT

Arousal/Activation

In their work on cats, Moruzzi and Magoun (1949) discovered that afferent nerve impulses that reached the central nervous system's higher centers first affected part of the brain stem. This so-called reticular formation, in turn, seemed to raise the state of preparedness of the entire nervous system. A certain degree of reticular activation proved to be a precondition for every form of experiencing as well as behavior. The theory of reticular activation has since been modified in various ways.

Luria (1973) recognized three areas in which reticular activation plays an important role: metabolic processes, the orienting reflex, and intentional mental activity. In metabolic processes Luria included food getting and sexual behavior. His description of the second and third areas is, however, more relevant to the present discussion.

> Man lives in a constantly changing environment, and these changes, which are sometimes unexpected by the individual, require a certain level of increased alertness. This increased alertness must accompany any change in the environmental conditions, any appearance of an unexpected (and sometimes, even an expected) change in those conditions. It must take the form of mobilization of the organism to meet possible surprises, and it is this aspect which lies at the basis of the special type of activity which Pavlov called the orienting reflex and which, although not necessarily connected with the primary biological form of instinctive processes (food-getting, sexual, and so on), is an important basis of investigative activity. (p. 55)

The third area in which the reticular activation is of importance is described by Luria in the following way:

> Much human activity is evoked by intentions and plans, by forecasts and programmes which are formed during man's conscious life, which are social in their motivation and are effected with the close participation, initially of his external, and later of his internal, speech. Every intention formulated in speech defines a certain goal and evokes a programme of action leading to the attainment of that goal. Every time the goal is reached, the activity stops, but every time it is not reached, this leads to further mobilization of efforts. (p. 57)

Thus, it was recognized that reticular activation occurs not only through external impulses, but to an equal degree from higher nerve centers or, in other words, through mental activity. Accordingly, the reticular system could be divided into two functionally separate sections called the ascending reticular activation system (ARAS) and the descending reticular activation system (DRAS). The initial stage of activation seems to be of a rather general nature, involving cortical, autonomic, emotional, and motoric areas. However, it will almost immediately be canalized to the system in which it is best needed, that is, in one case to the cortex, in the other to the body muscles, and so on. As stated by Birkmayer (1965):

> Besides the cortical arousal reaction, reticular activation also gives rise to affective excitation which, in analogy with the former, may be called affective arousal reaction, as

well as to hypothalamic-vegetative excitation (vegetative arousal reaction) and, through the descending reticular system, also to a discharge of muscle fibres resulting in an increased tonus, especially in the extensor muscles (spinal arousal reaction). (p. 85)

Research in the 1960s and 1970s further modified our understanding of the reticular system. Activation can be divided into phasic and tonic arousal. Phasic arousal is the immediate response to stimulation (this is by some authors termed the *orientation reaction;* see Berlyne, 1960), whereas tonic arousal is the general and more long-lasting activation level of the individual. Depending on the occurrence of phasic arousal reactions, tonic arousal level will gradually be altered either upward or downward (van Olst & Orlebeke, 1967). Furthermore, activation turned out to be only one side of the reticular system, inhibition being the other. Several independent studies have shown that although sudden stimulation well above threshold level will lead to a generalized arousal reaction, monotonous stimulation close to the threshold level will give rise to reticular inhibition, rest, and sleep (Libby, Lacey, & Lacey, 1973; Pilleri, 1965).

Arousal theory has been strongly supported by two areas of research. Influenced by the concept of brain washing, Hebb and his associates in the early 1950s began their research on sensory deprivation. After a period of sleep or boredom, their isolated subjects showed symptoms of restlessness or excessive emotional response. They became irritated, had difficulty in thinking clearly, and lost their power of concentration; they also became increasingly susceptible to propaganda; they suffered reduced precision in locomotion and dexterity, disturbed color vision, had physiological alterations of brain wave frequency, odd sensations of their own bodies, and, in certain cases, hallucinations (Bexton, Heron, & Scott, 1954). Although some of these early results have not been fully confirmed, more recent research clearly demonstrates the importance of background stimulation mediated by the reticular activation system, for the normal functioning of the individual (Rasmussen, 1973; Schultz, 1965; Solomon et al., 1961; Suedfeld, 1980).

Even more astounding effects of sensory deprivation on adult rats were found subsequently. Kept a few months in a dull environment, the rats became stupid and their brains decreased in weight. This was remedied, however, when the rats were put back into a more stimulating environment. Occipital and total cortical brain weights increased significantly after enriched conditions, whereas subcortical regions seemed to be resistant to environmental influences (Riege, 1971). The results from this and other similar studies seemed to prove the immense importance of the physical environment. Actually, authorities on brain physiology suggested that we might expect similar effects of deprivation in people living in the monotonous housing areas of suburbia that emerged at the time (Ingvar, 1974).

In a similar way stress research helped identify various adverse effects of overstimulation. The importance of the stress concept for environmental psychology emanates from the definition of stress as a generalized response to environmental factors (Selye, 1956). It is generally assumed that stress is a response to overload, resulting in a shift in body physiology such as blood pressure, pulse rate, and the secretion of adrenalin, noradrenalin, and cortisol. In addition, there might be changes in perception, emotion, and behavior. However, this straightforward view on the relationship between overload and stress is now being replaced by more elaborate models in which cognitive or motivational factors are assumed to mediate the stress reaction.

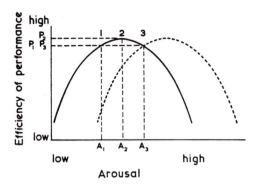

Figure 7.1. The relationship between arousal and performance for two tasks of different complexity. (After Corcoran, 1965.)

For instance, one study dealing with the effects of noise showed that helpfulness toward others diminished considerably in noisy environments (Mathews & Canon, 1975). Further support was obtained in a study by Evans et al. (1988) on a population in India, which showed that the adverse consequences of crowding on male adults' psychological health were mediated by a breakdown of social support systems.

Thus, the research on sensory deprivation and stress strongly supports the idea that the reticular systems will respond to overstimulation as well as to understimulation. By means of the reticular systems, the human arousal level will be maintained and attuned to the task. In a very general sense one may say that various activities demand various levels of tonic arousal. As illustrated in Figure 7.1, the arousal theory predicts that performance is best at moderate levels of tonic arousal but deteriorates when arousal is too low or too high (Hebb, 1949). However, to be performed well, simple, monotonous, or familiar activities demand a high level of arousal, whereas activities that are complex, varied, and novel demand a low level of arousal. This seeming paradox will be resolved when one conceives of the more complex activities as contributing more phasic arousal to the system as a whole. Actually, this relationship was expressed in somewhat different terms in a paper on habit formation by Yerkes and Dodson as early as 1908.

The high complexity of the reticular system explains why the results from environmental studies of arousal often seem contradictory. Results from our own research on the physiological effects of colors indicated cortical arousal and inhibition of heart rate simultaneously. In this study two rooms of totally different character were created. In one room we introduced many colors and patterns to create an environment of high visual complexity; the other room was entirely gray and monotonous. The results showed that colors and patterns stimulated the brain's activity, as shown by a pronounced alpha-attenuation of the EEG (Figure 7.2). In contrast, pulse rate was lowered in the complex room, which might be interpreted as a compensatory response to visual overstimulation (Küller, 1976, 1986). A similar contradiction between cortical and autonomic responses was obtained by Mikellides (1989), in a comparison between the impact of a red and a blue room. These two studies confirm a hypothesis put forth by Libby, Lacey, and Lacey (1973), that both pleasant and unpleasant environments that elicit attention will result in a parasympathetically dominated response that includes heart deceleration.

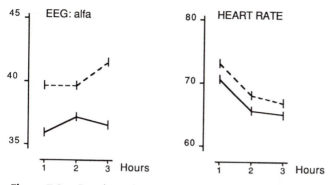

Figure 7.2. Paradoxical cortical and autonomic reactions of subjects sitting in two rooms, one of high (———), the other of low (---) visual complexity. (After Küller, 1986.)

To summarize, one basic hypothesis that we will have to consider in understanding environmental assessment is that there is a relationship between the amount of stimulation on one hand and reticular activation or inhibition on the other. A secondary hypothesis will be that every constellation of environmental factors, where the total amount of stimulation is too high or too low, will eventually result in a shift in tonic arousal level. Such reactions may be recognized as changes in the emotional state of activation, both by the individual and by his surroundings. Furthermore, such reactions in the long run may lead to adverse psychological, social, or even medical consequences.

Attention/Orientation

Our next neuropsychological concept may be defined either as the concentration of thought on an object, or close and careful observing or listening. In the former case we may speak of attention and in the latter of orientation. Any moderate change in the environment is likely to attract a person's attention. He or she will turn eyes, head, or body toward the source of stimulation. The significance of this mechanism was described by Pavlov in 1927 as the

> "What-is-it?" reflex. It is this reflex which brings about the immediate response in man and animals to the slightest changes in the world around them, so that they immediately orientate their appropriate receptor organ in accordance with the perceptible quality in the agent bringing about the change, making full investigation of it. The biological significance of this reflex is obvious. If the animal were not provided with such a reflex its life would hang at every moment by a thread. (p. 12)

Concerning attention, Berlyne (1960) pointed out that

> The word "attention" has had more varied usages than, perhaps, any other in psychology. It has, however, commonly been thought of as something with both intensive and selective aspects. On the one hand, it has been used to refer to processes that determine an organism's degree of alertness or vigilance, i.e., how effectively behavior is being controlled by the stimulus field as a whole. On the other hand, it has been applied to the processes that determine which elements of the stimulus field will exert a dominating

influence over behavior. These are logically two distinct functions, but it is widely felt that closely related processes must be responsible for both. (p. 45)

In my opinion what Berlyne calls the intensive aspect of attention coincides with arousal. We will instead focus on the selective aspect of attention.

The behavioral and cognitive duality of the two concepts orientation and attention may at first seem problematic. A similar duality existed for arousal (e.g., cortical vs. spinal arousal), and will be found to exist also for the concepts to be discussed below. I consider orientation and attention to constitute a unified process. I will assume that when mental attention is directed toward the surrounding environment, it will be accompanied, more or less automatically, by an orientation reaction, or even an approach in the physical sense of the word. This view is reasonably well supported by neurophysiological research. Reviewing the issue, Posner (1980) concluded that the relation between, for example, eye movement and attentional shifts is functional. It is usually the case that attention is needed in the same location to which one wants to direct one's eyes. Consequently, in all but the most contrived experimental settings, eye movements and attentional shifts are correlated.

Recent neurophysiological work also suggests that attention corresponds to a partial redistribution of activity in the brain. Attention to the visual modality, for instance, produces increased activity in the visual association cortex. In addition to specific effects such as this, certain cortical as well as subcortical areas may be related to attention in a more general way. Employing the powerful cerebral blood flow technique, Roland (1982) could demonstrate that whenever attention is shifted from one sensory modality to another, regardless of the modalities involved, there are also changes in the superior lateral part of the prefrontal cortex. Some data suggest hemispheric specialization in attention to pattern versus spatial location. Furthermore, they suggest that attention to location precedes attention to other stimulus attributes (Robinson & Petersen, 1986). Thus, the attention or orientation reaction is accompanied by a temporary increase in arousal, that is, a phasic arousal reaction, which is likely to be sustained and eventually canalized if orientation leads to exploration, conflict, approach, or withdrawal. Frequently the phasic arousal reaction will be accompanied by mental feelings of curiosity, interest, and the like. On the other hand, when habituation occurs, there is no increase in arousal and no feeling of interest (Berlyne, 1971, 1974).

Intense arousal is generally accompanied by an equally intense orientation reaction. Attention is completely directed toward the new and unexpected. At the same time the width of attention decreases. This has sometimes been referred to as the funnelling effect (Bursill, 1958). Drowsiness on the other hand leads to a drift in attention and the person becomes easily distracted. During moderate arousal the width of attention may vary in a more flexible way (Figure 7.3).

Research within the field of cognitive psychology has clearly established that selective attention can be based on semantic characteristics of the message as well as stimulus characteristics (Hirst, 1986). According to Kaplan (1987) environments that are boring, distracting, or unsafe require extensive use of directed attention, leading ultimately to mental fatigue, whereas restorative environments, including wilderness, gardens, and moving water, may permit the recovery of directed attention. Even if

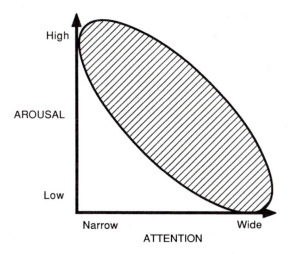

Figure 7.3. Hypothetical relationship between arousal and width of attention.

hypotheses such as this demand further support before they can become fully accepted, the selective aspect of attention will have to be considered in our model of environmental assessment.

Reward and Aversion

Five years after the work on formatio reticularis had been published by Moruzzi and Magoun, two classic papers appeared, which shed new light on the brain's reactions to external stimulation. Studies by Olds and Milner (1954) and Delgado, Roberts, and Miller (1954) indicated the existence of specific centers in the brain for reward and punishment. Later work, by among others Olds and Olds (1965), made it clear that the pleasure or displeasure brought about by stimulation may depend on the activities in three separate parts of the brain and the interaction of these parts. They have been called the primary reward system, the aversion system, and the secondary reward system. Berlyne (1971) pointed out that

> The primary reward and aversion systems are . . . closely connected, and at least partially identifiable, with the brain structures controlling the manifestations of heightened arousal. . . . The secondary reward system, on the other hand, seems to be more or less identical with the trophotropic or de-arousal system. . . . The secondary rewarding system inhibits the aversion system, which in its turn inhibits the primary rewarding system. Activation of the secondary rewarding system thus produces reward by releasing the primary rewarding system from inhibition. (pp. 84–85)

Briefly, Berlyne's model suggested that a moderate increase of low arousal, as well as a reduction of high arousal, will be experienced as pleasant (Figure 7.4). Levi (1972) presented a somewhat different model based on the stress concept. According to Levi an increase in stress level accompanies both pleasant and unpleasant emotions (Figure 7.5). Although the two models were not fully consistent, both pointed to the interesting fact that a change in physiological arousal level often is accompanied by a change in pleasantness. These findings in themselves do not explain what it actually

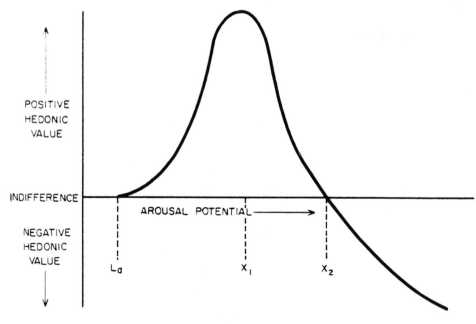

Figure 7.4. The relationship between arousal and reward and aversion. (After Berlyne, 1971.)

is that we like or dislike in our environment—or why. However, Rolls (1976) has speculated that one of the functions of limbic reward sites is related to learning to associate environmental events with rewards and punishments.

To understand the underlying significance of pleasantness, we must consider the fundamental biological urge to survive, grow, and multiply. To accomplish this, all higher animals must possess some kind of system by means of which they can detect, classify, evaluate, and take appropriate action against certain elements in the environment that impinge on them. Seen in this perspective, pleasantness may be considered as a projection onto the environment of an assessment process based on three

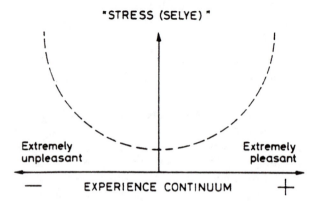

Figure 7.5. Levi (1972) suggests both pleasant and unpleasant emotions are accompanied by an increase in physiological arousal.

crude values—good, harmless, and bad—refined into what is commonly known as the hedonic or evaluative emotional dimension. Thus, after the initial arousal and orientation, one of several things can occur. If the object of attention is difficult to perceive or classify, there may follow a prolonged period of exploration, but eventually an evaluation is likely to occur on a conscious or subconscious level. If the assessment is good it will be followed by an approach, physically or mentally. If it is bad the reaction will be withdrawal, which again may take a physical or mental form. A third possibility is a double assessment, good and bad, usually known as conflict. However, in most cases the assessment will be harmless, of no significance, and the subject will turn away and shortly forget about the experience. What remains is a lasting tendency to disregard whatever caused the initial orientation reaction. This tendency has been termed habituation.

The scientific study of positive, neutral, or negative assessment is usually referred to as aesthetics. It has been treated extensively, not only within the field of psychology, but also in the study of the arts and philosophy (e.g., Arnheim, 1954). Under the heading "The new experimental aesthetics" Berlyne and others in 1974 presented work in which the concepts of arousal and reward had been applied in studies of paintings. At about this time the same concepts were introduced into studies of architecture (Acking & Küller, 1973; Mehrabian & Russell, 1974; Wohlwill, 1974). In recent model building, among others Kaplan (1982) made extensive use of the preference concept:

> Environmental preference is the outcome of what must be an incredibly rapid set of cognitive processes which integrate such considerations as safety, access and the opportunity to learning into a single affective judgement. . . . Viewed in the context of evolution. . . . preference guides behavior and learning. Preference fosters the building and use of cognitive maps. . . . The guidance of the organism's moment to moment behavior is substantially influenced by affect. The direction of locomotion, the selection of foods, the selection of a mate are all influenced by the "attractiveness" of the stimulus patterns. Attractiveness in turn can be analyzed in terms of the interest and pleasure elicited by the particular pattern. (pp. 186–187)

Thus the neuropsychological construct of reward and aversion seems to be the very foundation for human evaluations, both of a purely aesthetic and a more profane nature. It is, in fact, difficult to conceive of any aspect of human affairs that is completely free from reward or aversion. It will be imperative to consider this construct in any model of environmental assessment.

Coping/Control

Lazarus (1975) defined coping as an essential intervening factor for the regulation of emotional states. He divided coping into two main kinds of processes: direct actions on the person–environment relationship, which are motoric in nature and actually produce a change in the objective situation, and intrapsychic processes, which are internal and cognitive. Thus, again we encounter the duality that seemed to characterize the previous concepts. On the neurophysiological level coping is related to the limbic-striatal system with links both downward to the brain stem and upward to the cortex (Henry et al., 1975). However, in physiological terms coping may best be described as a return of the nervous system to normal conditions, for instance, the decrease in arousal after strong excitation. Berlyne (1971) approached this interpretation when he suggested that an increase in low arousal, or a reduction of high arousal, would be experienced as pleasant.

To the individual the main purpose of coping is to obtain control over the situation. Every major event in the external environment probably calls for some coping and the same may well be true for major mental events. Coping may be observed both as a decrease in physiological arousal and a shift in emotional tone. The understanding of coping has benefited from recent research on stress. Initially, stress was regarded as more or less proportional to the level of stimulation. A more modern view was taken by among others Ursin (1980): "Activation depends on the individual perception of the stimulus situation, the available response, and the previous experience with stimuli and responses. Processes identified as defense and coping are of decisive importance for the resulting activation, and hence the internal state of the organism" (p. 275). Levi (1972) suggested that control of the psychosocial environment might reduce both stress and disease, and Frankenhaeuser (1981) stated that "a moderately varied flow of stimuli and events, opportunities to engage in psychologically meaningful work, and to exercise personal control over situational factors, may be considered key components in the quality-of-life concept" (p. 491).

Research consistently shows that environmental stressors such as noise, heat, air pollution, and crowding cause greater stress when the individual is unable to cope with them. Actual or perceived control over a stressor often leads to fewer negative consequences than exposure to stressors that are uncontrollable (Averill, 1973; Glass & Singer, 1972; Lazarus & Folkman, 1984). Negative consequences associated with lack of control include negative affect, cognitive deficits, and reduced motivation to behave instrumentally when the option is available (Seligman, 1975). A study by Dalgard (1981) might illustrate the consequences of lack of control. Dalgard interviewed about 500 adults from Oslo with respect to mental health, occupational experience, and a number of social variables. Special emphasis was placed on closeness of supervision at work. A rather strong correlation between mental health problems and the degree of closeness of supervision was found. The stronger the external control at work, the higher the risk of mental health problems, even when controlling for a number of variables such as age, education, income, type of work, and quality of neighborhood.

The inability to cope may lead to emotional outbursts of anger or fright or to permanent states of anxiety. Evans and Cohen (1987) considered this to be a shift in coping strategies from problem-focused to emotional-focused coping. They also suggested that the chronic exposure to environmental stressors that are uncontrollable may produce greater susceptibility to learned helplessness. In children this may be exemplified by regression or stereotyped behavior. Actually, Lazarus (1975) pointed out that "much of the coping is anticipatory; it is initiated before a confrontation with harm when something in the environment or within the person signals the future possibility or inevitability of harm" (p. 58).

Thus, the experimental evidence suggests that the canalization of arousal in terms of coping or control is an essential component in the individual's interaction with the environment. Evidently a person will be able to handle quite high activation levels as long as he or she is able to control the situation. On the other hand, even sensory deprivation might be disastrous when there is no way of coping.

TOWARD A MODEL OF ENVIRONMENTAL ASSESSMENT

The Dimensions of Emotion

The neuropsychological concepts described above have all been employed in environmental assessment, at times in a rather straightforward way. Still, they constitute parts of a more complex emotional process that need to be further analyzed. I will first discuss how the concepts have been employed in attempts to extract various dimensions of emotion, and then try to expand on this previous work by proposing that they all fit into one coherent emotional process, which, in turn, may serve as the core for a model of environmental assessment. (For more general reviews on emotion, refer to Buck, 1986, and LeDoux, 1986.)

In the activation theory of emotion formulated by Lindsley (1951), the individual's emotions and motivations are considered to fall along an arousal continuum, with drowsiness at one end and strong emotions at the other. Several writers criticized this model for being too simple. "The activation theory of emotions has one obvious failing; it deals only with the intensive dimension, and takes no account of differentiation among the various emotions" (Schlosberg, 1955, p. 26). However, Lindsley did anticipate this difficulty: "What of the milder emotions, the so-called pleasant and relaxed states or mildly exciting emotions?" (1951, p. 509). Schlosberg (1954) brought the issue one step further. In addition to activation, he included two more dimensions, pleasantness–unpleasantness and attention–rejection.

Applying factor analysis to assessment by means of semantic rating scales, Mehrabian and Russell (1974) studied the emotional impact of environments, and obtained three basic dimensions, which they called pleasure, arousal, and dominance. Later, however, Ward and Russell (1981) on the basis of multivariate analyses of data from several independent studies concluded that the two "pleasure and arousal dimensions will be considered sufficient to characterize the affective meaning of place" (p. 137). In addition to restrictions inherent in the sampling of environments and response scales, these writers may be criticized because of their unwillingness to distinguish between emotions and environmental descriptors. It is only by studying the emotions of people in real-life situations that we may hope to obtain some understanding of the sublime relationship between emotions and environmental characteristics.

Since the beginning of the 1970s our research group has been engaged in a series of studies on self-rated emotions by means of semantic scales (Sorte, 1970; Küller, 1972). This technique of emotional assessment has proved to possess a high degree of clinical validity (Hentschel & Klintman, 1974). Selecting salient scales from previous research, a set of 36 bipolar scales was employed in a recent study of a meteorological work station at the Sturup Airport, Malmö (Janssens & Küller, 1989). By means of factor analysis it was possible to extract the basic emotional dimensions that lie behind the individuals' response patterns. As shown in Table 7.1, the analysis resulted in four factors that were interpreted as arousal/activation (IV), attention/orientation (II), reward/aversion (I), and coping/control (III). Even if the resulting

Table 7.1   Principal Component Analysis of Self-Rated Emotions for 28 Meteorologists in Various Situations at Sturup Airport

Adjective scales	Factor[a]			
	I	II	III	IV
Angry–friendly	.77			
Unfamiliar–familiar	.76			
Restless–calm	.75			
Displeased–satisfied	.66			
Worried–carefree	.64			
Sad–happy	.63			
Aggressive–placid	.63			
Selfish–helpful	.60			
Anxious–secure	.54			
Dependent–independent	.53			
Tense–relaxed	.51			
Indifferent–curious		.77		
Unconcerned–engaged		.77		
Lazy–energetic		.76		
Bored–interested		.75		
Drowsy–alert		.63		.53
Hesitant–eager		.51		
Quiet–talkative			.74	
Introverted–extroverted			.69	
Ordinary–original			.68	
Thoughtful–spontaneous			.66	
Serious–joking			.64	
Lonely–companionable			.63	
Submissive–dominating			.62	
Reserved–sociable			.60	
Little–big			.55	
Tired–rested				.64
Sleepy–wide awake				.59
Exposed–inaccessable				.53
Proportion of total variance (%)	18	15	14	8

[a]Oblique rotation. Only loadings >.50 are included.
Source: After Janssens and Küller (1989).

factor structures are not always as clear as this (Watzke, 1986), empirical work indicates that at least four separate dimensions are needed to account for the variance of emotions in real-life situations.

A Definition of the Basic Emotional Process

The neuropsychological evidence discussed earlier indicates that an emotion is not a state, but a process that evolves in stages. I will call this the basic emotional process. I will also suggest that this process proceeds in four steps corresponding to the neurophysiological events of arousal/activation, attention/orientation, reward/aversion (I prefer to use the term evaluation here), and coping/control. Further support for this view is provided by the factor analyses of self-rated emotions cited above. The basic emotional process implies that every impulse, irrespective of its coming from within or without, causes a brief temporary arousal reaction (phasic arousal). Depending on the nature of the impulse it may also give rise to an orientation reaction accompanied by a certain degree of reward or aversion. As a result of repeated impulses, the tonic arousal level may be altered upward to an ever higher (or downward to an ever lower) level. This change in the emotional state of the organism results in a growing preparedness to react to the upcoming situation. Once control is established, the basic emotional process may be said to be concluded. However, the process will be repeated over and over again, as a response to minor or major changes in the human–environment relation.

Although some basic emotional processes may take only seconds to complete, others may last for hours, days, or even years. The briefest type of process occurs, for instance, as a response to a phone call, when one lifts the receiver and says hello; a process of moderate length may be exemplified by having a meal when hungry; a long lasting process may be the saving of money to get a better house for the family. In the latter case, of course, activation, orientation, and evaluation will have to be represented at the cognitive level, and a special strategy developed to increase one's savings. Any long lasting basic emotional process may influence the individual's thinking as well as behavior for a prolonged period of time. It is likely that two or more basic emotional processes may proceed simultaneously but at different levels of consciousness.

The basic emotional dimensions must not be confused with the various emotions per se. Although some fundamental emotions (Plutchik, 1962; Izard, 1977) such as joy, interest, and fear bear close resemblance to our basic dimensions, others such as shame or contempt do not. This apparent inconsistency may be resolved by the fact that most human emotions constitute complex combinations of the basic dimensions. Depression may for instance be described in terms of low activation, diffuse orientation, moderate aversion, and lack of control. Furthermore, human emotions are often related to both past experiences and the present situation. They may therefore be difficult to interpret in the absence of a cognitive and contextual framework.

A Model of Human–Environment Interaction

I will propose that the basic emotional process described above constitutes the very foundation of people's assessment of their environments. Is the view through your window stimulating or boring? Are the people you work with friendly or hostile? Questions such as these may be analyzed in terms of activation, orientation, evaluation, and control. On the basis of these concepts I now introduce a model of the interaction between a person and the environment (Figure 7.6). According to this model the basic emotional process is partly affected by the physical environment, for instance, the dwelling, or the work environment, and partly by the social environment. It is further influenced by the activities the person engages in during the course of work and free time. This influence, which varies in extent over time, is modified by personal resources, constitution, experience, and so on. Although the environment

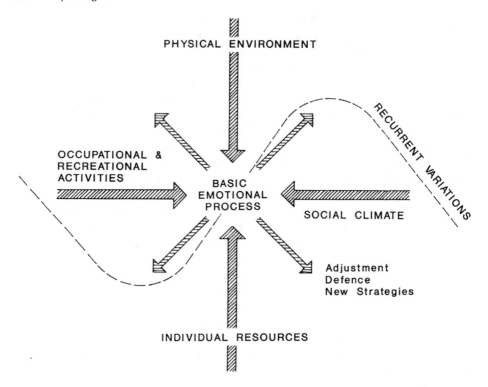

Figure 7.6. A model of human–environment interaction showing various factors that affect and are affected by the basic emotional process. (Modified after Küller, 1976.)

activates in various ways, the individual will endeavor to retain control over his/her situation. This will lead to various strategies of adaptation, defense, and coping.

The actual interaction proceeds in four steps: activation, orientation, evaluation, and control. All events that prevent this basic process from running smoothly will result in adjustment on behalf of the person, whereas strong or prolonged disturbance might lead to maladjustment. What the model indicates is, in part, that activation from various sources must be adapted to the resources of the individual. Inadequate activation can, in the long run, give rise to emotional disturbances. On the other hand, the activation must not become so intense that the individual is overwhelmed and loses control over his situation.

The model has been employed in studies of various kinds of environments, for example, theatres, ships, work places, and housing for the elderly (Janssens & Küller, 1989; Küller, 1977, 1980b, 1988a,b; Küller & Mattsson, 1986). Examples from this research will be given below. One obvious advantage of models of this kind is that they force the applied researcher as well as the planner and architect to take note of several factors simultaneously. I will now leave the core of the model represented by the basic emotional process and instead discuss the remaining parts of the interaction model.

THE MEDIATING ROLE OF REACTION TENDENCIES

Personality and the Environment

The person's mental and behavioral strategies in the environment express a personal style. In differential psychology numerous attempts have been made to develop systems that relate the personality of the individual to tendencies to react toward the environment. Concepts such as extraversion and neuroticism (Eysenck, 1952), field dependence (Witkin et al., 1954), and sensation seeking (Zuckerman et al., 1964) reflect such attempts. For instance, in Eysenck's model introverts are supposed to possess a more easily excitable nervous system than extraverts. Thus, extraverts have a need for intensive stimulation, and they are also likely to enjoy lively, noisy, and colorful environments and experiences (Eysenck, 1967). For the extreme extravert, understimulation may lead to a stimulus hunger with pronounced pathological features. Introverts, on the other hand, because they are sensitive even to very mild stimulation, will have a pronounced need of privacy and calmness, while overstimulation may result in recurrent anxiety or psychosomatic reactions. Eysenck's second major dimension, neuroticism, represents the individual's tendency to react with affect. The neurotics are constitutionally predisposed to intense sympathetic reactions in stressful situations. Recently, Eysenck's model has received considerable experimental support, but there have also been some important modifications (Stenberg, 1990).

Mehrabian and Russell (1974) analyzed a great number of verbal items to assess various aspects of the tendency toward arousal seeking, and came up with the following five factors: arousal from change, arousal from unusual stimuli, arousal from risk, arousal from sensuality, and arousal from new environments. McKechnie (1977) developed an even more elaborate Environmental Response Inventory, defining subscales such as environmental trust, antiquarianism, urbanism, environmental adaptation, stimulus seeking, pastoralism, need for privacy, and mechanical orientation. (A review of personality and the environment is given by Little, 1987.)

Unfortunately, many of the scales developed to assess environmental dispositions have exactly the same drawbacks as the conventional psychological tests, where the characteristics of an individual are described as more or less permanent. We must be extremely careful not to condemn people to become airplane pilots because they score high in arousal seeking. Neither must it be recommended that they move to cities if they score high in urbanism or remain in the countryside if they score high in pastoralism. Lewin (1951) expressed this criticism very clearly: ''in other words, to understand or to predict behaviour, the person and his environment have to be considered as one constellation of interdependent factors'' (pp. 239–240).

Emotionality and Excitability

To avoid the use of the personality construct as a set of more or less fixed characteristics of the individual, I prefer to speak of reaction tendencies. A reaction tendency predisposes the individual to feel or behave in a certain way. But more importantly, this tendency will force the individual to develop coping strategies to avoid becoming too emotional or too excited on one hand, or, on the other, too deprived of excitation and emotion. Therefore, a reaction tendency will seldom be directly tied to a particular behavior. Instead, reaction tendencies may be regarded as functional characteristics of the nervous system. They may at the simplest level be described by two neuropsychological concepts: emotionality and excitability.

Emotionality reflects a balance between the two parts of the autonomic nervous system, the parasympathetic and the sympathetic. The sympathetic part constitutes an emergency system that puts the organism in a state of alarm, inhibiting digestion, while pulse and breathing as well as stress hormones are exhilarated. Sympathetic innervation prepares the individual to confront a dangerous situation. The parasympathetic part works in the opposite direction by slowing down the pace of breathing and pulse beat, thus allowing the organism to function quietly and peacefully. The second concept, the excitability of the nervous system, is related to the reticular formation system with its activating and inhibiting constituents.

It is obvious that reaction tendencies will influence environmental assessment. Mehrabian and Russell (1974) demonstrated that arousal seekers had a greater desire for affiliation and high exposure to interpersonal cues. They also showed that persons who scored high on trait anxiety and neuroticism were affected to a greater extent by the unpleasant and arousing qualities of their environment. In studies on the physiological effects of color, Küller (1976, 1986) found subjects responded to overstimulation by means of a reduction in heart rate. As predicted, this reduction was much larger for introverts (11%) than for extraverts (4%).

On the other hand, environmental assessment will influence the strategies an individual develops to cope with the environment. In his classic book, *The Organization of Behavior,* Hebb (1949) first presented a theoretical analysis of the role of the environment in the development of the individual, in which he placed great emphasis on the importance of stimulation. According to Hebb, environmental stimulation may be regarded as a continuum ranging from deprivation at one end to enrichment at the other. Wachs and Gruen (1982) extended this model by stressing the importance of an optimal level of stimulation, beyond which further stimulation may act to interfere with the development. Even if the mutual influence between reaction tendencies and strategies and environmental assessment is of special significance for the developing child, it may be regarded as a life-long interaction. (For a review on environment and child development, see Wohlwill & Heft 1987.)

As the present model suggests, the interaction between environment and the individual is mediated through the basic emotional process. One can speculate about what this mediation may be like. High emotionality may dispose a person for extreme reactions in terms of reward and aversion. Such a person may show strong positive or negative emotions, resulting in extreme assessments of the environment. However, such a person may also develop efficient strategies to prevent his or her emotions from becoming too extreme. Again, high excitability may dispose a person to avoid the arousing situations of daily life; low excitability may promote arousal-seeking strategies.

Based on the model of environmental assessment, we recently attempted to analyze the relationship between reaction tendencies and environmental assessment in elderly persons. This was done by means of a projective technique, in which the person was shown pictures representing everyday situations containing potential conflicts. The administration and scoring system combines both spontaneous and probe stages in an effort to elicit a subject's acknowledgment of problems, projections of emotions on the protagonists, and solutions for any conflict seen in the drawings. In one study, the well-adjusted group of elderly (fewer signs of emotionality) acknowledged more problems, gave more solutions, and rated the environmental situations as more pleasant than did the maladjusted group (Watzke & Küller, 1986). In a second study on women only, the solutions were classified according to the model into those involving the built environment, the social setting, choice of activity, or internal personal strategies. The commonest way of controlling a conflicting situation was to suggest a social solution. However, after retirement this way of adapting to the situation became somewhat less common. The least usual way of controlling was to involve the built environment, but after retirement the women suggested this adaptive mechanism more often. Solutions by means of change of activities also became somewhat more frequent after retirement (Küller & Steen, 1988).

Reaction tendency models are now becoming increasingly common, especially in health psychology, where the aim is to identify potential risk groups. For example, the type A behavior concept may reveal a disposition for cardiovascular disease (Friedman & Rosenman, 1974). Type A individuals are recognized by extreme competitiveness, impatience, and aggression. In contrast, type B individuals lack these characteristics. It has been suggested that the type A behavior in adults has its roots in childhood experiences (Matthews & Angulo, 1980). Cloninger (1987) developed another model based on inherited factors that determine a specific individual pattern of hormone secretion. According to this system, high concentrations of serotonin enhances reactions to danger and avoidance learning and helps the person to withdraw from unpleasant situations, whereas low concentration prevents such learning. Another hormone, noradrenalin, facilitates the learning of rewarding events; a person with low concentrations of noradrenalin will be characterized by social alienation, high self-esteem, and lack of emotionality. Finally, dopamine concentration is directly related to novelty seeking; high concentrations lead to impulsiveness and exploratory behavior, but also to distraction and carelessness, that is swings in temperament.

THE IMPACT OF ACTIVITIES

The model assumes the existence of close links between a person's emotions and the activities he or she engages in. One side of this link, that is, the impact of the environment on human efficiency, has been thoroughly studied since the time of the Second World War (Poulton, 1970, 1980; Sundstrom, 1987). Successful performance presupposes an optimal level of arousal as well as an appropriate span of attention. When the tonic arousal level is high the attention span will become narrow and important cues may be missed. This may be exemplified by the hurried driver who is already late but still tries to get to an important meeting during rush hours. In this case, ascending as well as descending arousal builds up to a dangerous level. Again, when tonic arousal is low, attention will tend to drift, and the person may find it difficult to concentrate or will even begin to feel drowsy. This means there is mutual influence between environment and performance, and this influence is mediated through the basic emotional process.

Human activities may be divided into three gross categories, the first related to sleep, with predominantly slow and subdued physiological processes. Sleep activities demand a quiet and stable environment, free from strong, sudden, or irregular stimulation. The second category is the activities of everyday life. In this medium arousal state the organism's capacity to handle varied stimulation of all kinds reaches its peak. The third category includes extremely difficult or dangerous activities that put a heavy demand on concentration at the expense of all irrelevant information. This so-called vigilance performance is accompanied by a high or very high state of tonic arousal.

According to the present model of environmental assessment, not only the ongoing activities but also the physical environment and the social environment will contribute to activation. Thus, the model implies that different activities put different demands on the system as a whole. Paradoxically, it is the most monotonous activities that demand the highest activation, while the more interesting tasks demand lower activation. However, if one imagines that the interesting tasks in themselves add a certain degree of activation to the ongoing process, this seeming paradox is resolved. As a practical consequence of this, designers must contemplate what activities will take place in an environment before they decide on the actual design. Because creative or complex activities provide more activation, such environments should be kept more subdued than environments in which monotonous routine activities will take place.

For instance, Rissler and Elgerot (1980) investigated accommodation to work in an open-space office in three groups of insurance employees who had different work tasks. Difficulties of adjustment were clearly traceable to the type of work content and also were related to different coping reactions. During the months immediately after changing the work environment from the more enclosed type of private offices to a more open office-landscape design, employees with routine and service tasks were physiologically mobilized, but their difficulties in adaptation were temporary. However, a group of employees with complex problem-solving tasks had considerable problems adjusting to the open space. They were troubled much more than the other groups by auditory and visual disturbances that interfered with efficient work completion. This group coped by maintaining a high physiological activation level at the cost of qualitative and quantitative performance deterioration. They also expressed more psychological and physiological disturbances after a day's work than the other groups. These symptoms were not alleviated even after working 15 months in the open-space office.

However, the impact of activity characteristics on environmental assessment is a neglected area of research. In an attempt to analyze the role of activities, people working on merchant vessels were asked to assess their main occupational activity (Küller, 1980b). The data were subjected to factor analysis, which showed that the different activities varied in at least four respects: work load, satisfaction, routine, and variation. The different personnel categories varied widely as to how they experienced their job on board. Among others, it became evident that the mates were much more satisfied with their jobs than the rest of the crew. The subjects were also asked to assess different parts of the ship interiors, the private cabins, the mess rooms, the day rooms, recreational areas, corridors and stairs, and work stations. The mates evaluated all parts of the ship interior more highly than the rest of the crew, even those spaces that are shared by all the crew members. This might be due to a carryover from general satisfaction since the mates also evaluated their work activities and the work situation in general much more favorably than the rest of the crew.

In another study that aimed at improving the work environment for the meteorologists at the Sturup Airport, the job characteristics mentioned above were related to the basic emotional process. The overall evaluation was positively correlated to work satisfaction and negatively correlated to work load, while control was positively correlated to the satisfaction with one's work (Janssens & Küller, 1989). Even if much of the evidence to date is indirect, it seems plausible that there is a close connection between activity characteristics and environmental assessment. In addition to work activities, recreational and other free time activities need to be considered in future research.

ASSESSING THE SOCIAL CLIMATE

Crowding and Arousal

Work on the hidden dimension by Hall (1966), personal space by Sommer (1969), psychosocial stress by Levi (1971), and defensible space by Newman (1973) raised an interest in social factors among environmental psychologists. Today the study of the social environment is often referred to in terms such as human spatial behavior (Aiello, 1987), territoriality (Brown, 1987; Malmberg, 1980) and crowding (Baum & Paulus, 1987). One common denominator in this research is the idea that humans have a need for some space of their own (personal space) and if conditions get too dense (crowding) stress may result. To prevent this from happening, space should somehow be divided between persons (territoriality).

It is evident from this description that the social environment may influence arousal, and also induce various coping strategies. This link between crowding and the basic emotional process draws support from a great number of studies. For instance, Aiello, Epstein, and Karlin (1975) monitored skin conductance under laboratory conditions and found that arousal increased over time for crowded but not for uncrowded subjects. D'Atri (1975) found that the enforced crowding prevailing in prison dormitories, often paired with an athmosphere of threat and conflict, resulted in higher blood pressure levels than for those inmates who stayed in single or double occupancy cells. Eye contact between two persons also enhances arousal (Gale et al., 1972). Evans (1978) concluded: "there are several lines of evidence in support of the hypothesis that crowding and invasions of personal space are stressors that are mediated by high arousal" (p. 291).

This evidence makes it imperative that we include crowding in our model of environmental assessment. But what exactly does this concept mean? Stokols (1972) differentiates between crowding and density, with density representing physical conditions, and crowding implying the experience of these conditions. However, Stokols also differentiates between social crowding and nonsocial crowding, with the latter implying "spatial factors, including the amount and arrangement of space, stressor variables such as noise or glare which heighten the salience of physical constraints, and personal characteristics including idiosyncratic skills and traits" (p. 75). According to the present model, these aspects refer to the built environment and to reaction tendencies. Even if these factors do interact with crowding, they should not in themselves be considered as such.

According to Rapoport (1975) crowding is neither physical nor perceptual but affective. This makes sense, especially when one considers studies in which crowding has been shown to be related to physiological reactions. However, the crowding concept might benefit by being specified in rigorous yet general neuropsychological terms. I will suggest that crowding occurs when the tonic arousal level increases because of the presence of others in the perceptual or cognitive field. Two important inferences follow from this proposition:

1. If one is temporarily exposed to a high-density situation but the tonic response is lacking, because somehow one manages to control the situation, then there will be no reason to speak of crowding.
2. Although crowding implies an increase in tonic arousal level, this does not necessarily imply something negative. In cases in which the tonic level initially was very low, an increase may instead mean that the individual achieves a more adequate level. Only when the crowding effect is combined with an already optimal or high level of arousal may the effect of this combination become clearly negative. This explains a number of apparently contradictory results, such as why crowding sometimes leads to improved performance (Küller, 1979b).

Psychosocial Factors

The great interest in crowding research among environmental psychologists may lead us to think that crowding were the sole important aspect of the social environment. This is certainly not true. There is growing evidence that the positive qualities of the social environment, usually referred to as social support, play an immense role not only in everyday life, but also for people who face an acute crisis (Cohen & Syme, 1985). The importance of social support has been widely recognized in studies of child development (Parke, 1978). In a study of children's cognitive development, Bradley and Caldwell (1982) demonstrated that the choice of coping strategies differed from one type of environment to another. The social qualities of the child's home environment were the most important for healthy development. In studies of elderly people, social isolation and lack of social support have proven detrimental (e.g. Fiske Lowenthal, 1968) and increasing emphasis is being placed on social support in neighborhood intervention projects and in long-term care for the elderly (Küller, 1988a,b; Küller & Mattsson, 1986). Also in research on work environment the positive impact of social support is receiving more recognition (Levi, Frankenhaeuser, & Gardell, 1981). In this kind of research the social environment is often referred to as psychosocial factors. It may seem reasonable from an environmental psychology viewpoint to try to identify various salient factors of the social environment.

One attempt in this direction is the Family Environment Scale developed by Moos

(1975). This scale was developed by administering 200 items related to social issues to more than 1000 individuals from 300 families with varying religious, educational, and ethnical backgrounds, including a group with a clinical history. The Family Environment Scale consists of 90 statements, divided into 10 subscales designed to measure the press dimensions of the family's social environment in terms of relationships, personal growth, and system maintenance.

In our own research, descriptions of social situations were subjected to factor analysis in a study that included both large and small groups, in formal as well as informal contexts (Küller, 1978). From a list of 600 Swedish words, which could be used to characterize various qualities of social situations, 48 were selected and represented in the form of semantic rating scales. The scales were also translated into English and Italian, and administered to visitors at two public places in Stockholm (Kungsträdgården and Sergels torg) and two places in Rome (Piazza della Rotonda and Piazza Navona). In both cities, American tourists were used as controls to ascertain the degree of cross-cultural validity of the scales. In a second part of the study, the scales were administered to groups of students and visitors at the School of Architecture in Lund. Treating the data by means of factor analysis revealed a striking correspondence between the two parts of the study. In both instances the following five factors emerged: social intensity, interpersonal stability, familiarity, coherence, and friendliness of the situation. These dimensions may be used to define more precisely various situations of crowding and social support. In terms of the basic emotional process, social intensity may be thought of as conducive to high arousal, while coherence and familiarity may instead reduce arousal. Interpersonal stability as well as familiarity and friendliness may be rewarding and contribute to an overall positive assessment. Allegedly, these relations are at present hypothetical. Still, some empirical support was found in the recent study of meteorologists by Janssens and Küller (1989).

ASSESSING THE ENVIRONMENT

The one factor of the human–environment interaction that remains to be described is the physical environment. Environmental assessment first began to take shape in the 1960s. In the early studies, psychophysical scaling methods were used to assess various aspects of the environment such as odors (Berglund, 1974), shapes of space (Gärling, 1969), and room sizes (Holmberg, Küller, & Tidblom, 1966). In 1957, Osgood, Suci, and Tannenbaum published their work on the measurement of meaning, which influenced environmental psychologists all over the world. Osgood and his associates were mainly interested in measuring the semantic meaning of various concepts, but they also did studies in aesthetics. By means of factor analysis they obtained three salient dimensions, evaluation, activity, and potency, as well as another four dimensions that were more difficult to interpret. They were less successful, however, when trying to measure the dimensions in a uniform way for different research areas.

By limiting the area of measurement to perception of man-made environments, psychologists hoped to obtain dimensions that would be easier to interpret and more meaningful when attempting to evaluate an environment. This approach was taken by, among others, Acking and Küller (1967, 1968), Canter (1969), Craik (1971), Feimer (1984), Hershberger (1972), Honikman (1971), Horayangkura (1978), Kaplan (1972), Kasmar (1970), and Oostendorp and Berlyne (1978). Like Osgood et al., we used in our own research seven-point semantic scales, but instead of defining these by opposed pairs only one adjective was used for each scale. This approach facilitated the scale construction as well as the interpretation of the factors, and most likely improved the validity of the assessment instrument that was later developed. Other main features were the systematic sampling of adjectives from the Swedish language, and the wide range of environments and subject groups employed (Acking & Küller, 1973; Küller, 1971, 1972, 1973).

Using a total of about 200 adjectives on a wide range of environments and subjects of different age, sex, and occupation, factor analysis revealed that each of the adjectives related to one or more of the following eight dimensions: pleasantness, complexity, unity, enclosedness, potency, social status, affection, and originality (Table 7.2). The most reliable of the rating scales have been compiled into an instrument where pleasantness is measured by eight different scales and the remaining dimen-

Table 7.2   Eight Dimensions of Environmental Assessment Obtained by Means of Factor Analysis of Semantic Ratings in Different Studies

Pleasantness: The environmental quality of being pleasant, beautiful and secure	Descriptive evaluation (Honikman, 1971) Evaluation (Hershberger, 1972) Friendliness (Canter, 1969) Hedonic tone (Oostendorp & Berlyne, 1978) Valency (Franke & Bortz, 1972)
Complexity: The degree of variation or, more specifically, intensity, contrast, and abundance	Activity (Canter, 1969; Hershberger, 1972) Uncertainty (Oostendorp & Berlyne, 1978) Variation (Franke & Bortz 1972)
Unity: How well all the various parts of the environment fit together into a coherent and functional whole	Coherence (Canter, 1969) Order (Oostendorp & Berlyne, 1978)
Enclosedness: A sense of spatial enclosure and demarcation	Spatial quality (Hershberger, 1972; Honikman, 1971)
Potency: An expression of power in the environment and its various parts	Arousal (Oostendorp & Berlyne, 1978) Potency (Hershberger, 1972; Honikman, 1971)
Social status: An evaluation of the built environment in socioeconomic terms, but also in terms of maintenance	Comfort (Franke & Bortz, 1972)
Affection: The quality of recognition giving rise to a sense of familiarity, often related to the age of the environment	Familiarity (Oostendorp & Berlyne, 1978)
Originality: The unusual and surprising in the environment	Aesthetic/novelty factor (Hershberger, 1972)

Source: After Acking and Küller (1967, 1968) and Küller (1971, 1972, 1973).

sions by four scales each (Küller, 1972, 1975, 1979a). Gärling (1976) successfully validated these dimensions by means of multidimensional scaling. Kwok (1979) conducted a cross-cultural replication on one population in London and another in Singapore with the same semantic scales. An amazingly high cross-cultural stability of the scales was recently demonstrated by Zhao (1987) (Figure 7.7). The instrument has been used in the assessment of urban places (Küller, 1988c), work environments (Janssens & Küller, 1989), simulated environments (Janssens & Küller, 1986), and color spaces (Mikellides, 1989).

Traditional Chinese buildings in the Yunnan province.

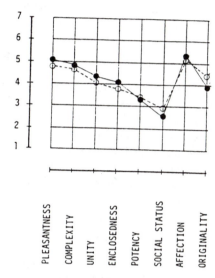

Modern housing area in Lund.

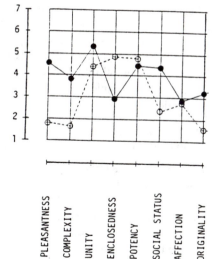

Figure 7.7. Chinese (●) and Swedish (○) subjects generally conformed in their assessment of the traditional buildings, but differed when confronted with modern Western architecture. (After Zhao, 1987.)

As a result of numerous validation studies, including the comparison of perceptual and neurophysiological responses, knowledge about the eight dimensions has increased considerably during the last few years. The relationship to the basic emotional process has been described in detail by Küller (1980a). Naturally, one should not expect any one-to-one relation between emotions and the perceived qualities of the environment. You might, for instance, consider your living room to be very pleasant. Sometimes, when you look around it you feel pleased and happy. At other times you hardly notice the room, but even at times of sadness or depression, you are not likely to find the room unpleasant. Although emotions may shift quite rapidly, the qualities projected onto the environment remain much more stable.

Pleasantness

Attempt at predicting pleasantness have made use of key concepts such as harmony, rhythm, complexity, uncertainty, and mystery, and often imply a search for the appropriate or optimal stimulus situation. Many of these attempts have been based on physiological considerations. The existence of a close link between arousal and reward and aversion has been discussed above. There is also some evidence of a link between pleasantness and attention. Janssens and Küller (1989) found that meteorologists who assessed their office as pleasant reported a higher level of interest and attention.

Complexity and Unity

Together, the complexity and unity of an environment form a higher order variable, which may be thought of as information rate. If complexity is far exceeded by unity, the result is a dull and monotonous environment, whereas if the difference goes the other way, the environment appears too chaotic. This is exemplified by our previously mentioned study of the colorful and gray rooms (Küller, 1976, 1986). Not only did the subjects have a higher physiological arousal level in the colorful room, but they also felt much more introverted in that room than in the gray one, as reflected by self-rated emotions. The experiment therefore underlines the impression that a change in the complexity of the built environment can be accompanied by a change in emotional control.

Enclosedness

The spatial characteristic of an environment termed enclosedness may also have emotional consequences mainly through mediation of crowding and privacy. For instance, the tenseness and lack of control people experience in an elevator may be counteracted if the elevator has a window. Increasing the enclosedness by closing the door may also be a means of filtering out part of the stimulation from the environment, that is of lowering one's arousal level. Again, a person who feels rested and in full control is apt to open up the filter more than if he or she feels tired and introverted. An appropriate use of enclosedness in the design of housing areas has also proven to promote a "defensible space" by means of increased social control (Newman, 1973).

Potency

Miron and Osgood (1966) considered potency as an expression of the amount of physiological effort it would take for the individual to come to terms with the stimulus situation. Thus, a building of high potency would be, initially, more difficult to incorporate in a physiological sense or, in emotional terms, to control mentally. Janssens and Küller (1989) found that meteorologists who perceived their office environment to be high in potency actually reported a lack of emotional control. Allegedly, at present this may be nothing more than a hunch, though an interesting one because of its far-reaching implications. It would mean, for instance, that the typical high-rise housing area merely through its visual character might make it more difficult for people to establish emotional control over their environment—perhaps an invitation to vandalism.

Social Status

No experimental studies seem to exist that throw light on the emotional significance of social status in the built environment. However, there is no doubt that social classification relates to basic human needs, and therefore social status may serve as a kind of criterion to our basic emotional evaluations. Several authors have also suggested a link between social status as upkeep or maintenance and absence of vandalism (Pablant & Baxter, 1975).

Affection and Originality

Affection implies a kind of recognition, an impression of familiarity, not necessarily because we have been in a particular place before, but perhaps as a result of our biological and cultural inheritance. For instance, there seems to be a wide register of readily identifiable environments, suggesting, perhaps, archetypes stored in the collective unconscious. As well as this kind of immediate recognition there is also a process of continuous familiarization. There are the environments we were born in, grew up in, and in some cases spent the whole of our lives in. People not only get used to new things, but may also develop, after some time, an affection for them.

Originality, meaning fresh and unusual as well as initial, first, is something of a counterbalance to affection. However, it is not the opposite of this quality. An original piece of architecture, which will be original even after the passage of time, may come to provoke an expression of affection; conversely, of course, total lack of originality is no guarantee that affection will be felt. For these reasons, I have avoided the terms novelty and familiarity, because these would have suggested a continuum, in which a building would start off as novel and end up as familiar.

The emotional impact of affection and originality may be considered in terms of orientation and habituation. In a place of high originality numerous strong orientation reactions will initially occur, but owing to habituation they will eventually level off. If originality is the only quality present, there will be nothing left to attend to. However, if there is "something more," that is something that we recognize because of its biological, cultural, or personal significance, the place will continue to hold our interest. Thus, affection will serve to sustain emotional attention. In a place of high affection—the landscape of the native country, the old town center with its typical buildings, the familiar room filled with personal belongings—there will always be things to recognize.

Limitations Imposed by the Method

Can we be certain that the eight dimensions of assessment described above are true? Have we found the atoms of assessment? I believe the answer to this lies in appropriate sampling. Since we are dealing with variances between environments judged by individuals, we must make certain the sample is wide and random. Actually, any restriction on randomness may result in spurious or unique factors. For instance, when Zhao (1987) restricted himself to architecture from China and Sweden, he obtained an additional factor that could be interpreted in terms of cultural identity (with high loadings in the scales Chinese and Western). When Sorte (1982) asked his subjects to assess physical objects such as roofs, doors, windows, and furniture, rather than environments, he obtained a set of 11 factors. When Olsson-Jonsson (1988) employed Sorte's method to assess windows only, she obtained an additional factor pertaining to the standing versus reclining proportions of the windows. Students of color perception generally come up with three to five salient factors (Hogg, 1969).

Many researchers, however, shun the restrictions imposed by a fixed set of assessment characteristics. One suggestion for the solution of this dilemma was proposed by Canter (1973). In a study of lighting, ventilation, heating, daylight, and view, he employed the personal construct technique originally developed by Kelly (1955), thereby obviating the need for fixed characteristics. Kelly argues that elements and constructs have a functional relationship to one another and that the same idea can behave as an element or a construct. One difficulty with this approach is that each time the investigator will have to begin afresh with adequate constructs. However, this may also be a strength, since it ensures a certain correspondence between the research problem and the problems of real life. More serious is the lack of conceptual clarity of such an approach. Will we in the long run be satisfied to represent element/construct interactions as points in a nonparametric space? To me, a concept such as environmental complexity not only makes theoretical sense but can also be of direct use in environmental design.

So far I have discussed only one side of the assessment concept, what Craik and Feimer (1987) in their review call observer-based environmental assessment; the other is technical environmental assessment. This second category may seem of little interest to psychologists. However, to architects, assessment, be it observer-based or not, will always have to be transformed into technical specifications. The difficulties in bridging this application gap becomes obvious in literature from the expanding area of postoccupancy evaluation (Preiser, Rabinowitz, & White, 1988). Looking at the elements of building performance listed in this literature as technical, functional, and behavioral makes its evident that the question remains what to assess in the environment.

CONCLUSIONS

The focus of psychological assessment has shifted away from the exact measurement of stimulus–response relations toward the study of complex processes characterized by mediated interaction. The theoretical framework presented in this chapter constitutes one such attempt. Based on the neuropsychological concepts arousal/activation, attention/orientation, reward/aversion, and coping/control, it models the interplay between humans and their environment. According to the model a person is partly affected by the physical environment, for instance, the dwelling and work environment, and partly by the social environment. In addition, he or she will be influenced by the activities engaged in during work and leisure. This influence, which varies in extent over time, is modified by the person's resources, constitution, experience, and so on. Although the environment activates in various ways, the person at the same time endeavors to retain control over the situation. What the model indicates is, in part, that activation from various sources ideally should match the resources of the individual. At times, this may call for the development of new coping strategies. Furthermore, a transfer is assumed between the living environment, work, and leisure sectors, so that positive experiences in one sector are passed on to the others, while negative experiences may possibly result in attempts to isolate that sector from the others.

The idea that many factors interact in the assessment process may be easy to accept, at least in principle. Most of us will agree that the psychosocial climate, say in a family, may be different to the various members of that family. However, the built environment is generally considered as more or less similar to different observers. For instance, a living room is considered to possess a definite size, color, temperature, style, and atmosphere. In environmental psychology this view is no longer tenable. To the little child the living room may seem very large, to the Eskimo very warm, to the owner very familiar. We must be prepared to accept that all characteristics of the environment are interactive. The fact that different individuals do appear to agree about most everyday environments rather depends on similarity between the individuals than any inherent unity of the environments. It is only when seen through the eyes of the physicist that the living room becomes a fairly objective phenomenon.

What evidence is there of true interactional effects? More than 30 years ago, Maslow and Mintz (1956) demonstrated that the character of the environment had an effect on how people are perceived. Subjects who spent 10 to 15 minutes rating a series of facial photographs in a beautiful room rated the faces as having significantly more energy and well-being than did subjects tested in either an average or ugly room. There is also some evidence from studies in which subjects looked at color slides of various environments and were asked how they thought they would feel in them. In a study by Sorte (1970), subjects were presented with one set of landscapes and one set of living room interiors. The subjects suggested that the more pleasant environments would contribute to an increase in calmness and security as well as to a reduction of aggressive feelings. Also, the subjects believed that the more pleasant interiors would make them feel more agile, independent, talkative, extroverted, and sociable. Küller (1972) tested a group of teachers of domestic economy with a personality inventory (EPI) by which means they could be divided into extroverts or introverts and stable or neurotic. The teachers were then asked to evaluate how they thought various environments would influence them. They generally believed they would become more extroverted in pleasant environments than in unpleasant environments. They also thought they would become more stable in pleasant environments. The more stable individuals further considered they would be favorably affected in environments of low complexity.

Mehrabian and Russell (1974) summarized a number of studies that showed that the social setting, including free food and drink, and also the spatial arrangement, may influence not only the assessment process but also the affiliative and hostility behavior of the subjects. The studies cited earlier, on differential reactions to a high complexity environment (Küller, 1976, 1986), noise and helping behavior (Mathews & Canon, 1975), crowding and stress (Evans, 1978), and the study of meteorologists by Janssens and Küller (1989), lend further support to the interaction thesis. In the meteorologists study all the components of the interactional model were studied, and it became possible to weigh their relative impact on the emotional well-being of the employees. The results showed that the work activities and the psychosocial climate were most important, but also that the work environment had an impact.

Another attempt at integrating several different components was recently undertaken in a study of environmental activation of old persons suffering from senile dementia (Küller, 1988a). Two collective housing units, each for nine patients, were built at the Kroksbäck housing area in Malmö. Both the therapeutic activities, the psychosocial climate, and the interior design emphasized the qualities of routine, familiarity, and affection, to match the mental resources of the patients. The intention was to follow the patients for 2 months while at the geriatric hospital and then for another 4 months after they had moved to the collective housing units. In senile dementia parts of the patient's brain have for various reasons been destroyed, which makes the learning of new habits and the recognition of new environments difficult. It was hypothesized that a familiar environment would activate old habits established through lifelong experience, thus increasing the functional and social competence of the patients.

To test this hypothesis the units were designed in a way that would be easily recognized as a home as opposed to an institutional environment. Among others, this meant a rather strict adherence to a style from the 1930s and 1940s. The decoration of the private rooms was supported by a special program that included interviews and counseling with the relatives of the patients. Thus, the patients would become tenants and able to continue a fairly normal life surrounded by their private belongings and their own friends and relatives. The assessment of the environmental impact was made by means of systematic observations of the patients' behavior and also included a control group who remained at the geriatric hospital for the whole period of 6 months. The results showed that collective housing in small units, especially if the environment was decorated in an old and familiar style, had an activating effect on patients with old age dementia. It actually provided a much better therapeutic environment than the conventional geriatric hospital.

In this chapter I have discussed research in which emotions are considered to play a central role as mediators of environmental assessment. The theoretical and empirical material referred to was selected to illustrate some of the major ideas within this research, and it is therefore far from inclusive. However, the material was chosen not only to support, but also to point out some of the inconsistencies that still prevail. One main conclusion that emerged is that more research is urgently needed where many different aspects of the human–environment interaction are brought together. Another conclusion is that there should be more research of a field-experimental kind, for instance, in the form of intervention studies. Only then will it become possible to achieve an understanding of the dynamics of environmental assessment. A third conclusion, finally, is that the field of environmental assessment would benefit by absorbing the results from recent neuropsychological work, especially on hormones and neurotransmitters. Not only would this help throw new light on concepts such as arousal and coping, which are now sometimes employed in a rather loose fashion, it would also considerably increase our understanding of the environment's long-term impact on human health and development.

ACKNOWLEDGMENTS

The writing of this chapter was made possible through grants from the Swedish Council for Building Research and the Swedish Work Environment Fund.

REFERENCES

Acking, C.A., & Küller, R. (1967). *Faktorer vid perception av interiörer. Bedömning från diabilder (Factors in the perception of interiors. Assessment of colour slides.)* (Work report No. 2). Lund, Sweden: Department of Theoretical and Applied Aesthetics, Lund Institute of Technology.

Acking, C.A., & Küller, R. (1968). *Faktorer vid perception av exteriörer. Bedömning i fullskala (Factors in the perception of exteriors. Assessment of full scale environments.)* (Work report No. 3). Lund, Sweden: Department of Theoretical and Applied Aesthetics, Lund Institute of Technology.

Acking, C.A., & Küller, R. (1973). Presentation and judgement of planned environment and the hypothesis of arousal. In W.F.E. Preiser (Ed.), *Environmental design research* (Vol. 1, pp. 71–83). Stroudsburg, Penn.: Dowden, Hutchinson & Ross.

Aiello, J.R. (1987). Human spatial behavior. In D. Stokols & I. Altman (Eds.), *Handbook of environmental psychology* (Vol. 1, pp. 389–504). New York: Wiley.

Aiello, J., Epstein, Y., & Karlin, R. (1975). Effects of crowding on electrodermal activity. *Sociological Symposium, 14,* 43–58.

Arnheim, R. (1954). *Art and visual perception.* London: Faber & Faber.

Averill, J.R. (1973). Personal control over aversive stimuli and its relationship to stress. *Psychological Bulletin, 8,* 286–303.

Baum, A., & Paulus, P.B. (1987). Crowding. In D. Stokols & I. Altman (Eds.), *Handbook of environmental psychology* (Vol. 1, pp. 533–570). New York: Wiley.

Berglund, B. (1974). Quantitative and qualitative analysis of industrial odors with human observers. *Annals of the New York Academy of Sciences, 237,* 35–51.

Berlyne, D.E. (1960). *Conflict, arousal and curiosity.* New York: McGraw-Hill.

Berlyne, D.E. (1971). *Aesthetics and psychobiology.* New York: Appleton-Century-Crofts.

Berlyne, D.E. (Ed.). (1974). *Studies in the new experimental aesthetics.* New York: Wiley.

Bexton, W.H., Heron, W., & Scott, T.H. (1954). Effects of decreased variation in the sensory environment. *Canadian Journal of Psychology, 8,* 70–76.

Birkmayer, W. (1965). Vegetativ-affektiva störningar och deras samband med den retikulära formationens funktion. (Vegetative-affective disorders as related to the function of the reticular formation.) In W. Birkmayer & G. Pilleri (Eds.), *Hjärnstammens reticulära formation och dess betydelse för de vegetativa funktionerna och affektlivet* (pp. 81–107). Basel: F. Hoffman-La Roche & Co.

Bradley, R.H., & Caldwell, B.M. (1982). The consistency of the home environment and its relation to child development. *International Journal of Behavioral Development, 5,* 445–465.

Brown, B.B. (1987). Territoriality. In D. Stokols & I. Altman (Eds.), *Handbook of environmental psychology* (Vol. 1, pp. 505–531). New York: Wiley.

Buck, R. (1986). The psychology of emotion. In J.E. LeDoux & W. Hirst (Eds.). *Mind and brain. Dialogues in cognitive neuroscience* (pp. 275–300). Cambridge: Cambridge University Press.

Bursill, A.E. (1958). The restriction of peripheral vision during exposure to hot and humid conditions. *Quarterly Journal of Experimental Psychology, 10*(3), 113–129.

Canter, D. (1969). An intergroup comparison of connotative dimensions in architecture. *Environment and Behavior, 1,* 37–48.

Canter, D. (1973). Evaluating buildings: Emerging scales and the salience of building elements over constructs. In R. Küller (Ed.), *Architectural psychology. Proceedings of the Lund Conference* (pp. 214–238), Stroudsburg, Penn.: Dowden, Hutchinson & Ross.

Cloninger, C.R. (1987). A systematic method for clinical description and classification of personality variants. A proposal. *Archieves Genetic Psychiatry, 44*(6), 573–588.

Cohen, S., & Syme, L. (Eds.) (1985). *Social support and health.* San Francisco: Academic Press.

Corcoran, D.W.J. (1965). Personality and the inverted-U relation. *British Journal of Psychology, 52,* 267–273.

Craik, K.H. (1971). The assessment of places. In P. McReynolds (Ed.), *Advances in psychological assessment* (Vol. 2, pp. 40–62). Palo Alto, Calif.: Science and Behavior Books.

Craik, K.H., & Feimer, N.R. (1987). Environmental assessment. In D. Stokols & I. Altman (Eds.), *Handbook of environmental psychology* (Vol. 2, pp. 891–918). New York: Wiley.

Dalgard, O.S. (1981). Occupational experience and mental health, with special reference to closeness of supervision. *Psychiatry and Social Science, 1,* 29–42.

D'Atri, D.A. (1975). Psychophysiological responses to crowding. *Environment and Behavior, 7,* 237–252.

Delgado, M.M.R., Roberts, W.W., & Miller, N.E. (1954). Learning by electrical stimulation of the brain. *American Journal of Physiology, 179,* 587–593.

Evans, G.W. (1978). Human spatial behavior: The arousal model. In A. Baum & Y. Epstein (Eds.), *Human response to crowding* (pp. 283–302). Hillsdale, N.J.: Erlbaum.

Evans, G.W., & Cohen, S. (1987). Environmental stress. In D. Stokols & I. Altman (Eds.), *Handbook of environmental psychology* (Vol. 1, pp. 571–610). New York: Wiley.

Evans, G.W., Palsane, M.N., Lepore, S.J., & Martin, J. (1988). Crowding and social support. In H. van Hogdalem, N.L. Prak, T.J.M. van der Voordt, & H.B.R. van Wegen (Eds.), *Looking back to the future. Proceedings IAPS 10* (Vol. 2, pp. 125–132). Delft, Netherlands: Delft University Press.

Eysenck, H.J. (1952). *The scientific study of personality.* London: Routledge & Kegan Paul.

Eysenck, H.J. (1967). *The biological basis of personality.* Springfield, Ill.: Thomas.

Feimer, N.R. (1984). Environmental perception: The effects of media, evaluative context, and observer sample. *Journal of Environmental Psychology, 4,* 61–80.

Fiske Lowenthal, M. (1968). Social isolation and mental illness in old age. In B.L. Neugarten (Ed.), *Middle age and aging* (pp. 220–234). Chicago: The University of Chicago Press.

Franke, J., & Bortz, J. (1972). Beiträge zur Anwendung der Psychologie auf den Städtebau. *Zeitschrift für experimentelle und angewandte Psychologie, 19,* 76–108.

Frankenhaeuser, M. (1981). Coping with stress at work. *International Journal of Health Services, 11,* 491–510.

Friedman, M. & Rosenman, R.H. (1974). *Type A behavior and your heart.* New York: Knopf.

Gale, A., Lucas, B., Nissim, R., & Harpham, B. (1972). Some EEG correlates of face-to-face contact. *British Journal of Social and Clinical Psychology, 11,* 326–332.

Gärling, T. (1969). Studies in visual perception of architectural spaces and rooms. *Scandinavian Journal of Psychology, 10,* 250–256.

Gärling, T. (1976). A multidimensional scaling and semantic differential technique study of the perception of environmental settings. *Scandinavian Journal of Psychology, 17,* 323–332.

Glass, D.C., & Singer, J.E. (1972). *Urban stress. Experiments on noise and social stressors.* New York: Academic Press.

Hall, E.T. (1966). *The hidden dimension.* New York: Doubleday.

Hebb, D. (1949). *The organization of behavior.* New York: Wiley.

Henry, J.P., Ely, D.L., Watson, F.M.C., & Stephens, P.M. (1975). Ethological methods as applied to the measurement of emotion. In L. Levi (Ed.). *Emotions. Their parameters and measurement* (pp. 469–497). New York: Raven.

Hentschel, U., & Klintman, H. (1974). *Twentyeight-variable semantic differential. II. On the validity as reflected by the relation of the scales to some personality constructs* (Psychological Research Bulletin, Vol. 14, No. 5). Lund, Sweden: Lund University.

Hershberger, R.G. (1972). Toward a set of semantic scales to measure the meaning of architectural environments. In W.J. Mitchell (Ed.), *Environmental design: Research and practice* (pp. 6.4.1–6.4.10). Los Angeles: University of California Press.

Hirst, W. (1986). The psychology of attention. In J.E. LeDoux & W. Hirst (Eds.). *Mind and brain. Dialogues in cognitive neuroscience* (pp. 105–141). Cambridge: Cambridge University Press.

Hogg, J. (1969). A principal component analysis of semantic differential judgements of single colors and color pairs. *Journal of General Psychology, 80,* 129–140.

Holmberg, L., Küller, R., & Tidblom, I. (1966). *The perception of volume content of rectangular rooms as a function of the ratio between depth and width* (Psychological Research Bulletin, Vol. 6, No. 1). Lund, Sweden: Lund University.

Honikman, B. (1971). An investigation of a method for studying personal evaluation and requirement of the built environment. In B. Honikman (Eds.), *Proceedings of the Architectural Psychology Conference at Kingston Polytechnic 1970.* London: RIBA Publications.

Horayangkura, V. (1978). Semantic dimensional structures. A methodological approach. *Environment and Behavior, 10*(4), 555–584.

Ingvar, D. (1974). Staden och hjärnan [City and brain] In C.A. Acking & R. Küller (Eds.), *Bygg mänskligt* (pp. 75–82). Stockholm: Askild & Kärnekull.

Izard, C.E. (1977). *Human emotions.* New York: Plenum.

Janssens, J., & Küller, R. (1986). Utilizing an environmental simulation laboratory in Sweden. In R.C. Smardon, J.F. Palmer & J.P. Felleman (Eds.), *Foundations for visual project analysis* (pp. 265–275). New York: Wiley.

Janssens, J., & Küller, R. (1989). *Vädertjänstens arbetsmiljö. Miljöpsykologisk studie av förhållandena vid Sturups flygplats. (Meteorologists' work environment. A psychological study of the conditions at Sturup Airport.)* (Environmental Psychology Monographs No. 7). Lund, Sweden: School of Architecture, Lund Institute of Technology.

Kaplan, R. (1972). The dimensions of the visual environment: Methodological considerations. In W.J. Mitchell (Ed.), *Environmental design: Research and practice.* Los Angeles: University of California Press.

Kaplan, S. (1982). Where cognition and affect meet: A theoretical analysis of preference. In P. Bart, A. Chen, & G. Francescato (Eds.), *Knowledge for design. Proceedings Environmental Design Research Association Conference 1982* (pp. 183–188). Washington, D.C.: EDRA.

Kaplan, S. (1987). Mental fatigue and the designed environment. In J. Harvey & D. Henning (Eds.), *Public Environments. Proceedings Environmental Design Research Association Conference 1987* (pp. 55–60). Ottawa, Canada.

Kasmar, J.V. (1970). The development of a usable lexicon of environmental descriptors. *Environment and Behavior, 2,* 153–169.

Kelly, G.A. (1955). *Psychology of personal constructs* (Vols. 1–2). New York: Norton.

Küller, R. (1971). The perception of an interior as a function of its colour. In B. Honikman (Ed.), *Proceedings of the architectural psychology conference at Kingston Polytechnic 1970.* London: RIBA Publications.

Küller, R. (1972). *A semantic model for describing perceived environment* (Document No. 12). Stockholm: Swedish Council for Building Research.

Küller, R. (1973). Beyond semantic measurement. In R. Küller (Ed.), *Architectural Psychology. Proceedings of the Lund Conference* (pp. 181–197). Stroudsburg, Penn.: Dowden, Hutchinson & Ross.

Küller, R. (1975). *Semantisk miljöbeskrivning (SMB). (Semantic description of environments.)* Stockholm: Psykologiförlaget.

Küller, R. (1976). The use of space—some physiological and philosophical aspects. In P. Korosec-Serfaty (Ed.), *Appropriation of space. Proceedings of the Strasbourg Conference* (pp. 154–163). Louvain-la-Neuve: CIACO.

Küller, R. (1977). Psycho-physiological conditions in theatre construction. In J. F. Arnott, J. Chariau, H. Huesmann, T. Lawrensen, & R. Theobald (Eds.), *Theatre Space* (pp. 158–180). München: Prestel Verlag.

Küller, R. (1978). Den sociala närmiljön på Piazza Navona och i Kungsträdgården. (The social climate of Piazza Navona and Kungsträdgården.) In G. J. Sorte (Ed.), *Architecture and Environmental Psychology (part 6)*. Lund, Sweden: School of Architecture, Lund Institute of Technology.

Küller, R. (1979a). A semantic test for use in crosscultural studies. *Man-Environment Systems, 9,* 253–256.

Küller, R. (1979b). Social crowding and the complexity of the built environment: A theoretical and experimental framework. In M.R. Gürkaynak & W.A. LeCompte (Eds.), *Human Consequences of Crowding* (pp. 139–146). New York: Plenum.

Küller, R. (1980a). Architecture and emotions. In B. Mikellides (Ed.), *Architecture for people* (pp. 87–100). London: Studio Vista.

Küller, R. (1980b). Differing demands on interior space in naval environments. In J.G. Simon (Ed.), *Conflicting experiences of space. Proceedings of the 4th IAPS, July 1979* (Vol. 2, pp. 645–654). Louvain-la-Neuve, Belgium: Catholic University of Louvain.

Küller, R. (1986). Physiological and psychological effects of illumination and colour in the interior environment. *Journal of Lighting and Visual Environment, 10,* 33–37.

Küller, R. (1988a). Environmental activation of old persons suffering from senile dementia. In H. van Hoogdalem, N.L. Prak, T.J.M. van der Voordt, & H.B.R. van Wegen (Eds.), *Looking back to the future. Proceedings IAPS 10* (Vol. 2, pp. 133–139). Delft, Netherlands: Delft University Press.

Küller, R. (1988b). Housing for the elderly in Sweden. In D. Canter, M. Krampen, & D. Stea (Eds.), *Environmental policy, assessment and communication. Ethnoscapes* (Vol. 2, pp. 199–224). Aldershot, U.K.: Avebury.

Küller, R. (1988c). Upplevelse av torgrum. (The perception of public squares.) In K. Åström (Ed.), *Stadens rum. Torget—gestalt, upplevelse, användning.* (Report No. 59, Appendix 1.) Stockholm: Swedish Council for Building Research.

Küller, R., & Mattsson, R. (1986). The dining room at a geriatric hospital. In M. Krampen (Ed.), *Environment and human action. Proceedings IAPS 8* (pp. 137–141). Berlin: Hochschule der Kuenste.

Küller, R., & Steen, G. (1988). *Age retirement in women. Psychological and environmental aspects.* (Unpublished manuscript). Lund, Sweden: School of Architecture, Lund Institute of Technology.

Kwok, K. (1979). Semantic evaluation of perceived environment. A cross-cultural replication. *Man-Environment Systems, 9,* 243–249.

Lazarus, R.S. (1975). The self-regulation of emotion. In L. Levi (Ed.), *Emotions: Their parameters and measurement* (pp. 47–67). New York: Raven.

Lazarus, R.S., & Folkman, S. (1984). *Stress, appraisal and coping.* New York: Springer.

LeDoux, J.E. (1986). The neurobiology of emotion. In J.E. LeDoux & W. Hirst (Eds.), *Mind and brain. Dialogues in cognitive neuroscience* (pp. 301–354). Cambridge: Cambridge University Press.

Levi, L. (Ed.). (1971). *Society, stress and disease. Vol. 1. The psycho-social environment and psychosomatic diseases.* London: Oxford University Press.

Levi, L. (Ed.) (1972). Stress and distress in response to psychosocial stimuli. *Acta Medica Scandinavica, 191* (Suppl. 528).

Levi, L., Frankenhaeuser, M., & Gardell, B. (1981). Work stress related to social structures and processes. In G.R. Elliot & C. Eisdorfer (Eds.), *Research on stress and human health.* New York: Springer.

Lewin, K., 1951. *Field theory in social science. Selected theoretical papers.* New York: Harper.

Libby, W.L., Lacey, B.C., & Lacey, J.I. (1973). Pupillary and cardiac activity during visual attention. *Psychophysiology, 10*(3), 270–294.

Lindsley, D.B. (1951). Emotion. In S.S. Stevens (Ed.), *Handbook of experimental psychology* (pp. 473–516). New York: Wiley.

Little, B.R. (1987). Personality and the environment. In D. Stokols & I. Altman (Eds.), *Handbook of environmental psychology* (Vol. 1, pp. 205–244). New York: Wiley.

Luria, A.R. (1973). *The working brain.* Harmondsworth: Penguin.

Malmberg, T. (1980). *Human territoriality.* The Hague: Mouton.

Maslow, A.H., & Mintz, N.L. (1956). Effects of esthetic surroundings: I. Initial short-term effects of three esthetic conditions upon perceiving "energy" and "well-being" in faces. *Journal of Psychology, 41,* 247–254.

Mathews, K.E., & Canon, L.K. (1975). Environmental noise level as a determinant of helping behavior. *Journal of Personality and Social Psychology, 32,* 571–577.

Matthews, K.A., & Angulo, J. (1980). Measurement of the Type A behavior pattern in children: Assessment of children's competitiveness, impatience-anger, and aggression. *Child Development, 51,* 466–475.

McKechnie, G. (1977). The environmental response inventory in application. *Environment and Behavior, 9,* 255–276.

Mehrabian, A., & Russell, J.A. (1974). *An approach to environmental psychology.* Cambridge, Mass.: MIT Press.

Mikellides, B. (1989). *Emotional and behavioural reaction to colour in the built environment.* Ph.D. Thesis, Oxford: Oxford Polytechnic.

Miron, M.S., & Osgood, C.E. (1966). Language behavior. The multivariate structure of qualification. In R.B. Cattell (Ed.), *Handbook of multivariate experimental psychology* (pp. 790–819). Chicago: Rand McNally.

Moos, R.H. (1975). Assessment and impact of social climate. In P. McReynolds

(Ed.). *Advances in psychological assessment* (Vol. 3, pp. 8–41). San Francisco: Jossey-Bass.

Moruzzi, G., & Magoun, H.W. (1949). Brain stem reticular formation and activation of the EEG. *Electroencephalography and Clinical Neurophysiology, 1,* 455–473.

Newman, O. (1973). *Defensible space. Crime prevention through urban design.* New York: Macmillan.

Olds, J., & Milner, P. (1954). Positive reinforcement produced by electrical stimulation of septal area and other regions of rat brain. *Journal of Comparative Physiology, 47,* 419–427.

Olds, J., & Olds, M. (1965). Drives, rewards and the brain. *New directions in psychology II.* New York: Holt, Rinehart & Winston.

Olsson-Jonsson, A. (1988). *Förbättring av fönsters värmeisolering samt upplevelse av fönsterbyten. (Improvement of thermal insulation of windows and perception of window replacements.)* (Report No. 40). Stockholm: Swedish Council for Building Research.

Oostendorp, A., & Berlyne, D.E. (1978). Dimensions in the perception of architecture: I. Identification and interpretation of dimensions of similarity. *Scandinavian Journal of Psychology, 12,* 73–82.

Osgood, C.E., Suci, G.J., & Tannenbaum, P.H. (1957). *The measurement of meaning.* Urbana: University of Illinois Press.

Pablant, P., & Baxter, J.C. (1975). Environmental correlates of school vandalism. *Journal of the American Institute of Planners, 41,* 270–279.

Parke, R.D. (1978). Children's home environments: Social and cognitive effects. In I. Altman & J. F. Wohlwill (Eds.), *Human behavior and the environment* (pp. 33–81). New York: Plenum.

Pavlov, I.P. (1927). *Conditioned reflexes.* Humphrey Milford: Oxford University Press.

Pilleri, G. (1965). Hjärnstammens formatio reticularis: anatomi, fysiologi och patologi. (The reticular formation of the brain stem: anatomy, physiology, and pathology.) In W. Birkmayer & G. Pilleri (Eds.), *Hjärnstammens reticulära formation och dess betydelse för de vegetativa funktionerna och affektlivet* (pp. 9–80), Basel: F. Hoffman-La Roche & Co.

Plutchik, R. (1962). *The emotions: Facts, theories and a new model.* New York: Random House.

Posner, M.I. (1980). Orienting of attention. *Quarterly Journal of Experimental Psychology, 32,* 3–25.

Poulton, E.C. (1970). *Environment and human efficiency.* Springfield, Ill.: Thomas.

Poulton, E.C. (1980). *The environment at work.* Springfield, Ill.: Thomas.

Preiser, W.F.E., Rabinowitz, H.Z., & White, E.T. (1988). *Post-occupancy evaluation.* New York: Van Nostrand Reinhold.

Rapoport, A. (1975). Toward a redefinition of density. *Environment and Behavior, 7,* 133–158.

Rasmussen, J.E. (Ed.). (1973). *Man in isolation and confinement.* Chicago: Aldine.

Riege, W.H. (1971). Environmental influences on brain and behavior of year-old rats. *Developmental Psychobiology, 4,* 157–167.

Rissler, A., & Elgerot, A. (1980). *Omställning till arbete i kontorslandskap. (Ac-*

commodation to work in open space office.) (Rep. No. 33). Stockholm: Psykologiska Institutionen, Stockholms Universitet.

Robinson, D.L., & Petersen, S.E. (1986). The neurobiology of attention. In J.E. LeDoux & W. Hirst (Eds.). *Mind and brain. Dialogues in cognitive neuroscience* (pp. 142–171). Cambridge: Cambridge University Press.

Roland, P.E. (1982). Cortical regulation of selective attention in man. A regional cerebral blood flow study. *Journal of Neurophysiology, 48,* 1059–1078.

Rolls, E.T. (1976). The neurophysiological basis of brain-stimulation reward. In A. Wanguier & E.T. Rolls (Eds.). *Brain-stimulation reward* (pp. 250–290). Amsterdam: North Holland.

Schlosberg, H.S. (1954). Three dimensions of emotion. *Psychological Review, 61,* 81–88.

Schlosberg, H.S. (1955). Three dimensions of emotion. In H.A. Abramson (Ed.), *Problems of consciousness. Transactions Fifth Conference 1954* (pp. 26–32). New York: Josiah Macy, Jr., Foundation.

Schultz, D.P. (1965). *Sensory restriction. Effects on behavior.* New York: Academic Press.

Seligman, M.E.P. (1975). *Helplessness.* San Francisco: Freeman.

Selye, H. (1956). *The stress of life.* New York: McGraw-Hill.

Solomon, P., Kubzansky, P.E., Leiderman, P.H., Mendelson, J.H., Trumbull, R., & Wexler, D. (Eds.) (1961). *Sensory deprivation.* Cambridge, Mass.: Harvard University Press.

Sommer, R. (1969). *Personal space. The behavioral basis of design.* Englewood Cliffs, N.J.: Prentice-Hall.

Sorte, G.J. (1970). *Perception av landskap. Studie beträffande hur individen tror sig påverkas av olika miljöer (Landscape perception. A study of the experienced influence from different environments.)* (Work report No. 2). Lund, Sweden: Department of Theoretical and Applied Aesthetics, Lund Institute of Technology.

Sorte, G.J. (1982). *Visuellt urskiljbara egenskaper hos föremål i den byggda miljön. (Visual qualities of objects in the built environment.)* (Report No. 5). Stockholm: Swedish Council for Building Research.

Stenberg, G. (1990). *Brain and personality. Extraversion/introversion and associated traits in relation to EEG, evoked potentials and regional cerebral blood flow.* Doctoral dissertation. Lund, Sweden: University of Lund.

Stokols, D. (1972). A social-psychological model of human crowding phenomena. *Journal of the American Institute of Planners, 38,* 72–83.

Suedfeld, P. (Ed.) (1980). *Restricted environmental stimulation.* New York: Wiley.

Sundstrom, E. (1987). Work environments: Offices and factories. In D. Stokols & I. Altman (Eds.), *Handbook of environmental psychology* (Vol. 1, pp. 733–782). New York: Wiley.

Ursin, H. (1980). Personality, activation and somatic health. In S. Levine & H. Ursin (Eds.), *Coping and health* (pp. 259–279). New York: Plenum.

van Olst, E.H., & Orlebeke, J.F. (1967). An analysis of the concept of arousal. *Nederlands Tijdschrift voor de Psychologie, 22,* 583–603.

Wachs, T.D., & Gruen, G.E. (1982). *Early experience and human development.* New York: Plenum.

Ward, L.M., & Russell, J.A. (1981). The psychological representation of molar physical environments. *Journal of Experimental Psychology: General, 110,* 121–152.

Watzke, J.R. (1986). *The psychological assessment of Swedish retired persons coming from urban and non-urban environments* (Environmental Psychology Monographs No. 5). Lund, Sweden: School of Architecture, Lund Institute of Technology.

Watzke, J.R., & Küller, R. (1986). *The conflict situations technique: A projective method for elderly persons* (Environmental Psychology Monographs No. 4). Lund, Sweden: School of Architecture, Lund Institute of Technology.

Witkin, H.A., Lewis, H.B., Hertzman, M., Machover, K., Meissner, P.B., & Wapner, S. (1954). *Personality through perception.* New York: Harper.

Wohlwill, J.F. (1974). Human adaptation to levels of environmental stimulation. *Human Ecology, 2,* 127–147.

Wohlwill, J.F., & Heft, H. (1987). The physical environment and the development of the child. In D. Stokols & I. Altman (Eds.), *Handbook of environmental psychology* (Vol. 1, pp. 281–328). New York: Wiley.

Yerkes, R.M., & Dodson, J.D. (1908). The relation of strength of stimulus to rapidity of habit formation. *Journal of Comparative Neurology and Psychology, 18,* 459–482.

Zhao, X. (1987). *Attributions of architectural form.* (Unpublished Ph.D. thesis). Lund, Sweden: Lund Institute of Technology, Architecture II & Environmental Psychology Unit.

Zuckerman, M., Kolin, E.A., Price, L., & Zoob, I. (1964). Development of a sensation-seeking scale. *Journal of Consulting Psychology, 28,* 477–482.

8

Spatial Cognition as Events

ANDERS BÖÖK

This chapter deals with the question of how adults process information about large-scale physical features and their spatial relations during navigation between places. The presentation is based on the presumption that single acts of cognition are comparatively unimportant in real-life travel. Accordingly, sequential relations between acts are emphasized, which is the reason for the term event in the title. In general, ways of seeing how spatial cognition is organized in time and space should further the search for connections between the fields of spatial cognition, environmental assessment and action. However, the latter prospect is beyond the scope of this chapter. The aim—to make explicit the sequence aspect of cognitive acts in several problem areas of spatial cognition—is pursued in a spirit of inductive analysis in that a number of act sequences are discussed as examples of important spatial cognition events. The approach is first described in broad outline.

SPATIAL COGNITION AND THREE LEVELS OF MENTAL FUNCTIONING

Processing of large-scale spatial information may entail different theoretical perspectives on levels of mental functioning. Basic mechanisms and operations that underlie the occurrence of cognitive acts represent one level, being the main focus of contemporary theory construction and model building. Further, cognitive acts are reflected in conscious activity and self-consciousness, which represent a second level. Finally, a third level emerges to the extent that cognitive acts are reliably ordered continuously in time and space.

Common categories of acts in large-scale spatial cognition are perceptual identification, encoding, recognition, and recall of environmental information, judgments of topological, projective, and metric spatial relations, spatial inference, visual–spatial imagery, and spatial choice. Detailed processing underlying these cognitive acts is progressively unraveled by means of refined task paradigms, deductive reasoning, mathematics, and procedures for controlling subjects' behavioral and mental activities. This kind of knowledge is sparse in the field of large-scale spatial cognition (Pick, 1985). Independent variables in experiments have been related as often to issues of development, the structure of location information in cognitive maps, methodology, or application as to the nature of processing per se (cf. Evans, 1980). In the long run, theory about underlying processing is indispensible for any of these concerns, including the event approach to be presented here.

Limited processing mechanisms underlie the performance properties of cognitive acts that determine the basic achievements of large-scale spatial cognition. These achievements are maintenance of spatial orientation, effortless route following, flexible wayfinding, rapid route learning, and economical representation of metric spatial knowledge. Increasing facts, conceptual distinctions, and models in basic cognition research should be applied in a productive way to further understanding of large-scale spatial cognition. However, how to achieve this may be difficult because of the possible unique nature of large-scale spatial cognition. To understand the underpinnings of the basic achievements may require that analyses are directed toward hypothetical properties of conscious activities rather than mechanisms closely related to a neurophysiological level. This means that the functional roles of cognitive acts in their sequential organization should be highlighted. Explanatory value is implied as far as avoidance, occurrence, and resolution of travel difficulties depend immediately on factors at this level of mental functioning.

The Sequential Level of Mental Functioning

To say that the unfolding of interrelated cognitive acts is analogous, or even equivalent, to processing of information may sound counterintuitive. However, there is a vertical as well as a horizontal perspective on processing (cf. James, 1890). This has been illustrated in Figure 8.1. In the vertical perspective, processing at specific points in time and space is traced along the path connected by a specific input, a specific cognitive act, and a specific system of inferred mechanisms and operations. In comparison, the horizontal perspective entails an extensive but limited space–time section of goal-related mental functioning (cf. Neisser, 1976). The enormous complexity of the resulting total processing is reducible to manageable analyses if questions are focused on what the hypothetical composition and interrelations of cognitive acts are likely to be, given our present knowledge and intuitions about spatial cognition. Further, specifications of subsets of cognitive acts, their complete or partial orders, and a minimum of performance characteristics should be tantamount to the description of and reference to kind of information processing. Finally, in this processing, cognitive and behavioral acts, such as body displacements, turns, and looking around, are conceivable as sequence constituents on a par with each other. Production of external and internal information change, which is advantageous to travel performance, is a consequence of each type of act. Similarly, each type is a means to eliminate or reduce the occurrence of information change which is disadvantageous.

Events of Spatial Cognition

In the following, the construct of an event of spatial cognition is envisaged. It is intended to differ from complex cognitive units, such as plans, scripts, procedures, and routines. These units are assumed to be stored permanently. As a kind of complex units, events of spatial cognition are assumed to be emergent phenomena lacking direct correspondence to stored action or processing units. Events emerge due to a

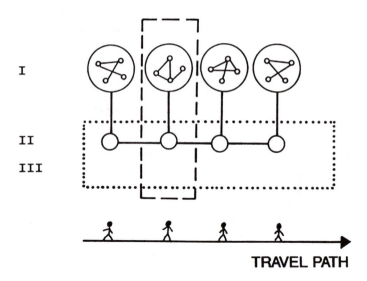

TRAVEL PATH

I Basic mental level: Systems of operations and mechanisms

II Conscious level: Unfolding sequence of interrelated cognitive acts

III Environment: Large-scale spatial information

Figure 8.1. Illustration of the vertical (dashed rectangle) and the horizontal (dotted rectangle) perspectives on processing of spatial information.

number of constraints that jointly shape the short-term course of spatial cognition in problematic travel situations. Some basic constraints are recurrent types of physical–spatial structures (e.g., building forms, street intersections), a limited set of cognitive acts as a basis for controlled processing (Allen, 1985), and knowledge in cognitive maps, variable in accuracy, and amenable to distortions. For these reasons, spatial cognition events are hypothetical phenomena in a theory of large-scale spatial cognition. The event examples to be proposed are previewed in Table 8.1.

The events will also be illustrated by means of figures. All events are assumed to originate in problematic travel situations due to incomplete learning of the environment. Acts of remembering environmental information are basic in the first three events, whereas direction judgments are central in the three last examples. Event examples 3 and 4 emphasize the large-scale nature of spatial information, which is also a starting point for the event example 5. Event examples 5 and 6 represent act sequences that have the consequence of improving the accuracy of an initial judgment. Several examples are possible to describe as containing transitions between subevents. Thus event example 1 implies two alternative recognition preconditions that lead to different continuations of the sequence. Event example 4 contains a transition between two sequences of judgments related to different cognitive goals.

Table 8.1   A Set of Spatial Cognition Events, Summarized as Partial or Complete Orders of Constituent Cognitive and Behavioral Acts

---

Example 1. Recall of environmental information > distance judgment > perception of travel distance > distance comparison > recognition or omitted recognition of initially recalled information > adequate judgment or inadequate perceptual search

Example 2. Recall > distance judgment > perceptual search > encoding of features conditional on recall failure

Example 3. Recognition acts *i,j,k* . . .

Example 4. Direction judgments *i,j,k* . . . > size and form apprehension of a large-scale pattern of small targets > updating judgments *i,j,k* . . . of the large-scale unit

Example 5. Inaccurate direction judgment of target *i* > accurate direction judgment of tarjet *j* > imagery acts > improved judgment of target *i*

Example 6. Decision to change stationpoint due to poor visual access > anticipation of new stationpoint > recognition contingent on increased access > direction judgment

---

Finally, events may occur as subevents in other events. For instance, event example 3 may occur as part of event example 6.

EXAMPLE 1. RECOGNITION IN A CONTEXT OF DISTANCE MONITORING

In the first example, illustrated in Figure 8.2, an event consisting of the sequence recall, distance judgment, recognition, and two different consequential continuations is proposed. It begins with a traveler's recall of previously encoded information about, for instance, a building or a street intersection. The recalled environmental unit is

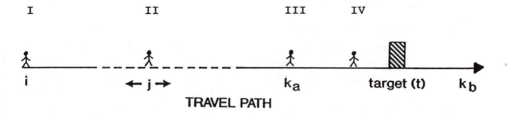

I   Recall of target, distance judgment d_{ik}, and expectation to view target

II   Perception of travel distance d_{ij} and comparison $d_{ik}-d_{ij}$

III No recognition of target, mismatch $d_{ik}-d_{jk}=0$

IV   Recognition of target, mismatch $d_{ik}-d_{jk}>0$

Figure 8.2.   Recognition in a context of distance monitoring (example 1).

expected to be encountered later after a certain distance of travel ahead. This distance is explicitly judged in connection with the recall act. The recall and judgment acts should create a readiness to perceive and recognize information about the unit. This readiness is assumed to consist of distance monitoring, specifically comparisons between the continuously perceived travel distance, increasing from the point of recall, and the distance judged at that point. According to one alternative course of the event, the recognition of the recalled and judged unit is associated with feelings of surprise. The reason is that, at this point, the perceived travel distance is experienced as shorter than the distance judged. Thus recognition occurred too early relative to expectation. Another type of distance mismatch is also possible. The decreasing distance difference may be canceled at a point during travel before the point where the environmental unit is possible to perceive and recognize. Thus the unit does not appear in view when expected to appear.

The two types of mismatches are likely to be associated with different continuations of the event. Too early recognition relative to distance monitoring may evoke a series of corrective judgments that should restore the sense of spatial orientation. Recognition that is omitted but expected may evoke decisions to search for missed information in the wrong route direction. Thus, depending on performance aspects of acts in the event, environmental learning is furthered or travel difficulties are increased.

In sum, the event entails continuity between acts of recall and recognition due to an environmental unit in common to the two acts. Further, continuity is sustained by interrelated acts of distance cognition about a common physical distance. It should be possible to investigate memorized distance and distance perceived during actual locomotion in conditions in which the former can influence the latter. A further research problem is to measure where recognition and recall occur relative to object positions, in conditions of self-selected or prescribed objects.

EXAMPLE 2. AN ACQUISITION EVENT AND VIEW–ACTION–VIEW STRUCTURE

The event construct presupposes short-term persistence of activated representations of external units subsequent to the occurrence of cognitive acts. Persistence accounts for processing continuity and grouping of acts into meaningful partial or complete act orders. Persistence is limited (Thomson, 1983). In general, the lower persistence capacity, the less space–time extension, and the less probable occurrences of transitions between subevents. On the other hand, limited short-term persistence and, further, long-term memory forgetting may create events with implications for questions about acquisition, as follows.

Common Notions about Environmental Encoding

Route knowledge reflects a linear-order type of procedural representation (cf. Anderson, 1985) that may be based on view–action–view units (Allen, 1987; Kuipers, 1983; Smyth, Morris, Levy, & Ellis, 1986). The view element represents organized bundles of environmental features that give a distinct appearance to specific objects and sometimes ground structure. The action element represents instructions to continue travel according to specified distances and turns. The selection and identification of view elements, and the consequent order and distances between them have been assumed to be perceptually, conceptually, or inferentially based (Allen, 1985, 1987; Allen, Siegel, & Rosinski, 1978; Heft, 1983; Kaplan, 1976). For example, encoding may be due to selective perception of salient objects appearing suddenly at occluding edges; specific buildings and places may be directly interpreted to be useful landmarks or units with unusual or significant meaning; remembered information located in adjacent, not visible regions (Kaplan, 1976) may be used as contrasting information for encoding purposes. Common to these notions is the assumption that acts of encoding are associated with distinctive aspects of information. Although this seems reasonable, limited short-term persistence and long-term memory forgetting may create acquisition events that offset distinctiveness as a dominant principle in acquisition of view elements. The following event is consistent with this possibility.

Self-Regulated Remembering Events

Before routes are followed routinely, travelers use acts of recall and distance judgment frequently as a means to maintain spatial orientation. The use of these acts is likely to be structured as events, for example, as illustrated in Figure 8.3. The acts of recall are assumed to include information about recently passed and encoded environmental units as well as information about units located further ahead on the route. Pairs of acts of recall and distance judgment are likely to occur at distinct points in time, but acts for units passed and units located ahead may occur simultaneously. In this event recall may fail frequently, meaning that recurrent questions about what was recently seen and what will be seen soon cannot be answered clearly. When recall fails, travelers are apt to search immediately for substitute information to compensate for forgotten information. Thus encoding acts should increase temporarily. Conversely, when remembering succeeds, encoding acts decrease and remain low for some time. Given that self-produced recall prompts and thus consequent

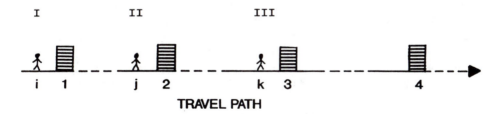

I   Encoding of target 1

II   Recall of target 1, judgment of distance d_{j1}, and
     encoding of target 2 iff recall fails

III Recall of target 4, judgment of distance d_{k4}, and
     encoding of target 3 iff recall fails

Figure 8.3. A self-regulated remembering event (example 2).

encoding acts occur independently of the distinctiveness of surrounding information, the following implication for knowledge acquisition appears reasonable. Encoding of nondistinctive information should occur in proportion to recall failures, whereas opportunities to encode distinctive information should be missed in proportion to recall successes. Thus the performance dynamics of the event should affect the information content of accumulating route knowledge. In particular, the extent to which distinctiveness is a property of acquired view elements may depend on self-regulated remembering in addition to objective factors in the surrounding. Admittedly, perception and encoding of distinctive information may occur independently of an event context.

It may be objected that a high rate of forgetting can be counteracted by an increase of the recall acts, which, if extreme, may change the event to a rehearsal process. However, it seems likely that competition for resources with unrelated but important ongoing mental activities should limit this possibility in practice (Kuipers, 1983; Norman & Bobrow, 1975). A further objection might be that route knowledge in early learning is structured differently compared to asymptotic learning. However, this may only imply that acquired information is reorganized at some stage in learning (Evans, Marrero, & Butler, 1981; Rumelhart & Norman, 1975). The economy in the knowledge system, commonly assumed, may be related to gradual learning to perceive surroundings as nonarbitrary layouts (Gibson, 1979).

EXAMPLE 3: RECOGNITION AND MATCHING OVER TIME

Recognition during Flexible Route Following

Recognition memory tasks are frequently used in environmental cognition research. The methods used have mainly been picture walks and edited films of walks (Allen et al., 1978; Evans, Skorpanich, Gärling, Bryant, & Bresolin, 1984; Heft, 1983). Important questions have concerned which features of surroundings determine selection and encoding of landmarks, relationships between landmark potential and judgments of route distances, and effects of visual transition information at travel turns.

In a recognition perspective, route following is mainly a process of matching acquired view elements against perceptual information. As has been suggested, the process may reflect a two-level hierarchy of procedural knowledge including view–action–view units and a basic level of sensorimotor associations. However, some intermediate level may be needed to account for dynamic factors, contextual factors, and factors of function and consequence, which were strongly emphasized by Siegel and White (1975) and Kaplan (1976). The route follower is hardly a kind of human robot who mechanically uses view–action–view orders invariantly whenever the same route is followed. This would underestimate the facts of flexibility and variability that are not necessarily inconsistent with automatized behavior and information use. The meaning of habitual behavior is not primarily repeated but adaptive behavior, which implies functional equivalence and substitution in behavior and information use. For example, feature information used in different instances of the same route following may only overlap, and use of features may occur at quite distinct path locations. In addition, flexible route following may be created due to experience of varying object distances, object orientations, occlusion patterns, and so on. Finally, variable conditions due to unreliable organismic factors need not increase encoding and recognition difficulties. For example, information that depends on viewpoint is orientation specific, which should be useful to perceptual search for specific object locations and computation of directions (cf. Böök, 1988). Evidence suggests that viewer-centered information may be directly stored in long-term memory (Biederman, 1987; Jolicoeur & Kosslyn, 1983; Pinker, 1984). However, relevant research on route following and wayfinding conditions is lacking (cf. Gopal, 1988).

It may be objected that travelers are busy thinking about things that are more important to them than the travel task (Kuipers, 1983), and that mental resource limitation is consistent with an extremely standardized utilization of route knowledge. However, it seems equally possible that the architecture of the representational system is fitted to varied external conditions in a way that allows for flexible route following. This should require a less rigid structure than a two-level hierarchy of view–action–view units and basic sensorimotor associations. This notion is elaborated in the following.

Recognition-over-Time Events

In the event perspective, recognition and route-following flexibility are taken into account because an organizing role for recognition experience is ascribed to the temporal dimension of travel. A single act of recognition of a single unit (e.g., a building, an intersection) may often have only marginal consequences except for units being part of goal places. The practical value of recognition may theoretically correspond to familiarity integration across several such elementary acts occurring in sequence over limited but extended time. Due to the required continuity aspect implied, a representational system rich in coded units and features must be assumed (cf. Tversky, 1981). This richness is increased if features such as size and color contrasts, figure-ground saliency, and meaning attributes are quantitative input variables, the simultaneous presence of which might converge on a common storage dimension of information strength. Further, if the variables are only moderately intercorrelated, the representational system should be consistent with a wide range of information strength, and, consequently, probabilities of search, attention, encoding, and recognition. On this account, two local environments may differ from each other, even if both are categorizable as familiar.

Richness and variability make possible grouping into distinct subsets of recognized elements defined at the level of objects. It will be argued that such subsets as sequenced correspond to a kind of recognition-over-time events. Two conclusive points will first be mentioned. First, the subset-and-sequence notion implies varying levels of distinctiveness. Second, the extended event character of recognition does not correspond to procedural units coded in permanent storage. What is relatively fixed in storage may only be a hierarchy of information units, from which a subset of units is actualized probabilistically in sequence within time limits suitable for familiarity integration. These two points are consistent with flexible route following, to some extent in opposition to a view–action–view conceptualization. In the following, the appropriateness of the construct of an event will be elucidated.

In a sequence of recognition acts, already matched information elements should loose their impact on the feeling of familiarity in proportion to the limited capacity for persistence of activated representations. A firm feeling of familiarity requires that such losses are compensated for by additional matches as travel proceeds. However, during many intervals of travel the number of matched units in a persistingly active state of representation may be quite low. For example, scarcity may be determined by poor visibility in the immediate environment. Further, periods of high attentiveness to acquired feature structures may interchange with periods of low attentiveness (cf. Wagner, Baird, & Barbaresi, 1981). This cyclic process may be coordinated with the current rate of change of the number of representations persisting in an active state. In addition, new series of matches after periods of low attentiveness may overcompensate for loss of persistence. The periodic nature of the entire process should thus be articulated. Finally, variation in organismic stress (Evans et al., 1984) may further contribute to the periodic nature. According to this account, a recognition-over-time event begins at the turning point in the cyclic process where the number of matches starts to increase. It ends where successive matches exceed some limit of time delay, above which successive recognition acts are truly independent acts.

The recognition-over-time event may be compared to the self-regulated remembering event in example 2. In the former event, the traveler has some degree of control over matching rates, in the latter event over encoding rates, in both cases due to forgetting and associated increase of attention and search. Further, richness of information in the representational system is a prerequisite for the former event but may be furthered by the latter event. Finally, both events imply flexible rather than stereotyped route following processes.

EXAMPLE 4. FORMATION OF LARGE-SCALE UNITS AND UPDATING

Large-Scale Factors

The distinction between small-scale and large-scale spaces (Acredolo, 1981; Evans, 1980) refers to single versus multiple views, top-down versus horizontal perspectives, and the necessity to move or not. These basic factors imply extensive object information at great distance. This suggests that the distinction may be important also for understanding the target construct, viewed as a theoretical construct. This point is developed in the following passages and further analyzed in connection with event example 5.

The notion of large-scale units in spatial representation systems is important in theoretical and empirical analyses. For example, in Kuipers' (1978) simulation model, targets, such as, for instance, street intersections, may be located by means of a topological reasoning process, through which regions bounded by street segments are successively eliminated until a small target area remains. Kaplan (1976) assumed that travelers use knowledge about adjacent, not visible regions to infer the relative distinctiveness of currently perceived information. Further, Allen (1985) has presented evidence for a process of cognitive segmentation of routes that was shown to facilitate judgments of proximity relations. Large-scale units are also central to the construct of the cognitive map. A central notion is that cognitive maps are regionalized according to a hierarchical organization of abstracted large-scale units (Couclelis, Golledge, Gale, & Tobler, 1987). Closely related is the finding that errors of judgments tend to be distorted in a direction consistent with relations between superordinate regions (Stevens & Coupe, 1978).

In some contrast to these notions, target locations used in experiments are often extremely small scale. This is true whether physical size or subtended angle at the vantage point is measured. In brief, targets have corresponded to approximate points. A reasonable criterion for a point type of target may be an angle size smaller than about 5° or 6°. A target measuring 10 horizontally and located 100 m away fulfills this criterion. It is probably very difficult to perform pointings that hit targets at this level of size because the latter corresponds to no more than about 6 or 7 cm movement of the stretched out arm. The levels of required precision in real-world conditions may frequently be less severe. In particular, this may follow if targets are cognitively constructed and not only selected. Further, target construction may entail implicit consideration of appropriate size for achievement of accurate judgments. These suggestions are explicit in the following large-scale formation and updating subevents.

An Economic Updating Subevent

Maintenance of spatial orientation in not yet familiar environments may require that several targets are judged in succession. The spatiotemporal properties of such sequences may sometimes conform to events for formation of large-scale units and subsequent updating of directions. These subevents are illustrated in Figure 8.4. Thus the first part of the hypothesized event consists of a sequence of judgments of different point types of targets during a period of short travel displacement. The judged locations are likely to be spatially separated, because moderate separation is more informative than spatial concentration. The pattern of locations should therefore subtend an angle at the vantage point substantially larger than the previously suggested level for the point type of target. Due to persisting activity in the representational system, the traveler may immediately apprehend the pattern as a large-scale unit. It has properties of location, size, and form. The size of the unit should depend mainly on the number of points in the sequence. However, the rate of judgments is important because it determines the extent of displacement. Therefore, slow rates may lead to patterns with too large spatial separation among points for apprehension of unity to occur. Although less probable, too rapid rates, combined with few judgments, may lead to patterns that remain similar to a point type of target.

Although construction of target units may occur as independent acquisition events, a likely continuation is a series of updating acts. The following statements are not intended to mean that travelers never update directions to single point type of targets, as has usually been the requirement in experimental tasks (Böök & Gärling, 1981; Rieser, 1983). However, updating of constructed large-scale units should be more advantageous because comparatively extended displacement may occur without subjective experience of great change of direction to the large-scale unit. Formally, this requires the assumption that a large-scale unit represents an infinite number of implicit points, which are used interchangeably during updating. Consequently, each position along the displacement path is associated with a continuum of spatial vec-

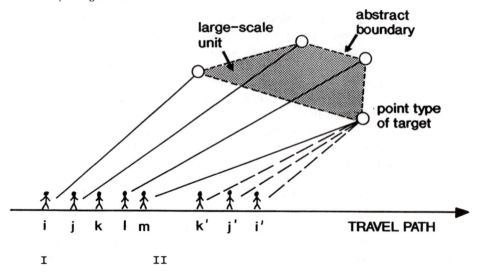

Figure 8.4. Large-scale formation and updating subevents (example 4). (Note: *i'*, *j'*, etc. denote points of maximum displacement, at which directions equal to those at points *i*, *j*, etc. are obtainable.)

tors, the point set of which coincides with the abstract boundaries or the internal area of the unit. Therefore, even continua associated with quite separate traveler positions may share specific distance and direction values. Thus, constancy or reduced change of direction is mentally imposed on the structure of objectively changing relations for specific points. The event should make possible economic updating computations, although the gains compared to single point targets are a function of several factors. In particular, the size of large-scale units, the general distance to them, and the displacement distance should limit possible gains. For example, when distance increases, preservation of the large-scale nature of the updated unit presupposes that points are sampled in a larger region of space, in compensation for decreased angle at the vantage point. Finally, the general form and orientation of the constructed unit should be important. If points are selected closer to the direction of the displacement path than the perpendicular to the path, the resulting large-scale form is elongated. Assuming that similar distances to selected points represent the prototypical case, the main axis of the unit is oriented to the advantage of the economic updating possibility.

The central feature of this event, achievement of relative direction constancy, is a principle that may have a wider context of application, for example, as part of perception of travel distance (Sadalla & Magel, 1980; Sadalla & Staplin, 1980; Sadalla, Staplin, & Burroughs, 1979). An important dimension of reference systems, such as buildings, is their horizontal extent (cf. Evans & Pezdek, 1980). Sensitivity to displacement change may in general decrease during passing because similar relative direction constancy as in the proposed event seems possible. This leads to the hypothesis that perceived travel distance is a negative function of the size of nearby buildings in sequence. The number of important things, such as intersections along routes (Sadalla & Staplin, 1980), has been shown to affect perceived travel distance. A number of large objects in combination with their size pattern is a further basis for identification of variables.

EXAMPLE 5. THE TARGET CONSTRUCT AND EVENTS FOR ERROR CORRECTION

An important question of generalization is whether accuracy of direction judgments, obtained in experiments, is compatible with accuracy required in real-world wayfinding situations. Experimental and real-word situations have often been similar. Incompatibility therefore seems unlikely from the outset. However, experimental situations have not been modeled on the basis of act sequences. Similar situations are therefore an insufficient basis for generalization to settings in which path choices are a natural component besides judgments. The generalization problem is discussed first in two subsections, the second of which refers once more to the possible importance of large-scale targets. By way of conclusion, the criticism is reconsidered in the light of a possible event for self-correction of judgment errors.

How Useful Are Direction Judgments?

Unsigned direction errors have varied between 20° and 30° under a wide range of experimental conditions and settings: large rooms (Böök & Gärling, 1981; Rieser, 1983), buildings or campus areas with target distances from about 30 to 200 m (Cousins, Siegel, & Maxwell, 1983; Kozlowski & Bryant, 1977; Thorndyke & Hayes-Roth, 1982), and exterior spaces extending several hundred meters from the subject (Gärling, Lindberg, Carreiras, & Böök, 1986; Moar & Carleton, 1982; Sholl, 1987). Effects of familiarity have generally been reliable but too small to be important for questions about usefulness. Perhaps, methods must be changed before truly substantial effects can be revealed. Furthermore, different targets often result in a wide range of accuracy. For example, Kirasic, Allen, and Siegel (1984) found a range of approximately 10°. In addition, individual differences might be large. However, dispersion measures are rarely reported. Finally, specific judgments are associated with degrees of experienced uncertainty. For example, means for 90% angular confidence intervals, have varied from about 20° to 30° (Gärling, Böök, Lindberg, & Nilsson, 1981; Gärling et al., 1986; Lindberg & Gärling, 1982). In sum, a considerable proportion of direction judgments appears to be of small practical value, given no further contextual specifications. However, the issue of usefulness can not be answered safely unless consequences for path choices are identified.

A preliminary analysis has been illustrated in Figure 8.5. The distance limit of the useful perceptual field is represented by arcs of circles with radii of 50 or 100 m from the stationpoints. Accuracy and spatial confidence intervals of 20° or 30° delimit arcs with specific lengths. For 20° and 50 m the computed arc length is about 35 m. It increases to about 105 m for 30° and 100 m. The expected number of perceivable

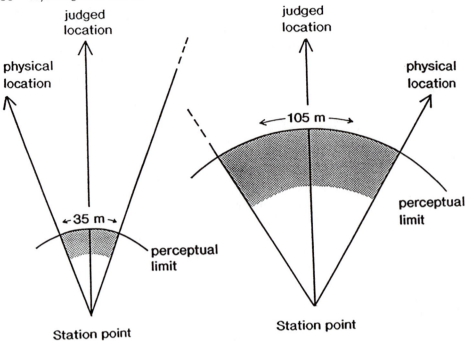

Figure 8.5. Conditions for path selection based on 20° (left) and 30° (right) judgment errors and associated confidence, for sight distances assumed to be 50 m (left) or 100 m (right). (Note: The dark areas denote areas for search of path information.)

paths in a representative sample of decision situations in urban environments might increase substantially in the domain of 35 to 105 m. Thus, if the choice of a path alternative within a wide angle sector is not better than a guess, severe consequences should occur. A traveler may believe that a target is approached but may soon find that a state of disorientation more serious than before the decision point has occurred. A possible fault with the preceding reasoning may be that the real nature of utilized targets has been misconceived. This possibility is discussed next.

What Is a Target?

What do travelers in the environment really judge? A point type of location, or a large-scale type of location? For example, does the location of the parking place correspond to the target or does the particular car correspond to it? Does it correspond to the location of a department in a building or the department entrance? Or should the basic question be formulated: When during travel is one or the other type of target primary? A possible resolution of these questions may have to do with the target selection process. The argument in the following is that target selection entails consideration of size in ways that increase usefulness.

The advantage of using the point type of target for measurement purposes is clear. However, acknowledging target selection as an important process, targets ought to be conceived as theoretical constructs, the spatial properties of which have to be discovered. For example, a possible assumption is that travelers do not ordinarily judge the point type of targets simply because they are too small and thus difficult to judge. The location of a parking place may be judged first and the location of a specific car later on when the traveler is closer. At that point in time, the distance to the car target may be so short that the subtended angle conforms to the previously suggested criterion for a large-scale target.

As discussed in event example 4, travelers are likely to impose spatial organization and economy through constructions of large-scale locational units. The advantage for updating has already been mentioned. Another specific reason is perceptual fuzziness or absence of physically salient boundaries (Allen, 1987). Finally, individuals may be more or less continuously aware of their positions in a system of nested large-scale locations, places, and more extended regions (cf. Neisser, 1976). For a consistent spatial cognition system, selection of large-scale targets ought to be primary. Therefore, the latter should be studied in research.

Even when a point type of location is recalled occasionally, this does not necessarily reflect a selection preference for this type of target. An alternative interpretation is that size of selected physical targets does not increase enough with increased distance so that the decrease of subtended angle is compensated for. However, within a critical distance range, for instance up to 500 m, target information may be selectively recalled so that large-scale targets are obtained frequently. That is, recall strategies may be rule based: Physical size of targets may increase with increased target distance. A simple hypothesis is that selected physical size is confined to a quite limited range of subtended angles, all consistent with large-scale targets. An important implication should be that knowledge about the physical size of object structures and places is acquired from travel experience to play a causal role in later selection and judgment processes.

A common experimental procedure is to guide subjects in large buildings to different rooms and to point out tiny objects for use as targets in later test conditions. At station points, the subtended angles of the surrounding rooms, corridors, entrances, and so on have been comparatively large for many combinations of targets and station points (Evans, Fellows, Zorn, & Doty, 1980; Thorndyke & Hayes-Roth, 1982). In agreement with the previous reasoning, it is possible that subjects have a good knowledge of the locations of these superordinate units. Further, and consistent with the notion of a hierarchical cognitive map, subjects may also know the locations of point targets but only in relation to superordinate units. In this account, the reason for large errors of point judgments may be due to a rotation factor. That is, the superordinate unit as a whole has a specific orientation relative to the visual surrounding of the stationpoint. Only one relevant study on this type of rotation knowledge appears to exist in the literature (Gärling et al., 1986). The results suggested that knowledge about how two places are permanently rotated relative to each other was poor, although two pictures of the places were presented in immediate succession.

In sum, the experimental observation of large errors is difficult to reconcile with the reasonable belief that judgments are quite useful in real-world conditions. This difficulty may be apparent only because we lack knowledge about target selection processes, thus what the real definition of targets is.

In the following, an alternative approach to usefulness is presented. Single judgments of the point type of target are assumed to be accompanied by further cognitive acts, the goal of which is to correct inaccuracy. An event is first described for conditions of stationary individuals, then a similar event including displacement as a complicating factor.

An Event for Error Correction

Assume that a traveler a moment ago has judged the location of a point type of target. The traveler cannot possibly immediately know how accurate the judgment is. Some feedback is needed. Subjective experience of confidence may play the role of feedback. Further, the latter may be an attribute of stored knowledge and correlated with accuracy. Given this, an inferential basis for the likely levels of errors should exist. Direct empirical evidence about the required correlation is lacking, but Gärling et al. (1981) found a fairly close correspondence between angular confidence intervals and accuracy across a set of different experimental conditions. A further assumption is that selected targets are frequently not substitutable. However, the initial judgment might be possible to correct. A sequence of acts capable of producing correction is illustrated in Figure 8.6.

First, the traveler recalls auxiliary information (T_a) that he or she is able to judge with high confidence. At this point, he or she is assumed to utilize knowledge in two different cognitive map frames of reference: either information in a viewer-centered frame, which is preliminary in the event (cf. Neisser, 1976), or an objective environmental frame, which is appropriate primarily for reasoning and communication purposes. The immediate goal of the traveler is to retrieve auxiliary knowledge in the latter frame. According to the following correction phase, the distance between the important and the auxiliary target locations (d_{ia}) is such knowledge.

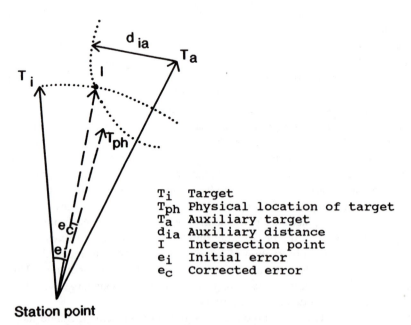

Station point

Figure 8.6.   An event for error correction based on vector rotation (example 5).

The correction phase begins with an operation for transposing the retrieved distance (d_{ia}) into the viewer-centered map frame and anchoring it at the judged location of the auxiliary target (T_a). The subsequent spatial-imagery act consists of simultaneous rotation of two vectors. One vector corresponds to the anchored auxiliary distance (d_{ia}) and the other to the direction and distance to the initially judged target. The two vectors are rotated in opposite directions until an intersection point *(I)* is obtained. This point implies a correction of the initially judged location, to a degree that depends on the accuracy of the auxiliary pieces of knowledge relative to the initial error. If, in addition, the distance component of the latter should be quite large, an intersection point will be lacking. However, the area where the two rotation paths are closest to each other should be small and thus be a good substitute.

A similar process of convergence through vector rotation may be part of related events in which displacement is a complicating factor. For example, a target vector may be anchored perceptually at a distinct reference object in the perceptual field. This vector may be experienced as unreliable. After a short displacement another reference object may be attended to but the target vector anchored in that object may also be experienced as unreliable. Therefore, both vectors to the same target may be used in combination to increase accuracy. That is, the two vectors anchored in their respective perceptual objects might be rotated as in the previous event. However, this imagery act may be difficult in a dynamic context of movement. An auxiliary imagery act may be needed before rotation can start. It should be similar to the task of pointing to targets from only imagined stationpoints, which is a quite difficult task (Rieser, 1983; Rieser, Guth, & Hill, 1982; Thorndyke & Hayes-Roth, 1982). However, this difficulty may be less in an event situation due to a comparatively short displacement between the two points on the path where the two vectors are actualized, and, further, due to the possibility to perceive the first point including the reference object from the second point. Finally, an additional connection to experimental work should be the triangulation technique for collecting and analyzing data (Cousins et al., 1983; Evans et al., 1980; Hardwick, McIntyre, & Pick, 1976; Kirasic et al., 1984). This technique might be modified for the purpose of empirical simulation of correction events.

In sum, single direction judgments of the point type of target may not play a dominant role in early learning because they are too inaccurate. On the other hand, self-imposed error correction may be possible because a few judgments may be feasible to combine in accordance with differences in knowledge of targets. In contrast to other events (examples 4 and 6), displacement is a complicating factor.

EXAMPLE 6. SPATIAL RETRIEVAL AS PART OF EXPLORATIVE EVENTS

Retrieval processes in connection with direction judgments comprise more than activation of knowledge elements in cognitive maps. The perceptual field is possibly a source of potential retrieval cues. Perceptual fields change with acts of looking around, turns, and displacements. In not yet familiar surroundings, these dynamic factors are part of the complete retrieval process. It begins and ends with specific but complex perceptual inputs, which directs and is directed by internal activation, respectively.

This process is articulated in explorative events. Before an explore-and-judge event is discussed, relevant research about visual factors is reviewed in a selective way.

Visual Factors and Judgments

An important variable, especially in an applied perspective, has been access to the visual surrounding (Lindberg & Gärling, 1981; Rieser et al., 1982; Rieser, Lockman, & Pick, 1980). A problem with this variable is that retrieval and acquisition is difficult to disentangle as interpretation alternatives. This would require more refined definitions of quantitative and qualitative access variables by means of visual-access reduction techniques. A step in that direction was taken by Gärling and colleagues (Gärling et al., 1986; Gärling, Lindberg, & Mäntylä, 1983). In a first study Gärling et al (1983) utilized a goggle technique that reduced visual access during walks in an unfamiliar building to a sector of about 30° and 10 m ahead. Compared to full vision, this condition decreased accuracy for different targets, all judged from a common stationpoint at the building entrance. The access-reduction technique ought to be used more extensively because spatial retrieval could be directly studied as a process of interaction between visual perception as a dynamic system and storage. For example, sighting tubes can be constructed for manipulation or measurement of available momentary spatial extent, direction of looking, and exposure times. Further, the retrieval versus acquisition problem might be approached by independent manipulation of access during walks and at station points.

In a further study Gärling et al. (1986) investigated direction judgments of preexperimentally familiar targets. Three conditions were compared: presentation of verbal labels of targets and station points, presentation of pictures of the same places, and visits to the real-world places and judgments at the camera positions. The two visual conditions were superior to the verbal condition, in particular the field condition. The results suggest that visual cueing increases retrieval efficiency, and, possibly, that amount of visual access is important.

These results are in accordance with the conception that spatial retrieval extends from identification of cueing information to response conversion including selective looking and associated perceptual input. Furthermore, this suggests that the selection of station points is crucial in experimental procedures. Usually, carefully standardized conditions are utilized. However, important information about how much and what information is accessible, how far away clear vision is possible, is often lacking in method sections of reported research. The relationship between station points and these lacking aspects is essential to the following types of explorative events.

Explore-and-Judge Events

Visual surroundings are clear or cluttered to various degrees. Clarity and easy layout perception may be required for rapid and accurate direction judgments. This means that visual retrieval cues should frequently be inadequate at the moments when judgments are needed. Furthermore, inadequate cues may tend to evoke these needs because a continuous kind of automatic spatial coordination may be weakened. Acts of looking around, turns, and displacements must therefore be used systematically to optimize visual access to useful information. This is assumed to occur in the explore-and-judge event, illustrated in Figure 8.7.

A particularly important condition for reliable occurrence of the event is movement into a bounded place (Acredolo, 1981), which limits vision substantially in all directions. The resulting discontinuity in layout perception may cause a loss of the spatial coordination of visually perceived and nonperceived adjacent regions. The need to compensate for this through judgments should be strong but first a period of perceptual exploration that restores lost coordination is required. Consequently, acts of search and moves to positions that are expected to provide increased visual access should be initiated. Positions close to windows or openings between occluding surfaces should be given priority. To what degree a series to changed vantage points is efficient should depend on the available knowledge about the adjacent but invisible spatial layout in a wide sector of directions. This adjacency knowledge should guide acts of anticipation of where in space visual access is believed to increase substantially, or, alternatively, where increased recognizable information is believed to accompany increased access.

Explore-and-judge events may occur also in less bounded surroundings. The space between edges of large sight-occluding objects is a kind of natural window that may invite explorative perception. For example, when a traveler approaches the far edge

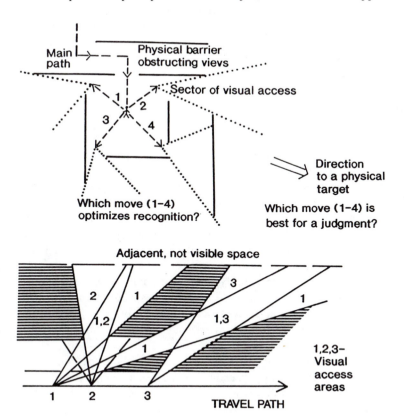

Figure 8.7. Explore-and-judge events in two situations varying in degree of visual boundedness (example 6).

of a close building, extensive ground, for example, a park, may gradually come into view before the process reverses as the occluding edge of the next building comes closer (cf. Gibson, 1979). Salient landmarks are sometimes possible to perceive in the background. In addition, such viewing opportunities may be unique along routes. Natural windows have size and form like real windows in buildings. Further, they may be arranged in close sequence and, in addition, be nested within each other in the viewing direction. Acts of attention to the successive background information available in such window patterns are essential parts of explore-and-judge events.

It follows that some instances of explore-and-judge events should be similar to recognition-over-time events (example 3). When position changes before the final judgment are extended, recognition-over-time events may occur as subevents in explore-and-judge events. However, critical information properties may differ. Spatial properties and perspectives should be part of the retrieval cues in the explore-and-judge event. Nonspatial properties, such as color and meaning, are equally important in recognition-over-time events.

In sum, explore-and-judge events are special in that behavioral acts are crucial. Insufficient exploration may be a common limitation of purposeful action when good judgments are needed (cf. Tolman, 1932). The accuracy, speed, and strategies of judgments may therefore be related in important ways to factors of visual access. Some questions for research are: Are subjects able to change positions efficiently so that visual access increases rapidly? Similarly, are subjects able to perform this task so that familiar information increases more rapidly than unfamiliar information? To which extent are judgments improved as a function of position change in these tasks?

CONCLUSIONS

An event approach to the analysis of spatial cognition under real-world conditions has been presented. The main assumption was that large-scale spatial cognition is a system of interrelated, cognitive acts at the level of consciousness. It has been assumed that understanding how spatial problems arise and are resolved requires the construct of spatial cognition events. It means that acts are grouped and sequenced in systematic ways as a product of individuals' efforts to adjust and adapt to the changing space–time conditions during locomotion. Basic mental processing of spatial information underlies the performance aspects of each specific act in such sequences. The event approach suggests that a complementary conceptual framework is needed. A primary goal should be to identify functional connections during locomotion between consciousness, perception, and large-scale spatial information. A subsidiary goal is to identify external and internal conditions assumed to account for specific grouping and sequencing. In the following, more specific conclusions are reiterated.

A recurrent question concerned what travelers need to know about the large-scale environment. The distinction between targets as large-scale versus point type of units was considered a possible ecological–experimental inconsistency. Several possibly neglected aspects of knowledge, such as rotation relationships between two places, objective size, or subtended angle of large-scale units, were discussed. Finally, knowledge specifications that account for flexible route following were called for.

A recurring theme was the importance of visual factors. Variable views and perspectives were assumed to further flexibility of human navigation. Usefulness of direction judgments was evaluated in terms of sectors of visual access and perception of path choice. Behavioral acts were assumed to be important means to optimize visual access or amount of recognized information.

Learning was not confined to the incremental aspect of acquisition of environmental information. Self-regulation was an important aspect of learning in several events. It was analyzed as error correction and utilization of knowledge inconsistencies. Similarly, occurrence of encoding acts was assumed to be contingent on recall performance.

Three methodological aspects should be mentioned: the role of independency of observations, derived variables, and dependent variables that reflect selection processes. First, the present event approach means that performance aspects of acts are dependent on each other. This was exemplified at many points during the presentation. Therefore, experimental observations in event-simulating conditions should deliberately be allowed to become dependent on each other. As an element of observation the single act is less important than relations between pairs of acts. To infer order and performance relationships on the basis of independent observations is indeed a difficult task, perhaps impossible from certain point of departures, such as systems analysis. Second, derived variables were often suggested, for example, relationships between distance, size of physical units, subtended angles in perspectives, and travel speed. Further, rate of change of matched or recognized information was an important aspect of recognition-over-time events and explorative events. Third, cognitive or behavioral selection of units represents an important variable category, apart from accuracy aspects of cognition. Examples were number of units recognized, number of point targets judged, number of retrieved spatial relations used to correct judgments, number of perceived path alternatives, and number of stationpoints to reach final judgments.

REFERENCES

Acredolo, L. (1981). Small- and large-scale spatial concepts in infancy and childhood. In L.S. Liben, A.H. Patterson, and N. Newcombe (Eds.), *Spatial representation and behavior across the life span* (pp. 63–81). New York: Academic press.

Allen, G.L. (1985). Strengthening weak links in the study of the development of macrospatial cognition. In R. Cohen (Ed.), *The development of spatial cognition* (pp. 301–321). Hillsdale, N.J.: Erlbaum.

Allen, G.L. (1987). Cognitive influences on the acquisition of route knowledge in children and adults. In P. Ellen and C. Thinus-Blanc (Eds.), *Cognitive processes and spatial orientation in animal and men* (pp. 274–283). Dordrecht: Martinus Nijhoff.

Allen, G.L., Siegel, A.W., & Rosinski, R.R. (1978). The role of perceptual context in structuring spatial knowledge. *Journal of Experimental Psychology: Human Learning and Memory, 4,* 617–630.

Anderson, J.R. (1985). *Cognitive psychology and its implications.* San Francisco: Freeman.

Biederman, I. (1987). Recognition-by-component: A theory of human image understanding. *Psychological Review, 94,* 115–147.

Böök, A. (1981). *Maintenance of environmental orientation during locomotion.* Doctoral dissertation. Department of Psychology, University of Umeå, Sweden.

Böök, A. (1988). The role of perspective in recognition of real-life scenes. In H. van Hoogalen, N.L. Prak, T.J.M. van der Voordt, & H.B.B. van Wegen (Eds.), *Looking back to the future. Proceedings of the 10th Conference of the International Association for the Study of People and their Physical Surroundings,* Delft, The Netherlands, July 5–8, 1988.

Böök, A., & Gärling, T. (1981). Maintenance of orientation during locomotion in unfamiliar environments. *Journal of Experimental Psychology: Human Perception and Performance, 7,* 995–1006.

Couclelis, H., Golledge, R.G., Gale, N., & Tobler, W. (1987). Exploring the anchor-point hypothesis of spatial cognition. *Journal of Environmental Psychology, 7,* 99–122.

Cousins, J.H., Siegel, A.W., & Maxwell, S.E. (1983). Way-finding and cognitive mapping in large-scale environments. A test of a developmental model. *Journal of Experimental Child Psychology, 35,* 1–20.

Evans, G.W. (1980). Environmental cognition. *Psychological Bulletin, 88,* 259–287.

Evans, G.W., Fellows, J., Zorn, M., & Doty, K. (1980). Cognitive mapping and architecture. *Journal of Applied Psychology, 65,* 474–478.

Evans, G.W., Marrero, D., & Butler, P. (1981). Environmental learning and cognitive mapping. *Environment and Behavior, 13,* 83–104.

Evans, G.W., & Pezdek, K. (1980). Cognitive mapping: Knowledge of real-world distance and location information. *Journal of Experimental Psychology, 6,* 13–24.

Evans, G.W., Skorpanich, M.A., Gärling, T., Bryant, K.J., & Bresolin, B. (1984). The effects of pathway configuration, landmarks and stress on environmental cognition. *Journal of Environmental Psychology, 4,* 323–335.

Gärling, T., Böök, A., Lindberg, E., & Nilsson, T. (1981). Memory for the spatial layout of the everyday activities in large-scale environments: Factors affecting rate of acquisition *Journal of Environmental Psychology, 1,* 263–277.

Gärling, T., Lindberg, E., Carreiras, M., & Böök, A. (1986). Reference systems in cognitive maps. *Journal of Environmental Psychology, 6,* 1–18.

Gärling, T., Lindberg, E., & Mäntylä, T. (1983). Orientation in buildings: Effects of familiarity, visual access, and orientation aids. *Journal of Applied Psychology, 68,* 177–186.

Gibson, J.J. (1979). *The ecological approach to visual perception.* Boston: Houghton Mifflin.

Gopal, S. (1988). *A computational model of spatial navigation.* Doctoral dissertation, Department of Geography, University of California, Santa Barbara.

Hardwick, D.A., McIntyre, C.W., & Pick, H.L., Jr. (1976). The content and manipulation of cognitive maps in children and adults. *Monographs of the Society for Research in Child Development, 41,* 1–55.

Heft, H. (1983). Way-finding as the perception of information over time. *Population and Environment: Behavioral and Social Issues, 6,* 133–150.

James, W. (1890). *Principles of psychology.* New York: Holt.

Jolicoeur, P., & Kosslyn, S.M. (1983). Coordinate systems in the long-term memory representation of three-dimensional shapes. *Cognitive Psychology, 15,* 301–345.

Kaplan, S. (1976). Adaptation, structure, and knowledge. In G.T. Moore and R.G. Golledge (Eds.), *Environmental knowledge* (pp. 32–45). Stroudsburg, Penn.: Dowden, Hutchinson & Ross.

Kirasic, K.C., Allen, G.L., & Siegel, A.W. (1984). Expression of configurational knowledge of large-scale environments. *Environment and Behavior, 16,* 687–712.

Kozlowski, L.T., & Bryant, K.J. (1977). Sense of direction, spatial orientation, and cognitive maps. *Journal of Experimental Psychology: Human Perception and Performance, 3,* 590–598.

Kuipers, B. (1978). Modeling spatial knowledge. *Cognitive Science, 2,* 129–153.

Kuipers, B. (1983). The cognitive map: Could it have been any other way? In H.L. Pick, Jr. and L.P. Acredolo (Eds.), *Spatial orientation: Theory, research, and application* (pp. 345–359). New York: Plenum.

Lindberg, E., & Gärling, T. (1981). Acquisition of locational information about reference points during blindfolded and sighted locomotion: Effects of a concurrent task and locomotion paths. *Scandinavian Journal of Psychology, 22,* 101–108.

Lindberg, E., & Gärling, T. (1982). Acquisition of locational information about reference points during locomotion: The role of central information processing. *Scandinavian Journal of Psychology, 23,* 207–218.

Moar, I., & Carleton, L.R. (1982). Memory for routes. *Quarterly Journal of Experimental Psychology, 34A,* 381–394.

Neisser, U. (1976). *Cognition and reality.* San Francisco: Freeman.

Norman, D.A., & Bobrow, D.G. (1975). On data-limited and resource-limited processes. *Cognitive Psychology, 7,* 44–64.

Pick, H.L., Jr. (1985). Foreword. In R. Cohen (Ed.), *The development of spatial cognition* (pp. ix–xi). Hillsdale, N.J.: Erlbaum.

Pinker, S. (1984). Visual cognition. *Cognition, 18,* 1–63.

Rieser, J.J. (1983). The generation and early development of spatial inferences. In Pick, H.L., Jr. and Acredolo, L. (Eds.), *Spatial orientation: Theory, research, and application* (pp. 39–71). New York: Plenum.

Rieser, J.J., Guth, D., & Hill, E. (1982). Mental processes mediating independent travel: Implications for orientation and mobility. *Journal of Visual Impairment and Blindness, 76,* 213–218.

Rieser, J.J., Lockman, J.J., & Pick, H.L., Jr. (1980). The role of visual experience in knowledge of spatial layout. *Perception and Psychophysics, 28,* 185–190.

Rumelhart, D.E., & Norman, D.A. (1975). Accretion, tuning, and restructuring: Three modes of learning. In J.W. Cotton and R.L. Klatzky (Eds.), *Semantic factors in cognition* (pp. 37–53). New York: Wiley.

Sadalla, E.K., & Magel, S.G. (1980). The perception of traversed distance. *Environment and Behavior, 12,* 65–79.

Sadalla, E.K., & Staplin, L.J. (1980). The perception of traversed distance: Intersections. *Environment and Behavior, 12,* 167–182.

Sadalla, E.K., Staplin, L.J., & Burroughs, W.J. (1979). Retrieval processes in distance cognition. *Memory and Cognition, 7,* 291–296.

Sholl, M.J. (1987). Cognitive maps as orienting schemata. *Journal of Experimental Psychology: Learning, Memory and Cognition, 13,* 615–628.

Siegel, A.W., & White, S.H. (1975). The development of spatial representation of large-scale environments. In H.W. Reese (Ed.), *Advances in child development and behavior* (Vol. 10, pp. 9–55). New York: Academic Press.

Smyth, M., Morris, P., Levy, P., & Ellis, A. (1986). *Cognition and action.* Hillsdale, N.J.: Erlbaum.

Stevens, A., & Coupe, P. (1978). Distortions in judged spatial relations. *Cognitive Psychology, 10,* 422–437.

Thomson, J.A. (1983). Is continuous visual monitoring necessary in visually guided locomotion? *Journal of Experimental Psychology: Human Perception and Performance, 9,* 427–443.

Thorndyke, P.W., & Hayes-Roth, B. (1982). Differences in spatial knowledge acquired from maps and navigation. *Cognitive Psychology, 14,* 560–589.

Tolman, E.C. (1932). *Purposive behavior in animals and men.* New York: Appleton-Century-Crofts.

Tversky, B. (1981). Distortions in memory for maps. *Cognitive Psychology, 13,* 407–433.

Wagner, M., Baird, J., & Barbaresi, W. (1981). The locus of environmental attention. *Journal of Environmental Psychology, 1,* 195–206.

9

Beyond Rationality:
Clarity-Based Decision Making

STEPHEN KAPLAN

The study of how people make decisions has long been dominated by the economic man or rationality model. In recent years researchers have extended the study of decision making into the spatial context. Given the pervasive role of the rationality model it was not surprising to see reliance on it in this new domain as well (Golledge & Timmermans, 1987; Timmermans, this volume). There are, however, at least two reasons why one might have hoped for a broader perspective.

First, given its obvious kinship to the area of environmental cognition, research on spatial decision making could have reflected the concern for cognitive structure central to the wayfinding literature.

Second, the rationality model has increasingly been the subject of searching questions and criticism. Cracks have been appearing in the once near-monolithic support for this model. A number of psychologists have been quite articulate about what they see as serious deficiencies in this approach (Einhorn & Hogarth, 1985; Herrnstein & Mazur, 1987; Kruglanski & Ajzen, 1983; Simon, 1957; Wallach & Wallach, 1983). Even economists have expressed serious reservations (Bell & Kristol, 1981; Earl, 1983a; Eichner, 1983; Kuttner, 1985; Lutz, 1987).

Decision theorists have not been insensitive to these concerns; many modifications have been proposed (see Jungermann, 1983, for an extensive review). If there is a consensus among them, it is far from obvious. In the absence of such a consensus, many stalwart investigators (including economists and planners) continue within the comfortable and familiar confines of the classical framework.

In the discussion that follows, the term "rationality" will be used to refer to the classical rationality position that still endures in many quarters, and that still serves as a center of gravity for the multitude of dissatisfied revisionists. In its simplest form, the position can be summarized as stating that people have perfect knowledge and that they strive to maximize their gains.

A most interesting analysis of the increasingly obvious inadequacy of the rationality model and of how planners are coping with this state of affairs is provided by E.R. Alexander (1984). The picture he paints is essentially one of a paradigm decline, with heroic efforts on the part of practitioners to carry on nonetheless. His message is quite clear: nothing short of a new paradigm will be sufficient to move people from their current postures. Until a new paradigm emerges they will continue in this mode, denying that anything is wrong, fiddling with details of the current paradigm, or proclaiming that we really do not need a guiding theory afterall.

Whether or not a new paradigm is called for, the rationality model at the very least requires some major revision. The purpose of this chapter is to propose such a modification in the portion of the model in which decision theory and environmental cognition most clearly overlap. Despite the many modifications that have been proposed in recent years, this part of the model appears to have been largely neglected.

THE RATIONALITY APPROACH TO CHOICE

The rationality approach must be an unusually attractive model to have endured for well over 100 years. It does, in fact, have a number of desirable features. It is simple and easy to remember. It greatly facilitates the expression of key aspects of choice in mathematical form. It deals with some difficult aspects of choice in a most convenient form. And finally, it greatly simplifies the combination of cognitive factors (such as probability and distance) and affective factors (the value of the outcome).

The rationality model is at its core a model of how decisions are made. A decision is seen as occurring when one has a choice among two or more alternatives. An *alternative*, in turn, is viewed within this context as consisting of two components. The *value* of the outcome refers to how desirable the alternative is; in other words, how good or how bad is the payoff. The other component, the *probability*, represents how likely it is that one would obtain that value if one chose that alternative. A simple example would be a lottery in which one could win $100 (the value), but one's chances were only 1 in 20 (the probability).

Although probability has been the traditional way of expressing how remote one is from the desired outcome, other factors besides probability can play a similar role. Thus in environmental cognition, *distance* has replaced probability. One might, for example, study the choice of a shopping center as a function of its distance from home. In other contexts (highway design, for example), the time it takes to get to one's goal replaces probability. Although I shall refer to this notion of remoteness from the goal as "probability," its traditional name, it is important to remember that it is a broader construct than that term might suggest.

The identification of value and probability (or an appropriate surrogate) as the components of an alternative does not, of course, constitute a theory of decision. There are some additional questions that must be answered. At the very least, one would want to know (1) what it is that people are trying to achieve when they make decisions and (2) on what basis the decision is made. The rationality model has simple and direct answers to these questions. These answers are in the form of three underlying assumptions. The first concerns the concept of *gain*. This is an aggregate of values that allows one to trade off the advantages and disadvantages of different alternatives with respect to a single standard of "goodness." The second assumption is that people attempt to *maximize* this gain; in other words, they make choices that will yield the highest possible quantity of this "goodness." The third assumption is that in making a decision, people have whatever information they might possibly need; they are assumed, in other words, to have *perfect knowledge*. What this means is that people not only know all the pertinent alternatives, but also their corresponding values and probabilities.

Some Criticisms

The classic rationality model is thus elegantly simple. It is based on two constructs (value and probability) and three assumptions. Of these the maximization assumption has received the greatest attention. Simon (1970) has most convincingly made the point that people often *satisfice* rather than maximize. In other words, they often choose what is good enough, rather than holding out for the best.

Even before one can maximize, there must be something to maximize; there must be some way to combine what may well be incommensurate concerns into a single result. This in turn depends on the possibility of substituting more of something in exchange for less of something else. For example, if one likes camping and likes movies, one should be willing to exchange one's planned camping trip for an additional film series. Foa (1971) has perceptively demonstrated that even among a limited set of desirables (goods, money, status, love, information, service) translation cannot occur without a substantial loss. It is widely recognized, for example, that money is not an adequate substitute for love; comparably goods are rarely considered an adequate trade for a loss of status. Thus the idea of substitutability, which is essential for the gain concept to function properly, is also suspect.

In the context of the rationality model, the gain concept not only depends on substitutability, it also relies on the perfect knowledge assumption. It requires people to know the value of all potential alternative choices. However, as Midgley (1978) has pointed out, it is often difficult to place a confident value on a choice even after it has been made. Thus perfect knowledge of value before the fact seems rather unlikely.

The probability concept is an essential element of decision making, since it addresses the irreducible uncertainty in the process of making a choice. Although probability is an important component of this uncertainty, it is, by itself, too narrowly drawn. Einhorn and Hogarth (1985) provided an important broadening of the concept by demonstrating that information about what determines the probability is also subject to uncertainty. They point out, for example, that circumstances with the same probability of outcome can be strikingly different in ambiguity. If urn A contains 50 red and 50 black balls and urn B contains 100 black and red balls in uncertain proportion, most people consider the probability of drawing a red ball to be the same, that is, .5, for each urn. The ambiguity, however, is far greater in the case of urn B, and people will, all other things being equal, tend to avoid such an alternative.

A further broadening of the probability concept has occurred, as we have seen, in applications of the model to spatial contexts, where distance has come to replace probability. Many of these applications treat distance as an attribute of an alternative. In other words, a given destination has a particular attractiveness value and a particular value on a scale of distance. Work on travel plans (Gärling, Böök, & Lindberg, 1984; Böök, this volume) points to the centrality of cognitive maps in understanding cognitions of distance. Rather than being considered an attribute of a place, distance takes on structural properties. Instead of being treated as if it were a single value, it becomes an extended conceptual space with all the richness that any cognitive map of any extended space might have.

Although these various complications undermine the refreshing simplicity of the probability concept, this is an aspect of the classical rationality model in which major change is long overdue. It is noteworthy that of all the information about the state of the world one might consider, the rationality model has chosen probability. Probability, as it turns out, is a concept that people handle rather badly, to judge from the extensive literature on cognitive bias (Kahneman, Slovic, & Tversky, 1982; Nisbett & Ross, 1980). *It seems most unlikely that something that people deal with that poorly would be a keystone of the way people make decisions.*

Another area in which the probability concept should be broadened concerns the domain of ignorance. Surely choice must be influenced not only by the content of the knowledge one has, but also by the realization that potentially relevant information may be lacking. Plunging into a circumstance in which one lacks salient knowledge, and in which one is ignorant and inexperienced, could readily lead to trouble. Within the rationality context, however, avoiding situations of confusion and helplessness is a concern that receives little notice.

Admittedly the rationality theorist might claim that "trouble" would have a strong negative value, and hence would play an obvious role in the rationality calculus. But this would be a misreading of the issue. Consider, for example, a situation in which there is an opportunity to invest in some oil wells that, one is assured, have a very high probability of a very high payoff. Although some people do indeed make such investments, others find the lack of knowledge about who they are dealing with or why they are being blessed with such an amazing opportunity sufficiently uncomfortable to decline to participate. For those who think such foolish investments are only made by the unsophisticated, consider those who invested in the U.S. stock market shortly before October 1987 when the values were increasing rapidly and the probabilities were considered excellent. At the same time the lack of understanding as to what was going on was deeply troubling to some investors. In other words, one must be sensitive to the state of one's knowledge in making a decision, because attempting to function despite confusion *might* lead to trouble.

Some Criteria

Much as these various flaws of the rationality model are serious and pervasive,[1] the fact that the model is clear and explicit is a great advantage. It provides an excellent context for identifying the criteria that are desirable to include in an improved model. These can be organized around two themes: the inadequacies in the treatment of knowledge and the adaptive constraints on choice (and especially on choices that might get one in over one's head).

Knowledge-Related Criteria. There are three limitations in the way in which the rationality model treats knowledge that need to be corrected in any viable alternative:

1. It should be *integrative* or synthetic with respect to kinds of knowledge. It is undoubtedly convenient to manipulate a single factor such as probability or distance or time. Such mutual exclusivity, however, fails to capture the rich range of issues that people are likely to consider in a given situation. Much

more than probability or distance cr time goes into the knowledge structure about a given topic, and much of that knowledge is pertinent to a decision.

2. It must incorporate the issue of *ignorance*. Ignorance is an important aspect of one's knowledge about a given topic, and hence is an appropriate input into the decision-making process. The assumption of perfect knowledge is tantamount to denying the role of cognition in decision making.

3. It must be possible to distinguish what one *knows* from what one is *told*. In the context of the rationality framework, if a person is given a probability of a specified outcome, it is expected that that probability will be used in subsequent decision making. But being told such a "fact" may have very little to do with the individual's knowledge. People tend to find concrete experience more persuasive. They even find reports of the concrete experiences of others far more compelling. Thus in traditional decision-making research when participants are "given" probabilities they generally fail to use them effectively (Kahneman et al., 1982). Experience (and its corresponding structure in the head) is hard won, and not easily transferred.

Adaptive Criteria. For knowledge to play an adaptive role, it must not only support gainful activity but must also help avoid difficulty by encouraging individuals to stay away from situations in which they will be unprepared or incompetent. Therefore a new and improved model must also meet these criteria:

1. First and foremost an adaptive decision must include an assessment of *how much pertinent knowledge an individual has*. In other words, a crucial aspect of a decision is how much one knows about what one is getting into. One needs to take into account some assessment of how well one could cope with whatever uncertainties might arise at a later time.

   Such a concern about future uncertainties implies a disbelief in the pervasiveness of instant gratification. Rather, it assumes that real (as opposed to laboratory) decisions often do not lead directly to payoff. Being confident that one can function effectively during the course of traversing what may be an extended route on the way to one's goal (see Böök, this volume) must be a nontrivial aspect of making a good decision.

2. It follows from the previous requirement that the assessment of the adequacy of one's knowledge in a given situation should be *readily translatable into affect*. In other words, one must have feelings about one's knowledge with respect to a given alternative that is combinable with the feelings about the value of the alternative. (This is vital on adaptive grounds as well as being a theoretical necessity.)

3. This assessment must also be achieved *quickly and intuitively:* It should not call for great effort lest the process of making routine decisions be slowed down to the point of adaptive failure.

TOWARD AN INFORMATION-CENTERED
MODEL OF CHOICE

What is needed to correct these many difficulties and meet these various criteria is a concept that is two faceted. It must be cognitive in the sense that it reflects an individual's state of knowledge or ignorance. At the same time it must have affective consequences; possessing pertinent knowledge must engender positive feelings and encourage action while ignorance must have the opposite effect. The concept that possesses these necessary qualities is *cognitive clarity*. Intuitively this concept refers to the clear state of mind that accompanies comprehension and that is acutely lacking during states of confusion. At a more theoretical level it concerns the strength and extent of the person's knowledge pertinent to the problem at hand.

In 1877 the eminent pragmatist philosopher Charles Sanders Peirce identified what is essentially the same concept, which he cast in terms of "doubt."

> Doubt is an uneasy and dissatisfied state from which we struggle to free ourselves and pass into the state of belief: while the latter is a calm and satisfactory state which we do not wish to avoid, or to change. (p. 10)

As Tedeschi, Schlenker, and Bonoma (1971) suggest, "For Peirce, the sole object of individual inquiry was the settlement of doubtful opinions, to attain beliefs, and thus restore a comfortable state of mind" (p. 685). Several theorists have proposed the search for clarity as a basic human need since Peirce's perceptive description (Gibson, 1966; Kaplan, 1978; Kelly, 1963; Maslow & Diaz-Guerrero, 1971; Schachter, 1959; Woodworth, 1947, 1958). Although it is not known that any of these proponents of clarity were aware of Peirce's work on this subject, the concepts are essentially similar.

From the point of view of the rationality model, a particularly pertinent discussion of the motivating effect of cognitive clarity is set in the context of the resistance to a paradigm shift in economics. Earl (1983b) proposes six motives or "goals" to explain why academic economists have not abandoned the traditional (rational) economic model despite its evident inadequacy. One of these goals is "to keep situations of unfamiliarity within particular tolerance bounds (anxiety-avoidance aspiration)" (p. 94). That Earl is here referring to something closely akin to clarity is evident from his book, *The Economic Imagination* (1983a), in which he states "human behaviour can usefully be seen not as evidence of hedonistic, 'utility seeking' activities but as the manifestation of attempts by people to reduce the mysterious nature of the world around them" (p. 146).

Some examples might be helpful at this point to provide concrete imagery, and to give a sense for the pervasiveness of clarity's influence on decision making. Due to this very pervasiveness, these examples may seem at first glance to lack coherence. Helplessness, antisocial behavior, nonuse of desirable facilities in the urban environment, and failure to participate in curbside recycling may appear to have little to do with each other, and even less to do with clarity. There is, however, a common bond here. Each of these examples points to the powerful impact of the lack of knowledge, even knowledge of a rather simple and rudimentary kind, on the decisions people make.

Example 1. Children from low-income families are provided with a preschool program of instruction. One group is taught using a formal teacher-directed approach. The other is taught in a way that emphasizes child-initiated activities. This latter group is encouraged to learn such skills as how to plan and how to find the information they need. Years later when these children are in junior high school, the latter group has less delinquency, fewer pregnancies, and less involvement with drugs (Bales, 1987; Schweinhart, Weikart, & Larner, 1986).

Example 2. People in an ethnic neighborhood in Los Angeles are asked to draw maps of their environments. They draw only their immediate neighborhood and apparently have no knowledge of the many facilities and resources elsewhere in their city. Presumably they make little or no use of such resources (Orleans, 1973).

Example 3. A comparison of people who recycle and people who do not shows no difference in attitudes, but a significant difference in knowledge. The nonrecyclers were significantly less clear as to exactly how one goes about the recycling process (De Young, 1988–89).

Example 4. Teachers of environmental education are asked to describe how they teach and whether their students continue to be active in any way with respect to environmental issues. Although it was expected that students who had been involved in major class projects would be the most active, the two strongest predictors of subsequent activity were presenting case studies and discussion of how other people have handled environmental problems (Monroe & Kaplan, 1988).

These otherwise disparate situations appear to have two themes in common. First, they demonstrate the power of a *lack* of information in the decision making process. From the point of view of a clarity-oriented model, what is striking is that the lack of clarity is not the result of low probability or long distance, but a lack of familiarity or knowledge. People avoid situations in which they might become confused, where they might not know how to behave. There is also the additional social aspect of functioning in public without adequate information: People do not want to appear foolish or helpless or ignorant.

As these examples suggest, the proposed clarity-based approach to decision making can be summarized quite simply. People both prefer and benefit from making decisions that put them in domains in which they can use what they know and in which their hard-won cognitive structure can make a difference. Correspondingly they dislike, and tend to avoid, situations in which they feel they have insufficient information to guide their behavior.

At this point one could imagine an adherent of the rationality position commenting, ''Well, if clarity is that important why don't we simply add it to the rationality equation?'' There are two reasons why this is not an appropriate resolution:

1. Clarity is at a different level from the traditional rationality concepts; it is not one of these concepts but is *about* them. One can be unclear about the probabilities involved (as Einhorn & Hogarth, 1985, point out), or about the values involved (as Midgley, 1978, points out). One can even be unclear as to whether the issues one is taking into account are the relevant ones in the long run. Clarity is thus a metaconcept.

2. As one might expect with respect to a concept at a different level, clarity does not behave the same way as do the other components of a decision. Rather, it follows its own rules. It is something that not only may be given away freely; but that people actually *enjoy* giving away. And giving it away does not reduce one's own supply; on the contrary, giving it away may actually strengthen one's own level of clarity.

CLARITY AND COGNITIVE STRUCTURE

This section concerns the factors that influence choice. To make a choice between two or more alternatives one has to know how much one likes (or values or prefers) each of the alternatives. One must, in other words, have a way of evaluating the "goodness" of the alternatives. Two sorts of factors are involved here. The first is the perceived value of the outcome; the second involves the somewhat more complex issue of clarity.

It is hard to argue with the traditional rationality assumption that an essential component of the evaluation of an alternative must be the desirability of the outcome, or more technically, its affective value. (Our analysis here is directly parallel to the "value" assessment of the rationality model. In keeping with the preceding arguments, however, neither perfect knowledge nor perfect substitutability is assumed.) In the context of the framework developed in this section, it is assumed that when one experiences something pleasant, a mental code for pleasure becomes associated with the corresponding memory, and, similarly, a negative code for painful experiences. Thus affective value is determined by the direct pleasure or pain code associated with it.

The other component of the "goodness" of an alternative is its clarity. Understanding this concept requires a brief excursion into the way cognitive structure relates to choice.

Cognitive Structure

The simplest (although not necessarily the most useful) way of looking at the structural basis of choice is in terms of a *link*, a simple instrumentality, as diagrammed in Figure 9.1a. (Following traditional psychological notation, the "*" represents a

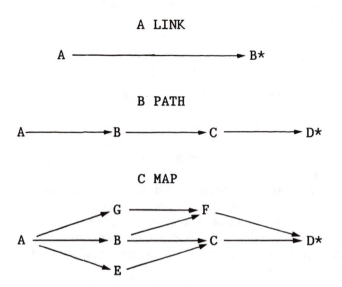

Figure 9.1. Alternative structural bases of choice.

reward, goal, or payoff.) Thus choice of "A" will lead to outcome "B." The bond between them will have a certain strength, which can intuitively be thought of as representing the confidence that "A" will in fact lead to "B."

Although its simplicity is delightful, such a pared down model of choice has only limited applicability. In reality one's goals are rarely that close at hand. A choice is more likely to lead to a first step in an extended sequence than to an immediate reward. It is frequently necessary to commit oneself to a *path* that one hopes will lead eventually to the desired outcome. Many psychological treatments of problem solving speak of such paths as intervening between start and goal (Figure 9.1b). Purposive behavior in general seems better represented by a path than a simple link.

When one deals with environmental realities, however, even a path is an inadequate model. A path of any substantial length is bound to have surprises. The bridge may be out or the road blocked. The likelihood that unexpected problems will arise is one of the primary reasons for involving humans in the guidance of spaceships; otherwise computers would be quite satisfactory. As soon as one acknowledges that surprises can occur, it becomes essential to look into alternative ways to reach one's goal. Whether there are other possibilities should the favored path fail to work can make a major difference in one's decision. Here the schematic diagram is considerably more complicated (Figure 9.1c).

One way to deal with such a situation is to think through all possible alternative routes. One not only considers A–B–C–D, but also A–G–F–D and A–E–C–D and so on. The difficulty with such a procedure is that with an environment of any complexity, an exhaustive enumeration of all the possible sequences becomes prohibitively costly of time and effort. There is a hypothetical example based on the game of chess that makes this point quite dramatically. Imagine a chess-playing machine that made its moves based on a consideration of all possible next moves, and all possible moves after that, and so on to the completion of the game. Even if the consideration of each board configuration took only a millisecond, it would take longer than the universe has been in existence to make a single move.

What this means is that one cannot approach this more realistic (and more complicated) way of framing a problem by considering each specific possible path; rather one has to evaluate the space as a whole. The "space" referred to here can be either literal or conceptual. It includes the knowledge one has of where one is, where one wishes to go, and the various paths or segments of paths inbetween. The convention in the problem-solving literature of referring to such a body of connected information as a "problem space" seems equally appropriate in this context.

Some spaces allow more alternatives if something should go wrong; some spaces are friendlier because one knows more about them. The admonition, "Ya gotta know the territory," reflects this recognition that effective behavior depends on knowledge of a larger space, even though it is impossible to predict what aspect of this knowledge will be useful. The cognitive structure that reflects knowledge of such a space corresponds remarkably well to what is usually referred to as a *cognitive map.*[2]

"Match" and Connectedness

Based on the discussion of links, paths, and maps, we can now turn to the role of clarity in the perceived "goodness" of a possible choice. Put simply, clarity of choice depends on the cognitive structure that represents the extensive problem space in which the choice is embedded. The *strength* (or connectedness) of the cognitive structure and the quality of its *match* to reality are the two essential components of clarity. Let us examine the concept of "match" first.

No matter how strong one's cognitive structure, one's confidence can be undermined if one's expectations do not correspond to perceived reality. Thus the quality of the "match"[3] of one's knowledge to the environment is necessarily a significant factor in how one feels about a situation. Some environments are arranged in ways that make it easy to achieve a good match even when one knows relatively little about them. Such environments might be said to be more compatible with human requirements. The compatibility of person and environment (S. Kaplan, 1983) is, in general, a powerful contributing factor to the achievement of clarity.

The other component of clarity is the strength or connectedness of the cognitive structure itself. The cognitive structure of interest here is the problem space (or cognitive map) in which a given choice is embedded. This particular cognitive structure has certain properties in common with cognitive structures in general. It consists of elements and relations. The elements in this case would stand for things in the world; the relations are associations or connections between these elements. The associations stand for the experienced ease of going from one thing to the next. A structure of high strength in this framework is one in which it is easy to get from one thing to any other thing in the same structure. Thus the more strongly connected the structure, the greater the likelihood that any two points in the structure will be connected. This corresponds to the ease of getting from one point to another in the space it represents. The more connected the structure, in other words, the greater the likelihood that any two points in the space will be connected.

Although relatively straightforward to characterize at an intuitive level, connectedness is a matter of considerable complexity because of the many factors that contribute to it. These various factors can be shown to reduce to associative strength when viewed at a more molecular level. Unfortunately, however, this analysis is considerably more technical than that which preceded it; readers who are comfortable with the relatively intuitive description already provided may wish to skip the Technical Analysis section that follows.

Technical Analysis

As already suggested, the degree of association of the various aspects of the link (or path or map) necessarily reflects a diversity of factors. Not only is there the issue of the probability or distance between a choice and its outcome, there is also the degree of familiarity and the sense of mastery (or conversely, the feeling that one is ignorant about what is going on). All of these factors influence the sense of confidence in a choice.

The theoretical challenge is to express probability and familiarity in terms of a common coin, in a way that permits one to combine them. One way to approach doing this is to consider how these factors might be represented in a cognitive structure.

Let us begin with an analysis of the most basic component of cognitive structure, namely the internal representation (S. Kaplan, 1973; Neisser, 1966; Posner, 1973) that stands for an object or landmark. If one knows and understands things at the basic object level, one has a good foundation for a knowledge structure that will be both useful and confidence inspiring. The impact of familiarity at this level is straightforward. The more familiar one is with an object, the more its many different aspects or features will be associated in the corresponding internal representation.

The impact of probability on the connectedness of the object representation, by contrast, may seem less intuitive. In fact, the very meaning of the probability concept may appear to have changed in this context. Probability as described in the context of the rationality model refers to the likelihood of a particular valued outcome, given a particular choice. But as the concept became more general in the context of distance, ambiguity, and the like, it came to refer to the likelihood of some event predicting the occurrence of some other event. At the scale of an object, the entities that do or do not predict each other are not events, but the features by which the object is known.

Perhaps a hypothetical comparison would be helpful. Consider an object whose features can be counted on to be reliably associated with that object. One can count on the presence of one of the features to predict the presence of the others, day in and day out, independent of varying conditions. Such an object is an easy object to get to know. By contrast consider an object whose appearance changes under various circumstances. It looks different depending on lighting conditions and viewing angles. Building a well connected cognitive unit (i.e., an internal representation) to stand for such a variable object is far more difficult. Since the probability of experiencing any given feature of an object, given some other feature, is low, the object will be difficult to recognize and to feel confident about.

When an object's parts or aspects are well connected, when the object is familiar, and when one knows what to do with it, the corresponding cognitive structure is strongly connected. *This strength of association characterizing a cognitive structure thus provides the desired common coin that permits one to integrate across various factors.*

Cognitive structures represent more than objects; an important aspect of cognitive structure is the relationship among objects. In our analysis above, three relationships were distinguished—a link, a path, and a map (see Figure 9.1). Each of these relationships can vary in its strength of associative structure or connectedness. Each of them, then, is a potential contributor to the overall associative strength of the cognitive structure in question. The connectedness of the object representation, together with the connectedness of the larger associative structure (whether link or path or map), constitutes the total strength of connection for a given alternative.

Putting the Pieces Together

What this analysis has yielded so far, then, are the key components of a cognitive structure that participate in clarity-based decision making. The next step in the argument is to determine how these components might be combined into a decision. There must be some way for these components of choice to come together to yield a composite value. Figure 9.2 shows how this might take place.

The cognitive structure (composed of units and the relationships among them) contributes to clarity in two distinct ways. It contributes both through its aggregate

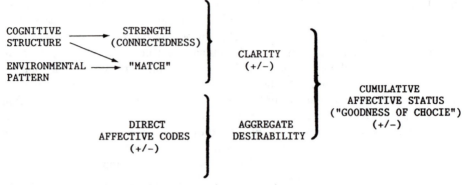

Figure 9.2.   Cascades of influence in a decision-making process.

associative strength and through the degree to which it constitutes a good match to the current environmental pattern. *Clarity, then, is defined in terms of mental activity in a strongly connected structure that is at the same time a good match to the environment or to the same problem at hand.*

Clarity, in turn, has two implications for choice. First, there will be a tendency to avoid any situation that is low in clarity. This means that if one can avoid the domain of the choice entirely one will do so. Although this may be considered equivalent to making a choice, as we have seen, it is psychologically, as well as functionally, quite distinct.

Consider, for example, two individuals who are intrigued by the idea of travel abroad. Each explores the possibilities and decides against going. For one, the decision is based on economic issues. The other finds the conflicting information, the uncertainties, and the endless contingencies overwhelming, and, with a sense of relief, drops the entire matter. Although the outcome is the same in both cases, the differences are far from trivial. Certainly the feelings toward traveling abroad are very different for the two individuals. In addition, the willingness to consider such a possibility in the future is vastly different.

A second implication of the clarity concept for choice is the fact that it carries with it an affective code. The strength of the structure, in combination with the quality of the match, yields a certain intensity level of cognitive activity *that is automatically translated by the system into affective terms.* The details of this proposed physiological mechanism need not concern us here. In rough and ready terms, pleasure units in the brain are organized in such a way as to respond to well-focused cortical activity of the kind characteristic of clarity. Correspondingly, the arrangement of pain units leads them to be responsive to the diffuse activity one would expect from such a lack of clarity.[4] As a result of this mechanism, patterns high in clarity are experienced as pleasurable, and those low in clarity are painful. In this way the associative aspects of choice are converted into the common coin of affect.

Figure 9.2 brings together these various components that bear on the cumulative affective status, or "goodness" of a choice. As discussed previously, one aspect of the goodness of a potential choice is the desirability of the outcome, a concept directly parallel to the "value" assessment of the rationality model. As Figure 9.2

suggests, this is an aggregate across all the affective codes $(+/-)$ involved in making a given choice.

On the clarity side of the ledger, by contrast, the affective code appears relatively late in the process. The various cognitive components (cognitive structure, strength, and quality of "match") ultimately influence clarity, and only then does the affective consequence emerge. Thus in Figure 9.2, the "$(+/-)$" code is associated with clarity but not with any of its components.

The overall assessment of the "goodness" of a choice is thus the result of the combination of values inherent in the choice and the clarity of the cognitions related to it. The critical step in this analysis is the hypothesis that *clarity generates an affective reaction that makes it directly combinable with the affective value of the outcome.*

SOME CONTRASTING POSTULATES

The clarity concept represents a marked contrast to the classical rationality position. It might be helpful to try to make this comparison explicit. It should be noted, however, that the correspondence will necessarily be imperfect. It is difficult to account for the vicissitudes of human choice behavior with a theory as simple as the rationality model.

MOTIVATIONAL POSTULATE
> *Clarity:* People are trying to do many things; one of the important ones is to comprehend the confusing world around them.
> *Rationality:* People are trying to maximize their expected gain.

KNOWLEDGE POSTULATES: LEARNING
> *Clarity:* Knowledge is acquired slowly through the integration of many particular experiences or instances.
> *Rationality:* A person can be "given" knowledge by being told.

KNOWLEDGE POSTULATES: IMPERFECTION (relative to a particular decision)
> *Clarity:* Knowledge is necessarily incomplete.
> *Rationality:* People know all they need to know.

REALITY POSTULATES: EXTENDED PATH
> *Clarity:* Most decisions involve a committment to an extended path; gratification is rarely immediate.
> *Rationality:* No comment.

REALITY POSTULATES: ENVIRONMENTAL UNCERTAINTY
> *Clarity:* One never can be sure what will happen next. If something can go wrong, it is reasonably likely to do so.
> *Rationality:* This is taken care of by the probability component.

PRUDENT DECISION POSTULATE
> *Clarity:* Knowledge makes a difference in one's effectiveness, especially if all does not go as planned. Therefore if one does not know what one is

doing; if one is not clear as to what is going on, it may be best to stay away.

Rationality: No comment.

At this point it might be useful to pause for a moment to review what has been achieved so far. The goal has been to identify a replacement for the limited and distorting treatment of knowledge utilized in the rationality model. Cognitive clarity has been nominated as this replacement. It meets the knowledge structure criteria of being synthetic; it achieves this by reflecting the strength of interconnection of a cognitive map, whether this strength is due to probability, or distance, or familiarity, or any combination of these and related concepts. It incorporates ignorance: When one is ignorant, there will be a shortage of strong interconnections and clarity will be correspondingly low. And "being told" does not in and of itself suffice; such information is quite inadequate for building the necessary interconnections.

The clarity concept meets the adaptiveness criteria as well. It includes an assessment of pertinent knowledge by reflecting the strength of the relevant cognitive structure. We know on empirical grounds that it readily translates into affect; the pain and distress associated with being lost or disoriented or confused are widely recognized. Indeed, clarity would be unlikely to have been so widely recognized as a human motive were it not for its striking affective consequences. Finally, the assessment of clarity is quick and intuitive. One need not take much time to determine that one feels lost or confused.

CONCLUSIONS

There are certain things the proposed model does, and certain important things that it does not attempt to do. Hopefully it will provide a better fit with a broad range of real world data than does the rationality model. Clearly it suggests a quite different emphasis as far as understanding what a humane environment is, and in terms of how to aid people in functioning more reasonably and effectively. It also suggests that one cannot simply compute the value people place on a particular choice as a prelude to taking action on their behalf. Such a computation must incorporate the prevailing level of clarity. Clarity, however, is not a fixed entity, but highly susceptible to an exchange of information.

Achieving an exchange of information does, of course, run counter to taking action on behalf of others. Instead it requires a form of public participation that is, explicitly and intentionally, a two-way process. In such a procedure participants are assumed to require information before they can provide a useful response. For a discussion of the rationale and practice of this approach, see R. Kaplan (1979) and S. Kaplan & R. Kaplan (1989).

Helplessness can be a direct response to a lack of clarity. Thus, the proposed approach highlights how close the relationship between information and helplessness can often be. A lack of information, even a lack of an objectively small amount of information, can be sufficient to convince individuals of their helplessness. There are two implications here. First, a little information (of the right kind) can make a great deal of difference. Second, although a feeling of helplessness is often assumed to arise out of prior experiences of helplessness (Seligmann, 1975), this need not be the case. It can occur as an outcome of assessing one's relevant knowledge. In such cases "perceived helplessness" may equally well be described as "objective but correctable ignorance." Another contribution of the proposed approach is to underscore the very real possibility of expressing one's lack of clarity by ignoring a decision rather than facing it. People may be hesitant to enter an entire domain (be it computers or the library or the woods) because of their lack of knowledge as to what to do, even how to begin. Thus, as the examples mentioned earlier illustrated, what may appear from the outside to be a negative or even hostile reaction may actually be an expression of discomfort in the absence of sufficient information.

Since it is easy (and not uncommon) for experts to belittle such timidity in the face of unfamiliar situations, it is important to point out that the expert's willingness to take on uncertainty is on a quite different level. Facing small confusions is far easier to accept when embedded in a larger context of knowledge and competence. While this is typically invisible to the expert (Kaplan, 1977), it strikingly demonstrates the power of information to make potentially difficult situations manageable.

Despite these various implications, it should be emphasized that this position is descriptive, not normative. It does not assert that clarity is good, but only that it plays an important role in decision making. Clarity is, in fact, a double-edged sword; people's motivation to achieve it is so strong that they will sometimes do appalling things in a desperate quest for clarity. Fromm's (1941) *Escape from Freedom* can be read as a description of the attractiveness of the simplistic clarity offered by Hitler to a people reeling from the chaos and confusion of post-War War I Germany. Becker's (1975) *Escape from Evil* provides a more general statement of a similar theme. His brilliant analysis probes the causes of evil, where his focus is not on the individual and idiosyncratic evil, but on large-scale evil (like the Holocaust), which is practiced by an entire society. Ironically, one of the factors he identifies as a central cause of evil is the commitment to "stamp out evil." His examples raise the strong possibility that the "evil" that is to be "stamped out" is typically the confusing, the different, the discrepant. It is, in other words, an important source of unclarity.

The downside of clarity expresses itself in various ways, many not as dramatic and appalling as the examples discussed by Fromm and Becker, but costly nonetheless. The attractiveness of cults shows, among other things, the power of the yearning for clarity, as do simplistic and uninformative presidential campaigns. As Christopher Alexander (1965) has demonstrated in his "City is not a tree," there is a human bias toward thinking about how the world is organized in a way that favors clarity over reality. Thus although the bias toward clarity is often adaptive, it can be expressed in unfortunate, and even in disastrous ways. But whether this pervasive need leads to good or to evil, it seems essential that so powerful a fact of human motivation and experience be identified and studied.

Clarity-based decision making is thus purely descriptive; there is no claim to speak to normative issues. By contrast, the rationality model is both descriptive and normative; it not only claims to be a theory of how people decide, it also speaks to how people *should* decide. Whereas playing both sides of the fence has often been a source of confusion, it does have certain advantages. As E.R. Alexander (1984) has argued, it is not enough to demonstrate that the rationality model is inadequate, or even to provide a model that does a better job of describing human behavior. It is also necessary to offer a viable normative position, to speak to the issue of the ideal as well as the real.

Perhaps, however, a normative theory is not needed. One can ask whether people are making appropriate enough decisions without any help from a normative model. Nisbett and Ross (1980) asked a similar question in their excellent review of decision making. After surveying a vast array of human tendencies to depart from rationality, they stepped back for a moment to ask how much difference it all makes in real world functioning. They concluded, apparently to their surprise, that in reality people do remarkably well afterall. Unfortunately, however, this conclusion is based on a rather narrowly circumscribed view of human activities. The impartial observer of the state of the environment and how we have cared for it knows all too well that this optimistic perspective is seriously misleading.

Thus although rationality is not an option, leaving the system to its own devices is not acceptable either. What is needed is a reality-respecting alternative that deals with such difficult but essential issues as uncertainty, future orientation, and frameworks for stewardship. Such an alternative must be concerned with the power of information as well as the doubled-edged sword of clarity. It should also find a way to unleash human creativity in the search for better solutions. A proposal for "Adaptive Muddling" offers a beginning for what will necessarily be a difficult and extensive dialogue. This approach assumes that it is possible to explore (and hence achieve clarity about) future alternatives without the necessity of committing to them first (De Young & Kaplan, 1988).

The human organism has many assets, not the least of which are a great potential for problem solving and the capacity—when appropriately informed—for reasonable behavior. The original basis of the rationality model is the acknowledgment of human selfishness and the assumption that the collective outcome of individual selfishness would be an "invisible hand" that would act for the greater good. It is becoming increasingly clear that the invisible hand has failed us, and that we can and must call on our fellow humans in a more thoughtful and effective way.

NOTES

1. There are other important characteristics of human decision making in addition to these that disturb many people. Most salient among these are the tendency to emphasize individual as opposed to group benefits, and the tendency to overvalue short-term as opposed to long-term goals. These are important concerns but they are not criticisms of the rationality model but of human behavior per se. They thus constitute a separate set of problems from those under discussion here.

2. The preceding analysis of the cognitive structure underlying the clarity concept arises out of a position once relatively widely shared among students of environmental cognition, namely the cognitive map model. The version of that model employed here (S. Kaplan, 1973; S. Kaplan & R. Kaplan, 1982) is, in turn, part of a long tradition of "associative" models in psychology (Attneave, 1962). Associative models have, however, been in eclipse for some time now, largely because of the pervasiveness of the "mind as computer" analogy that has played such a powerful role in the cognitive revolution. Recently, however, associative models have experi-

enced a resurgence in popularity, in part because of the development of what are called "connectionist" models (Rumelhart et al., 1986; Waltz & Feldman, 1988) and in part because of support for the older associative position (Hebb, 1949, 1982) coming from work in neurophysiology (Brown, Chapman, Kairiss, & Keenan, 1988; Segal, 1988). Quite a range of connectionist models have been proposed; we have called the version that underlies the present discussion "Active Symbol Connectionism" (S. Kaplan, Weaver, & French, 1990). Of particular interest to students of environmental cognition in this area is the simulation work by Levenick (1985) and O'Neill (1989) who explored the remarkable power of an associative cognitive map in solving wayfinding problems.

3. The idea of a match between some mental structure and an environmental pattern derives from an old theoretical conception that posited an internal template that did or did not fit the environmental pattern. This theory has been shown to be unsatisfactory. It requires a very large number of comparisons to recognize an object, and the more one knows, the longer it would take. Further there is the implication that some intelligent agent must be present to decide in each case whether a match has been made. By contrast, in terms of the connectionist framework underlying the present analysis, the way the goodness of fit between environmental patterns and internal structures is evaluated involves a process of parallel growth of activity of neural networks that might be pertinent, along with competition among these alternatives based on the strength of activity. This approach is highly parallel and rapid, and requires no "intelligent agent." The term "match," while convenient and appropriate as a loose analogy, is quite unsatisfactory as a theoretical construct.

4. The hypothesized physiological mechanism for translating clarity into pleasure and confusion into pain depends on two assumptions. First pleasure and pain units are assumed to be mutually inhibitory. Second, pleasure units are assumed to have a higher threshold value than pain units. Thus diffuse cortical activity (corresponding to confusion) stimulates the low threshold pain units. Activity characteristic of clarity is not only more focused but also more intense because of the greater focus. This intense activity stimulates pleasure units, which in turn inhibits pain units. The result, then, is the experience of pleasure as a consequence of clarity.

ACKNOWLEDGMENTS

The contributions of Gary Evans, Tommy Gärling, Lashon Booker, Rachel Kaplan, and Lisa Bardwell to the development of this chapter are greatly appreciated. I would also like to thank the Seminar in Environmentally Sensitive Adaptive Mechanisms (SESAME) for their intellectual support throughout the process.

REFERENCES

Alexander, C. (1965). A city is not a tree. *Architectural Forum, 122,* April 58–62, May 58–62.

Alexander, E.R. (1984). After rationality, what? *Journal of American Planning Association, 50,* 62–69.

Attneave, F. (1962). Perception and related areas. In S. Koch (Ed.) *Psychology: A study of a science* (Vol. 4). New York: McGraw-Hill.

Bales, J. (1987 April) Prevention at its best. *American Psychological Association Monitor*, 18–19.

Becker, E. (1975). *Escape from evil*. New York: Free Press.

Bell, D., & Kristol. I. (1981). *The crisis in economic theory*. New York: Basic.

Brown, T.H., Chapman, P.F., Kairiss, E.W., & Kennan, C.L. (1988). Long-term synaptic potentiation. *Science, 242*, 724–728.

De Young, R. (1988–89). Exploring the difference between recyclers and nonrecyclers: The role of information. *Journal of Environmental Systems, 18*, 341–351.

De Young, R., & Kaplan. S. (1988). On averting the tragedy of the commons. *Environmental Management, 12*, 273–283.

Earl, P.E. (1983a). *The economic imagination*. Armonk, N.Y.: Sharpe.

Earl, P.E. (1983b). A behavioral theory of economists' behavior. In A.S. Eichner (Ed.) *Why economics is not yet a science*. Armonk, N.Y.: Sharpe.

Eichner, A.S. (Ed.) (1983). *Why economics is not yet a science*. Armonk, N.Y.: Sharpe.

Einhorn, H.J. & Hogarth, R.M. (1985). Ambiguity and uncertainty in probabilistic inference. *Psychological Review, 92*, 433–461.

Foa, U.G. (1971). Interpersonal and economic resources. *Science, 171*, 345–351.

Fromm, E. (1941). *Escape from freedom*. New York: Farrer & Reinhart.

Gärling, T., Böök, A., & Lindberg, E. (1984). Cognitive mapping of large-scale environments. *Environment and Behavior, 16*, 3–34.

Gibson, J.J. (1966). *The senses considered as perceptual systems*. Boston: Houghton Mifflin.

Golledge, R.G., & Timmermans, H. (Eds.) (1987). *Behavioral modeling approaches in geography and planning*. London: Croom Hell.

Hebb, D.O. (1949). *The organization of behavior*. New York: Wiley.

Hebb, D.O. (1982). *Essay on mind*. Hillsdale, N.J.: Erlbaum.

Herrnstein, R.J., & Mazur, J.E. (1987, Nov.–Dec.). Making up our minds. *The Sciences*, 40–47.

Jungermann, H. (1983). The two camps on rationality. In R.W. Scholz (Ed.) *Decision making under uncertainty*. North-Holland: Elsevier.

Kahneman, D., Slovic, P.L., & Tversky. A. (1982). *Judgment under uncertainty: Heuristics and biases*. Cambridge: Cambridge University Press.

Kaplan, R. (1979). A methodology for simultaneously obtaining and sharing information. In *Assessing amenity resource values*. USDA Forest Service General Technical Report RM-68.

Kaplan, S. (1973). Cognitive maps in perception and thought. In R.M. Downs & D. Stea (Eds.), *Image and environment* (pp. 63–78). Chicago: Aldine.

Kaplan, S. (1977). Participation in the design process: A cognitive approach. In D. Stokols (Ed.) *Perspectives on environment and behavior: Theory, research and applications* (pp. 221–234). New York: Plenum.

Kaplan, S. (1978). Attention and fascination: The search for cognitive clarity. In S. Kaplan & R. Kaplan (Eds.) *Humanscape: Environments for people* (pp. 84–90). (Republished by Ann Arbor, Mich.: Ulrich's, 1982.)

Kaplan, S. (1983). A model of person-environment compatibility. *Environment and Behavior, 15,* 311–332.

Kaplan, S., & Kaplan, R. (1982). *Cognition and environment: Functioning in an uncertain world.* New York: Praeger. (Republished by Ann Arbor, Mich.: Ulrich's, 1989.)

Kaplan, S., & Kaplan, R. (1989). The visual environment: Public participation in design and planning. *Journal of Social Issues, 45,* 59–86.

Kaplan, S., Weaver, M., & French R. (1990). Active symbols and internal models: Towards a cognitive connectionism. *AI and Society, 4,* 51–71.

Kelly, G.A. (1963). *A theory of personality.* New York: Norton.

Kruglanski, A.W., & Ajzen, I. (1983). Bias and error in human judgment. *European Journal of Social Psychology, 13,* 1–44.

Kuttner, R. (1985, Feb.). The poverty of economics. *Atlantic Monthly,* 74–84.

Levenick, J.R. (1985). *Knowledge representation and intelligent systems: From semantic networks to cognitive maps.* Doctoral Dissertation, University of Michigan.

Lutz, M.A. (1987). The economic relevance of selflessness. *The Human Economy Newsletter, 8,* 4, 1–5.

Maslow, A.H., & Diaz-Guerrero, R. (1971). Adolescence and juvenile delinquency in two different cultures. In A.H. Maslow (Ed.), *The farther reaches of human nature.* New York: Viking.

Midgley, M. (1978). *Beast and man: The roots of human nature.* Ithaca, N.Y.: Cornell University Press.

Monroe, M.C., & Kaplan, S. (1988). When words speak louder than actions: Environmental problem solving in the classroom. *Journal of Environmental Education, 19,* 38–41.

Neisser, C. (1966). *Cognitive psychology.* New York: Appleton-Century-Crofts.

Nisbett, R., & Ross, L. (1980). *Human inference: Strategies and shortcomings of social judgment.* Englewood Cliffs, N.J.: Prentice-Hall.

O'Neill, M.J. (1989). *Computer simulation of cognitive mapping for the evaluation of architectural legibility.* Doctoral Dissertation, University of Wisconsin–Milwaukee.

Orleans, P. (1973). Differential cognition of urban residents: Effects of social scale on mapping. In R.M. Downs & D. Stea (Eds.), *Image and environment* (pp. 115–130). Chicago: Aldine.

Peirce, C.S. (1877). The fixation of belief. *Popular Science Monthly.* (Reprinted in J. Buchler, Ed., *Philosophical writings of Peirce.* New York: Dover.)

Posner, M.I. (1973). *Cognition: An introduction.* Glenview, Ill.: Scott, Foresman.

Rumelhart, J.L., McClelland, L., & the PDP Research Group (1986). *Parallel distributed processing: Explorations in the microstructure of cognition.* Cambridge, Mass.: MIT Press.

Schachter, S. (1959). *The psychology of affiliation.* Stanford: Stanford University Press.

Schweinhart, L.J., Weikart, D.P., & Larner, M.B. (1986). Consequences of three preschool curriculum models through age 15. *Early Childhood Research Quarterly, 1,* 15–45.

Segal, M.M. (1988). Neural network programs. [Review of *Explorations in parallel distributed processing.*] *Science, 241,* 1107–1108.

Seligmann, M.E.P. (1975). *Helplessness: On depression, development, and death.* San Francisco: Freeman.

Simon, H. (1957). *Models of man: Social and rational.* New York: Wiley.

Simon, H. (1970). Style in design. In J. Archea & C. Eastman (Eds.), *EDRA 2* (pp. 1–3). Stroudsburg, Penn.: Dowden, Hutchinson and Ross.

Tedeschi, J.T., Schlenker, B.R., & Bonoma, T.V. (1971). Cognitive dissonance: Private ratiocination or public spectacle? *American Psychologist, 26,* 685–695.

Wallach, M.A., & Wallach, L. (1983). *Psychology's sanction for selfishness.* San Francisco: Freeman.

Woodworth, R.S. (1947). Reinforcement of perception. *American Journal of Psychology, 60,* 119–124.

Woodworth, R.S. (1958). *Dynamics of behavior.* New York: Holt.

Waltz, D., & Feldman, J. (Eds.). (1988). *Connectionist models and their implications: Readings from cognitive science.* Norwood, N.J.: Ablex.

10

Understanding, Assessing, and Acting in Places: Is an Integrative Framework Possible?

DAVID CANTER

THREE SEPARATE HABITATS

The field of environmental psychology appears to maintain three rather different habitats, that have not so far been formed into a coherent ecology. One is the area from which this book drew its central inspiration. That is the study of environmental cognition. The processes by which people perceive and know their physical surroundings. As made clear and presented in some detail in Chapter 1, this research has its roots in two interrelated traditions: the "cognitive mapping" tradition that is usually traced to the work of Lynch (1960), and the "environmental meaning" tradition that grew out of the studies of Osgood, Suci, and Tannenbaum (1956), especially as they were developed by Berlyne (1971). In many ways the great significance of Kaplan and Kaplan's (1978) contribution, developed in Chapter 9, is the way Kaplan has integrated these two strands and thereby enriched our perspectives on environmental knowing.

At the heart of this domain is the cognitive psychology belief that knowledge of the world is integrally linked to the perception of it. Neisser (1976) has done most to elaborate this view and argue for epistemic perception as the starting point for understanding human transactions with the world. In providing this emphasis the laboratory-based, experimental tradition out of which it is derived is never completely forgotten. The transactions are with simple, concrete entities that exist outside the laboratory but could be readily simulated within it. This inheritance from an earlier generation of perceptual theorists is an important one, to which I shall return. I see it as the major reason why prospects for theoretical integration, even though they have been opened up by fruitful developments in cognitive theory, still escape us.

The second distinct habitat in environmental psychology has far weaker theoretical roots and a less well-established vocabulary. It used to be called "building appraisal" (Canter, 1966), it then became the more alliterative "environmental evaluation" (Zube, 1980), and now is drifting into "assessment." The origins of this domain are in the pragmatic requests of architects, planners, and environmental policy makers for information on how good their decisions have been. As a consequence, early research had to struggle to free itself from a framework drawn from public opinion surveys, in which environmental benefit is equated with percentage endorsement.

What has been notable is that the concepts and methods of the evaluation literature, until very recently, have had virtually no overlap with those of the environmental cognition literature. So although, for example, S. Kaplan emphasized the value of clarity in our environmental schemata as long ago as 1973, postoccupancy evaluations have studiously avoided asking questions about this. Reciprocally, although appraisals of environments have slowly moved toward reasonably precise descriptions of, say, comfort or satisfaction, these notions have been absent from the great majority of studies of environmental cognition.

One crucial anomaly serves to illustrate the power of the rift between environmental evaluations and studies of environmental cognition. This is the way in which environmental preference has been equated with aesthetics and both aesthetics and preference have been firmly placed in the cognitive corner of the field. Yet what people prefer or enjoy might reasonably have been expected to overlap with their evaluations. The research literature has generally not explored this possible overlap (although Küller in Chapter 7 has started to make some interesting steps in this direction). Yet, for example, in Nasar's recent book on *Environmental Aesthetics* (1988), even though he equates aesthetics with preference and quality, terms such as "annoyance," "comfort," and "satisfaction" are absent from his book and do not even appear in the index. The wide-ranging and intellectually stimulating papers in his book owe their allegiance almost entirely to the cognitive psychology tradition.

In other words, I would suggest that the rift between studies of evaluation and cognition is so great that even domains such as aesthetics, that might be expected to bridge them, must fall onto one side or the other. The habitat itself must become more coherent before hybrids can survive in a variety of niches. That is one of the reasons why this is so important. For the first time there is a conscious attempt to encompass environmental assessment and cognition.

If theoretical integration is to be achieved, however, it is essential to encompass a large enough domain to allow a viable intellectual ecology to evolve. The environmental psychology literature reveals a third distinct range of issues and theories that was absent from the conference agenda out of which this book emerged, yet must surely be relevant to environmental knowledge and evaluation. These are the studies of personal space, crowding, privacy, and territoriality. For many people these studies are the essence of environmental psychology, yet they are notably absent from studies of environmental cognition and assessment. Can they really be irrelevant?

Integration with Action

One important feature of the studies of personal space, crowding, and the like, sets them apart from studies of cognition and evaluation. They are firmly grounded in the behavioral tradition. The conduct of these studies focuses on what people do when they use environments. In this regard the early behavioral mapping studies of Proshansky and his colleagues (1970) are part of the same genre of studies as those of personal space. The concern of researchers who carry out these studies is to account for any patterns they find in the observations they make of spatial behavior.

The most behaviorally oriented of these studies are those of Barker and his colleagues (1968), carried out when they were developing their own brand of ecological psychology. Although later writers in this tradition, most notably Wicker (1987), have eschewed a purely behavioral focus, their emphasis is still on observable phenomena. The emphasis is on what people do, whether it be their attendance or participation.

Yet these behavioral studies of place use must surely tell us something of how well regarded a place is, or indeed of how it is known. But with an important exception the literature on personal space, territoriality, crowding, and ecological psychology tells us little of the structure of environmental cognition, or of the criteria for environmental evaluation. Likewise most searches of the environmental cognition and evaluation literature for indications of how people behave in their surroundings will prove fruitless.

One exception to this barren state is the seminal work of Altman (1979). By positing privacy as a central objective for spatial behavior Altman builds a slim but sturdy bridge between the concepts that people have about their environment and their behavior within it. Of more importance than the particular bridging concept that Altman uses, privacy, is the indication he gives us of how many other bridges may be built. He shows that by considering the personal objectives that shape both a person's cognitive framework and their behavior, we can understand the links between these two aspects of human experience.

In a more general sense, Altman illustrates the power of adjusting the focus from behavior to a focus on the system of purposes and aspirations of which that behavior is a part, in other words, a focus on environmental, goal-directed action (Canter, 1988). It is because the notion of action involves conscious direction that it embraces cognitive processes. Because it also embraces the possibility of the achievement of some goal it encapsulates an evaluative potential.

The direction indicated by the writings of Altman has resonance with the work of S. Kaplan to which reference has already been made. They have chosen to emphasise work at different environmental scales and in differing areas of concern, Altman leaning more toward smaller scale domestic environments and Kaplan toward the larger-scale natural landscape, but the seeds of theoretical integration lie in the ground they have in common. But before I can elaborate on this it is necessary to take a detour so that we can obtain a clearer view of the field we are studying.

AN ARISTOTELIAN TRIAD

There is a philosophical inevitability to identifying cognition, evaluation, and action as three distinct domains of environmental psychology. This classification is as old as Western philosophy. In so far as our ways of thinking about the world have been shaped by the early Greek philosophers, the distinctions made by Aristotle when considering the major aspects of human processes are the distinctions to which it is still natural to drift.

In his psychological work *De anima*, Aristotle identified two aspects to human psychology. One was essentially a process of discrimination. This concept of fundamental "dianoetic" processes in human actions is still accepted as being at the base of cognitive processes. So although later philosophers have done much to enhance our understanding of the active, structuring processes inherent in cognition, it is to Aristotle that we owe the recognition of the central role of cognitive processes as a distinct aspect of human functioning.

Aristotle contrasted the dianoetic aspects with orectic aspects. These are the desires and appetites that maintain the person within their context. Two functions can be distinguished within these desires. The one relates to the emotional constituents that underlie the making of choices. The second relates to movements and actions on the world. The orectic processes thus subsume the evaluations and actions that can be recognized as distinct areas of environmental research.

This highly simplified distillation of Aristotle's profundity is necessary to emphasize that it is philosophically essential to recognize that the three processes of cognition, evaluation, and action are part of one integrated system. In some senses, the development of Western psychology has been the exploration of how these processes do integrate. Environmental psychology is, at last, finding its way into the same debates.

In a tentative, hesitant way I made an attempt over 10 years ago to draw attention to the need for this integration (Canter, 1977). The essence of my argument there was that the heart of environmental psychology was the study of "places." These "places" were presented as integrations through our experience of an understanding of the physical form of given locations, together with an evaluation of them, in combination with the actions characteristic of them.

Although it was not as clear in 1977 as it is now, the plea for theories that would link these three constituents was a plea to develop our understanding in the environmental context of the links between cognition, actions, and the emotional essence of evaluations. The progress toward this goal requires us to absorb the implications of the purposive emphases in the arguments of Altman and of S. Kaplan, the latter emphasized in his chapter in the current volume.

PURPOSE AS INTEGRATOR

For Aristotle the distinguishing characteristic of life was movement. The very term *anima* indicated the moving force of the soul and from it we have absorbed such fundamental concepts as "animal" and "animate." This drive to action has been a recurring theme throughout philosophy, often revolving around the discussion of what is the ultimate objective for humankind in all this movement. In recent philosophical history it was probably Hegel who did most to represent this movement as an evolving process in which individual and social dynamics interplay to produce new levels of civilization. Marx took this idea further in arguing that it was the interplay of the individual with the material artifacts of society that shaped both the individual's consciousness and the nature of society.

This brief reference to major figures in the history of human thought is intended only to draw attention to the fact that there are central philosophical issues at the core of any attempt to integrate different strands of environmental psychology theory. Furthermore, although the epistemological questions around the distinction between psychology and environment are important, it seems to me that questions about what it means to interact with the environment hold a better prospect as a source for a coherent theory. This is because interaction involves notions of action and change. It is at least implicit in any discussion of environmental interactions or transactions that the processes being studied are moving toward or away from some preferred outcome. Indeed, in Chapter 8, Böök gives a form to many complex issues in spatial perception by focusing on navigation between places rather than being a static receiver of environmental stimuli. His arguments are therefore in direct descent from Aristotle.

This purposive theme has also been present in psychological theories since the writings of William James and William McDougall. But its incorporation into recent psychological theories probably received most impetus from George Kelly's (1955) Personal Construct Theory. Within Kelly's framework people are constantly "seeking to predict and control the course of events" with which they are involved. Flux and change are what characterizes people and their experiences. It is the attempts to deal with those dynamics that provides the motive force for human actions.

It is especially curious that it has taken environmental psychologists so long to look to human agency and personal purposes as an integrating focus for a theoretical account of person–environment transactions. After all, one of the primary reasons for the existence of the field is the requests made by those who shape our environments for guidance on how it may be most effectively modified. Planners, architects, policy makers, and all the other environmental decision makers are active agents shaping the physical surroundings in relation to implicit or explicit objectives. Why should such purposive agency be ignored in our considerations of the people who will use and experience those surroundings?

Taking human agency as a core for place experience provides a basis for integrating the three domains of environmental psychology because each of those domains is itself enriched directly be considering purposive aspects. For example, Ward, Snodgrass, Chew, and Russell (1988) have recently shown that environmental cognitions are shaped by the individual's plans. Such an approach has great potential for elaboration. In the same paper Ward and his colleagues point to similar processes for affective responses to places, thereby reflecting an earlier argument (Canter, 1983) that place evaluations are best understood in terms of the purposes those places may be seen to support.

The third aspect of our triad, actions in places, also has greater utility when its purposive components are elaborated. The very term "action," as opposed to "behavior," has served to give emphasis to human agency (Canter, 1986). Behavior can be observed of a person as an object, but to understand the actions that the behavior constitutes, the goals of the actions need to be addressed.

When the details of these purpose oriented aspects of place experience are considered, it becomes more obvious that each aspect depends on the others for its form and content. A systemic model of place experience evolves out of these details that has both pragmatic and theoretical implications. By drawing on the developments in environmental psychology theory over the past 10 years, the earlier three component metaphor of place (Canter, 1977) is converted into a working prototype, with the intention of helping to shape the new paradigm that is beginning to characterize environmental psychology.

RULES OF PLACE

As has been mentioned, any overview will reveal that besides studies of environmental cognition and assessments there is a large body of studies, probably the majority, that examines the use that people make of places. These studies focus on human behavior, looking at matters such as interpersonal distances, density, the distribution of people over space, and the social structuring of human activities. This rather disparate range of topics has been given some coherence by two separate theoretical streams: the work of Altman and of Barker.

Although there have been some important criticisms of Barker's (1968) ecological psychology perspective (notably by Kaminski, 1983), the central contribution of identifying units of social behavior that have a natural occurrence, behavior settings, cannot be overemphasized. This structuring of the social world of the individual into discrete units that have a finite existence in time and place, together with a recognizable set of actions and roles that maintain that setting, provides a powerful description of place-related actions.

Barker's original work was fundamentally descriptive, but more recently Wicker (1987) started to give some account of how settings emerge and are controlled. The processes by which behavior and settings shape each other are also being explored. Yet it is still the case that the actual physical use of space is rarely examined within the context of Barker's ecological psychology. Settings are defined in terms of their physical boundaries, but beyond that the considerations of behavioral ecology are firmly within the social and organizational framework.

By contrast Altman's (1975) social-systems approach examines the physical distribution of people in space. In doing this he linked together explorations of crowding, territoriality, and personal space by arguing that they all derive their significance from successful or unsuccessful attempts to produce an acceptable level of input in relation to output. This balance Altman saw as being the maintenance of appropriate levels of privacy.

By providing a focused objective for a variety of spatial behaviors Altman turned the coercive, setting-dominant, and fundamentally behavioral orientation of Barker into a more dynamic, psychologically richer model. It is the predilections that the individual brings to the social context that are the prime movers in the use of space according to Altman. Ten years later, in reviewing theoretical orientations for the handbook that he co-edited, Altman developed these seeds by giving special support to what he calls a "transactional" world view (Altman & Rogoff, 1987). This emphasizes holistic studies of change, in which the observer is seen as part of the phenomena under study, never as a separate "subject" or "respondent."

The transactional view still owes much to the social-systems perspective of Barker, but has lost some of the purposive strengths of Altman's model of privacy. By contrast Wicker's (1987) elaboration of Barker's framework, in the same handbook, now recognizes the significance of human cognitions in the creation and maintenance of settings. What is of especial interest is Wicker's statement that it is the programs of settings for which people have the strongest and richest mental representations.

It is this attention to programs that help to indicate what it is that is being studied in the many examinations of interpersonal distance, territoriality, crowding, and their associated matrix of social interactions. What is it that keeps people at various distances from each other or maintains the spatial distribution that is characteristic of particular behaviour settings? In other words, what purposes organize human spatial actions? I would like to suggest that it is the desire to make use of settings in ways appropriate to a given individual's goals that is the prime organizer.

The effective use of a setting implies that it has in Barker's terms a "program." In other words a set of expected roles, relationships between people, and rules for how those roles are acted out. Within this framework the studies of spatial behavior are studies of the socially formed, rules of place use. Certain distances are learned as being appropriate for certain types of activities in certain settings.

In other accounts these have been called "rules of place" (Canter, 1985) to draw attention to the ways in which human actions fit into the place in which they occur. The use of the term "rules" probably lacks the subtlety necessary to capture the mixture of percepts, customs, and habits associated with place use, and future research will undoubtedly need to elaborate this concept. Nonetheless, the idea of place rules serves to summarize the extent to which the study of spatial behavior has discovered forms and patterns of place use, and the extent to which these patterns are embedded in social and cultural processes.

By seeing the social processes as the dominant theme in this spatial composition it is possible to recognize that people are acting in places by relating to the rules of place use. These rules are followed, implicitly or explicitly, though, in order to act within (or against) the actions that are physically or socially possible in that place. Rules are feasible as a structuring device only because enough people aspire to play the game. Empirical studies have also shown that some of these "games" have remarkably consistent rules (Canter, 1985). Indeed, when the demands of a group task are consistent across cultures, as for instance in the requirements of a lecture, then the spatial rules are likely to be very similar in very different settings. However, when similar institutions, such as religious institutions, have very different expectations of their participants, then the associated place rules will be very different. Intriguingly, domestic patterns in the developed world may have higher-order place rules that transcend cultural differences (Canter, 1985).

The discovery of place rules may be seen in a number of very different types of studies. For example, from its earliest use, behavioral mapping (Ittelson, Rivlin, & Proshansky, 1976) has demonstrated that behavior is not randomly distributed across spaces. This is true even if those spaces are relatively undifferentiated and not bound by very strict precepts about their use. Different types of people or different activities tend to cluster in different areas of any space. From this the self-fulfilling cycle elaborated in Canter (1977) can be seen to emerge, giving rise to the observed patterns of place use.

The emergence of patterns of place use with their associated rules and interpersonal expectations provides a different perspective on a number of studies. For example, it raises many questions about the study of interpersonal distances and the cultural and contextual parameters that give those distances their meaning (Aiello

1987). The very interesting results reported by Küller (1988), based upon his study of rearranging the furniture in an old people's home dining room, can be given a very different interpretation if a place rule perspective is applied. Introducing different, more informal furniture may have created the opportunity for different types of interactions between staff and patients and for the emergence of different expectations and rules of place, so producing the dramatic changes in patient behavior. This perspective provides a social interpretation that compliments the essentially cognitive, complexity, and familiarity hypotheses that Küller presents.

One further example of the operation of place rules is important to mention because it also serves to illustrate how physical form and layout can be generated by these rules. Hillier and Hanson (1984) showed that a small number of spatial rules about the relationship between buildings and the opportunities for moving between them can be used to generate layouts that are very similar to those that are observed in vernacular housing. The examples they cite in Southern France appear virtually random and certainly have no formal plan to them, but nonetheless analysis reveals a clear structure. Of particular significance is that the spatial rules that generate these layouts quite clearly carry implications for the interactions between people.

In one set of examples described by Hillier and Hanson, for instance, all houses open straight onto a public pathway, implying direct social contact between households and the street. The pathway itself does not differentiate between areas of the hamlet, forming a ring with no obvious beginning and end and no especially large open spaces into which it moves. This implies no hierarchical arrangement of houses or of areas within the hamlet. These patterns are presented not as geometric artifacts but as the product of "the social logic of space," but unfortunately no details are given of what the social processes are that are revealed by these spatial patterns.

COGNITIVE ECOLOGY

The emphasis on rules of place, rather than simply patterns of space use, has the special value of providing a strong link to environmental cognition. Putting it at its most elementary level of analysis, rules of place use would not emerge and remain if there were not some shared understanding of their existence. This does not require that people are necessarily aware of the rules or can articulate them, but it does require that they can recognize appropriate environmental cues, relevant to the patterns of place-related behavior. In other words the behavioral patterns and the environmental cognitions are interdependent. One cannot occur without the other. Without appropriate environmental cognitions people would not participate in recognizable spatial patterns. Without those patterns people would not develop an environmentally appropriate behavioral repertoire.

Another way of expressing the environmental significance of place-relevant cognitions is to suggest that if place rules do generate the observed behavioral ecology, then there must at least implicitly be a "cognitive ecology" on which each person can draw. This cognitive system enshrines expectations about what does and may happen where and who is likely to carry out the actions in those places. In systems terms it is the cognitive ecology that grows and is shaped by the system of rules of place, which it also shapes (as summarized in Figure 10.1). This interaction may be

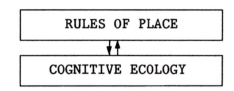

Figure 10.1. The interaction of place rules with a cognitive ecology.

understood more fully by considering the ways in which children develop an understanding of place use. Initially, through overt teaching and implicit observation they will learn that certain activities are restricted to certain settings. This will be part of a growing understanding of what types of physical requirements are appropriate for any particular events; an open space for a game of football, a hidden corner to do forbidden things, and so on.

In the area in which they live children quickly become aware of what opportunities are provided by different places to which they have access. In other words, they develop internal representations of their environment that include knowledge of physical forms as well as of the possibilities for action that those forms offer, a "cognitive ecology." There has been very little research on the components of these internal representations of places and how they develop, but there can be little doubt that by adulthood people have a rich understanding of what is possible where.

This understanding is an aspect of what Kelly (1955) called a personal construct system. As with all such construct systems, a person's sane survival in society is a function of how closely that construct system is supported by the actual activities in which a person takes part. A person who urinates on the pavement outside Buckingham Palace would be regarded as either antisocial or mentally disturbed. So the cognitive ecology does itself help to perpetuate the particular patterns of palace use from which it is derived. There will therefore always be a behavioral ecology to interact with the consensus of cognitive ecologies. In Indian villages, for example, urination in public streets is more generally apparent so the role of this activity in resident's internal representations will be rather different than for public places in Britain.

The hypothesis of two interacting systems raises some critical questions about the nature of the cognitive ecology. For instance, is it a primary system? Or is it a derived from the active interpretation of perceptual information? Can it be regarded conceptually as the aggregate of a number of individual, personal cognitive systems, or is it more appropriate to think of it as existing within a social group? Questions of the development of the cognitive ecology also become very important not least because the individual experiences very different places during development and has varying degrees of access as a direct function of maturation.

The notion of a cognitive ecology, though, does enable us to reconsider much of the environmental cognition literature. We can examine the almost 30 years of research to see what form cognitive ecologies might take. In other words, studies of "mental maps" and studies of "meaning" are worth reexamining for what they tell us about the cognitive processes that generate the spatial modeling of place rules and their implications.

The study of mental maps is usually traced to Lynch's (1960) small scale studies of Boston, Los Angeles, and Jersey City, but as reviewed, for example, by Canter

(1977), empirical considerations of the internal representations people have of their environments can be traced back to the turn of the century when scientific studies of the mind and its processes were beginning to gain momentum. As long ago as 1913 Trowbridge wrote about "Imaginary Maps" and discussed the way in which "artificial training" leads to the use of different cues for environmental orientation than those that are naturally available to "all living creatures, other than civilised man."

The critical point, though, in relation to the argument here, is that from the earliest discussions of these internal representations, attention was paid to evolutionary survival value. S. Kaplan (1973), for instance, argued that the ability to develop cognitive maps has a direct evolutionary advantage to a highly mobile animal, such as *Homo sapiens*. In other words, these mental representations have always been discussed in terms of their functional significance to the individual or the group. Furthermore, mismatches (usually referred to as errors) between accounts of a person's representation of the environment and a professional, geographic representation, have been considered quite consistently as a function of the activities and experiences of the individual, not as some distortion in perceptual processes. In his excellent review of this literature, Golledge (1987) draws attention to the simple fact that familiarity is the best predictor of "accuracy" in environmental cognition.

So although most of the studies of environmental cognition have focused on the accuracy of mental representations, the underlying theme has been the contribution that these representations make to the achievement of individual goals and objectives. Indeed, in Chapter 9 S. Kaplan argues that the very search for clarity of representation is natural to human beings. This link to purposes and the functional utility of perceptions and cognitions has the best of pedigrees in Gibson's (1979) account of "affordances." In his framework perceptions involve a virtually direct recognition of what human actions they make possible. A few environmentally oriented studies have explored the possible development of this conceptualisation (Evans, Brennan, Skorpanich, & Held, 1984; Sixsmith, Sixsmith, & Canter, 1988), but at present it serves best as an emphasis on the purposive significance of environmental cognitions.

Golledge (Chapter 3) has contributed further to our understanding of the purposive components of environmental cognition by emphasizing the value of drawing on the vocabulary and methods of artificial intelligence. In particular he points to the distinction between procedural and declarative knowledge. Procedural knowledge embraces those aspects of knowledge that enable us to modify our interactions with the world. This type of knowledge emphasizes the rules that can be used to produce intended changes of state.

Much of spatial knowledge, then, may be seen as ways of summarizing production rules. In essence this sees much of the map-like component of environmental cognition as a summary of the possibilities for route finding, planning, traveling, or more generally acting on the world. Referring back to rules of place, procedural knowledge may be seen as knowledge of the physical and temporal processes whereby the experience of one set of rule systems may be transferred to another.

Declarative environmental knowledge encapsulates that aspect of place experience that informs us of what a place is. Since Osgood et al.'s (1957) early use of bipolar adjectival scales to describe colors it has been accepted that knowledge of what something is also covers knowledge of what it is and is not like. This associative network, as many would now call it, has been summarized as the "meaning" of a place. Environmental meaning has grown as a self-contained subarea of environmental psychology, but its place within environmental cognition is difficult to challenge.

What is fascinating to explore is whether, just as procedural knowledge may be knowledge about acting on the world, declarative knowledge may be knowledge about being in the world. In other words, this is knowledge about the personal significance of places, about their relevance to us, and their consequences for our actions. Recent publications have shown the strength of this perspective. For example, Ward et al. (1988) demonstrated that the plans a person has for using a place modify the conceptualization of that place.

These conceptualizations relate places to the person. The meanings that a person sees in a place are declarative in the sense that they inform the person of who might be expected in that place, what the experience of that place might be. These are Osgood's connotative dimensions, elaborated by Russell and Lanius (1984), but are always implicitly about the significance of the environment to the person. Even the much vaunted measure of complexity that Berlyne (1971) introduced may be regarded in this light as an index of the extent to which the images being examined carry some identifiable meaning to the observer.

All of current cognitive psychology, then, accepts that meaning is an integral part of perception. Nothing can be seen without some significance being assigned to it. Indeed the paradox that must be resolved in the training of painters derives from the need to try and unlearn this natural way of seeing, even though their art depends on their ability to recapture the meanings of what they see.

If places have meanings and these derive from their significance to people, then the exploration of place identity is a natural part of environmental cognition. Proshansky, Fabian, and Kaminoft's (1983) examination of the place identity concept drew attention to its importance, but the question of what aspects of physical forms contribute to the establishment and maintenance of place identity remain unanswered.

This question of the interrelationship between the physical forms and the meanings they carry for people has remained problematic throughout the 20 years or so that environmental psychologists have been studying environmental meaning. However, the location of meaning within the active, goal directedness of the individual serves to illustrate why general, all pervasive rule systems that are virtually context free are unlikely to be established, except at a very superficial level. The link between meaning seen as declarative rules and meaning seen as procedural rules also indicates that these two rules systems are likely to interact. Knowledge of where something is (or how to get there) is likely to influence knowledge of what it is and vice versa. As there has already been cause to mention, there has been little research into the relationship between these two aspects of environmental meaning.

It should perhaps not be surprising that the two aspects of environmental knowing are treated so differently. If future research could provide further understanding of the links between the declarative and procedural aspects of environmental cognition it would also open the way to understanding how these two aspects of internal representations of the physical surroundings connect with the patterns of physical space use and the rules of place which govern those patterns. This is an ambitious but important task.

PURPOSIVE EVALUATION

It has been argued that the interplay between rules of place and the cognitive ecology (in its declarative and procedural forms) is motivated by human agency. Indeed, the basis of the interplay is that to follow place rules, knowledge of the cognitive ecology is essential and the cognitions themselves summarize the rules that are expected to apply and their likely consequence for the rule follower. However, this must be an evolving process as has been discussed in detail elsewhere (Canter, 1988). The evolution will arise, in part, out of the assessment individuals and groups make of the fit between their knowledge of the rule systems in operation and their understanding of what is possible, appropriate, and desirable in a given place. This process of assessment with some purposive implications has an implicit assumption central to it. Action and purpose imply at least the possibility of a goal or objective to which the action is directed. In those situations in which such objectives can be derived the fit between the knowledge and the actions can be assessed.

It is proposed that this is at the heart of any environmental evaluation. The evaluation is an assessment of the extent to which the rules and the cognitions are congruent. This has been called purposive evaluation (Canter, 1983) to indicate that a place evaluation makes sense only when viewed in relation to the purposes for which the place is being evaluated. A lecture theater will be evaluated very differently when being considered as a place to lecture compared with being considered for a party.

The way in which evaluation is a product of the interplay between rules of place and the cognitive ecology is represented in Figure 10.2. The diagram deliberately puts evaluation at a higher position in the hierarchy of relationships then the two other processes because it would seem that evaluation requires their existence before it has any real meaning of its own.

Empirical evidence for the links between meaning and assessment is, of course, present in the earliest semantic differential studies of meaning. The principal component in these studies is invariably one of evaluation or preference. Yet the artificial derivation of orthogonal dimensions is based on the assumption that the other factors are independent of evaluation. But evaluation must be a central aspect of the pattern of meanings, not something totally separate and distinct. Indeed, in one account of his work Osgood (Snider & Osgood, 1969) admits to the difficulty in some domains of distinguishing between denotation and connotation. He complains of "denotative contamination," whereby certain descriptions carry meanings beyond the mere physical presence of the object. But, as has been indicated, for places at least, although

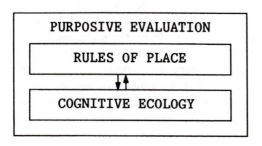

Figure 10.2. The relationship of evaluations to place rules and cognitive ecology.

probably in other domains too, the system of meanings that are associated with the physical artifacts is what is being studied, it is not a "contamination" but an "essence."

Although Osgood made this statement many years ago, there is still the habit within environmental research to act as if it holds. This consists of considering the ratings of buildings, or landscapes, as if this were an exercise very different from evaluating them. Indeed, in an amusing and challenging article some years ago, Heath (1974) pointed out that most studies of evaluation were really studies in the tradition of empirical aesthetics, dealing with evaluative meaning.

ENVIRONMENTAL ROLES

It seems possible that one reason why evaluation has been separated from studies of environmental cognitions has been the power of the laboratory model of research. In this model the respondent is seen as a context-free subject of experimental manipulation. The reasons or purposes the person has for taking part in the study, or the particular orientation they bring to bear on the task they are given, is considered irrelevant. As a consequence the whole framework of purposes, goals, and intentions is removed from laboratory exploration.

The subjects of the many environmental experiments in which they are shown slides and asked to rate them are actually responding in a purposeless limbo. Their task is fundamentally ambiguous. It would not be surprising, therefore, if they tackled it by regarding the task they are set as a problem-solving one in which they try to guess the characteristics for which they should be looking and therefore draw on readily available stereotypes. In effect, they are likely to take on the role of the distant art critic searching out the picturesque.

Studies carried out by Leff, Gordon, and Ferguson (1974) served to illustrate the way in which responses to slides could be modified notably by changing the perspective of the rater to the task of rating. What their instructions did was to change the purpose for looking at the slides. In other words they used instructions to change the role respondents played as subjects. This study, then, like the study of Wards et al. (1988) on the impact of plans on environmental cognitions, helps to show how different orientations to places may be reflected in different cognitions.

The cognitive and social traditions in psychology have both ignored variations between people. The physiological roots of the study of cognitions have led to an emphasis on those processes that are seen as being common to all people with similar nervous systems. On the other hand, the ecological psychology framework of Barker (1968) has seen the group processes as so coercive that variations outside of those processes have been ignored. Yet, many studies of place use and understanding, as well as of place evaluation, reveal differences between people. The aggregation of data and the calculations of measures of central tendency and variation would be unnecessary if everyone were identical. To dismiss these variations as random noise is to undervalue the commitment that people bring to their participation in our research.

Yet the purposive model of action and place does enable quite clear hypotheses to be derived about the differences between people in their dealings with the physical surroundings. The argument is that people differ in their reasons for being in places

(Canter, 1977). Therefore they have different purposes and goals in those places. It follows that their patterns of action and their associated cognitions in those places will be different. Taken together, then, it is being proposed that the experiences that relate a person to a place, that give that person a reason for being in that place, are the key distinguishing features that lead to individual differences in regard to place experience.

Most of these purposes and goal-directed actions derive from the social organization of which a person is a part and, for this reason, as a shorthand, I have suggested "environmental role" as a description of these aspects of individual variation. Further, these role differences would be hypothesized to be most pronounced in relation to the evaluation of places. For it is in evaluation that the difference between people in their objectives may be most strongly revealed. The diagram of the system being evolved here therefore places the other aspects within the environmental role framework (Figure 10.3).

There is certainly considerably evidence for the power of these role variations (Canter, 1986). But it is clear that simple organizational designation may not be the best predictor of matters of environmental significance (Canter, 1988). It is also interesting to note that there may be differences in the conceptualizations of different role groups, such as husbands and wives, without any overall differences in their average ratings (Canter & Rees, 1982). A further point worth elaboration in future research is the extent to which role differences are best considered in terms of the person's own self-identification of the role they play rather than some external, organizational definition.

Some role differences, of course, are likely to be of more significance than others. The most interesting distinction to be explored at present is that between the inhabitants of a place and the people who create that place: designers and users. The model being proposed here would predict that because their purposes in relation to a place are so different, their experiences and evaluations of that place will also be very different. This does, of course, pose important problems for matters such as design participation.

PHYSICAL FORMS

The discussion of the cognitions, actions, and evaluations that constitute the experience of places inevitably takes the emphasis away from physical aspects of places

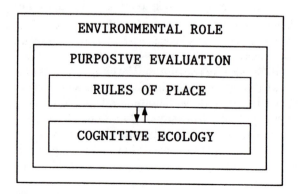

Figure 10.3.   The placement of evaluations in the framework of environmental roles.

and looks toward personal and social processes. Yet one intention has been to clarify the picture of place experience well enough to allow the role of the physical environment to be more specifically identified.

It is certainly clear that whatever the perceptual processes that distort the human experience of the environment, the significance of the physical attributes of place is a complex product of their context within a social–psychological matrix. Two separate aspects of the physical context are indicated by the model here. These relate, on the one hand, to those aspects of places that represent and reflect the people (and their activities) who experience those places. On the other hand, they draw on the relationships between places that provide the framework within which the social rule systems operate.

The first set of relationships can be seen as rooted in the declarative knowledge that people can draw from their transactions with places. This is knowledge about the people and actions that are either housed within or associated with places. This might be expected to include such ideas as knowledge of how a place was created, as reflected in its use of materials or other details of it, or knowledge of the way relationships between places imply relationships between people. Within this framework the size and shape of places take on a significance that derives from their implications within the social matrix. An old school hall, as a place to sleep, will have different consequences, depending on whether people are forced to sleep there because their home is flooded, or whether they have converted it into a bijou residence. Research needs to unpack these associations and the ways they are modified by the actions and aspirations of those who hold them.

The second set of physical implications derives from the procedural relationships between spaces and the associations they carry for the rule systems of place use. To tackle this approach to physical form we need to develop a more elaborate understanding of the rule systems that structure place use. Such research would explore the various types of rules that exist and how rules relate to each other, forming the matrix of expectations and limitations that underlies any social network. Undoubtedly, there will be parallels in the network of interpenetration of spaces to the matrix of rules. But these parallels will become apparent only once we can incorporate the social and personal objectives, from which those places derive their meaning, into our models of design.

The physical shape and form of the environment, then, do not have direct significance for cognition, action, and evaluation. Its significance comes from the ways in which it enshrines procedural and declarative knowledge about the people and actions that the place can or may encompass. As S. Kaplan argues in Chapter 9, we may often perceive a clarity in our environment that is not actually supported by the detailed evidence. Environmental psychology, in general, may have fallen into this same illusion by searching for distinct, clear links between environment and behavior. The literature of the past 20 years has shown how difficult it is to establish such relationships. The *Handbook of Environmental Psychology* (Stokols & Altman, 1987) gives only meager indication of any substantive, specific role for identifiable environmental variables in human experience, within the range determined by human physiological responses.

Figure 10.4, therefore, shows physical forms as orthogonal to the processes of place experience that have been considered in this chapter, metaphorically on a different plane. Conceptually, a multidimensional structure is being proposed. There are

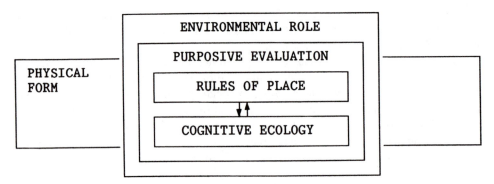

Figure 10.4.   The orthogonal relationship of physical form to the process of place experience.

perspectives from which physical forms can be seen to be psychologically significant, but this significance is derived from the social processes with which they interact. Such a proposal is at variance with the perspectives revealed in the chapters by Böök, S. Kaplan, and Küller. They argue for the fundamental primacy of environmental perception, although it is shaped by cognitive processes. I am arguing for the primacy of the human being as a social creature that learns to see the world through social processes. These two perspectives are probably complimentary rather than competitive, but they are weak and distorted reflections of major philosophical debates over the centuries, between Aristotle and Plato, between Locke and Kant, between Russell and Sartre. It is unlikely that we will resolve them in one generation of environmental psychology.

SUMMARY AND CONCLUSIONS

It is virtually 30 years since Lynch's (1960) *Image of the City* was published and rather longer since Osgood et al. (1957) introduced the semantic differential into psychology. It is salutary to reflect that after all this time environmental researchers are still using sketch maps and bipolar adjectival scales as dominant research methodologies. Indeed, over the short history of the field, as revealed throughout this book, environmental psychologists have tended to use those limited range of methodologies that first emerged in the early days of its development from the main stream of psychology. So although computers have made these procedures quicker and more sophisticated, structured questionnaires and simple performance tasks such as map drawing and distance estimation still dominate with a smattering of rather atomistic observational studies. Biologists, economists, sociologists, and anthropologists, for example, all have a scientific interest in understanding, assessing, and acting on environments and a much wider range of methodologies than considered in the present volume.

By contrast to the methodological conservatism of the environmental psychology, the evolution of theoretical models has been very rapid over recent years, especially with the self-conscious attempt to integrate various themes in environmental research.

An important landmark in the development of an integrative perspective was Altman's (1975) arguments that many aspects of spatial behavior interconnected in the search for appropriate levels of privacy. A second and very distinct contribution, developed in Chapter 9 of the present volume, was the work of S. Kaplan and R. Kaplan, published in book form in 1982. For the Kaplans the emphasis is on the central objectives of the cognitive processes that enable us to make appropriate spatial decisions. They argue for appropriate levels of clarity, and as S. Kaplan emphasizes in Chapter 9, the judgment of appropriateness should not be assumed to be a linear, rational process.

What both Altman and Kaplan have in common is the recognition that it is human action on the world that shapes human understanding; the action is aimed at the creation of appropriate levels of privacy in Altman's case and the search for clarity in a confusing world in Kaplan's case. In the present chapter, these purposive, active characteristics have been taken as the start for sketching out the directions in which a model may be found that integrates environmental cognition, evaluation, and action. In providing this sketch, emphasis has been given to the need to consider and model human use of space, because it is this aspect of place experience, revealed directly in behavior, yet only obliquely considered in other chapters of this book, that provides a key to unraveling the significance of cognitions and evaluations.

By directing attention to purposive behavior, action on and in the world, it has been argued that environmental cognitions contain declarative information of who does what in which places, and procedural information about the temporal, spatial, and social relationships that exist between places. This interplay between cognitions and actions has been summarized as transactions between a cognitive ecology and place rules, evaluations emerging as an assessment of the effectiveness of this interplay in any specific place.

The purposive orientation, though, leads back to the question of what the objectives of such an assessment are. It is proposed that the answer to that question lies in the social matrix of which a person is a part. The person's "role" provides the framework for understanding their environmental evaluations. A fundamental question emerges from this hypothesis. Which is primary in environmental cognition, the role-related purposes and rules or the direct experience of acting on the world? A systemic model would suggest that both are primary at different points in time.

The implications of the attempt at an integrative model, as outlined in the present chapter, go beyond psychology. They suggest that anthropology and indeed archaeology, as well as other social sciences and design disciplines will have something to teach us about human environmental understanding and assessment, but until psychologists can talk to each other in a systematic way about these issues it is unlikely that we can have really fruitful and intelligent dialogue with those from neighboring disciplines.

REFERENCES

Aiello, J. (1987). Human spatial behavior. In D. Stokols & I. Altman (Eds.), *Handbook of environmental psychology* (Vol. 1, pp. 385–504). New York: Wiley.

Altman, I. (1975). *The environment and social behaviour: Privacy, personal space, territory, and crowding*. Monterey, Calif.: Brooks Cole.

Altman, I. (1979). Privacy as an interpersonal boundary process. In M. von Cranach, K. Foppa, W. Lepenies, & D. Ploog, (Eds), *Human ethology: Claims and limits of a new discipline* (pp. 95–132) London: Cambridge University Press.

Altman, I., & Rogoff, B. (1987). World views in psychology: Trait, interaction, organismic, and transactional perspectives. In D. Stokols & I. Altman (Eds.), *Handbook of environmental psychology* (Vol. 1, pp. 7–40). New York: Wiley.

Barker, R.G. (1968). *Ecological psychology: Concepts and methods for studying the environment of human behavior*. Stanford: Stanford University.

Berlyne, D.E. (1971) *Aesthetics and psychobiology*. New York: Appleton-Century-Crofts.

Canter, D.V. (1966). On appraising building appraisals. *Architects' Journal*, 21 December, 881–888.

Canter, D.V. (1977). *The psychology of place*. London: Architectural Press.

Canter, D. (1983). The purposive evaluation of places: A facet approach. *Environment and Behaviour*, *15*, 659–698.

Canter, D.V. (1985). Intention, meaning and structure: Social action in its physical context. In M. Von Cranach, G.P. Ginsburg, & M. Brenner (Eds.), *Discovery strategies in the psychology of action* (pp. 171–186). London: Academic Press.

Canter, D.V. (1986). Putting situations in their place. In A. Furnham (Ed.), *Social behaviour in context* (pp. 208–239). Boston: Allyn and Bacon.

Canter, D. (1988). Action and place: An existential dialectic. In D. Canter, M. Krampen, & D. Stea (Eds.), *Environmental perspectives* (pp. 1–17). Aldershot: Avebury.

Canter, D., & Rees, K. (1982) A multivariate model of housing satisfaction. *International Review of Applied Psychology*, *31*, 185–208.

Evans, G.W., Brennan, P., Skorpanich, M.A., & Held, D. (1984). Cognitive mapping and elderly adults: Verbal and location memory for urban landmarks. *Journal of Gerontology*, *39*, 452–457.

Gibson, J.J. (1979). *An ecological approach to visual perception*. Boston: Houghton Mifflin.

Golledge, R.G. (1987). Environmental cognition. In D. Stokols & I. Altman (Eds.), *Handbook of environmental psychology* (Vol. 1, pp. 131–174). New York: Wiley.

Heath, T. (1974). Should we tell the children about aesthetics, or should we let them find out in the street? In D. Canter & T. Lee (Eds.), *Psychology in the built environment* (pp. 179–183). London: Architectural Press.

Hillier, B., & Hanson, J. (1984). *The social logic of space*. Cambridge, England: Cambridge University Press.

Ittelson, W.H., Rivlin, L.G., & Proshansky, H.M. (1976). The use of behavioral maps in environmental psychology. In H.M. Proshansky, W.H. Ittelson, & L.G. Rivlin (Eds.), *Environmental psychology: Man and his physical setting* (pp. 340–350). New York: Holt, Rinehart & Winston.

Kaminski, G. (1983). Enigma of ecological psychology. *Journal of Environmental Psychology*, *3*, 85–94.

Kaplan, S. (1973). Cognitive maps in perception and thought. In R.M. Downs & D. Stea (Eds.), *Image and environment* (pp. 63–78). Chicago, Ill.: Aldine.

Kaplan, S., & Kaplan, R. (1978). *Humanscape: Environments for people.* North Scituate, Mass.: Duxbury.

Kaplan, S., & Kaplan, R. (1982). *Cognition and environment: Functioning in an uncertain world.* New York: Praeger.

Kelly, G.A. (1955). *The psychology of personal constructs.* New York: Norton.

Küller, R. (1988). Housing for the elderly in Sweden. In D. Canter, M. Krampen, & D. Stea (Eds.), *Environmental policy, assessment and communication* (pp. 199–224). Aldershot: Avebury.

Leff, H.S., & Gordon, L.R., & Ferguson, J.G. (1974). Cognitive set and environmental awareness. *Environment and Behavior, 6*(4), 395–447.

Lynch, K. (1960) *The image of the city.* Cambridge, Mass.: MIT Press.

Nasar, J.L. (1988). *Environmental aesthetics: Theory, research and applications.* New York: Cambridge University Press.

Neisser, U. (1976). *Cognition and reality.* San Francisco: Freeman.

Osgood, C.E., Suci, G.J., & Tannenbaum, P.H. (1957). *The measurement of meaning.* Chicago: University of Chicago Press.

Proshansky, H.M., Ittleson, W.H., & Rivlin, L.G. (eds.) (1970). *Environmental psychology: People and their physical settings.* New York: Holt, Rinehart & Winston.

Proshansky, H.M., Fabian, A.K., & Kaminoff, R. (1983). Place-identity: Physical world socialisation of the self. *Journal of Environmental Psychology, 3*(1), 57–83.

Russell, J.A., & Lanius, U.F. (1984). Adaptation level and the affective appraisal of environments. *Journal of Environmental Psychology, 4*(2), 119–136.

Sixsmith, A., Sixsmith, J., & Canter, D. (1988). When is a door not a door? A study of evacuation route identification in a large shopping mall. In J.D. Sime (Ed.), *Safety in the built environment* (pp. 62–74). London: E. & F.N. Spon.

Snider, J.G., & Osgood, C.E. (Eds.). (1969). *Semantic differential technique: A source book.* Chicago: Aldive.

Stokols, D., & Altman, I. (1987). *Handbook of environmental psychology.* New York: Wiley.

Ward, L.M., Snodgrass, J., Chew, B., & Russell, J.A. (1988). The role of plans in cognitive and affective response to places. *Journal of Environmental Psychology, 8*, 1–8.

Wicker, A. (1987). Behavior settings reconsidered: Temporal stages, resources, internal dynamics, context. In D. Stokols and I. Altman (Eds.), *Handbook of environmental psychology,* (Vol. 1, pp. 613–654).

Trowbridge, C.C. (1913). On fundamental methods of orientation and imaginary maps. *Science, 38*, 888–897.

Zube, E.H. (1980). *Environmental evaluation: Perception and public policy.* Monterey, Calif.: Brooks/Cole.

11

Conceptualization and Application: Psychological Processes in Environmental Cognition and Assessment

GERALD D. WEISMAN

Effective research application has always been an important but illusive goal in environment–behavior research. However, the fact that we have not been entirely successful in realizing this goal should not be a source of particular surprise or dismay. Problems of effective research utilization are not at all unique to environment–behavior studies; they are common across disciplines and professions that endeavor to link knowledge and action (Weisman, 1983). Such difficulties are a reflection of fundamentally different ideas of what constitutes effective research application.

Assessment of the applicability of the models of psychological processes presented by Böök, Küller, and S. Kaplan (this volume), therefore, is not a simple or entirely straightforward task. It is necessary to first consider the quite different yet useful ways in which application has been defined. After this discussion of application, each of the models in this section will be briefly reviewed, and some conclusions drawn regarding their applicability to environmental planning and design. Throughout this chapter, particular emphasis is placed on the need to confront the physical environment in theoretically meaningful terms and the ways in which this can advance our ability to link environmental knowledge and action.

CONCEPTS OF APPLICATION

Application may be viewed in many different ways. For some practitioners, research utilization is defined in terms of "instrumental application" (Weiss, 1980). This straightforward view focuses on "the direct application of a research finding in a project, program, policy or administrative decision" (Seidel, 1985, p. 50). Such instrumental application, however, is not the only nor necessarily the most significant avenue for research application. Almost 30 years ago, in a particularly thoughtful article, policy analyst Max Millikan explored the relationship of knowledge and action. Decision makers, Millikan suggested, "commit their elementary error in an inductive fallacy—the assumption that the solution of any problem will be advanced by the simple collection of fact." "This is easiest to observe," Millikan noted, "in government circles, where research is considered as identical with 'intelligence' " (1959, p. 163).

Following Millikan, it may be suggested that another goal of research application—in addition to, or perhaps instead of, trying to provide answers—should be "to deepen, broaden and extend the policy maker's capacity for judgements. . . . the payoff (for the decision maker) will usually be . . . in the argument rather than in the conclusions" (p. 167). Criteria for effective research application may be extended to include guidance in and tools for the decision-making process as well as assistance in the formulation of problems in new ways in which decision makers may be more responsive (cf. Kantrowitz, 1985).

Thus, we may define three interim landmarks along the path from knowledge to action (Table 11.1), and three possible criteria for assessment of environmental design applicability: (1) contributions to new and more integrative ways of thinking about environment–action relationships; (2) contributions to the process of environmental design decision making; and, finally, (3) contributions to instrumental application. Note that these three criteria are not discrete; new ways of conceptualizing a problem area should lead to new processes for design and research decision making, resulting in data relevant to specific problems. The following review of each of the three models under consideration will briefly touch on these criteria; the concluding section of the chapter will develop such concepts in greater detail.

POINT OF ORIGIN: AFFECT, KNOWLEDGE, AND ACTION

The chapters by Küller, Böök, and S. Kaplan clearly reflect their respective locations within the overall organizing scheme for this book (i.e., environmental assessment, cognition, and action). But each chapter also does something more; each conceptualization extends its respective paradigm in interesting and potentially fruitful directions. The following review of each model highlights these extensions.

Küller's Neuropsychological Model of Human–Environment Interaction

Küller presents a broad framework, and moves beyond what is typically included within the assessment paradigm. Consistent with the paradigm, there is discussion of

Table 11.1   Three Forms of Application in Moving from Knowledge to Action

Knowledge of psychological processes	Application	Environmental planning, programming, and design
↓	↓	↓
Problem formulation	Guidance in design decision making	Direct research utilization

individual differences—referred to as reaction tendencies—and consideration of systems such as introversion/extroversion, sharpeners/levelers, and arousal seeking that relate the personality of the individual to tendencies in environmental response. Also in keeping with the paradigm, he reviews various perceptual qualities of the built environment—pleasantness, complexity, enclosedness, potency, social status, affection, and originality—which have provided the basis for many studies. However, Küller's neuropsychological model also extends environmental assessment work in significant ways, specifically with respect to issues of physiological arousal, stress, coping, and control.

> The basic emotional process implies that every impulse . . . causes a brief temporary arousal reaction . . . Depending on the nature of the impulse it may also give rise to an orientation reaction accompanied by a feeling of pleasantness or unpleasantness . . . This change in the emotional state of the organism results in a growing preparedness to react to the upcoming situation. Once control is established, the basic emotional process may be said to be concluded. (Küller, this volume, p. 123)

Thus cognition, assessment, and action may be seen as embedded within the "basic emotional process" as Küller presents it.

Böök's Spatiotemporal Events of Environmental Cognition

Böök reviews many issues that have been central to the study of environmental cognition. However, in the process of considering six hypothetical "events of spatial cognition," he reaches a number of significant conclusions that raise fundamental questions regarding conventional wisdom in environmental cognition research.

Böök emphasizes that "route learning, route following, and wayfinding occur under the pressures of resource limitations." As a consequence of these functional pressures, "travelers are busy with a lot of processing, unrelated to spatial cognition, much of which may be more important" (Böök, this volume). This concern with conflicting information processing demands leads him to consider the kinds of environmental information travelers attend to, and the kinds of spatial judgments they make. Böök suggests that travelers do not employ "point" locations of the kind typically employed in experimental distance and direction estimation tasks; rather, they make judgments with respect to larger-scale locations, which in turn are composed of a subset of judgments of point type locations. This reconsideration of the assumption of point-target judgments may provide a potential explanation for the large errors typically observed in distance and direction estimation: While acknowledging the measurement advantages of the point-based approach in cognition research, Böök emphasizes that "the concepts of target information and target location should be regarded as theoretical constructs, the significant spatial properties of which have to be discovered" (Böök, this volume, pp. 160–161). Indeed, Böök's chapter extends the cognition paradigm precisely through such efforts to understand the "significant spatial properties" of the physical environment.

Kaplan's Adaptive, Knowledge-Oriented Approach to Decision Making

The traditional rationality paradigm for decision making holds that alternatives are selected on the basis of value and probability, with people endeavoring to *maximize* value received. However, building on what has been learned about cognitive structure in the study of wayfinding and environmental cognition more generally, Kaplan proposes a rather different model. He suggests that, as a consequence of functional demands and limited information, "people often *satisfice* rather than maximize . . . they often hold out for what is good enough rather than holding out for the best (Kaplan, this volume, p. 173).

At the same time, people have a strong need for what Kaplan characterizes as "cognitive clarity . . . the clear state of mind that accompanies comprehension and that is acutely lacking during states of confusion" (Kaplan, this volume, p. 176). Attention is thus directed to the mechanisms, both cognitive and behavioral, by which such cognitive clarity is achieved. The acquisition of knowledge of the environment, through the formation of an internal representation comprised of nodes and the paths that connect them, emerges as the primary cognitive mechanism. This cognitive structure is then extended to the realms of affect and decision making.

> People both prefer and benefit from making decision that put them in domains where they can use what they know, where their hard won cognitive structure can make a difference. Correspondingly they dislike and tend to avoid situations where they feel they have insufficient information to guide their behavior. (Kaplan, this volume, p. 177)

LINKING AFFECT, KNOWLEDGE, AND ACTION IN THE ENVIRONMENT

Problem Formulation

Having briefly reviewed each of the three models under consideration, it is now possible to move on to an assessment of conceptual application. Does each of these three chapters contribute to new ways of thinking about the processes that mediate between the environment and human action? The initial answer to this question of conceptual application would seem to be a qualified "yes." Each chapter can usefully contribute to the formulation of a richer, more complex, more physical, albeit less precise conceptualization of the nature of environmental knowledge.

The Less Than Precise Nature of Environmental Knowledge. Strategies for the attainment of cognitive clarity, as developed by Kaplan, together with Böök's conclusions regarding the kind of rough approximation and estimation employed in orientation and wayfinding, suggest a new and quite different formulation of environmental knowledge. The expectations we hold of what environmental knowledge "should" be—reflected in the tasks, such as distance and direction estimation, with which participants in experiments are typically presented—tend to be based on high levels of both abstraction and precision. We assume that competence and performance should be equivalent. By way of example, Gärling and Golledge (1989), after reviewing empirical research on content and properties of cognitive maps, conclude:

> All this seems to suggest that people have the competence to represent distance and direction in ways they are represented in cartographic maps, but that many factors may cause performance to be *suboptimal* [emphasis added] in actual environments. (p. 210)

Perhaps in a world of less than perfect information, with pressures on information processing capacities, some form of "satisficing" in knowledge acquisition and representation may be, if not optimal, then certainly adaptive. Indeed, Böök suggests that travelers may take advantage of accuracy differences in their knowledge in order to correct single judgments of point locations.

The More Physical Nature of Environmental Knowledge. Böök, drawing on Gibson's theoretical framework, emphasizes the need to confront and engage in systematic analysis of the structure of the physical environment. Indeed, there have been a number of recent examples in the environment–behavior literature of just such efforts to come to terms with the physical world.

Moeser (1988) reports a series of studies that elicited and assessed the environmental knowledge of nursing students in an especially complex health sciences center. She contrasts the consistently "poor" performance of these students with the assumption "throughout the cognitive mapping literature . . . that a person's mapping system of the environment automatically develops into a more complex representation as that person gains experience" (p. 46).

> The question that needs to be asked is why these nursing students failed to develop survey mapping systems when so many studies have shown that most people do develop such survey systems. The answer must be in the design of the building. (p. 47)

Both Heft (1988) and Bryant (1984) advocate more detailed conceptualizations and operationalizations of physical variables in studies of acquisition of environmental knowledge. In exploring the relationship between cognitive and individual-difference perspectives on environmental representation, Bryant concludes that it is necessary to extend the paradigm currently employed in experimental tasks and to consider the physical properties of target locations. He speculates that, as a consequence of specific environmental attributes, some locations may show systematic individual differences in the accuracy of their cognitive representation and others will not.

The Spatially and Temporally Extensive Nature of Environmental Knowledge

This aspect of environmental knowledge is clearly reflected in Böök's conceptualization of "events."

> Events of spatial cognition emerge due to a number of simultaneous constraints . . . Some basic constraints are: Recurrent types of physical-spatial structure . . . a limited set of personally controllable cognitive acts . . . and lawfully incomplete spatial knowledge. (Böök, this volume, pp. 149–150)

His consideration of the unfolding of environmental experience and decision making

over time and space leads to a potentially very valuable analysis of patterns of occlusion and opening in the visual field and the impact of target size on locational judgments.

The Differential Nature of Environmental Knowledge. Is it possible that much of
the variance observed in the distance and direction estimation tasks employed in
much environmental cognition research is a consequence not of "error," but of differential strategies for the acquisition and representation of environmental knowledge? Küller presents a number of potentially productive approaches to individual
differences (e.g., sharpeners/levelers, stimulus seekers); might these represent different approaches to the achievement of cognitive clarity?

Bryant (1984) has undertaken detailed investigation of individual difference and
cognitive perspectives on environmental representation. He concludes that there is
"little evidence . . . to suggest . . . a unified mental representation of the geographical environment" (Bryant, 1984, p. 43). Note, however, that his analyses are
based solely on directional errors in pointing and mapping tasks, and, as indicated
above, there is no systematic analysis of the impact of physical variables associated
with each target location.

The Affective Character of Environmental Knowledge. Kaplan focuses on cognitive
clarity and the anxiety that accompanies its absence, while Küller discusses stress,
control, and individual differences in the seeking of information. Although Böök
does not focus on stress directly, there is at least a limited literature (Evans et al.,
1984; Moeser, 1988; Nelson-Shulman, 1983–84) that links stress to focal and incidental environmental learning, and thus presumably back to individual differences as
well. One might also speculate on the impact of preference on the acquisition and
representation of environmental information. Smith (1984), for example, reports a
positive relationship between judged pleasingness of landmarks and accuracy of cognitive distance estimation tasks.

The linking of stress to environmental knowledge and behavior appears to represent a new problem formulation for decision makers; it can contribute to the salience
of issues of environmental clarity and legibility, particularly in inherently stressful
institutional settings such as hospitals (Carpman, Grant, & Simmons, 1985).

THE PROCESS OF ENVIRONMENTAL DESIGN AND
ENVIRONMENTAL DESIGN RESEARCH

If it is indeed possible to develop a more functional and more physically based conceptualization of the nature of environmental knowledge, how can it then assist in
meeting our second criterion of application: guidance in and/or new tools for environmental-design decision making?

One such tool—with clear utility for both research and design—is provided by
environmental simulation. Gaining adequate control over a range of environmental
variables is not easily accomplished; Gärling and Golledge (1989), for example, note
"practical problems, unavoidable confounding of different factors, and an unknown
degree of generalizability of the results to other environments" (pp. 216–217).

Such simulations can be computational, as developed by Golledge and associates

(1985), physical, or visual in nature. One dynamic, visual simulation (Weisman, O'Neill, & Doll, 1987) validated wayfinding performance in a real-world setting against performance in a computer graphic simulation of that same environment. In over three-quarters of comparisons there were no significant differences between wayfinding performance in real and simulated environments; similar trends were found for three performance measures in both conditions. Equally important, this simulation utilized inexpensive, low-technology computer graphics to provide study participants with the ability to make real-time wayfinding decisions. Participants were highly engaged by this sequence of "spatiotemporal events" and were seemingly untroubled by the absence of detail in the simulated environment.

Simulation studies of this sort can provide experimental control over physical variables. Over the longer term, they represent a mechanism for coming to understand the potentially complex interplay between physical features of the environment (cf. Evans et al., 1984; Gärling, Böök, & Lindberg, 1986).

Such recent advances in the realm of microcomputers suggest that simulation techniques are also viable as tools for actual design decision making. Carpman, Grant, and Simmons (1985) employed such simulation techniques to determine locations at which drivers entering a large medical center were most likely to attend to directional signage; thus it was possible to anticipate and respond to patterns of environmental learning and behavior in as yet unbuilt environments.

INSTRUMENTAL APPLICATION: QUESTIONS AND ANSWERS

Having taken this long and somewhat circuitous path, it would be gratifying to now point to clear and well-substantiated areas of application of the three psychological models presented in this section of the book. There clearly are promising linkages, and new and hopefully more general conceptualizations of environmental assessment, cognition, and action. These conceptualizations, in turn, are suggestive of approaches to and tools for the process of design decision making (Table 11.2). The consequences of these new conceptualizations and processes of design application, however, have not yet materialized. To the extent the three conceptualizations of psychological processes under review do not provide information directly relevant to environmental-design decision making, they may be judged to lack instrumental applicability. While this absence of instrumental application may in part be a consequence of the authors' prescribed focus on psychological processes, it is not, I would submit, simply an artifact of the organization of this book. It also reflects the dilemma within environment–behavior studies, noted by many authors (Moore, 1979; Evans, 1980; Weisman, 1982), of little of the existing research confronting the physical environment in theoretically significant terms. Böök's analysis—and his emphasis on the relationships between distance, environmental extent, subtended angles in perspectives, and size of physical reference systems—is particularly promising in its focus on physical variables.

In summary, it should not be concluded that there is no guidance to be provided to design-decision makers. Indeed, much of the literature cited throughout this chapter is of relevance. It may be, however, that problems in application reflect assumptions even more fundamental than the inductive fallacy described by Millikan (1959),

Table 11.2   Potential Applications to Environmental Knowledge and Action

Knowledge of psychological processes ↓ Problem Formulation	Application ↓ Guidance in design decision making	Environmental planning, programming, and design ↓ Direct Research utilization
Less precise environmental knowledge	Sampling of settings	Environmental education
Spatiotemporal structure of physical environment	Environmental simulation Rationale for research utilization	Planning/design participation
Individual differences in environmental perception and knowledge		
Affective content and coding of environmental information		

assumptions reflected in the very distinction between "theory" and "application." For our purposes, valid and viable conceptualizations of processes that mediate between environmental knowledge and action must be equally rooted in both of these end points. From such conceptualizations can come research that systematically analyzes and samples the physical environment and recognizes the impact of the environment not just on action but on the very processes and structures by which we acquire and represent environmental information. We will then find application to be a productive, and fundamental, aspect of our work.

REFERENCES

Bryant, K. (1984). Methodological convergence as an issue within environmental cognition research. *Journal of Environmental Psychology, 4*, 43–60.

Carpman, J., Grant M., & Simmons, D. (1985). Hospital design and wayfinding: A video simulation study. *Environment and Behavior, 17*, 296–314.

Evans, G. (1980). Environmental cognition. *Psychological Bulletin, 88*, 259–287.

Evans, G., Skopanich, M., Gärling, T., Bryant, K., & Bresolin, B. (1984). The effects of pathway configuration, landmarks and stress on environmental cognition. *Journal of Environmental Psychology, 4*, 323–335.

Gärling, T., Böök, A., & Lindberg, E. (1986). Spatial orientation and wayfinding in the designed environment: A conceptual analysis and some suggestions for postoccupancy evaluation. *Journal of Architectural and Planning Research, 3*, 55–64.

Gärling, T., & Golledge, R. (1989). Environmental perception and cognition. In E. Zube & G. Moore (Eds.), *Advances in environment-behavior research* (Vol. 2, pp. 203–236). New York: Plenum.

Golledge, R., Smith, T., Pellegrino, J., Doherty, S., & Marshall, P. (1985). A conceptual model and empirical analysis of children's acquisition of spatial knowledge. *Journal of Environmental Psychology, 5,* 125-152.

Heft, H. (1988). The vicissitudes of ecological phenomena in environment-behavior research. *Environment and Behavior, 20,* 92–99.

Kantrowitz, M. (1985). Has environment-behavior research made a difference? *Environment and Behavior. 17,* 25–46.

Millikan, M. (1959). Inquiry and policy: The relation of knowledge to action. In D. Lerner (Ed.), *The human meaning of the social sciences* (pp. 158–180). New York: Meridian Books.

Moeser, S. (1988). Cognitive mapping in a complex building. *Environment and Behavior, 21,* 21–49.

Moore, G. (1979). Knowing about environmental knowing. *Environment and Behavior, 11,* 33–70.

Nelson-Shulman, Y. (1983–84). Information and environmental stress: Report of a hospital intervention. *Journal of Environmental Systems, 13,* 303–316.

Seidel, A. (1985). What is success in E & B research? *Environment and Behavior, 17,* 47–70.

Smith, C. (1984). The relationship between the pleasingness of landmarks and the judgment of distance in cognitive maps. *Journal of Environmental Psychology, 4,* 229–234.

Weisman, G. (1982). Developing man-environment models. In M. Lawton, P. Windley, & T. Byerts (Eds.), *Aging and the environment: Theoretical approaches* (pp. 69–79). New York: Springer.

Weisman, G. (1983). Environmental programming and action research. *Environment and Behavior, 15,* 381–408.

Weisman, G., O'Neill, M., & Doll, C. (1987). Computer graphic simulation of way finding in a public environment: A validation study. In J. Harvey & D. Henning (Eds.), *Public environments* (pp. 74–80). Washington, D.C.: Environmental Design Research Association.

Weiss, C. (1980). *Social science research and decision-making.* New York: Columbia University Press.

III

LIFE-SPAN DEVELOPMENT

Another point of focus in research on environmental cognition, environmental assessment, and decision making and action in real-world environments has been individual differences. What role might interindividual variation play as people interact with the molar, physical environment? The most highly developed and extensively studied individual difference factor has been age. As Lynn Liben aptly notes herein, interest in organism age stems from a more fundamental question: How do underlying physical, cognitive, and sociocultural changes in the individual that age merely marks interrelate to human interactions with the environment? Another reason that developmental issues have predominated is because they are highly intertwined with a theoretical and methodological perspective called life-span development. We share Liben's view that this perspective reflects a commitment to study the organism in terms of its constructive engagements with the surrounding physical and social world. Moreover, life-span research leads to a methodological perspective emphasizing dynamic, interactive organism-environment relations that are reciprocal and multicausal.

Chapter 12, by Giovanna Axia, Erminielda Mainardi Peron, and Rosa Baroni, utilizes the concept of cognitive schemata to suggest a strong link between individuals' evaluations of places and their ability to recognize and comprehend the basic elements in a scene, their location, and their function. Given that schemata of place result from experience with both specific exemplars of place and an overall knowledge of the category of place types in which a particular locus falls, a ready connection is made with the life-span perspective. Axia and colleagues show how the roles of experience and changing cognitive skills influence environmental assessment across the life span. Moreover, the contribution of emotion is shown to vary with age, which in turn appears to alter the relation between cognition and assessment.

Liben's chapter on environmental cognition provides a careful analysis of the role of several physical, socioemotional, cognitive, and experiential–historical factors that may partially account for changes in environmental cognition over the life course. Among these hypothetical factors are locomotion, physical stature, self-object differentiation, attachment, negative affect, thinking skills (including memory and language), and extent of familiarity. Liben concludes with a call for more attention to the potent role of environmental representations in environmental cognition research. She notes that although many people, and in particular children, experience places via representations in maps, pictures, diagrams, and the like, we know very little about how this affects the development of cognitive representations.

Roger Hart and Michael Conn in Chapter 14 address the largely neglected topic of the development of decision making and action in real-world environments. They call for a more expanded, holistic view of human–environment transactions that would rely heavily on a functional analysis of what is necessary to behave competently in different real-world situations. Hart and Conn believe that several viable theoretical constructs already exist that could be adapted profitably. Finally, they argue strongly for more case study analyses to illuminate more completely the role of decision making and action in people's knowledge and assessments of their physical surroundings.

The two discussion chapters by Christopher Spencer and Gary Moore focus, as in the previous parts, on the problems of conceptual integration across assessment, cognition, and action, and on the application of this literature to environmental planning, design, and policy.

12

Environmental Assessment Across the Life Span

GIOVANNA AXIA, ERMINIELDA MAINARDI PERON,
AND MARIA ROSA BARONI

Before trying to analyze environmental assessment throughout the life span, let us briefly consider what environmental assessment means. Craik (1971), for instance, distinguishes five kinds of place assessment: physical and spatial properties of places, number and variety of artifacts in a place, traits of places, behaviors typically occurring in a place, and institutional attributes or social climate of places. In general, models of environmental assessment can be considered place centered, while environmental appraisal relates more to observer-centered variables. Gifford (1987) stresses how environmental appraisal refers to different personal impressions, such as descriptions, evaluations, emotional reactions, meanings, and attitudes of concern. In his recent review of environmental psychology, Holahan (1986) includes under assessment studies relating to the affective appraisal of the environment (Russell & Lanius, 1984), place evaluation envisioned in terms of the degree to which a place is seen as helping to achieve goals (Canter, 1983), the cognitive components in environmental assessment and the ''supporting environment''—that is, an environment in which the information necessary for making decisions is readily available and interpretable (Kaplan, 1982), preferences for places and their attractiveness (Nasar, 1983; Zube & Pitt, 1981), residential satisfaction and neighborhood attachment (Fried, 1982; Galster & Hesser, 1981), and identification of standards of quality for various settings (Craik, 1981). Thus environmental assessment includes a variety of factors and/or of processes, ranging from the mere perception of a place to affective/emotional evaluations of it. Even if all of the components of assessment are relevant, not all of them will be considered here. We will focus mainly on cognitive aspects of environmental assessment. This means perception, cognitive evaluation, affective/emotional evaluation, and preference for places. These aspects are all interrelated to the concept of ''place schema'' (we will use ''schema'' when referring to one single schema, and ''schemata'' when referring to the plural). A place schema is abstract and hierarchically organized knowledge about places. Perception of a place can be viewed as the mere fact of coming into contact with a setting through the senses. Perception may also include the categorization and/or the conceptualization of a place, and it can also mean to form or use place schemata. As for place evaluation, it can deal with a "cognitive" evaluation of a place in terms of rational, logical thinking, an evaluation of the affective/emotional aspects of a place, and an evaluation in terms of supportive environment. This latter evaluation too is mainly determined by possible range of behaviors that a particular environment can readily sustain.

PLACE SCHEMATA

Perception of a place is the first step for any other form of knowledge about places, and can be studied using various techniques (cf. Evans, 1980; Gärling, 1976a, b, 1980; Gärling & Golledge, 1989). Perception is often guided by many factors, including previous knowledge about places (Baroni, Job, Mainardi Peron, & Salmaso, 1985), individual goals when coming into contact with a place (Salmaso, Baroni, Job, & Mainardi Peron, 1981), subject's attention level—either spontaneous or induced by instructions—(Baroni, Job, Mainardi Peron, & Salmaso, 1980), and mode of interaction with the place (Job, Mainardi Peron, Salmaso, & Baroni, 1981). Furthermore, to perceive a place as "a place," and not merely as an array of items, requires organization into a meaningful unit. Thus place perception proceeds from mere perception to the categorization and/or the conceptualization of what has been perceived.

The notion of schema has been introduced in environmental psychology as a consequence of Gibson's (1966, 1979) ecological theory of perception, which challenges the information-processing theories. Gibson's position has been partially adopted by Neisser (1976), who considers "schemata" as mental constructs that mediate perception. Schemata accept some components of perceptual information and direct attention toward specific aspects of perceptual information. In this process the schemata themselves are modified. Schemata then are both the origin of the experience of environments and the final product of such experience. This last point is stressed by Mandler (1984), who affirms that there are four types of mental organization of knowledge: categorical, matrix, serial, and schematic. The categorical or taxonomic structure mainly consists of a class-inclusion hierarchy. The matrix structure arranges elements according to two dimensions as it occurs, for example, in any double-entry table. The serial structure links the items in a unidirectional series, such as in the alphabetic order or as in a musical piece. Finally, there are schematic structures, which are sets of expectations (Rumelhart, 1980) about various aspects of everyday life experience, such as social routines, places, and stories.

If place schemata are abstract and hierarchically organized representations of knowledge about places, the passage from perception to categorization of places is linked to the schemata of places the individual already possesses or will form on that occasion. Schemata can guide categorization and conceptualization of places, but are in turn formed or modified on the basis of new information extracted from place perception. A place schema is considered more strongly structured—which does not necessarily mean more correct—if it is derived from encounters with different instances of that kind of place than if it derives from only a few instances. Schemata are also related to the cognitive evaluation of places as they determine, for instance, subjects' judgments about the general appearance and location of a particular place (e.g., if it should be large or small, internal or external, or where it should be located), about what items should or should not necessarily be present in it, about the locations of the items, and about whether and why that particular place is or is not a good or prototypical instance of that place category.

Knowledge of everyday life environments is considered to be organized into "scene" schemata (Mandler, 1984). In the literature the term scene schema has been used to indicate both a real environment or a reproduction of it, ranging from a colored photo to a sketch. For us the crucial variable is whether a scene is congruent, well organized, or either partially or totally incongruent or disorganized. Therefore, to simplify exposition, we will use the term place schema to refer to a congruent, real-life environment—either physically present or reproduced in some way.

Studies about place schemata have focused on recognition, categorization, and memory of information present in everyday arrangements of natural objects (cf. Biederman, 1981; Hock, Romanski, Galie, & Williams, 1978; Mandler & Parker, 1976). Other studies have focused more specifically on processing of information of everyday environments. Mandler (1984) proposes a distinction between *inventory information* and *spatial-relation information* in the place schemata. The inventory information refers to what objects typically appear in a place, while the spatial-relation information describes the typical spatial layout of a place. Mandler also considers a third factor, *descriptive information,* which is what objects look like. This factor, though less important than the other two, is also part of the place schema. For example, classrooms contain desks, benches, chairs, windows, doors, and so on (inventory information), but the distinctive features of desks and chairs, for example, can vary greatly (descriptive information). Also the spatial locations of furniture and people in a classroom (spatial information) follow a set of expectations. For example, we do not expect children to be sitting on the desk (spatial relation), nor do we expect benches and chairs to be grouped separately in two different parts of the room (spatial composition).

Mandler (1983) proposed five effects of place schemata on the processing of information. First, objects are coded more easily when presented in an organized, familiar scene. Second, well-organized scenes are recalled better and for a longer time. Third, when recalled, disorganized scenes are modified into more usual scenes. Fourth, anomalous objects and violations of physical laws are promptly recognized. Fifth, schema-relevant information is more accurately remembered than schema-irrelevant information, which is in turn better remembered than schema-opposed information. To fully understand this last point one has to consider the distinction among schema-expected, schema-compatible, schema-irrelevant, and schema-opposed items. Schema-expected items are necessary to define a particular place as an instance of a certain place schema (e.g., walls, ceiling, and floor are items necessary to define a place as an interior). Schema-compatible items are more optional items with respect to a certain place schema, though compatible with it (e.g., a table lamp can easily be found in an office, but even if absent, one can still recognize the place as an office); schema-irrelevant items are elements whose presence or absence in a given place is trivial in order to define it as an instance of a particular place schema (e.g., flowers in a living room). Finally, schema-opposed items strongly challenge the correctness of the activated schema (e.g., a bath basin should not be found in a dining room).

When encountering a place, one activates the place schema considered appropriate for the place in question. One then verifies the presence of the schema-expected elements—derived from the activated schema—before deciding whether that place is or is not an instance of that particular place category (Mandler, 1979). Therefore, more attention is devoted to the schema-expected elements, which are then deeply processed and therefore better remembered (see also Brewer & Treyens, 1981; Mandler & Parker, 1976; Mandler & Ritchey, 1977). However, contrasting results have also been found (Friedman, 1979). Bobrow and Norman (1975) suggest that information that is expected, or otherwise readily accounted for, would not require much processing and would therefore not be well remembered; instead, information discrepant from the schema should receive deeper processing and thus be remembered better.

Salmaso, Baroni, Job, and Mainardi Peron (1983) reported data on the relation between subjects' goals and memory for schematic information that may reconcile these two differing views on memory for schema-expected items. In their experiment subjects' incidental or intentional memory for interiors was tested, separately computing memory for structural elements (i.e., the schema-expected elements) and for furniture objects (i.e., the schema-compatible, more variable elements). Results showed that in the incidental condition structural features were remembered better than furniture objects, whereas the opposite was true in the intentional condition. These data stress the importance of considering not only the distinction between types of schematic information, but also subjects' goals. In the incidental condition, where features are processed superficially, the coding of expected elements might be related to sources of variability, whereas the coding of variable elements might include their identification. As a consequence, we might expect the physical features of structural elements to be memorized better than those of the variable elements, that is, the objects. In the intentional condition, on the other hand, the subject's attentive resources are used for the identification of variable elements, which will then be better remembered than the expected items. The influence on memory of the probability of finding certain objects in a given place according to that place schema has been investigated also by Vandierendonck and Schuurmans (1984) and by Schuurmans and Vandierendonck (1985).

We have argued that a place schema is the knowledge resulting from having encountered various instances of that place. Such encounters can have been, from an affective/emotional point of view, either trivial or important and impressive. We might expect then that the affective/emotional evaluation of places (environmental preference), which could also include aesthetic evaluations, should be more idiosyncratic than the cognitive evaluation of them. The more complete model of affective appraisal of places is that of Russell and Lanius (1984), which considers the two main dimensions of arousal and pleasure. We feel, however, that Purcell's model (1984, 1986, 1987) is the frame that offers a stimulating explanation not only of environmental preference but, more generally, of the links between cognition and emotions in environmental assessment. Purcell suggests that "affective responses occur when the attributes of the particular instance do not match or are discrepant from the default values in the relevant schema. The discrepancy results in interruption or blocking of ongoing perceptual, cognitive, and action sequences which in turn leads to autonomic nervous system (ANS) arousal. ANS arousal is a necessary part of the affective response and is followed by cognitive activity, the results of which will determine the type of affect experienced'' (Purcell, 1987, pp. 67–68). The larger the discrepancy from the schemata the greater the arousal and the cognitive activity associated with the affective experience: with moderate discrepancy beauty and excitement often result. In the case of extreme discrepancy, unsuccessful cognitive activity occurs, resulting in ugliness and unpleasantness. Thus place schemata contain—in addition to perceptual, cognitive, and action sequences—emotional experiences as well. Purcell's model also explains individual differences in response to the environment: ''[some] individuals could require larger discrepancies between an instance and the schema for greater preference or attractiveness to occur, with corresponding shifts in the amount of discrepancy required to create interest and the negative emotions'' (Purcell, 1987, p. 68), although an extensive overlap between individuals can be expected within a given culture.

Verbal Reports as a Means for Studying Environmental Assessment

Environmental assessment has been investigated using different tasks, including the reproduction of environments through maps, drawings, models, and so on (cf. Hart, 1979; Lynch, 1977; Matthews, 1985), route recognition (cf. Cousins, Siegel, & Maxwell, 1983), or verbal ratings (cf. Craik & Zube, 1976).

These tasks not only rely on practical use of materials by the subjects, and thus may be biased by technical abilities (Evans, 1980), but also reflect verbal instructions. Such instructions typically direct subject's actions during task execution, including the selection, use, and grouping of materials available during encoding. Therefore data on environmental assessment also reflect linguistic and communicative variables. Thus it is important to understand how verbal communication can affect performance. This is especially important in working with young children whose knowledge may exceed their verbal communication abilities.

The analysis of verbal reporting can be considered at least under three different perspectives (Klein, 1982): *cognitive, interactive,* and *linguistic*. The *cognitive* component is analyzed in other sections of this chapter. As for the *interactive* component, conversational rules (Grice, 1975; Perner & Leekam, 1986) have to be applied in contexts in which the content of the communication is the description of a place. Even in this case important factors in determining subject's performance are subject's developmental level (Axia, Baroni, & Mainardi Peron, 1988), both speaker's and addressee's aims and their coding of the social situation in which the interaction takes place (Mainardi Peron, Baroni, Job, & Salmaso, 1985), and their different knowledge of the places in question (Baroni, Job, Mainardi Peron, & Salmaso, 1985). Although adult subjects are generally good in adapting their descriptions of places to the situational context (Wunderlich & Reinelt, 1982), violations of communication rules are far from being rare, often resulting in a poor or wrong communication (Baroni & Mainardi Peron, 1987). For example, this happens when in selecting information subjects give either a surplus of useless data or a lack of needed information with respect to their interlocutor's previous knowledge.

Apart from individual differences, age undoubtedly affects the *linguistic* component of communication, as far as development of spatial concepts and specific communicative skills are concerned (Abkarian, 1982; Clark, 1973; Conner & Chapman,

1985; Cox & Ryder Richardson, 1985; Wanska, 1977; Windmiller, 1974). The correct use of simple concepts like "left" and "right," for instance, implies that the speaker is able to take into account the addressee's point of view (Waller, 1986).

The above aspects of verbal communication, although applicable to environmental descriptions, are not specific of this topic. Verbal reportings of places present some unique issues, however. First, a very important aspect of verbal communication about environments is *linearization:* the subject has to transpose the three-dimensional space of environment into the unidimensional space of speech (Ullmer-Ehrich, 1982). That is to say items contemporaneously present in the environment have to be mentioned in succession. One must choose the order in which to recite them, and what to say about each of them. When the subject describes the environment making an imaginary tour of it, this presents an additional temporal dimension to the unidimensional report. The analysis of the ordering of items in free recall can cast some light on organization of knowledge in children (Ackerman, 1985), as well as when spatial arrangement is investigated (Axia & Caravaggi, 1987). When producing a verbal description of a place, the speaker must solve several problems (Clark & Clark, 1977): *level,* for instance the level of specification of the items; *content,* that is, since one cannot include everything in the description, something must be omitted; *order,* for instance from left to right; and *relations* of the parts of the environment with respect to each other. Clark and Clark observe that in the study of Linde and Labov (1975), in which subjects were asked to describe their apartments, they solved this problem generally in the same way: instead of giving a map of the environment and then filling it with what was there, they described what could be found making an imaginary tour of their flats, as "the tour solves the problems of content, order and relation all at once" (Clark & Clark, 1977, p. 233).

The linguistic aspects of verbal reports can be viewed not only as limiting subject's performance, but also as a means for detecting some aspects of cognitive representations of places. For instance, in solving the *linearization* and *order* problems, subjects adopt an importance criterium (Mainardi Peron, 1985). They in fact start mentioning the items they consider to be more important and characteristic for the place in question, and then proceed describing the less important ones. The relative importance of the various aspects of a place—or variations in the importance the same item has if considered in different places—can then be more or less directly inferred from subject's report.

Some studies (Axia, Baroni, & Mainardi Peron, 1988; Mainardi Peron, Baroni, Job, & Salmaso, 1985) have shown that through the choices relating to the *level,* *content,* and *relations* of the reporting, it is possible to detect subjects' modifications of the cognitive representations of environments. These modifications can in turn be linked to their developmental level. In addition, the use of verbal reports has stressed how subjects' performance is biased by subjects' presuppositions about their addressee's knowledge of the place in question.

Let us consider in further detail one of the above-mentioned experiments, to better clarify what can be discovered about cognitive representation of places by means of verbal reportings. Axia, Baroni, and Mainardi Peron (1988) have compared verbal descriptions of familiar places by 8 year olds and adults. In particular, they focused on discourse organization, use of locatives (items specifications concerning their position, e.g., "the telephone on the table"), and use of verbs of motion (e.g., "then you go to your right''). The places considered were the entrance hall and the court-yard of a school. Subjects described both places under one of three experimental conditions: free recall, description from memory (i.e., a description based on data contained in memory and intended for a person not acquainted with the place), and direct description (i.e., a description given while looking at the place). The results yielded a difference in recall between places (the courtyard being better remembered) only in children. Both children and adults remembered primarily aspects of the places that were constant constraints to actions (e.g., walls, steps, gates). Discourse orga-nization varied according to task conditions, children giving more ''planned descrip-tions'' (although less than those given by adults) in the description from memory condition—in which the communicative goal is stressed—than in the free recall con-dition, which was characterized by a large majority of enumerations of unconnected items. Furthermore, children used locatives and verbs of motion mainly when de-scribing the interior. Compared with children's reports, adults' descriptions contained more locatives and less verbs of motion. The latter indexes confirm the fact that descriptions of actions characterize a particular developmental phase of environmen-tal knowledge, while specifications of item positions are more frequently found in adults' descriptions. On the other hand, these results show that 8-year-old children are well aware of the communicative functions of their descriptions.

The cognitive components of environmental assessment have been discussed up to this point in general. The main issues may be summarized as follows: knowledge about environments is organized in place schemata, which also involve memories about emotional experiences; the positive or negative evaluation of environments is linked to the degree of discrepancy between actual experience and the experience already stored in memory (schemata); preference for environments is related to easi-ness and availability of new information in the actual experience. In the following section we will discuss in more detail the importance of the above-mentioned points for the study of environmental assessment across the life span.

ENVIRONMENTAL ASSESSMENT

The main purpose of this section is to discuss modifications in environmental assess-ment that occur during life. As we have argued, environmental assessment is a hu-man activity composed of overlapping mental processes, ranging from perception to categorization, aesthetic and emotional judgments, and incorporating purposeful be-havior. Not surprisingly, few studies adopt a life-span perspective in this field, as it is difficult to account jointly for modifications intervening in each of these domains. In this section we will analyze the modifications over life of the above-discussed cognitive processes that are responsible for environmental assessment. As ''change'' over time is under examination here, the focus will primarily be on the periods of life when cognitive modifications are more dramatic. Thus children will be the major focus of this section. Because of the relative lack of specific evidence, some of our discussion will be speculative. We will try to integrate different pieces of evidence into a more general frame for environmental assessment, which can also suggest hypotheses for further research. In general, differences between children and adults in environmental assessment can be expected in three main cognitive domains: first, the development of understanding of environmental reality; second, the role of emotions in cognitive processing at various ages; and third, the modifications in environmental preference during the life time.

Representation of Environments in Childhood

During childhood, children come in contact with progressively wider domains of both physical and social reality. The study of children's representation of the world has a long tradition in developmental psychology (cf. Piaget, 1926). More recently, children's representation of social reality has received much attention (Flavell & Ross, 1981; Shantz, 1983) and much has been written on the development of spatial representation of environments (cf. Cohen, 1985; Liben, this volume; Liben, Patterson, & Newcombe, 1981). Less has been written on nonspatial components of children's environmental knowledge, that is, on the development of "representation of environments." Axia (1986) proposed a three-phase descriptive model of the development of representation of environments. Such a model incorporates the results of several studies that mostly employed verbal reports—this being the most widely used method in the study of children's representation of the world.

The first step in the representation of environments is knowledge of environmental elements of directly accessed places. At this stage children can attribute everyday objects to appropriate environments. Two year olds, for example, can distinguish between objects suitable for bathrooms and objects suitable for kitchens, although their classifications are far more "flexible" than the stricter criteria applied by 4 year olds (Ratner & Myers, 1981). At this latter age, conceptual definition for highly familiar environments such as home or kindergarten is accessed. Children can give a list of elements present in their homes and in their schools, but they can scarcely organize them either spatially or in terms of episodes or routines (Axia & Nicolini, 1989). Furthermore, 4 and 5 year olds show difficulties in distinguishing environments in a conceptual manner. For example, when asked to describe the courtyard of their kindergarten while looking at it, young children in fact name elements that are inside the courtyard, but also items that are outside it, this error disappearing in older children (Axia, 1986). Another typical example of young children's fuzzy environmental representation is the notion of "the place in which I live," which can be both home and city. Here is an example: "What is a city for?" the experimenter asks. "To go inside" is a 5 year old's answer "because outdoors is cold!"

The second step in environmental knowledge is composed of fairly well-organized chunks, which may lack relation with one another. By analogy with results obtained in spatial memory for familiar environments (Hart, 1981), children can represent home and school, but may have difficulties in describing the route that links the two places (Axia, 1986, pp. 200–215). From 5 to 7 years, children become increasingly confident in their descriptions of familiar environments. The most evident limits in this phase are difficulties in purposefully selecting relevant environmental information. For example, 6 year olds can provide complete descriptions of what they encounter during a walk in an urban environment. However, only children with highly developed conceptual abilities can select environmental features useful for orientation as they had been requested to do. Six-year-old children of average conceptual ability report "pebbles," "dogs," and "trucks" as having more informational value for orientation than "pedestrian crossing," "church," or "petrol station" (Axia, 1988). At this phase, children treat their environmental knowledge as unitary chunks that can barely be analyzed and reorganized according to different criteria. This type of knowledge is very close to the iconic representation proposed by Bruner, Olver, and Greenfield (1966), based on the predominance of mental images on logic-propositional representation (see also Kosslyn, 1980).

By the end of childhood children overcome most of the representational difficulties observed in the earlier phases (third step). They can clearly distinguish among directly accessed environments and show wide conceptual knowledge for different types of environments. The typical fuzziness and rigidness of young children's knowledge are less evident. In this respect there is no reason to consider children's knowledge at this stage different from that of adults. Of course, differences in experience still separate children's and adults' knowledge, but these differences are now more quantitative than qualitative. The following is an example of how 10 year olds represent the notion of city: Marta (10;9) in response to the question: "What is Padova?" "A city." "How do you know?" "Because there are many houses, because it is very inhabited. If there were just few houses, it would be not a city, but a small town, a village." This category-based, adult-like definition nicely contrasts with younger children's representations of the same notion. Here is an example drawn from the interview with Valentina (5;6): "What is Padova?" "It is a city which is named Italy." "How do you now?" "Mummy tells me." "What is a city composed of?" "Stones, otherwise, without stones it falls down!" One would suppose that individual or group differences from this age on will be related more to extracognitive factors such as interests, goals, and experience, than to intracognitive ones.

The above three steps summarize the main changes in content and organization of verbal representations of environments in childhood. It is noteworthy that the major turning points are consistent with those illustrated in the literature relating to the development of *spatial* representation of large-scale environments (Evans, 1980; Hart & Moore, 1973; Siegel & White, 1975).

Role of Emotions in Environmental Assessment

Apart from the cognitive representation of the environment, another important aspect that may differentiate children from adults is the role of emotions in environmental assessment. Emotions change from birth to adulthood. Campos, Barrett, Lamb, Goldsmith, and Stenberg (1983) proposed a distinction between basic emotions (joy, rage, sadness, fear, and interest), which can be observed during the first year of life, and complex emotions (shame, guilt, envy, and depression). Babies develop at first highly adaptive emotions, such as interest and joy, which induce them to explore the physical and social world (Izard, 1978). Displeasure too is a primitive emotion that guarantees caregiver's help and comfort, while other emotions develop later, when the child can use them adaptively, for example rage (4 to 6 months) and fear (6 months).

The complex emotions differ from the basic ones because they are related to goals that are uniquely human. The appearance of complex emotions is related to cognitive and social development. For example, the feeling of guilt is related to violations of one's moral standards, and develops later than fear or even shame (Campos, Barrett,

Lamb, Goldsmith, & Stenberg, 1983). Thus, some emotions require rather complex cognitive evaluations. For example, the evaluation of one's own ability to deal with an event influences the intensity and sometimes the quality of the emotion, as is the case, for instance, when fear turns into pride for having acted successfully in a risky situation (Mandler, 1975).

In brief, emotional development can be conceived as following three steps. Initially emotions can be elicited only by real events; for example, the baby cries during a medical examination. Later, children can feel emotions also from representations of future events; for example, the toddler can cry before entering the doctor's room. Finally, emotions can be derived from the knowledge the child has about emotions. For example, the fear a child experiences when entering the dentist's office may give rise to a new fear of not being quiet enough, so that the time of the disturbing visit could be prolonged because of one's own overemotional behavior (Saarny, 1978).

The relation between affect and cognition has recently received much attention. For example, Bower (1981) affirms that

> Human memory can be modeled in terms of an associative network of semantic concepts and schemata that are used to describe events. An event is represented in memory by a cluster of descriptive propositions. These are recorded in memory by describing the event. The basic unit of thought is the proposition; the basic process of thought is activation of a proposition and its concepts . . . The semantic-network approach supposes that each distinct emotion such as joy, depression or fear has a specific node or unit in memory that collects together many other aspects of the emotion that are connected to it by associative pointers. (pp. 134–135)

Environmental assessment may be related to semantic networks in long-term memory, where conceptual and emotional information is stored. The emotional nodes may play different roles in children and adults, both in terms of the emotional development itself and in the importance of emotional information in cognitive processing.

Emotional nodes in the semantic networks related to environments can vary with age according to the different nature of emotions during development. For example, perhaps young children tend to organize emotions about environments in simple associations, such as good versus bad. Older children might, however, be able to consider more complex emotional nodes such as, for instance, "the place which makes me feel shy" or "the place which is depressing for me."

Young children—but this might also apply to adults in nonliterate societies— conceive time, space, and the external world as intimately interwoven with their inner emotional reality (Werner, 1957). In addition, emotional nodes may be more important in retrieving events for children than for adults (Ackerman, 1985). As young children have more limited knowledge of the world, they may have to depend more on emotional nodes than older children and adults (Anooshian & Siegel, 1987).

The importance of the affective appraisal of the environment and its development over time have been demonstrated even for adults (Spencer & Dixon, 1982). The development occurring in emotions and in their integration into the cognitive system suggests two related hypotheses. On the one hand, if compared with adults', children's environmental assessment (perception, categorization, retrieval of stored knowledge, and so on) may rest more heavily on emotional information. On the other hand, children may prove to be less capable than adults to offer high-level evaluations of environments, as a complex integration of cognitive, social, and emotional knowledge is then required.

Development of Environmental Preference

Both semantic knowledge about environments and the integration of emotional-environmental information change in a variety of ways from infancy to adulthood. People's activity in the environment will not be analyzed here, although such analysis can offer important insights about environmental preferences, especially for preverbal children. This issue is discussed in some detail by Hart and Conn (this volume). Instead the focus here will be on judgments that involve conscious evaluation and mental effort.

Environmental preference has been related to successful adaptation, considered in an evolutionary perspective (Kaplan, 1987). For example, adults prefer environments that offer both "perspect" (e.g., a hill from which a large portion of landscape can be seen) and "refuge" (e.g., a place surrounded by trees) (Appleton, 1975). S. Kaplan and R. Kaplan (1982) suggest that preference is a dual factor of one's ability to make sense out of a scene and one's involvement or interest in the setting. Making sense is facilitated by the coherence or underlying thematic structure of elements in a setting plus the ease with which one can comprehend the general layout and spatial organization present (legibility). Interest or involvement is enhanced by moderate complexity and the promise of further exploration, as suggested, for example, by a partially occluded clearing.

Balling and Falk (1982) studied the development of preference for five types of natural environments (savannah, desert, deciduous forest, coniferous forest, pluvial forest) in subjects whose age ranged from 8 to 70 years. One of their most interesting results was that 8 and 11 year olds prefer the savannah (isolated and high trees, short grass, no undergrowth), while 15, 18, 35, and 70 year olds prefer savannah, deciduous forest, and coniferous forest. The pluvial forest and the desert are the least preferred; however, 8 year olds like the desert better than the other groups of subjects. According to Balling and Falk, preference for the savannah reflects genetically primitive, evolutionarily based needs and that is why it is more frequent among children, while adults prefer environments that are more familiar, giving more importance to sociocultural adaptation. The distributions of preference for the desert are very interesting: adults do not like desert, whereas young children do. Adults who live in cities dislike desert less than adults who live in the country. Relative preference in this case may reflect a sort of "hunger" for free space.

Balling and Falk's research poses a number of important issues, but just two of them will be discussed. First, further evidence for the notion that environmental preference changes as a function of age will be given. Second, the role of familiarity with environments on such changes will be analyzed.

Age-related differences in environmental preference have not received much attention. Children's preference for places may however change according to their age. For example, Zube, Pitt, and Evans (1983) found age-related differences in scenic quality assessment of landscapes. Six to 11 year olds' judgments are similar to one another, but they differ from young adults' judgments. In particular, children are less sensitive to human presence, to land-use compatibility, and to physical indexes of complexity of the landscape.

Social and emotional development originate different interests during the life span, which may account for differences in environmental preferences. For example, children's preference for open spaces is well documented. American children prefer outdoors to indoors, and in particular open spaces (lawns, playgrounds) are the most favorite (Hart, 1979; Moore, 1986). This tendency has been observed also in Italian 5 year olds living either in Venice or in the Venician hinterland (Axia & Nicolini, 1989). However, preference for open spaces may be typical of middle childhood, when many interests of children focus around play activities with peers. Toddlers in fact prefer corners or narrow, "closed" spaces in daycare centers—thus showing a strong need for intimacy and privacy (Nicolini, 1985). The need for closed spaces emerges again in late childhood and in adolescence. For example, in a vast cross-cultural study involving four countries (Argentina, Australia, Mexico, and Poland), Lynch (1977) found that preadolescents mention their room as one of the places they like best, followed by environments in which friends can be met, such as friends' homes, streets, parks, and so on.

In summary, when evaluating environments children select different environmental characteristics in relation to specific interests, needs, or values that vary as a function of age—preference for environments being related both to subjects' past experience and to their expectations for the future (Zube, 1987). Children's environmental assessment can be viewed as a holistic phenomenon in which cognition and emotions as well as plans and action are integrated (Hart & Conn, this volume). In adults, the behavioral goals and plans one has are a key factor in the assessment of an environment (Canter, this volume). Environmental assessment may thus be different in children and adults not only because of different interests during life, but also because of more profound reasons. We argued before that emotion about environments may be the key factor for children's environmental assessment. It could be hypothesized that the emotional nodes in the semantic network for environments constitute the database for children's action planning within environment. On the other hand, one would expect that adults would utilize a wider span of information for both assessing environment and action planning within it.

Another factor that can influence environmental preference is familiarity. To discuss this further, let us start with a classic quotation: "To become completely lost is perhaps a rather rare experience for most people . . . . But let the mishap of disorientation once occur, and the sense of anxiety and even terror that accompanies it reveals to us how closely it is linked to our sense of balance and well-being" (Lynch, 1960, p. 4). Familiarity with the environment is an important factor for positive assessment. According to S. Kaplan and R. Kaplan (1982), familiar environments are preferred to unfamiliar ones because they facilitate meaningful predictions. Children are influenced by familiarity with the environment in various ways. For example, Acredolo (1979, 1981) found that 9 month olds perform spatial tasks much better at home than in the laboratory. This difference disappears, however, when the children are given the opportunity to play in the lab with their mothers and the experimenter for 15 minutes before the experiment begins.

Familiarity also affects economy in mental efforts. As noted earlier, coding and recall of places are deeply influenced by the degree of congruence of the places with subjects' schemata. For example, Kirasic, Siegel, and Allen (1980) found that adults and 10 year olds recognize equally well a familiar environment presented as a whole and its landmarks presented separately. Five and 6 year olds, however, need more time to recognize the scene than to recognize separate elements of it.

According to R. Kaplan (1985, p. 162), "Humans, after all, respond not only to the 'things' but also to their arrangement, and not merely to the arrangement, but also to the inference of what such arrangement makes possible." Spatial relations in everyday environments inform people about which actions can be performed in a given place. Environments are typically used by people and objects are purposefully arranged in space. Thus spatial arrangement of a place is related also to memories of social or individual actions performed in a similar place. Such memories enter into the individual's place schemata and may orient preference. It would not be surprising that one tended to appraise places in which the spatial arrangement evokes memories linked to pleasant activities. Individual, age-related, and even cross-cultural differences in environmental preference may be attributed to differences in past experience organized in place schemata.

We have investigated the influence that spatial arrangement and complexity of furnishing have on the environmental preference of children and adults (Axia, Baroni, & Mainardi Peron, 1990). Subjects were requested to evaluate how much they liked each one of 8 photographs of the same classroom, which reproduced 4 different spatial arrangements of 10 benches. Each arrangement was presented both in a "low-complexity" and in a "high-complexity" version. Apart from the teacher's desk and the benches, in the high-complexity photos more didactic material and furnishing were present with respect to the low-complexity photographs.

As spatial arrangement is an important source of information about the social activity facilitated or inhibited by a given place, the arrangements here considered were chosen so as to (1) focus social interaction on the teacher, with all the benches facing the desk ("teacher-centered" classroom); (2) to favor communication between the participants, the benches having a horseshoe arrangement ("communication-aimed" classroom); (3) to have children work in small groups, with groups of three or four benches facing each other ("group work" classroom); and (4) to have children work and interact as they are all sitting at just one, long table, with half of the benches stuck in front of the others ("dining table" classroom). It should perhaps be explained that this last spatial arrangement can be found mainly in Italian schools located in historical buildings, where large corridors or rooms have been partially modified to locate small classrooms.

The above stimulus materials were used in two experiments. In the first two age levels (6 and 8 year olds) and two kinds of schools ("traditional" and "nontraditional") were examined. The "traditional school" groups were acquainted only with teacher-centered and with communication-aimed spatial arrangements of classrooms, while the "nontraditional school" groups were acquainted with all four types of spatial arrangement. In the second experiment adults in their twenties or in their sixties who were either primary school teachers or clerks were examined.

The results indicated that both 6 and 8 year olds prefer high-complexity to low-complexity classrooms, thus suggesting that richness of information is a generally preferred factor—at least at the age levels here considered. As for spatial arrangements, while "traditional school" children show a strong preference for the teacher-centered and the communication-aimed arrangements, "nontraditional school" children like all the four arrangements equally well. This result stresses how preference and experience of places are linked in children.

In the second experiment, teachers preferred high-complexity classrooms to low-complexity ones, while clerks do not show preference according to complexity. Preference for spatial arrangements is influenced both by type of job and by subjects' age. Teachers and clerks like the communication-aimed arrangement best, but although clerks appreciate the teacher-centered arrangement, young teachers particularly dislike it. In brief, these results confirm that both complexity and spatial arrangement are important factors in preference for places in children and adults. This study also indicates that age of subjects may be a badly defined factor if considered just in itself. A better approach would be to consider the relationships between age and other factors that may contribute to environmental preference. As Liben argues in this volume, in a life-span perspective age may simply be a marker for various underlying factors. For example, the above study indicates that type of environmental experience is a relevant factor for 6- and 8-year-old children, while type of job is important for younger and older adults. Teachers and clerks probably evaluated the classrooms presented in the experiment in relation both to the potentials for action offered by the places and to their own aims. It is likely that a teacher will primarily consider any classroom as related to his/her professional aims and beliefs. Such functional evaluation may be different for nonteachers. Future research should thus examine in greater detail the relation between functional appraisal and environmental preference, under the general hypothesis that functional appraisal of places changes according to one's own goals and aims—which are also modified by increasing age.

To further enlighten the relations between environmental assessment, age, and individual goals we will now briefly consider some aspects of environment and aging.

Environmental Assessment in Elderly People: Some Observations

Some environmental research has been devoted to investigations of elderly people. Mostly practical aspects were under examination, for example programs for the social integration of the elderly and housing for the elderly. Sometimes, the appreciable effort to ease old people's lives by planning specific environments—such as, for example, hospitals or housing—have had the spurious effect of overstressing the difficulties that some groups of old people may have. Research on elderly people should distinguish more clearly between phenomena that are due to a deteriorated mental and/or physical health (which is not necessarily related just to old age) and phenomena that are more intrinsically connected to old age per se. Evidence supporting this point of view can be found, for example, in the study by Walsh, Krauss, and Regnier (1981), which is aimed at assessing the relationships between environmental knowledge and the use of the environment in old people. The results have shown that for the spatial knowledge of the environment in old people stable predictors can hardly be found. In general, young adults draw better maps than old adults, but good health, education, and male gender are also good predictors for mapping accuracy. The area of neighborhood drawn by old people is related, among other things, to the subject's mobility index. Such extracognitive factors prevent the construction of testable hypotheses on environmental knowledge and on environmental use, which may be specific of old age. The poor graphic skills and the scarce motivation to experimental tests that are typical of elderly subjects add further problems to the above difficulties.

The great variability of results in research with elderly people is also due to the variety of interindividual differences between the subjects of this age group. Baltes (1979) argues that three types of factors influence the life-span development: "age graded," "history graded" (for example, the cohort effect), and "nonnormative" factors, which do not necessarily occur to all people through their life course. Such nonnormative factors are particularly strong in old age. Poor health, low income, and recent negative events are extracognitive factors. However, they play a strong role as "modifiers" in the relation between personal variables and environmental attributes—thus influencing also environmental behavior (Carp, 1987; Carp & Carp, 1984). Similarly, the "ecological model" proposed by Lawton (1982) stresses the vulnerability and the dependence from environmental conditions of the old people. When "competence" decreases, "environmental press" becomes a powerful factor for predicting environmental behavior.

Old age has been found to be a significant factor also in preference for landscapes. For example, Lyons (1983) partially replicated Balling and Falk's (1982) study, finding that preference scores decrease with age and drop for elderly subjects. Lyons concludes that "the development of landscape preference is a cumulative process that reflects the action, through the life cycle, of socially differentiating attributes such as age, gender, place of residence, and environmental experience" (p. 505).

In brief, it is difficult to describe specific patterns of place cognition and evaluation for old people, taking into account only the factor age. Thus, hypotheses for place cognition or evaluation cannot be proposed for the elderly per se, apart from specific difficulties already found for long-term memory or in time required to complete a task in the elderly (Coleman, 1986; Walsh & Thomson, 1978).

Because of their greater vulnerability, the elderly appear to be more sensitive to environmental characteristics than other age groups, as well as to residential satisfaction—as indicated by research on residential variables and subjective satisfaction (Carp & Carp, 1982; Christensen & Carp, 1987). However, idiosyncratic factors often appear in this age group. For example, when evaluating environments old people consider not only aesthetic and functional factors, as the other people do, but also autobiographical factors, such as attachment for places (Sixmith, 1988) or for home (O'Bryant & Wolf, 1983).

The emotional aspects of environment thus appear to be particularly important for the elderly and to have practical consequences. For example, when the hospital environment is modified so as to resemble the patients' past homes, old patients suffering from senile dementia improve in physical conditions, intellectual activity, and emotional conditions (Küller, 1987, 1988). However, as some stress due to physical environment is always present in hospitalization, it is rather difficult to separate the factor age from other factors such as loneliness, poor health, and insecurity, which may also account for lowered competence in the elderly.

In conclusion, contextual extracognitive factors have a preeminent role in old people's environmental assessment, for example in memory for urban landmarks (Evans, Brennan, Skorpanich, & Held, 1984). Little evidence can be found that old age is a significant factor per se for cognition and evaluation of places. We might then hypothesize that environmental knowledge organized in place schemata is not affected by age in late adulthood, although individual factors (such as, for example, type of job, physical health, environmental experience) can be of relevance in the cognitive processing of environments in old age. We might also suggest that in old age the emotional components of environmental assessment may be of greater importance than in adulthood.

FINAL REMARKS

This chapter has focused on the conscious evaluation of environments and its modifications according to age. We have suggested a distinction between "perception"— that is the process of coming in touch with environments and of categorizing or conceptualizing them—and "evaluation" of environments, which involves emotional and idiosyncratic aspects as well as cognitive ones. We have also argued that such conscious evaluation is related to subject's place schemata, which change according to age. Research on place schemata and on their development can inform us about the system of psychological processes involved in place assessment.

Figure 12.1 summarizes our point of view on the mental processes involved in environmental assessment. The major aspects involved are place cognition, emotional experience about places, and personal aims or interests. The relations between such aspects have a twofold nature. On the one hand, the various aspects partially overlap.

ENVIRONMENTAL ASSESSMENT

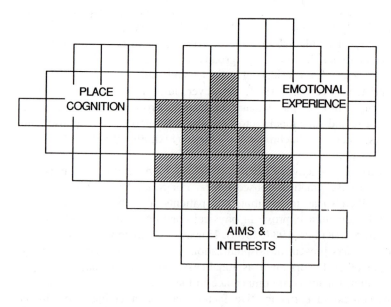

Figure 12.1.   A dynamic model for environmental assessment.

Each aspect has a specific domain, and it also overlaps with each of the other two aspects. The three aspects also share a common core domain. On the other hand, the relations between place cognition, emotion, and goals give rise to a *dynamic system* that integrates the mental processes responsible for environmental assessment. The system is dynamic because its parts are interrelated and modifications occurring in one aspect necessarily involve modifications in the other two. For example, since the system is not infinite, the relative importance (or "size") of each aspect inside the system influences the relative size of the remaining parts. When an aspect prevails, the other two are subdued or reduced in their importance.

This last notion may partially account for the difficulties in defining what environmental assessment is. In reviewing the literature one has the impression that each definition is a good one, yet the concept itself still remains slightly elusive. In fact, environmental assessment cannot be precisely defined because the location of the fulcrum changes within the system. Powerful sources of change are behavioral goals of the subject and developmental status. For example, research on environmental assessment can focus subject's attention on just one aspect of the system, as each aspect is rather complex in itself to study. The researcher induces changes in the location of the fulcrum and the equilibrium of the system rotates around it. The definition of environmental assessment thus may be more a matter of perspective.

Analysis of environmental assessment from a developmental point of view requires additional effort. Each of the parts of the system dramatically changes from birth to adulthood. In the literature ample evidence can be found that both spatial knowledge and place representation develop according to age. Place cognition thus changes both quantitatively and qualitatively. In general, place cognition has been widely studied, while children's emotional experience about environments and related interests have been comparatively scarce. An interesting transactional approach that aims at integrating research about children's emotions, goals, and action within environments is discussed by Hart and Conn (this volume). We suggest that goals and interests also change as a functional of age and that such modifications are relevant in accounting for differences between children and adults and even between adults in environmental preference. A promising line for future research would be the study of children's preferences for places in relation to their knowledge, emotions, and goals about places. Furthermore, the development of single aspects may not account for modifications of the system as a whole. The relations between place cognition, emotional experience, and goals or interests may change not only according to their different salience during life but also according to the idiosyncratic nature of development.

A relatively new domain for further research would be the role of emotions in environmental assessment. As a general hypothesis, young children should be more sensitive to emotional information in assessing environments than older children and adults. In other words, in young children the salience of emotions within the system should be larger than in later ages. In old age, also, emotional information may be more relevant than in adulthood for assessing environments. At the beginning and at the end of life, emotions apparently play an important role in assessing environments. The underlying processes are rather different in such distant periods of the life cycle. However, environmental vulnerability is a common factor for both young children and old people. The awareness of one own's dependence on some environmental factors may predispose persons to a strong emotional reaction to environment. Environmental assessment may thus change in the life span not only according to cognition and evaluation about the environment, but also according to cognition and evaluation about the self.

REFERENCES

Abkarian, G.G. (1982). Comprehension of deictic locatives: The object behind it. *Journal of Psycholinguistic Research, 11*, 229–245.

Ackerman, B.P. (1985). Children's retrieval deficit. In C.J. Brainerd, & M. Pressley (Eds.), *Basic Processes in Memory development* (pp. 1–45). New York: Springer-Verlag.

Acredolo, L.P. (1979). Laboratory versus home: The effect of the environment on the nine-month-old infant's choice of spatial reference system. *Developmental Psychology, 13*, 666–667.

Acredolo, L.P. (1981). Small and large-scale spatial concepts in infancy and childhood. In L.S. Liben, A.H. Patterson, & N. Newcombe (Eds.), *Spatial representation and behavior across the life span* (pp. 63–82). New York: Academic Press.

Anooshian, L.S., & Siegel, A.W. (1987). From cognitive to procedural mapping. In C.J. Brainerd & M. Pressley (Eds.), *Basic processes in memory development: Progress in cognitive development research* (pp. 47–101). New York: Springer-Verlag.

Appleton, J. (1975). *The experience of landscape*. London: Wiley.

Axia, G. (1986). *La mente ecologica. La conoscenza dell'ambiente nel bambino.* Firenze: Giunti.

Axia, G. (1988). Language and orientation: Memory for route elements in verbal descriptions by children and adults. In H. van Hoogdalem, N.L. Prak, T.J.M. van der Voordt, H.B.R. van Wegen (Eds.), *Looking back to the future. IAPS 10/1988*, (Vol. 2, pp. 513–522). Delft: Delft University Press.

Axia, G., Baroni, M.R., & Mainardi Peron, E. (1988). Representation of familiar places in children and adults: Verbal reports as a method for studying environmental knowledge. *Journal of Environmental Psychology, 8*, 124–139.

Axia, G., Baroni, M.R., & Mainardi Peron, E. (1990). Cognitive assessment of classrooms in childhood and early and late adulthood. *Children's Environments Quarterly, 7*, 17–25.

Axia, G., & Caravaggi, D. (1987). Effects of spatial arrangement on 4- and 6-years old children's memory. *Perceptual and Motor Skills, 65*, 283–293.

Axia, G., & Nicolini, C. (1989). *Image and description of home, school and town in Venetian children*. Unpublished manuscript.

Balling, J.D., & Falk, J.H. (1982). Development of visual preference for natural environments. *Environment and Behavior, 14*, 5–28.

Baltes, P.B. (1979). Life-span developmental psychology. In P.B. Baltes & O.G. Brim (Eds.), *Life-span development and behavior* (Vol. 2, pp. 255–279). New York: Academic Press.

Baroni, M.R., Job, R,. Mainardi Peron, E., & Salmaso, P. (1980). Memory for natural settings: role of diffuse and focused attention. *Perceptual and Motor Skills, 51,* 883–889.

Baroni, M.R., Job, R., Mainardi Peron, E., & Salmaso, P. (1985). *Recalling interiors and outdoors: Effects of familiarity.* Paper presented at the 16th Environmental Design Research Association Conference, New York.

Baroni, M.R., & Mainardi Peron, E. (1987). *Descriptions of an urban route in a natural setting: Effects of familiarity.* Poster presented at the Second European Conference for Research on Learning and Instruction, Tübingen, West Germany.

Biederman, I. (1981). On the semantics of a glance at a scene. In M.K. Kubovy & J.R. Pomerantz (Eds.), *Perceptual Organization* (pp. 213–253). Hillsdale, N.J.: Erlbaum.

Bobrow, D.G., & Norman, D.A. (1975). Some principles of memory schemata. In D.G. Bobrow & A.M. Collins (Eds.), *Representation and understanding: Studies in cognitive science* (pp. 131–149). New York: Academic Press.

Bower, G.H. (1981). Mood and memory. *American Psychologist, 36,* 129–148.

Brewer, W.F., & Treyens, J.C. (1981). Role of the schemata in memory for places. *Cognitive Psychology, 13,* 207–230.

Bruner, J.S., Olver, R.R., & Greenfield, P.M. (1966). *A Study on thinking,* New York: Wiley.

Campos, J.J., Barrett, K.C., Lamb, M.E., Goldsmith, H.H., & Stenberg, C. (1983). Socioemotional development. In M.M. Haith & J.J. Campos (Eds.), *Infancy and developmental psychology.* In P.H. Mussen (Ed.), *Handbook of child psychology* (Vol. 2, pp. 783–915). New York: Wiley.

Canter, D. (1983). The purposive evaluation of places: A facet approach. *Environment and Behavior, 15,* 659–698.

Carp, F.M. (1987). Environment and aging. In D. Stokols & I. Altman (Eds.), *Handbook of environmental psychology* (pp. 329–369). New York: Wiley.

Carp, F.M., & Carp, A. (1982). Perceived environmental quality of neighborhoods: Development of assessment scales and their relation to age and gender. *Journal of Environmental Psychology, 2,* 295–312.

Carp, F.M., & Carp, A. (1984). A complementary/congruence model of well-being and mental health for the community elderly. In I. Altman, M.P. Lawton, & J.F. Wohlwill (Eds.), *Elderly people and the environment. Advances in theory and research* (Vol. 7, pp. 279–336). New York: Plenum.

Christensen, D.L., & Carp, F.M. (1987). PEQI-based environmental predictors of the residential satisfaction of older women. *Journal of Environmental Psychology, 7,* 45–64.

Clark, H.H. (1973). Space, time, semantics and the child. In T.E. Moore (Ed.) *Cognitive development and the acquisition of language* (pp. 27–63). New York: Academic Press.

Clark, H.H., & Clark, E.V. (1977). *Psychology and language.* New York: Harcourt, Brace Jovanovich.

Cohen, R. (Ed.). (1985). *The development of spatial cognition.* Hillsdale, N.J.: Erlbaum.

Coleman, P.G. (1986). *Ageing and reminiscence processes*. Chichester: Wiley.

Conner, P.S., & Chapman, R.S. (1985). The development of locative comprehension in Spanish. *Journal of Child Psychology, 12,* 109–123.

Cousins, J.H., Siegel, A.W., & Maxwell, S.E. (1983). Way finding and cognitive mapping in large-scale environments: A test of a developmental model. *Journal of Experimental Child Psychology, 35,* 1–20.

Cox, M.V., & Ryder Richardson, J. (1985). How do children describe spatial relationships? *Journal of Child Language, 12,* 109–123.

Craik, K.H. (1971). The assessment of places. In P. McReynolds (Ed.), *Advances in psychological assessment* (Vol. 2). Palo Alto, Calif.: Science and Behavior Books.

Craik, K.H. (1981). Environmental assessment and situational analysis. In D. Magnusson (Ed.), *Toward a psychology of situations* (pp. 37–48). Hillsdale, N.J.: Erlbaum.

Craik, K.H., & Zube, E.H. (1976). *Perceiving environmental quality*. New York: Plenum Press.

Evans, G.W. (1980). Environmental cognition. *Psychological Bulletin, 88,* 259–287.

Evans, G.W., Brennan, P.L., Skorpanich, M.A., & Held, D. (1984). Cognitive mapping and elderly adults: Verbal and location memory for urban landmarks. *Journal of Gerontology, 34,* 4, 452–457.

Flavell, J.H., & Ross, L. (1981). *Social cognitive development*. Cambridge: Cambridge University Press.

Fried, M. (1982). Residential attachment: Sources of residential and community satisfaction. *Journal of Social Issues, 38,* 107–119.

Friedman, A. (1979). Framing pictures: The role of knowledge in automatized encoding and memory for gist. *Journal of Experimental Psychology: General, 108,* 316–355.

Galster, G.C., & Hesser, G.W. (1981). Residential satisfaction: Compositional and contextual correlates. *Environment and Behavior, 13,* 735–758.

Gärling, T. (1976a). A multidimensional scaling and semantic differential technique study of the perception of environmental settings. *Scandinavian Journal of Psychology, 17,* 323–332.

Gärling, T. (1976b). The structural analysis of environmental perception and cognition: A multidimensional scaling approach. *Environment and Behavior, 8,* 385–415.

Gärling, T. (1980). A comparison of multidimensional scaling with the semantic differential technique as methods for structural analysis of environmental perception and cognition. *Umeå Psychological Reports,* No. 155, Umeå, Sweden: Department of Psychology, University of Umeå.

Gärling, T., & Golledge, R.G. (1989). Environmental perception and cognition. In E.H. Zube & G.T. Moore (Eds.), *Advances in environment, behavior and design* (Vol. 1, pp. 203–236). New York: Plenum.

Gibson, J.J. (1966). *The senses considered as perceptual system*. Boston: Houghton Mifflin.

Gibson, J.J. (1979). *The ecological approach to visual perception,* Boston: Houghton Mifflin.

Gifford, R. (1987). *Environmental psychology. Principles and practice.* Boston: Allyn & Bacon.

Grice, H.P. (1975). Logic and conversation. In P. Cole & J.L. Morgan (Eds.), *Syntax and semantics; Speech acts* (pp. 41–58). New York: Academic Press.

Hart, R.A. (1979). *Children's experience of the place.* New York: Irvington.

Hart, R.A. (1981). Children spatial representation of the landscape: Lessons and questions from a field study. In L.S. Liben, A.H. Patterson, & N. Newcombe (Eds.), *Spatial representation and behavior across the life span* (pp. 195–236). New York: Academic Press.

Hart, R.A., & Moore, G.T. (1973). The development of spatial cognition. A review. In R.D. Downs & D. Stea (Eds.), *Image and environment* (pp. 346–388). Chicago: Aldine.

Hock, H.S., Romanski, L., Galie, A., & Williams, G.S. (1978). Real world schemata and scene recognition in adults and children. *Memory and Cognition, 6,* 423–431.

Holahan, C.J. (1986). Environmental psychology. *Annual Review of Psychology, 37,* 381–407.

Izard, C. (1978). On the ontogenesis of emotions and emotion-cognition relationships in infancy. In M. Lewis & L.A. Rosenblum (Eds.), *The Development of affect* (pp. 389–413). New York: Plenum.

Job, R., Mainardi Peron, E., Salmaso, P., & Baroni, M.R. (1981). Effects of mode of interaction and type of material on memory for objects. *Cahiers de Psychologie Cognitive, 4,* 481–487.

Kaplan, R. (1985). The analysis of perception via preference: A strategy for studying how the environment is experienced. *Landscape Planning, 12,* 161–176.

Kaplan, S. (1982). Where cognition and affect meet: A theoretical analysis of preference. In P. Bart, A. Chen, & G. Francescato (Eds.), *Knowledge for design* (pp. 183–188). Washington, D.C.: Environmental Design Research Association.

Kaplan, S. (1987). Aesthetics, affect and cognition. Environmental preference from an evolutionary perspective. *Environment and Behavior, 19,* 3–32.

Kaplan, S., & Kaplan, R. (1982). *Cognition and environment.* New York: Praeger.

Kirasic, K.C., Siegel, A.W., & Allen, G.L. (1980). Developmental changes in recognition in context memory. *Child Development, 51,* 302–305.

Klein, W. (1982). Local deixis in route directions. In R. Jarvella & W. Klein (Eds), *Speech, place and action* (pp. 161–182). New York: Wiley.

Kosslyn, S.M. (1980). *Image and mind.* Cambridge, Mass.: Harvard University Press.

Küller, R. (1987). Housing for elderly in Sweden. In D. Canter, M. Crempen, & D. Stea (Eds.), *Ethnoscapes: Transcultural studies in action and place* (Vol. 2, pp. 199–226). London: Gower Press.

Küller, R. (1988). Environmental activation of old persons suffering from senile dementia. In H. van Hoogdalem, N.L. Prak, T.J.M. van der Voordt, & H.B.R. van Wegen (Eds.), *Looking back to the future. IAPS 10/1988* (Vol. 2, pp. 133–139). Delft: Delft University Press.

Lawton, M.P. (1982). Competence, environmental press and adaptation. In M.P. Lawton, P.G. Windley, & T.O. Byerts (Eds.), *Aging and the environment* (pp. 33–59). New York: Springer.

Liben, L.S., Patterson, A.H., & Newcombe, N. (Eds). (1981). *Spatial Representation and behavior across the life span*. New York: Academic Press.

Linde, C., & Labov, W. (1975). Spatial networks as a site for the study of language and thought. *Language, 51*, 924–939.

Lynch, K. (1960). *The image of the city*. Cambridge, Mass.: M.I.T. Press.

Lynch, K. (1977). *Growing up in cities*. Cambridge, Mass.: M.I.T. Press.

Lyons, E. (1983). Demographic correlates of landscapes preference. *Environment and Behavior, 15*, 4, 487–511.

Mainardi Peron, E. (1985). *Choice and ordering of items in descriptions of places*. Paper presented at the 16th Environmental Design Research Association Conference, New York.

Mainardi Peron, E., Baroni, M.R., Job, R., & Salmaso, P. (1985). Cognitive factors and communicative strategies in recalling unfamiliar places. *Journal of Environmental Psychology, 5*, 325–333.

Mandler, G. (1975). *Mind and emotion*. New York: Wiley.

Mandler, J.M. (1979). Categorical and schematic organization in memory. In C.R. Puff (Ed.), *Memory organization and structure* (pp. 259–299). New York: Academic Press.

Mandler, J.M. (1983). Representation. In J.H. Flavell & E.M. Markman (Eds.), *Cognitive development*. In P.H. Mussen (Ed.), *Handbook of child psychology* (Vol. 3, pp. 420–494). New York: Wiley.

Mandler, J.M. (1984). *Stories, scripts, and scenes: Aspects of schema theories*. Hillsdale, N.J.: Erlbaum.

Mandler, J.M., & Parker, R.E. (1976). Memory for descriptive and spatial information in complex pictures. *Journal of Experimental Psychology: Human Learning and Memory, 2*, 28–48.

Mandler, J.M., & Ritchey, G.H. (1977). Long-term memory for pictures. *Journal of Experimental Psychology: Human Learning and Memory, 3*, 386–396.

Matthews, M.H. (1985). Young children's representations of the environment: A comparison of techniques. *Journal of Environmental Psychology, 5*, 261–278.

Moore, R.C. (1986). *Childhood's domain*. London: Croom Helm.

Nasar, J.L. (1983). Adult viewers' preference in residential scenes: A study of the relationship of environmental attributes to preference. *Environment and Behavior, 15*, 589–614.

Neisser, R.V. (1976). *Cognition and reality*. San Francisco: Freeman.

Nicolini, C. (1985). *Il comportamento spaziale nei bambini da zero a tre anni*. Paper presented at the International Symposium "Rischio Psichico e Rischio Sociale in Eé Evolutiva," Trento, Italy.

O'Bryant, S.L., & Wolf, S.M. (1983). Explanations of housing satisfaction of older homeowners and renters. *Research on Aging, 5*, 217–233.

Perner, J., & Leekam, S.R. (1986). Belief and quantity: Three year olds' adaptation to listener's knowledge. *Journal of Child Language, 13*, 305–315.

Piaget, J. (1926). *La représentation du monde chez l'enfant*. Paris: Presses Universitaires de France.

Purcell, A.T. (1984). The organization of the experience of the built environment. *Environment and Planning B: Planning and Design, 11*, 173–192.

Purcell, A.T. (1986). A schema discrepancy model of environmental perception and affect. *Environment and Behavior, 18,* 3–30.

Purcell, A.T. (1987). Landscape perception, preference, and schema discrepancy. *Environment and Planning B: Planning and Design, 14,* 67–92.

Ratner, H.H., & Myers, N.A. (1981). Long term memory and retrieval at ages 2, 3, 4. *Journal of Experimental Child Psychology, 31,* 365–386.

Rumelhart, D.E. (1980). Schemata: The building blocks of cognition. In R. Spiro, B. Bruce, & W. Brewer (Eds.), *Theoretical issues in reading comprehension* (pp. 33–58). Hillsdale, N.J.: Erlbaum.

Russell, J.A., & Lanius, U.F. (1984). Adaptation level and the affective appraisal of environments. *Journal of Environmental Psychology, 4,* 119–135.

Saarny, C. (1978). Cognitive and communicative features of emotional experience. In M. Lewis & L.A. Rosenblum (Eds.), *The development of affect* (pp. 361–375). New York: Plenum.

Salmaso, P., Baroni, M.R., Job, R., & Mainardi Peron, E. (1981). Aims, attention and natural settings: An investigation into memory for places. *Italian Journal of Psychology, 8,* 219–233.

Salmaso, P., Baroni, M.R., Job. R., & Mainardi Peron, E. (1983). Schematic information, attention and memory for places. *Journal of Experimental Psychology: Learning, Memory and Cognition, 9,* 263–268.

Schuurmans, E., & Vandierendonck, A. (1985). Recall as communication: Effects of frame anticipation. *Psychological Research, 47,* 119–124.

Shantz, T.U. (1983). Social cognition. In J.H. Flavell & E.M. Markman (Eds.), *Cognitive development.* In P.H. Mussen (Ed.), *Handbook of child psychology* (Vol. 3, pp. 495–555). New York: Wiley.

Siegel, A.W., & White, S.H. (1975). The development of spatial representation of large-scale environments. In H.W. Reese (Ed.), *Advances in child development and behavior* (Vol. 10, pp. 9–55). New York: Academic Press.

Sixmith, A.J. (1988). *Remembering-in-the-world: An analysis of the relationship between memories and home in later life.* Paper presented at the IAPS10 Conference, TU Delft, Netherlands.

Spencer, C., & Dixon, J. (1982). Mapping the development of feelings about the city: A longitudinal study of new residents' affective maps. *Transactions of the Institute of British Geographers, 8,* 373–383.

Ullmer-Ehrich, V. (1982). The structure of living place descriptions. In R.J. Jarvella & W. Klein (Eds.), *Speech, place and action* (pp. 219–249). New York: Wiley.

Vandierendonck, A., & Schuurmans, E. (1984). Interaction of incidental and intentional learning with frame usage. *Cahiers de Psychologie Cognitive, 6,* 405–418.

Waller, G. (1986). The use of "left" and "right" in speech: The development of listener-specific skills. *Journal of Child Language, 13,* 573–582.

Walsh, D., Krauss, I., & Regnier, V.A. (1981). Spatial ability, environmental knowledge, and environmental use: The elderly. In L. Liben, A.H. Patterson, & N. Newcombe (Eds.), *Spatial representation and behavior across the life span* (pp. 321–357). New York: Academic Press.

Walsh, D.A., & Thomson, L.W. (1978). Age differences in visual sensory memory. *Journal of Gerontology, 33,* 383–387.

Wanska, S.K. (1977). *The relationship of the development of spatial concepts to the acquisition of locative meaning* (Technical Report No. 415). Madison: Wisconsin Center for Cognitive Learning, University of Wisconsin-Madison.

Werner, H. (1957). *Comparative psychology of mental development.* New York: International Universities Press.

Windmiller, M. (1974). The relationship between a child's conception of space and his comprehension and production of spatial locations. In G. Lubin, J. Magary, & M. Poulsen (Eds.), *Piagetian theory and the helping professions* (pp. 146–152). Los Angeles: University of Southern California Press.

Wunderlich, D., & Reinelt, R. (1982). How to get there from here. In R.J. Jarvella & W. Klein (Eds.), *Speech, place and action* (pp. 183–201). New York: Wiley.

Zube, E.H. (1987). Perceived land use patterns and landscape values. *Landscape Ecology, 1,* 37–47.

Zube, E.H., & Pitt, D.G. (1981). Cross-cultural perceptions of scenic and heritage landscapes. *Landscape Planning, 8,* 69–87.

Zube, E.H., Pitt, D.G., & Evans, G.W. (1983). A lifespan developmental study of landscape assessment. *Journal of Environmental Psychology, 3,* 115–128.

13

Environmental Cognition through Direct and Representational Experiences: A Life-Span Perspective

LYNN S. LIBEN

The purpose of this chapter is to provide a review of past research and theory in environmental cognition from the perspective of life-span developmental psychology, to suggest future directions for work in this area, and to lay the groundwork for questions of application that are discussed elsewhere in this volume. Before it is possible to address these goals, however, it is essential to establish what is meant by "a life-span developmental approach to environmental cognition." The first section of the chapter is thus devoted to a discussion of these definitional issues.

The second section provides a selective review of past research. The research has been chosen to illustrate how changes in individual development in a variety of domains (e.g., development of logical classification skills in the cognitive domain, or development of interpersonal attachment in the socioemotional domain) may have consequences for environmental cognition.

The review of past work leads to the observation that most research has focused on how environmental cognition is derived from direct experience *in* environments. It is argued that another extremely influential source of environmental cognition is through exposure to representations *of* environments. Thus, the final section of the chapter contains discussions of the roles of environmental representations for environmental cognition, and descriptions of some recent research in this area.

DEFINITIONS

Defining Environmental Cognition

In the original conceptualization of the conference on which this volume is based, Evans and Gärling (1987) defined environmental cognition as

> the processes involved in the perception and cognition of *spatial* information in the real world. Most of this research has not examined preference or evaluation. Instead the focus has been primarily on understanding the cognitive processes themselves and how they are

influenced by person variables (e.g. age, gender, familiarity) and by environmental variables such as landmarks, path structures, or overall organizational factors. (p. 2)

This definition works well for the purpose intended, that is, for distinguishing environmental cognition from environmental assessment, on the one hand, and from decision making and action, on the other. In part, these distinctions are congruent with
a taxonomy developed earlier (Liben, 1981a), which similarly placed environmental
cognition in a broader context. Because that earlier taxonomy illuminates a number
of definitional concerns that are important for discussing environmental cognition
from the perspective of life-span development, it is described briefly here.

First, a preliminary distinction was drawn between *spatial behavior or activity*
and *spatial representation*. Spatial behavior refers to "behavior in space, that is, to
sensorimotor activity in the environment, such as the manipulations of objects in
space, or the locomotion of the self through the environment" (Liben, 1981a, p. 8).
Spatial representation in most general terms refers to anything that stands for space
in some way. As depicted graphically in Figure 13.1, spatial representation is further
divided into three *types*—spatial products, spatial thought, and spatial storage—and
two *contents*—specific and abstract space.

Spatial products are "the external products that represent space in some way,
[encompassing] any kind of external representation, regardless of medium, [e.g.,]
sketch maps, miniature models, and verbal descriptions" (p. 11). *Spatial thought*
"refers to thinking that concerns or makes use of space in some way. Spatial thought
is knowledge that individuals have access to, can reflect upon, or can manipulate, as
in spatial problem solving or spatial imagery" (p. 12). Finally, *spatial storage* "refers to any information about space contained "in the head" (and hence necessarily
"represented" in some way, as in neurophysiological structures) . . . The individual
is not cognizant of this information, however" (p. 13).

A further distinction was drawn between two *contents* of spatial representation.

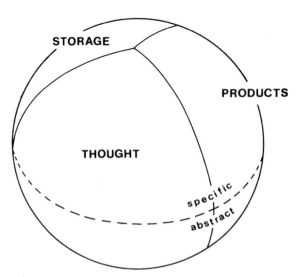

Figure 13.1. Types and contents
of spatial representation described by Liben (1981a).

One content focus is *environmental cognition,* or "information people have about space that enables them to maneuver in their environments, that is, individuals' knowledge about *specific* spaces" (p. 15). The second content focus, *spatial abstraction,* concerns "individuals' notions about space in the *abstract*" (p. 15), such as the topological, projective, and Euclidean concepts studied by Piaget and Inhelder (1956). Importantly, individuals make use of these abstract conceptual systems not only for abstract cognitive tasks (such as geometry), but also for conceptualizing specific environments.

In the context of the present volume, the distinction between spatial activity and spatial representation is particularly important because it is precisely the *interaction* between them that is of most interest to many environmental psychologists. How do one's spatial representations affect how one *acts* in the environment? These questions of integration are the specific focus of the contribution of Gary Moore (this volume).

The distinctions among the three types of representation are probably somewhat less important insofar as the focus here is on what people do in and to their environments as a function of their representations of those environments, regardless of the particular form that those representations may take. However, what is noteworthy about this taxonomy of types of representations is that they all refer to spatial knowledge that is in some way already "in the head," or produced and manipulated therein. Thus, these spatial types quite explicitly *exclude* information that is *currently* being picked up from the environment. Similarly, this chapter shall, for the most part, exclude "perception." This omission is motivated not by a belief that perception is irrelevant for spatial behavior, but rather by a conviction that it would be impossible to do justice to the issues involved in how we glean and construct spatial information from the environment in the first place, while also considering issues in how we store or use the information already available.

The distinction between abstract and specific spatial representation is also critical in delineating the content of the volume. The focus here is on what people know about *particular* places. Individuals' abstract spatial representations and systems of representations are relevant only insofar as these affect that environmental cognition. Thus, although much of the developmental literature in spatial cognition has concerned abstract systems, this work is discussed in the present chapter only when it is directly relevant to environmental cognition per se.

Defining Life-Span Developmental Psychology

The task of defining life-span developmental psychology is, unfortunately, not much simpler than the task of defining environmental cognition. Neither the term "development" nor "life span" is transparent.

As Overton and Reese began discussing some 20 years ago (see Overton & Reese, 1973; Reese & Overton, 1970), the definition of what is meant by "development" differs markedly for those working within mechanistic versus organismic models. In mechanistic models, the basic metaphor is the machine, which is "inherently at rest, and active only as a result of external forces" (Overton and Reese, 1973, p. 69). It is, in addition, reducible to its component parts. In mechanistic models in psychology, human behavior is similarly explained by reference to externally controlled experiences, all of which function through the same basic processes.

Researchers who study age-linked differences in behavior from a mechanistic perspective such as learning theory, attribute age differences to externally controlled experiences, functioning through age-independent learning mechanisms such as operant and instrumental conditioning. In these theories, the term "development" is merely shorthand for age-linked differences that occur, but only because as people get older, they have typically encountered and accumulated a different set of experiences. From this perspective, "development" is not really different from "learning" (see Liben, 1987). Indeed, Baer (1970), a researcher identified with this approach, explicitly suggested that there *is* no development, and that those who conceptualize and study age differences from the perspective of learning theory should probably not be considered developmental psychologists at all.

In contrast, the basic metaphor in organismic theories is the "living organism, an organized whole" (Overton & Reese, 1973, p. 69). In psychology, this translates into theories in which people are thought to be "inherently and spontaneously active; the organism is the source of acts, rather than being activated by external or peripheral forces" (p. 70). Furthermore, in contrast to the reductionist approach outlined above, parts are understood only in context of the whole organism (holism).

In an organismic developmental theory such as Piaget's, age-linked differences are thus understood as a consequence not only of external forces, but of internal forces as well. Individuals act to construct their own knowledge through interactions with the social and physical world, and maintain balance with that world through a self-regulating mechanism of equilibration (see Liben, 1981b, for a fuller discussion of these processes). Furthermore, because of the basic assumption of holism rather than reductionism, change is viewed as being qualitative as well as quantitative. Thus, rather than focusing research exclusively on efficient causality (i.e., identifying which environmental stimuli lead to which individual behaviors), "inquiry is directed toward the discovery of principles of organization" (Overton & Reese, 1973, p. 70). Age-linked differences in behaviors are thus interpreted as reflections of differences underlying organization (as when Piaget, 1970, attributes the differences between preadolescents' and adolescents' in performance on combinatorial reasoning tasks to the difference between concrete operational and formal operational structures).

The value of explicitly recognizing these major alternative world views and definitions of development is that they have differing implications for the conduct and interpretation of empirical research (see Overton, 1984; Pepper, 1942). Some kinds of research (such as examining environmental cognition in relation to unobservable organizational structures such as concrete operations) that are valued and essential under one approach (the organismic world view) are dismissed as bad science by another (the mechanistic world view). It should be made explicit that as a researcher sympathetic to organismic theories (see Liben, 1987), I have emphasized empirical work drawn from these theories in this chapter.

A discussion of the term "life-span developmental psychology" must address not only the word "development," but also the modifier "life-span." Unfortunately, this term, too, is difficult. Most often, it is simply interpreted to mean that the domain of inquiry includes people across the full life span. With this interpretation, one is not "doing" life-span developmental research unless one includes subjects across a wide range of ages. Interestingly, the judgment that a particular study is "life-span" is typically (and erroneously) made on the basis that elderly subjects are included in the sample.

More properly, however, what defines research as "life-span" is its focus on understanding the selected phenomenon in the context of the entire life course (see Huston-Stein & Baltes, 1976). Even a phenomenon that occurs at only a certain portion of the life course (e.g., the onset of walking) may be placed within the broader context of the life course (e.g., the role of self-directed locomotion).

Thus, the hallmark of life-span work is *not* its inclusion of subjects from infancy to old age, nor its focus on the elderly (which is no more "life-span" in and of itself than is the study of infants), but rather its concern for the life-span context of the phenomenon under study. A life-span developmentalist is interested in developmental processes or mechanisms at any point along the life course rather than just describing the species at difference ages. Any single "true" developmentalist might focus his or her work on a particular portion of the life span (such as infancy or old age), but this is a focus on an age group in the *context* of developmental processes across other age groups as well. (Those who study particular people of particular ages per se are better labeled by age-group terms such as "child psychologists" or "gerontologists." '

In this light, I should note that the particular studies and issues focused on in this chapter are weighted more heavily toward early and middle childhood, largely reflecting the focus of my own past work. But it should be clear that the developmental mechanisms are equally relevant for other age groups and could have been discussed emphasizing a different empirical literature instead.

Finally, another notable feature of the term "life-span developmental psychology" is the inclusion of the term "psychology." This term makes explicit that the focus in the present chapter is on the *psychological* development of individuals. This "personological" approach, as it has been called elsewhere (see Baltes, Cornelius, & Nesselroade, 1977), contrasts with a "life-span developmental" or "life-span human developmental" approach, which implies a more fully *interdisciplinary* perspective. Although scholars in life-span human development may be concerned with psychological development as well, they are simultaneously committed to studying that development in the context of changing societies, biological environments, historical changes, and so on. Thus, a human developmental approach is understood to include disciplines such as sociology, history, biology, and anthropology, as well as psychology. Again the decision to focus the current chapter on theory and research from psychology does not imply a belief that other disciplines are less relevant, but simply reflects practical constraints on what can be discussed in a single chapter.

Intersectng Definitions: A Life-Span Approach to Environmental Cognition

Having discussed the definitions of environmental cognition and life-span developmental psychology individually, it is possible to combine the concepts and consider what is gained by *using* a life-span approach to study environmental cognition.

First, developmental approaches are more likely than others to make the psychological model of the mature mastery of the domain explicit. Such descriptions provide the yardsticks by which progressions along the developmental path are measured. Second, the multidisciplinary tradition of life-span developmental work is necessarily sensitive to a wide range of influences on environmental cognition. Thus, life-span developmentalists typically include reciprocal and multiple causes, as, for example, in the diagram shown in Figure 13.2 (Liben, 1981a), which models influences on the development of spatial representation and behavior. Note that relevant variables are drawn not only from the *physical* environment (see Golbeck & Liben, 1988; Wohlwill, 1973a), but also from the biological and social domains.

A third contribution of a life-span developmental approach is its utility for identifying important individual differences. Even the most universalist of developmental theorists—Jean Piaget—who holds that cognitive development undergoes qualitatively similar structural changes across individuals and groups, posits that there are individual differences with respect to *rates of development,* to *final levels of development,* and to *domains* in which maximum development will be evidenced (Piaget, 1972). Although developmentalists typically characterize differences along these dimensions as differences in how far individuals have progressed along a developmental continuum, they may instead be conceptualized as individual differences among people at any given point in time (Liben, 1988).

Fourth, and most importantly, a life-span developmental approach—perhaps more than any other—focuses attention on the *processes* or *mechanisms* that effect and affect environmental cognition. That is, while much work by child psychologists is directed toward the undeniably important *descriptive* task of cataloguing age-linked differences in environmental cognition (see Cohen, 1985), the work by "true" life-span developmentalists is directed toward the *explanatory* task of understanding the mechanisms by which those age-linked changes occur. For the latter group, chronological age is not explanatory in and of itself, but rather serves as a *marker variable* for the factors that covary with age (see Baltes, Reese, & Nesselroade, 1977; Wohl-

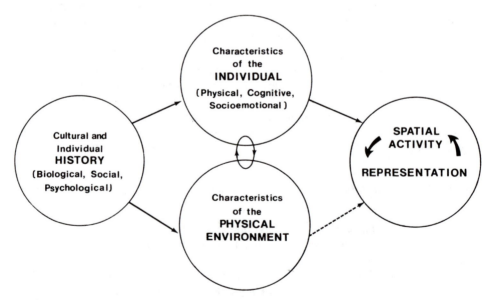

Figure 13.2. Influences on the development of spatial representation and behavior from Liben (1981a).

will, 1973b). Because this approach seems ultimately more likely to enable us to understand not only ontogenetic, but also microgenetic change in environmental cognition, it is this latter approach that is used to organize the selective review of developmental work on environmental cognition that follows.

THE DERIVATION OF ENVIRONMENTAL COGNITION FROM ENVIRONMENTAL EXPERIENCE

If chronological age is important as a marker for other variables, then it is essential to begin by asking what it is that age *marks*. The major dimensions include physical, socioemotional, cognitive, and experiential change. Given the vast nature of the changes in these domains, the chapter is limited to providing illustrative, rather than exhaustive, reviews of the relevant theoretical and empirical literatures. My goal is to illustrate the questions that have been asked and the kinds of methods that have been used, and to highlight the areas in need of greatest attention.

Physical Change

Perhaps the most obvious age-linked changes are those in the physical domain. Size increases, musculature becomes stronger, body proportions change, and so on. As infants become able to grasp objects, they can explore them, modify where they are located in space and in relation to their own bodies, and so on. These skills, which rest on physical (as well as cognitive) changes, have important implications for mastering a practical understanding of spatial relationships (see, especially, Piaget, 1954; Pick & Lockman, 1981).

Also critical for environmental cognition are those physical changes that allow increasingly independent and efficient locomotion. Newborn infants are passive recipients of others transporting them through their environments; older infants can scoot or crawl around, and still older infants or toddlers can walk. As individuals grow older, they have increased free range on foot or bike, public transportation, and private vehicles. As the aging process continues, limits on health may again limit mobility entirely, or reduce control over locomotion. What effects do physical changes have on environmental cognition?

In excellent reviews of the history of research on the relationship between motor and intellectual development in young children, both Kopp (1979) and Acredolo (1988) conclude that the early attempts to demonstrate the expected links failed because relationships were sought at too global a level (i.e., between rate of motor development in general and intellectual prowess in general). When more specialized relationships have been examined in recent work, however, the evidence does support the conclusion that changes in mobility are related to changes in environmental cognition (Bremner & Bryant, 1985).

For example, Bertenthal, Campos, and Barrett (1984) compared 8-month-old infants of differing mobility: those who could crawl, this who could not crawl but were experienced in using a walker to move through the environment, and those who had no means of independent locomotion. Using a methodology developed by Acredolo and Evans (1980), infants were first conditioned to turn to their right to see an interesting event following a buzzer. After training, infants were moved to the opposite side of the room. Infants who had preexperimental experience with independent locomotion (i.e., crawlers and walker-users) were more successful in making "landmark" rather than "egocentric" responses. That is, they were able to anticipate the correct direction—turning to their left—to see the interesting event. In contrast, infants who were not already independent at locomoting were far more likely to continue to turn to their right, thus failing to compensate for their changed position in the environment. Further support for the importance of mobility comes from the finding (Bertenthal et al., 1984) that an orthopedically handicapped child who had been in various body casts until about $8\frac{1}{2}$ months, showed high levels of egocentric responding until the first test following onset of crawling.

The importance of active rather than passive movement has also been demonstrated in older children. In a 6-month longitudinal study that began with 12-month-old infants, Acredolo, Adams, and Goodwyn (1984) used a paradigm similar to that described above, except that the toddler's task was to retrieve something from a well (positioned to the right or left) in a box rather than to turn to look for an interesting event. After learning the initial location (the well on the infant's right), infants were either carried (passive condition) or encouraged to crawl (active condition) to the other side of the box. Those who were carried showed higher levels of egocentric responding (i.e., selecting the well to their right) than did those who moved on their own. Importantly, active infants were also more likely to keep their eyes on the target as they moved to the other side of the box. By 18 months, this relationship no longer held, however. Little visual tracking was evident, and showed no relationship to success.

The conclusion that toddlers by this age are able to update self-landmark relationships mentally was supported by data from another study showing nonegocentric responding even when visual tracking was precluded. (Box walls were made opaque.) In summarizing her data, Acredolo (1988) emphasizes the importance of visual attention that accompanies infants' movement through environments. She suggests that visual tracking not only helps to solve individual problems, but also serves the child in building an understanding of space as a container, and self as simply one object within it.

One of the admirable features of the research reviewed above is that locomotion mechanisms are not confounded with chronological age: Investigators selected children who differed in locomotion within the same chronological age, or experimentally manipulated children's control of their locomotion. These data thus provide strong support for the conclusion that control of movement through one's environment is an important factor in the resulting environmental cognition. This conclusion is consistent with correlational data linking infants' "floor freedom" to later measures of IQ (see Wachs, 1978, 1979; Wachs & Gruen, 1982), with work in environmental psychology showing the powerful role of differential means of locomotion through environments (Appleyard, 1970; Hart & Berzok, 1982), with other work in child development showing the impact of self- versus other-directed exploration for reasons other than *physical* change (Feldman & Acredolo, 1979; Gauvain & Rogoff, 1986; Hazen, 1982; Poag, Cohen, & Weatherford, 1983), and with work in gerontology linking older adults' mobility to their performance on various environmental measures (see Evans, 1980; Walsh, Krauss, & Regnier, 1981).

Although considerable attention has been given to the physical changes that allow individuals freedom to move around their environments at all, there has been relatively little attention given to how physical differences in *size* may affect the form in which those environments are encountered. Simple differences in height, for example, have profound effects on what is seen in an environment. Perhaps the reason that children have less access to the relationships among objects in space (e.g., a room layout, see Liben, Moore, & Golbeck, 1982) is that they *see* fewer of these relationships simply because they are shorter!

Similarly, loss of sensory functioning in the elderly may decrease the availability of environmental information (Pastalan, 1973; Regnier, 1983). Reduced vision in older people may especially interfere with their access to environmental information under nonoptimal situations such as poorly lit corridors and illegible signs (Parr, 1980; Windley & Scheidt, 1980).

Socioemotional Change

Socioemotional changes may also be powerful in the development of environmental cognition. First, the very recognition that there *is* an environment at all may be understood as a reflection of the first critical socioemotional milestone, differentiation of self from nonself (see Lewis & Brooks-Gunn, 1979). At the empirical level, however, it is largely Piaget's *cognitive* analysis of this accomplishment that has motivated work related to environmental cognition. Piaget (1954) suggested that young infants only gradually comes to understand that objects exist apart from their own actions on those objects. Mastery of this object concept underlies developing success in infant search behavior (see Wellman, 1985) and the body–body, body–object, and object–object relationships so central to activity in, and representation of the environment (see Pick & Lockman, 1981).

A second concept from developmental theories of socioemotional development that should be a powerful one from the perspective of environmental cognition is the role of attachment. Surprisingly, however, although the importance of a secure emotional base—typically maternal—on exploration has received much attention in the animal literature (the work by Harlow & Harlow, 1969, on maternal deprivation), it has received relatively little attention in developmental research on environmental cognition.

The data that are available, however, support the importance of attachment. Ainsworth, Bell, and Stayton (1973), for example, found that securely attached babies showed more exploration than those who were not securely attached. In a more explicit test of the role of attachment for environmental cognition, Hazen and Durrett (1982) first judged 1-year-old infants' attachment to mothers using the standard "strange situation" procedure. In later measures of environmental exploration at 30 to 34 months, those children who had previously been rated as more securely attached showed more exploratory activity than those who had been rated as either anxious/avoidant or anxious/resistant. Importantly from the perspective of environmental cognition, the securely attached explorers also performed better on a detour-wayfinding task, tended to be better than the anxious/avoidant group in reversing a route, and were better able to manipulate acquired spatial information. These findings support the hypothesis that secure attachment provides an important foundation for environmental cognition, and suggests the potential utility of examining environmental cognition—much as intelligence has been studied—in relation to other factors that may affect the quantity and/or quality of early parent–child relationships (e.g., institutionalization, day-care).

Finally, it would also be useful to consider the extent to which environmental exploration and cognition are influenced by different affective associations of place. Research with elderly subjects has shown the importance of affective loading of place. Regnier (1983), for example, illustrates the importance of meaning by citing an elderly respondent who, when asked to produce a map of her neighborhood, included elements such as a trolley car line that had been gone for more than 20 years. Although aware that the trolley line was no longer there, she showed that it held great significance. This phenomenon was not limited to a single individual. At the group level as well, Regnier (1983) found that the most likely elements to surface in elderly individuals' composite sketch maps were not necessarily those identified by the city planners as the strongest symbolic, aesthetic, or visual elements, but rather those with the greatest functional meaning for the respondents. Evans, Brennan, Skorpanich, and Held (1984) similarly found that elderly subjects' performance on real-world memory tasks reflected individuals' own personal knowledge and history with the city.

There is also evidence that negative affect may have a deleterious effect on peoples' acquisition of knowledge of their environments and on their ability to demonstrate that knowledge. Evidence from the early portion of the life span comes from a study by Acredolo (1979). She observed that 9-month-old infants performed less egocentrically (that is, better) in their own homes than in either a relatively landmark-free laboratory environment or in a unfamiliar office environment that, like the home setting, contained many and varied potential landmarks. To evaluate the possibility that infants perform worse in lab settings because the unfamiliar environment is stressful, Acredolo (1982) tested additional infants in the lab, but began with a 15-minute play period prior to testing. During this time, the infant, mother, and experimenter played together to increase the infants' security in the experimental space. Consistent with the hypothesized importance of affect, only 3 of the 16 infants tested after this play session performed egocentrically, a pattern comparable to those infants tested at home rather than the lab environment in the earlier study.

At the opposite end of the life span there is also evidence that negative affect may be an important factor in environmental cognition. First, negative affect, especially fear, may limit the range of environmental experiences and hence environmental cognition. Fear of crime in the elderly, for example, may limit exploration of new environments and use of neighborhoods (see Lee & Lassey, 1980; Regnier, 1983; Rowles, 1983). Second, negative affect may also interfere with elderly subjects' abilities to demonstrate the environmental cognition and spatial skills that they do have. Ohta and Kirasic (1983), for example, found that whereas older adults generally perform more poorly than younger adults on spatial measures in laboratory settings, they perform just as competently in well-known, comfortable environments.

In conclusion, major concepts from theories of socioemotional development, as well as the limited empirical data that are available suggest that there are important relationships between socioemotional factors and environmental cognition.

Cognitive Change

The third major category of developmental change is cognitive change. Although at first glance it may seem circular to ask whether changes in *cognitive* development can explain developmental changes in environmental *cognition,* I would argue that it is not. The goal of such an analysis is to ask whether changes in underlying cognitive skills, in general, effect changes in the individual's ability to encode, remember, and manipulate information about environments in particular. I shall consider a sample of the aspects of cognitive development that might have an impact on environmental cognition.

Qualitative Cognitive Change. Piagetian theory provides the most complete theoretical model suggesting that cognitive structures undergo radical, qualitative changes from infancy through adolescence (Piaget, 1970). Although the use or activation of cognitive competence for a particular task may depend on a variety of factors (Overton & Newman, 1982), the competence that is potentially available for any particular task is critical.

What are some of the qualitative changes in reasoning identified in Piagetian theory that may be of relevance for environmental cognition? In answering this question, I shall focus on the progression from preoperational to concrete operational thought (thus characterizing the shift usually found between preschool and early elementary school years), although equally fascinating changes from other stage transitions could have been considered.

Although preoperational thinking is advanced over sensorimotor thought in that it allows the child to understand that one thing may represent another, it is simultaneously characterized by a number of restrictions. Critically, preoperational children's thinking is characterized by irreversibility of thought, that is, by an inability to recognize simultaneous relationships among logical operations such as addition and subtraction. This deficit is reflected in a number of more specific logical limitations such as the inability to categorize along more than one dimension simultaneously; an inability to understand proportionality; difficulty in understanding transitive relations (i.e., if A > B and B > C, then A > C), and, relatedly, seriated (ordered) relationships that require an understanding that on a particular dimension (e.g., length) a particular item is simultaneously larger than and smaller than other items; and failure to understand conservation, that is, that quantities remain unchanged despite changes in position or arrangement.

In addition to changes in logical thought, Piaget also identified changes during childhood with respect to "infralogical" thinking about space. Specifically, Piaget and Inhelder (1956) proposed that young children first come to understand topological spatial concepts, that is, those that remain unchanged even as the surface is stretched and bent (relationships such as proximity and enclosure, but not distance or angle). Only later do children master projective and Euclidean concepts, the former permitting an understanding of point of view (and hence, for example, that my left is your right when we face one another; or that in front of/behind relationships change with perspective); the latter permitting locations and distances to be related to an arbitrary but fixed reference system such as Cartesian coordinate axes (and hence, for example, allowing measurement and conservation of distance and angles).

Unfortunately, however, few investigators have structured their empirical research from the perspective of asking how qualitative cognitive changes might affect performance on environmental cognition tasks. Investigators rarely include children young enough to allow evaluation of the shift from preoperational to concrete operational thinking. (In much of the empirical work the youngest children tested are second graders, who, although easier to test than younger children, may be expected to have achieved concrete operational thinking.) Furthermore, investigators rarely include cognitive measures *other* than those used to test environmental cognition, thus allowing conclusions about environmental cognition in relation to chronological age only. As a result, there are actually very few studies that provide a test of the relations suggested here.

In one of the few relevant studies, Golbeck (1983) examined the relation between children's ability to categorize and their ability to reconstruct a room-size layout of furniture. Children ranging in age from 5 to 9 years were first given Piagetian classification tasks, and thereby classified as high, transitional, or low in their categorization skills. Children were later asked to reconstruct the layout of furniture in a room that varied with respect to logical organization (clustered vs. nonclustered) and spatial organization (meaningful vs. nonmeaningful). Children with more advanced classification skills did perform better with respect to general location. In a later study, Golbeck (1985) found significant relationships between first-grade children's performance on a Piagetian Euclidean spatial task and their ability to reproduce exact spatial locations of cardboard houses within a room, although again, the predicted relationship between the child's abilitiy to classify and to replace items in the room within the correct general area of the room was not obtained.

The empirical work to date is thus limited, and the findings provide only limited support for the hypothesized relationships. It would be helpful to study the impact of cognitive level on environmental cognition by using a number of other paradigms. Of particular promise is examining the relationship between children's classification skills and the extent to which their cognitive maps are affected by conceptual divisions within a space, such as those created by barriers within a room (Kosslyn, Pick, and Fariello, 1974; Newcombe & Liben, 1982), subdivisions along a route (Allen, 1981; 1982), or conceptual divisions of well-known, large environments such as state boundaries (Acredolo & Boulter, 1984).

Relationships between a number of other logical operations and environmental cognition have been suggested. Newcombe (1985), for example, reviewed a number of studies showing developmental changes in environmental cognition that might be understood in relationship to growing understanding of transitivity and conservation of distance, but notes that only our own pilot work (reported in Liben, 1982a) even attempted to provide a direct test of the relationships. Similarly, although we have speculated (Liben & Newcombe, 1988) about the potential role of seriation skills for judging relative distance rankings, we, too, have failed to examine this relationship empirically. In short, there are very few studies that offer data relevant to the relationship between qualitative cognitive structure and environmental cognition, but existing data and theory suggest many potentially important links worthy of investigation.

Quantitative Capacity. Apart from these qualitative changes in logical and infralog-ical systems, there are other major progressions in cognitive development that are candidates for affecting environmental cognition. Some developmentalists, for ex-ample, have suggested that as children get older, their quantitative capacity for hold-ing and manipulating pieces of information grows (Pascual-Leone, 1970; Case 1985). In a test of this theoretical position, for example, Dennis (1988) asked children to draw pictures of people engaged in specified activities (e.g., shaking hands) in spec-ified environments (e.g., a park). Although these were imaginary rather than actual environments, the analysis could presumably be applied to children's attempts to represent veridical environments instead. Dennis (1988) interpreted her results as supporting the hypothesis that with an increase in chronological age and its correla-tive increase in processing capacity (as measured independently), children are better able to depict multiple spatial relationships in their pictures.

A study of the potential role of quantitative capacity more directly within the research traditions of environmental cognition was conducted by Liben and New-combe (1988) using a paradigm devised by Kosslyn, Pick, and Fariello (1974). In this paradigm, subjects first learn the location of objects in a room, and are later asked to rank order objects' distances from a selected (referent) object. Adults per-form better on the rank-ordering measure than do young children (Kosslyn et al., 1974; Newcombe & Liben, 1982). To determine if adults' superiority simply re-flected a greater capacity to handle the 10 items in the task, a new sample of adults was tested, but this time with 20 items in the room rather than 10. Adults experi-enced difficulty learning the 20-item space that was much like the difficulty evi-denced by children with the 10-item space. Critically, however, although the absolute levels of adults' performance on the ranking task dropped somewhat, their perfor-mance remained generally high, and did *not* match the pattern found with children. This finding suggests that quantitative capacity per se is probably not an extremely powerful factor in explaining developmental differences observed in the original stud-ies.

These two sample studies document that the impact of age-linked differences in processing capacity is far from resolved. A similar controversy exists in other re-search areas (e.g., memory). It is, of course, possible that changes in ''capacity'' are themselves explicable by changes in other cognitive skills (e.g., developmental changes in conceptual chunking or in the depth and breadth of associates to the memory stimuli, see Chi, 1976; Liben, 1982b). Further research explicitly directed to these questions in environmental cognition would be useful.

Linguistic Skills. Another cognitive change that is of profound importance for cog-nition and social interactions that has been examined in relation to environmental cognition is the development of language. There is considerable research and theo-retical literature relating language development to spatial cognition. In a recent re-view focused on locatives, for example, Johnston (1988) suggests that despite differ-ences across languages with respect to the mechanisms used to express spatial information, and despite differences with respect to the ease of expression across languages, the evidence suggests that spatial concepts precede rather than follow linguistic mapping. However, ''words, once available, may constitute convenient interpretive programs that streamline real time processing." Again, empirical work is needed to determine whether children's growing linguistic facility in fact permits a better coding of environmental information.

Metacognitive Skills. Finally, children's age-related successes on environmental cognition tasks may be attributed to their increasing skills in monitoring their own cognitive processes, that is, to increasing skills in metacognition. As children get older they are better able to evaluate the difficulty of a problem and choose appropriately from among available strategies (Flavell & Wellman, 1977). In part, children's improvement on environmental cognitive tasks may stem from taking the problem seriously enough and exploiting available information.

Two studies provide direct demonstrations of the relevance of this skill. Liben, Moore, and Golbeck (1982) asked children to show the layout of their classrooms by arranging a scale model. As expected, overall performance was better when the classroom was in view than when it was out of sight. Interestingly, however, this group difference was accounted for by the subset of children who spontaneously looked back and forth between the model and the actual environment as they completed the task. A later study by Golbeck, Rand, and Soundy (1986) specifically manipulated children's attention to the actual environment in a similar modeling task. Preschoolers who were allowed to complete the task as they liked performed significantly worse than preschoolers who were required to point to the real furniture before placing the model furniture. Planning has also been shown to relate to success on other kinds of spatial tasks such as search (see Wellman, Fabricius, & Sophian, 1985).

Conclusion. There is regrettably little empirical work in which basic cognitive skills are measured independently from environmental cognition. Without such measures, we can conclude little more than that there are individual and age-linked differences in performance, and can only speculate about the possible reasons for these differences. Where they exist, I have mentioned studies in which subjects' environmental cognition is tested in relation to *some* underlying cognitive skill. By far, however, most investigators appear to be concerned with demonstrating simply that age-linked differences in environmental cognition exist. Many of these investigators manipulate the specific kind or amount of experience with the environment during the course of the experimental session. By implication, this approach suggests that these investigators attribute most of the age-linked differences in environmental cognition to preexperimental differences in accumulated experience. It is thus to the question of experience that I now turn.

Experiential Histories

The effect of environmental experience is, of course, one of the main foci of research in environmental psychology. Research with adults has demonstrated the power of repeated exposure to environments (Appleyard, 1970; Evans, Marrero, & Butler, 1981; Heft, 1979; Herman, Kail, & Siegel,1979). Research with elderly adults has similarly demonstrated the power of personal experience. Elderly subjects are less likely to recall buildings that are not directly accessible from the street (Evans, Brennan, Skorpanich, & Held, 1984) and include more information about their city environments in representations in relation to their mobility throughout the city (Walsh, Krauss, & Regnier, 1981).

Likewise, developmental psychologists (or developmental environmental psychologists) have shown the importance of similar variables for children. Repeated exposure to everyday environments leads to increasingly differentiated cognitive maps of those environments. Schouela, Steinberg, Leveton, and Wapner (1980), for example, studied sketch maps produced by four children (ranging in age from about 4 to 10 years) as they first entered a new environment, and then as they become increasingly familiar with it during a 9-month period. The children's sketch maps became increasingly differentiated, showed additional territory, and so on, similar to the microgenetic changes shown by adults as they become increasingly familiar with new environments (see Cohen & Cohen, 1985, for a review of much of the empirical literature).

Furthermore, there is suggestive (correlational) evidence from the literature on sex-related differences that exposure to a wide range of environments may be responsible for enhanced spatial and environmental cognition. Males, as a group, typically perform better than females, as a group, on spatial and environmental measures (see Linn & Petersen, 1985). Correlatively, boys are found to have a greater free range, for example, traveling further from home on bicycles (Hart, 1981), make fewer routinized trips (Coates & Bussard, 1974; Moore & Young, 1978), and use more space and more diverse areas in classrooms and playgrounds (Harper & Sanders, 1975).

The hypothesized relationship between experience in natural environments and environmental cognition is bolstered by findings from experimental work showing that repeated exposure to laboratory environments enhances environmental cognition. Siegel, Herman, Allen, and Kirasic (1979), for example, showed that children's performance in reproducing the locations of buildings in a room-size model town improved with repeated exposure.

Similar parallels between studies with adults and children may be found with respect to showing that environmental cognition is affected by the *means* (e.g., on foot vs. car) through which the environment is experienced (Appleyard, 1970; Golledge & Spector, 1978; Hart, 1981; Hart & Berzok, 1982; see Cohen & Cohen, 1985), and the *purpose* (e.g., goal directed vs. nondirected exploration) for which it is explored (Cohen & Cohen, 1982; Gauvain & Rogoff, 1986). These research efforts lead to the conclusion that the same general kinds of variables that affect environmental cognition in adults likewise appear to affect environmental cognition in children.

Another experience-related question addressed in developmental research is whether age-linked increments in environmental cognition may be attributed, at least in part, to the accumulation of *visual* experience in environments. In part, this question is addressed in the work by Acredolo et al. (1984) discussed earlier on infants' visual tracking. This question has also been addressed by comparing environmental cognition in individuals who have and have not—because they are blind—had visual experience.

In one program of research, Landau (1988) posits that visual experience per se is *not* important in the development of spatial cognition. She argues that spatial knowledge is dependent on an underlying structure in humans, which can be developed through experiences in *any* modality. In support of this position, she cites a young blind child's ability to make Euclidean spatial inferences after moving through a room-sized space and the child's success in using a tactile map to find objects in a room. However, Landau's conclusions have been criticized on both procedural and conceptual grounds (see Liben, 1988; Liben & Downs, 1989; Millar, 1988; but see Mandler, 1988, for a supportive position).

Most other researchers have noted important deficits in visually impaired subjects' environmental cognition. Reiser, Lockman, and Pick (1980), for example, asked congenitally blind and sighted subjects to make comparative distance judgments of pairs of locations in a highly familiar space. Both groups' spontaneous judgments tended to be relatively good with respect to functional or traveled distances between points. When subjects were explicitly asked to give straight-line or Euclidean distances between points, however, only the sighted subjects were able to modify their estimates accurately.

In a related study, Reiser, Guth, and Hill (1982) first taught adult subjects to point quickly and accurately from a home base to three locations within a room. After walking to one of the three locations, sighted, but not blind subjects, were still quick and accurate in pointing to the other locations in the room. (Neither sighted nor blind subjects were successful when asked to *imagine* themselves in a new location.) In reviewing this work, Pick (1988) suggests that "the constant exposure of sighted persons during their lives to perspective transformations as they move provides a background of sensitivity as to how the relative positions of locations to themselves change" (p. 154). Acredolo (1988) similarly stressed attributed to the importance of visual tracking in infancy:

> by watching objects as he or she moves, the infant acquires first-hand knowledge about space as a container and self as but one object in relation to others. Views are coordinated, distances are calibrated, and landmarks achieve significance. (p. 165)

Thus, although somewhat controversial, the weight of the evidence seems to support the position that environmental cognition rests heavily on a foundation established through visual experience (see also Golledge, this volume). As discussed earlier, other kinds of experience (e.g., exploration of environments) are also critical in expanding environmental cognition in children, just as they are instrumental in enhancing environmental cognition in adults.

Conclusions

It is clear that individuals change physically, emotionally, and cognitively as they move through the life course. They likewise acquire a host of important experiences that are important for developing both their abstract spatial concepts and their specific environmental knowledge. Although the major domains of developmental change—physical, socioemotional, cognitive, and experiential—have been discussed individually, it should be obvious that these interact in important and fundamental ways. When placed in a new environment, the individual's interaction with, and representation of that environment will depend not only on the sensorimotor skills available, but also on the degree to which that individual feels comfortable in exploring the space, can relate those explorations to already established cognitive schemata, the logical skills available to manipulate the incoming information, and so on. In short, although changes in domains were discussed separately, in actuality they are highly interdependent.

THE DERIVATION OF ENVIRONMENTAL COGNITION FROM ENVIRONMENTAL REPRESENTATIONS

The environmental cognition discussed above derives from individuals' direct exploration or perception of the actual environment. Although this direct source is undoubtedly the one that has received the most attention in the developmental literature, it is not the only important source of environmental cognition. People also acquire knowledge about environments through *representations* of environments. Representations may be verbal descriptions of places, static or dynamic photographs, drawings, three-dimensional models, maps, and so on. In this section I first discuss ways in which environmental representations may affect environmental cognition, and then review selected research on the development of understanding of environmental representations.

Functions of Environmental Representations

Environmental Representations as Substitutes for Direct Environmental Experience. One use of environmental representations is as an experimental tool to *simulate* direct experience in the environment. The use of representations rather than actual experience in the "real" environment is usually driven by practical considerations. It may be too difficult to take subjects into the actual environment (e.g., because of time, cost, exposure to risks), and/or it may be that the actual environment cannot be controlled adequately for the investigator's purpose (e.g., portions of the urban landscape may be obscured unpredictably by traffic).

Research on environmental assessment is often conducted using environmental representations. Rachel Kaplan (this volume), for example, has asked subjects to make a variety of environmental judgments from photographs of different natural vistas. Similarly, Küller (this volume) obtained preference ratings of interior and built environments using photographs; and Axia et al. (this volume) asked children to judge whether or not rooms are classrooms by employing photographic stimuli.

In research directed to learning how subjects select landmarks for route learning, trips through environments have been simulated by videotapes of travel through real or model environments, or by a series of still slides that show scenes along a route. Allen, Kirasic, Siegel, and Herman (1979), for example, were interested in determining whether children would be able to select informative landmarks as reminders for where they were along a slide-presented "walk." Thus, after viewing the whole "walk," 7 year olds, 10 year olds, and college students were asked to select pictures that would serve as good reference points. Interestingly, adults most often selected scenes that showed actual, or potential changes in headings (i.e., intersections), whereas children most often selected scenes that were *visually salient* (e.g., colorful awnings) but that were neither distinctive (e.g., there were several similar scenes along the route) nor informative about headings (being located in mid-block, for example, rather than at intersections with choice points). Apparently, individuals become increasingly adept at attending to relevant aspects of the available information.

In these illustrative studies, the critical information provided by the environmental representation is meant to be comparable to information available in the actual environment. That is, in the use of representations as *substitutes* for direct environmental experience, the goal is to create an experience as much like that in the real environment as possible. Were the two methods equally easy, the representation would not be used.

Environmental Representations as Amplifiers of Direct Environmental Experience. A conceptually more interesting function of environmental representations is to *amplify* direct environmental experience. In this sense, environmental representations provide information about the environment that would not otherwise be available to the individual. A number of purposes (not necessarily mutually exclusive) may be served.

First, environmental representations may act as *advanced organizers* that influence the impact of later direct experience in the environment. Environmental representations may provide an introduction to a place, giving people some sense of familiarity and comfort. Kaplan (1976), for example, showed environmental representations (e.g., aerial photographs, contour maps) to a group of junior high school students prior to taking them to the depicted natural environment. These students reported more confidence, less fear, and more enjoyment in their later explorations of that environment than did students not exposed to these representations. The opportunity to examine representations in advance of encountering a particular environment serves not only an affective function but an obvious cognitive one as well. Studying a map of an environment is undeniably useful for getting to a location *in* an environment, and for understanding and exploring that environment after getting to it. Even some 3 year olds seem to be able to profit from previewing a map prior to entering an environment (Uttal & Wellman, 1987).

Second, environmental representations amplify environmental cognition by conveying information about *unavailable environments*. Photographs, maps, or descriptions of Mars or Venus, for example, serve that purpose for virtually all adults; comparable representations of other continents, countries, regions, or even just towns and neighborhoods serve that purpose for many individuals, and, especially for children who are given endless lessons in social studies about distant lands.

Third, and perhaps both most important and least obvious, place representations provide a means of *realizing otherwise unknowable aspects of the environment,* that is, environmental cognition that cannot be derived from direct experience, not simply because a particular place has not *yet* been visited, but rather because of limits on the human perceptual or cognitive system. This argument has been developed most fully by Downs (1981) in his discussion of the function of maps.

Given that maps are not simply miniaturizations of the world but rather are creative statements about it, Downs (1981) argues that maps allow new ways of understanding or "realizing" the environment. Place representations expand our realization of the environment by overcoming the limits of our perceptual faculties. For example, we could never see the entire Earth at once because it is simply too big, but we can see a map of the entire Earth at once. Maps can be used to solve problems. For example, mapping the distribution of cholera cases allowed the realization that incidence was linked to water pumps, thereby leading to the discovery of the water-borne nature of dispersion. Maps can lead people to realize new relationships. Many of the maps included in the *Fortune Atlas for World Strategy* (Harrison, 1944) published during World War II led people to "know" new relationships. For example, the map of Europe from the east, shown in Figure 13.3, allows one to "realize" that Europe provides a corridor directly into Russia (or the reverse).

Conclusions: The Relevance of Environmental Representations. The argument just made suggests that an important source of environmental cognition is exposure to and use of environmental representations. It is not *only* that representations can be used as substitutes for actual environments in the attempt to make our scientific task easier. Importantly, environmental representations may also be instrumental in yielding environmental cognition that would be impossible from direct environmental experiences alone. Thus, to provide a more complete picture of the development of environmental cognition, it is crucial to consider the development of the ability to understand environmental representations. The work described below is drawn entirely from a fully collaborative effort with Roger Downs, and is described in more detail in Downs and Liben (1987, 1988) and in Liben and Downs (1986, 1989).

Understanding Environmental Representations: Definitional and Developmental Issues

The Conventional Wisdom. There is actually surprisingly little research on the development of the ability to understand place representations (see Liben & Downs,

Figure 13.3. Europe from the east, adapted from a map by Richard Edes Harrison, originally appearing in the *Fortune Atlas for World Strategy* (1944).

1989, for a review). A conventional wisdom has emerged, however, from the extant literature. The received view is that place representations—even cartographic maps— are understood even by very young children, even with very little effort, and even with little or no prior experience.

Landau (1986), for example, citing a 4-year-old blind child's successful use of a tactile map, proposed "that certain fundamental components of map use are accessible without specific prior experience in map reading, and without previous visual experience" (p. 201). Similarly, Blaut and Stea (1971) found that elementary school children were able to identify features on maps and aerial photographs, and thus concluded that "school-entering six-year-olds can read and make maps" (p. 390). Perhaps even more strikingly, they suggested that at least for some children, the emergence of these abilities is so early (by 2 and 3 years of age) that it could not be assessed by their interview methods. Similar conclusions about very young children's map competencies are drawn by other investigators as well (Blades & Spencer, 1986; Bluestein & Acredolo, 1979; Presson, 1982).

Questioning the Conventional Wisdom. The conclusion that place representations are understood early and easily, however, is surprising on the basis of theoretical arguments and empirical data. Two theoretical perspectives challenge the "easy and early" conclusion, one drawn from cognitive-developmental theory and the other from cartography.

First, Piagetian cognitive-developmental theory posits significant limitations on young children's representational skills. Specifically, although the representational function is said to be established very early—at about 2 years when the child progresses from sensorimotor to preoperational thought—the young child's representational skills are still constrained and fragile (see Piaget & Inhelder, 1969). Early in the preoperational period children do not fully appreciate the arbitrary nature of symbols and the complete separation of representation from referent. Thus, for example, preoperational children may treat a representation as if it were the referent itself (as in licking a photograph of an ice cream cone, see Beilin, 1983) or may fail to appreciate the representational function of something that is understood as an object in its own right (as when the $2\frac{1}{2}$-year-old child appears to be unable to treat a scale model of a room not only as a toy, but simultaneously as a *representation* of a full-size room, see DeLoache, 1987).

Second, Piagetian theory suggests that the *spatial* content of place representations should not be readily accessible to very young children. As discussed earlier, Piaget and Inhelder (1956) proposed that young children first come to understand topological spatial concepts, and only later master projective and Euclidean concepts. Projective concepts are essential for understanding many features of place representations, including viewing angle and azimuth, map projections, and relationships among self, representation, and place. Euclidean concepts are likewise essential, as in understanding scale, distance, angular relationships, and systems of coordinates.

In addition to Piagetian theory, aspects of cartographic theory also cast doubt on the received view that map understanding is early and easy. It is naive to think that maps (and, by extension, other modes of place representation) are "transparent" miniaturizations of the real world, automatically interpretable by the perceptual system (Downs, 1981). Cartographers recognize the diversity of possible representations—differing in projective system, symbols, differential content, and other map features—and thus appreciate the virtually limitless variety in the representation of place. Surely not all these varieties are automatically accessible through prewired perceptual systems. Indeed, the difficulty that untrained adults have interpreting many place representations—be they maps or aerial photographs—and the necessity for teaching map reading and map interpretation to cartographers, military personnel, pilots, and others (Lobeck, 1956) indicate the nontransparent nature of these representations. (See Downs & Liben, 1988, for a fuller development of this argument.)

In evaluating the conventional wisdom, it is relevant to consider not only cognitive-developmental and cartographic *theory*, but also the *empirical* basis on which the conventional wisdom rests. In particular, one might question the criteria that have been used to conclude that an individual has, or has not, understood a place representation. From the observation that young children could identify some features on a black-and-white vertical aerial photograph, Blaut, McCleary, and Blaut (1970) concluded that school-entering children can interpret vertical aerial photographs; from the finding that children could trace roads and houses onto acetate and then draw a pencil line route from one house to another, Blaut, McCleary, and Blaut (1970) concluded that these children could make and use abstract maps for route-planning problems. From the finding that a 4-year-old blind child was able to find specified landmarks following exposure to a tactile map of the room and landmarks, Landau (1986) suggested that "Certain fundamental components of map use are accessible without specific prior experience in map reading, and without previous visual experience" (pp. 201–202).

Are these empirical findings, however, sufficient for the conclusions drawn? One might argue (see Liben & Downs, 1989) that the data on young children's successes are misleading if viewed in isolation from the data on their failures, and if alternative paths for successful performance are not acknowledged. Blaut, McCleary, and Blaut (1970), for example, stressed children's successes in identifying features of the aerial photographs. But they did not discuss the *errors* that, on the basis of other reports, must have occurred. For example, using similar procedures, Spencer, Harrison, Darvizeh (1980) found that preschoolers recognized some geographic features such as roads, but made telling errors as well. None of the children recognized tennis courts on the aerial photograph. More critically, some misidentified them as doors, apparently finding "no inconsistency in seeing the lines as the panels on what would have been a pair of huge doors lying flat beside the minute blobs that they had previously identified correctly as being full sized trees" (p. 62). We have found similar kinds of errors in our work with preschoolers as well (Downs & Liben, 1987).

Similarly, one might question Landau's (1986) conclusion that Kelli, a blind child, understood a tactile map of a room, simply because she reached a target. As suggested elsewhere (Liben, 1988; Liben & Downs, 1989; Millar, 1988), Kelli may have relied on a variety of perceptual cues in solving the problem, and/or may have drawn on knowledge gained from prior experimental sessions in which a similar diamond-shaped layout of landmarks in a small room had been used.

In short, both on the basis of theoretical expectations from cognitive-developmental and cartographic theory, and on the basis of concern for the particular indices that have been used to assert "success," there is reason to question the "early and easy" conventional wisdom. At the very least, it is necessary to recognize that a young child's success in answering one particular question about one particular environmental representation should not be taken as an indication that the child has mastered environmental representations in general. To clarify what has and has not been mastered, it is important to address more explicitly what we mean by "understanding" environmental representations.

Our Understanding of "Understanding Environmental Representations." Two fundamental correspondences between environments and their representations must be understood to claim that someone has "understood" an environmental representation (Liben & Downs, 1989). First, one must appreciate *representational correspondences* that refer to the correspondence between the information that is to be presented (i.e., the particular aspects of the environmental referent chosen to be depicted) and the means for its portrayal (i.e., the symbolization system, be it cartographic, photographic, pictorial, etc.). Second, one must appreciate the *geometrical correspondences* that refer to the correspondence between the spatial relations contained in the environment itself and the spatial relations of the representation (e.g., the scale, viewing azimuth, viewing angle). Understanding these correspondences permits the individual to obtain information about the environment from the representation of the environment. To assert that there is true "understanding" of an environmental representation, one might also want to insist that the individual has "interpreted" as well as "read" the representation (see Lobeck, 1956). Brief discussion bearing on each of these kinds of understanding follows.

Understanding the Information Given: Representational and Geometric Correspondences. At the most basic level, an understanding of an environmental representation requires that the individual appreciate that the representation *stands for* the environment at the *holistic* level (Liben & Downs, 1989). For the most part, even young children do appear to be successful in recognizing environmental representations as showing places. When shown an aerial photograph of Chicago, for example, preschoolers uniformly recognized it as a place, although the precision of that recognition varied considerably (Downs & Liben, 1987). Some children, for example, recognized it as "a city," or "lots of buildings," whereas others, although recognizing it as a place, did so with less accuracy, saying it showed "the USA" and "the whole world." Similar levels of understanding were evident in reactions to a road map of Pennsylvania, which was varyingly identified as "states and stuff" and "part of Africa," and, by a single child, as "California, Canada, the West, and the North Coast." When faced with place representations that were less familiar, children often failed to recognize them as places at all. A tourist map of Washington, D.C., for example, readily identified as a map by adults (see Downs & Liben, 1987), was thought to be "a cage" and "a spaceship."

What is perhaps more telling, however, is that even having "understood" the representation in the holistic sense that it shows a place, young children often demonstrate a *lack* of understanding of specific pieces of the representation, what we have elsewhere referred to as *componential* understanding (Liben & Downs, 1989). Thus, even having understood that a particular graphic form (photograph or map) stands for a place, young children often interpret components of the representation for what they "look like" in an iconic sense. Sometimes these iconic interpretations are advantageous, as in recognizing roads on the Chicago aerial as roads "because they are gray" or the Susquehanna River as a river on the road map "because it's blue." But more often, such interpretations work against understanding, as when on the Chicago aerial a baseball diamond was recognized as "an eye" and "a guitar"; a semicircular field was said to be "cheese"; or when on the road map, the compass rose was identified as "the sun," "a basketball stadium," "feathers," and "the place where the lifeguard sits" [it was, after all, placed on Lake Erie!]; the yellow areal symbols actually used to represent built-up areas were said to show "firecrackers" and "eggs." (See Downs & Liben, 1987; Liben & Downs, 1989, for additional examples and detail about procedures.) These errors suggest that young children have only a fragile and limited understanding of the symbolic nature of the representation.

Similar limitations on children's understanding of the geometric correspondences between the environment and its representation are found. First, young children have difficulty in understanding the scale and size relationships and thus do not understand the dimensional systematicity of representations. Thus, for example, on the Chicago aerial, children who found buildings (despite the fact that they were small) also found "fish" [actually boats] on Lake Michigan; on the Pennsylvania road map, children rejected the suggestion that the lines could show roads because they were "not fat enough for two cars to go on." Further limits in understanding geometric correspondences are evident in children's difficulty in understanding perspective (viewing angle and azimuth). On the aerial photograph, for example, rows of railroad box cars were identified as "book shelves," an example like that cited earlier from Spencer et al. (1980) in which tennis courts were thought to be "doors."

In summary, although most environmental representations are identified as places by even very young children, some prove more difficult to interpret. Even those that are correctly understood as places, however, are misunderstood in significant ways, demonstrating children's difficulties with both the representational and geometric correspondences between environment and representation.

Going beyond the Information Given: Map Interpretation and Use. Recognition of the representational and geometric correspondences is critical for "reading" place representations, that is, for identifying their contents. However, environmental cognition is much more than identifying elements of an environment and/or of its representation. It extends beyond to understanding relationships implied by, or latent in, the representation. In using maps for wayfinding, for example, it is necessary not only to understand the geometric correspondences between the environment and the map, but, in addition, to understand the relationship among map, environment, and self.

There is considerable evidence that this aspect of understanding undergoes significant development during childhood. In our work (Liben & Downs, 1986), for example, many kindergarten, first-, and second-grade children appear to be oblivious to the need to align map and space either physically or mentally when showing locations on a map. Even when told directly of the need for this rotation (as when asked to indicate locations on a map of their classroom that was rotated 180°), many young children have serious difficulty.

Other researchers have likewise shown that young children have difficulty when map and space are unaligned (see Bluestein & Acredolo, 1979; Presson, 1982). Our current work with children in middle childhood (fifth through eighth graders, about 10 to 13 year olds) suggests that these older children are able to succeed on mapping tasks that require an understanding of alignment. The observed pattern of improvement is consistent with predictions derived from Piagetian theory concerning the gradual mastery of projective and Euclidean concepts. Even with these concepts, however, success is not complete. Misalignments continue to make map-reading tasks difficult as indicated by research on "You-are-here" maps showing that even adults have difficulty when the map and the space are misaligned (see Levine, 1982).

Similar findings may be cited concerning young children's growing ability to understand the conceptual implications of place representations. For example, an environmental representation such as a map of the United States contains within it information about relationships among different levels of places, including, for example, the geographic hierarchical relationships among city, county, state, region, and country. A true understanding of these logically nested relationships depends on the child's understanding of class inclusion, an accomplishment that is underdeveloped in preoperational children. Consistent with this view, Daggs (1986) found that young children had great difficulty in representing nested relationships of geographic hierarchies correctly either verbally or graphically (see also Downs, Liben, & Daggs, 1988).

These examples provide some indication that children's abilities to extract and go beyond the information contained in environmental representations develop dramatically across the life span. Just as a "true" life-span developmentalist asks what physical, socioemotional, cognitive, and experiential factors account for individuals' growing abilities to achieve "environmental cognition" from interacting directly with the environment, so too, the life-span developmentalist should ask how these same factors account for growing environmental cognition derived from *representations* of the environment. Unfortunately, there is very little research bearing on these relationships.

In our own work we have found significant correlations between performance on summary mapping scores and performance on projective and Euclidean tasks *even when* chronological age was partialled out (Liben & Downs, 1986). Similarly, Daggs (1986) found relationships between children's understanding of class inclusion and certain measures of their understanding of geographic hierarchies (see Downs, Liben, & Daggs, 1988). Far more research of this kind is needed, however, if we are to understand what developmental changes underlie children's growing abilities to learn about environments from representations of environments.

CONCLUSIONS

An extensive body of research assessing various aspects of environmental cognition at different points in the life span already exists. Not surprisingly, older children almost always do better than younger children. Elderly adults often show some deterioration of functioning. The problem with much of the extant research, however, is that although it *describes* age-linked differences in environmental cognition, it does not *explain* the mechanisms by which these improvements or deteriorations come about. To do so, it is necessary to include independent assessments of those variables hypothesized to underlie the developmental changes in environmental cognition. In this way it may be possible not only to explain developmental phenomena, but also to identify mechanisms responsible for individual differences and microgenetic change.

In addition, past research has predominately focused on how experiences in the environment foster environmental cognition. Although these experiences are critical, it has been argued here that experiences with *representations* of the environment also play a powerful role. Importantly, there are many functions served by environmental representations that simply *cannot* be served by direct environmental experience. If we are to develop a full understanding of the content and use of environmental cognition, and if we are to plan interventions that affect the ways that people interact with their environments, consideration of both sources is critical.

ACKNOWLEDGMENTS

I would like to express my thanks to Gary Evans and Tommy Gärling for organizing the Umeå Conference on Environmental Cognition and Assessment (July 1988) for which this chapter was originally prepared.

REFERENCES

Acredolo, L.P. (1979). Laboratory versus home: The effect of environment on the 9-month-old infant's choice of spatial reference system. *Developmental Psychology, 15,* 666–667.

Acredolo, L.P. (1982). The familiarity factor in spatial research. In R. Cohen (Ed.), *New directions for child development: Vol. 15. Children's conceptions of spatial relationships* (pp. 19–30). San Francisco: Jossey-Bass.

Acredolo, L.P. (1988). Infant mobility and spatial development. In J. Stiles-Davis, M. Kritchevsky, & U. Bellugi (Eds.), *Spatial cognition: Brain bases and development* (pp. 157–186). Hillsdale, N.J.: Erlbaum.

Acredolo, L.P., Adams, A., & Goodwyn, S.W. (1984). The role of self-produced movement and visual tracking in infant spatial orientation. *Journal of Experimental Child Psychology, 38,* 312–327.

Acredolo, L.P., & Boulter, L.T. (1984). Effects of hierarchical organization on children's judgments of distance and direction. *Journal of Experimental Child Psychology, 37,* 409–425.

Acredolo, L.P., & Evans, D. (1980). Developmental changes in the effects of landmarks on infant spatial behavior. *Developmental Psychology, 16,* 312–318.

Ainsworth, M.D.S., Bell, S.M.V., & Stayton, D.J. (1973). Individual differences in the strange-situation behavior of one-year-olds. In L.S. Stone, H.T. Smith, & L.B. Murphy (Eds.), *The competent infant.* New York: Basic Books.

Allen, G.L. (1981). A developmental perspective on the effects of "subdividing" macrospatial experience. *Journal of Experimental Psychology: Human Learning and Memory, 7,* 120–132.

Allen, G.L. (1982). The organization of route knowledge. In R. Cohen (Ed.), *New directions for child development: Children's conceptions of spatial relationships* (No. 15, pp. 31–39). San Francisco: Jossey-Bass.

Allen, G.L., Kirasic, K.C., Siegel, A.W., & Herman, J.F. (1979). Developmental issues in cognitive mapping: The selection and utilization of environmental landmarks. *Child Development, 50,* 1062–1070.

Appleyard, D. (1970). Styles and methods of structuring a city. *Environment and Behavior, 2,* 100–117.

Baer, D.M. (1970). An age-irrelevant concept of development. *Merrill-Palmer Quarterly, 16,* 238–246.

Baltes, P.B., Cornelius, S.W., & Nesselroade, J.R. (1977). Cohort effects in behavioral development: Theoretical and methodological perspectives. In W.A. Collins (Ed.), *Minnesota symposium on child psychology* (Vol. 11). Hillsdale, N.J.: Erlbaum.

Baltes, P.B., Reese, H.W., & Nesselroade, J.R. (1977). *Life-span developmental psychology: Introduction to research methods.* Monterey, Calif.: Brooks/Cole.

Beilin, H. (1983). Development of photogenic comprehension. *Art Education,* Special Issue, *The Arts and the Mind,* 28–33.

Bertenthal, B.I., Campos, J.J., & Barrett, K.C. (1984). Self-produced locomotion: An organizer of emotional, cognitive, and social development in infancy. In R. Emde and R. Harmon (Eds.), *Continuities and discontinuities in development* (pp. 175–210). New York: Plenum.

Blades, M., & Spencer, C. (1986). Map use by young children. *Geography, 71,* 47–52.

Blaut, J.M., McCleary, G.S., Jr., & Blaut, A.S. (1970). Environmental mapping in young children. *Environment and Behavior, 2,* 335–349.

Blaut, J.M., & Stea, D. (1971). Studies in geographic learning. *Annals of the Association of American Geographers, 61,* 387–393.

Bluestein, N., & Acredolo, L. (1979). Developmental changes in map-reading skills. *Child Development, 50,* 691–697.

Bremner, J.G., & Bryant, P.E. (1985). Active movement and development of spatial abilities in infancy. In H.M. Wellman (Ed.), *Children's searching* (pp. 53–72). Hillsdale, N.J.: Erlbaum.

Case, R. (1985). *Intellectual development.* New York: Academic Press.

Chi, M.T.H. (1976). Short-term memory limitations in children: Capacity or processing deficits? *Memory & Cognition, 4,* 559–572.

Coates, G., & Bussard, E. (1974). Patterns of children's spatial behavior in a moderate-density housing development. In R.C. Moore (Ed.), *Childhood city, man-environment interactions* (Vol. 12). D. Carson (General Ed.). Milwaukee: EDRA.

Cohen, R. (Ed.). (1985). *The development of spatial cognition.* Hillsdale, N.J.: Erlbaum.

Cohen, S.L., & Cohen, R. (1982). Distance estimates of children as a function of type of activity in the environment. *Child Development, 53,* 834–837.

Cohen, S.L., & Cohen, R. (1985). The role of activity in spatial cognition. In R. Cohen (Ed.), *The development of spatial cognition* (pp. 199–223). Hillsdale, N.J.: Erlbaum.

Daggs, D.G. (1986). *Pyramid of places: Children's understanding of geographic hierarchy.* Unpublished Masters Thesis, The Pennsylvania State University.

DeLoache, J.S. (1987). Rapid change in the symbolic functioning of very young children. *Science, 238,* 1556–1557.

Dennis, S. (1988). *A stage theory view of school-aged children's drawings.* Paper presented at the Conference on Human Development, Charleston, South Carolina.

Downs, R.M. (1981). Maps and mappings as metaphors for spatial representation. In L.S. Liben, A.H. Patterson, & N. Newcombe (Eds.), *Spatial representation and behavior across the life span: Theory and application* (pp. 143–166). New York: Academic Press.

Downs, R.M., & Liben, L.S. (1987). Children's understanding of maps. In P. Ellen & C. Thinus-Blanc (Eds.). *Cognitive processes and spatial orientation in animal and man. Vol. 2. Neurophysiology and developmental aspects* (pp. 202–219). Dordrecht: Martinus Nijhoff.

Downs, R.M., & Liben, L.S. (1988). Through a map darkly: Understanding maps as representations. *The Genetic Epistemologist, 16,* 11–18.

Downs, R.M., Liben, L.S., & Daggs, D.G. (1988). On education and geographers: The role of cognitive developmental theory in geographic education. *Annals of the Association of American Geographers, 78,* 680–700.

Evans, G.W. (1980). Environmental cognition. *Psychological Bulletin, 88,* 259–287.

Evans, G.W., Brennan, P.L., Skorpanich, M.A., & Held, D. (1984). Cognitive mapping and elderly adults: Verbal and location memory for urban landmarks. *Journal of Gerontology, 39,* 452–457.

Evans, G.W., & Gärling, T. (1987). Description of Conference on Environmental Cognition and Assessment, University of Umeå, Sweden.

Evans, G.W., Marrero, D.G., & Butler, P.A. (1981). Environmental learning and cognitive mapping. *Environment and Behavior, 13,* 83–104.

Feldman, A., & Acredolo, L. (1979). The effect of active versus passive exploration on memory for spatial location in children. *Child Development, 50,* 698–704.

Flavell, J., & Wellman, H.M. (1977). Metamemory. In R.V. Kail, Jr., & J.W. Hagen (Eds.), *Perspectives on the development of memory and cognition* (pp. 3–33). Hillsdale, N.J.: Erlbaum.

Gauvain, M., & Rogoff, B. (1986). Influence of the goal on children's exploration and memory of large-scale space. *Developmental Psychology, 22,* 72–77.

Golbeck, S. (1983). Reconstructing a large-scale spatial arrangement: Effects of environmental organization and operativity. *Developmental Psychology, 19,* 644–653.

Golbeck, S. (1985). Spatial cognition as a function of environmental characteristics. In R. Cohen (Ed.), *The development of spatial cognition* (pp. 225–255). Hillsdale, N.J.: Erlbaum.

Golbeck, S.L., & Liben. L.S. (1988). A cognitive-developmental approach to children's environmental representations. *Children's Environment Quarterly, 5,* 46–53.

Golbeck, S.L., Rand, M., & Soundy, C. (1986). Constructing a model of a large-scale space with the space in view: Effects on preschoolers of guidance and cognitive restructuring, *Merrill-Palmer Quarterly, 32,* 187–203.

Golledge, R.G., & Spector, A.N. (1978). Comprehending the urban environment: Theory and practice. *Geographical Analysis, 10,* 401–426.

Harlow, H.F., & Harlow, M.K. (1969). Effects of various mother-infant relationships on rhesus monkey behaviors. In B.M. Foss (Ed.), *Determinants of infant behavior* (Vol. 4). London: Methuen.

Harper, L.V., & Sanders, K.M. (1975). Pre-school children's use of space: Sex differences in outdoor play. *Developmental Psychology, 11,* 119.

Harrison, R.E. (1944). *Look at the world: The Fortune atlas for world strategy.* New York: Knopf.

Hart, R. (1981). Children's spatial representation of the landscape: Lessons and questions from a field study. In L.S. Liben, A.H. Patterson, & N. Newcombe (Eds.), *Spatial representation and behavior across the life span: Theory and application* (pp. 195–233). New York: Academic Press.

Hart, R., & Berzok, M. (1982). Children's strategies for mapping the geographic-scale environment. In M. Potegal (Ed.), *Spatial abilities: Development and physiological foundations* (pp. 147–169). New York: Academic Press.

Hazen, N.L. (1982). Spatial exploration and spatial knowledge: Individual and developmental differences in very young children. *Child Development, 53,* 826–833.

Hazen, N.L., & Durrett, M.E. (1982). Relationship of security of attachment to exploration and cognitive mapping abilities in 2-year-olds. *Developmental Psychology, 18,* 751–759.

Heft, H. (1979). The role of environmental features in route-learning: Two exploratory studies of way-finding. *Environmental Psychology and Nonverbal Behavior, 3,* 173–185.

Herman, J.F., Kail, J.V., & Siegel, A.W. (1979). Cognitive maps of a college campus: A new look at freshman orientation. *Bulletin of the Psychonomic Society, 13,* 183–186.

Huston-Stein, A., & Baltes, P.B. (1976). Theory and method in life-span developmental psychology: Implications for child development. In H.W. Reese (Ed.), *Advances in child development and behavior* (pp. 169–188). New York: Academic Press.

Johnston, J.R. (1988). Children's verbal representation of spatial location. In J. Stiles-David, M. Kritchevsky, & U. Bellugi (Eds.), *Spatial cognition: Brain bases and development* (pp. 195–205). Hillsdale, N.J.: Erlbaum.

Kaplan, R. (1976). Way-finding in the natural environment. In G. Moore & R. Golledge (Eds.), *Environmental knowing.* Stroudsburg, Penn.: Dowden, Hutchinson, & Ross.

Kopp, C.B. (1979). Perspective on infant motor system development. In M.H. Bornstein & W. Kessen (Eds.), *Psychological development from infancy: Image to intention* (pp. 9–35). Hillsdale, N.J.: Erlbaum.

Kosslyn, S.M., Pick, H.L., & Fariello, G.R. (1974). Cognitive maps in children and men. *Child Development, 45,* 707–716.

Landau, B. (1986). Early map use as an unlearned ability. *Cognition, 22,* 201–223.

Landau, B. (1988). Spatial knowledge in blind and sighted children. In J. Stiles-Davis, M. Kritchevsky, & U. Bellugi (Eds.), *Spatial cognition: Brain bases and development* (pp. 343–371). Hillsdale, N.J.: Erlbaum.

Lee, G.R., & Lassey, M.L. (1980). Rural-urban differences among the elderly: Economic, social, and subjective factors. *Journal of Social Issues, 36,* 62–74.

Levine, M. (1982). YOU-ARE-HERE maps: Psychological considerations. *Environment and Behavior, 14,* 221–237.

Lewis, M., & Brooks-Gunn, J. (1979). *Social cognition and the acquisition of self.* New York: Plenum.

Liben, L.S. (1981a). Spatial representation and behavior: Multiple perspectives. In L.S. Liben, A.H. Patterson, & N. Newcombe (Eds.), *Spatial representation and behavior across the life span: Theory and application* (pp. 3–36). New York: Academic Press.

Liben, L.S. (1981b). Contributions of individuals to their development during childhood: A Piagetian perspective. In R. Lerner & N. Busch-Rossnagel (Eds.), *Individuals as producers of their development: A life-span perspective* (pp. 117–153). New York: Academic Press.

Liben, L.S. (1982a). Children's large-scale spatial cognition: Is the measure the message? In R. Cohen (Ed.), *New directions for child development, Vol. 15. Children's conceptions of spatial relationships* (pp. 51–64). San Francisco: Jossey-Bass.

Liben, L.S. (1982b). The developmental study of children's memory. In T. Field, A. Huston, H. Quay, L. Troll, & G. Finley (Eds.), *Review of human development* (pp. 269–289). New York: Wiley.

Liben, L.S. (1987). Information-processing and Piagetian theory: Conflict or congruence? In L.S. Liben (Ed.), *Development and learning: Conflict or congruence?* (pp. 109–132). Hillsdale, N.J.: Erlbaum.

Liben, L.S. (1988). Conceptual issues in the development of spatial cognition. In J. Stiles-Davis, M. Kritchevsky, & U. Bellugi (Eds.), *Spatial cognition: Brain bases and development* (pp. 167–194). Hillsdale, N.J.: Erlbaum.

Liben, L.S., & Downs, R.M. (1986). *Children's production and comprehension of maps: Increasing graphic literacy.* Final Report to the National Institute of Education, #G-83-0025.

Liben, L.S., & Downs, R.M. (1989). Understanding maps as symbols: The development of map concepts in children. In H.W. Reese (Ed.), *Advances in child development and behavior* (Vol. 22, pp. 145–201). New York: Academic Press.

Liben, L.S., & Newcombe, N. (1988). *The appearance and disappearance of barrier effects in children.* Unpublished manuscript, The Pennsylvania State University.

Liben, L.S., Moore, M.L., & Golbeck, S.L. (1982). Preschoolers' knowledge of their classroom environments: Evidence from small-scale and life-size spatial tasks. *Child Development, 53,* 1275–1284.

Linn, M.C., & Petersen, A.C. (1985). Emergence and characterization of sex differences in spatial ability: A meta-analysis. *Child Development, 56,* 1479–1498.

Lobeck, A.K. (1956). *Things maps don't tell us.* New York: Macmillan.

Mandler, J.M. (1988). The development of spatial cognition: On topological and Euclidean representation. In J. Stiles-Davis, M. Kritchevsky, & U. Bellugi (Eds.), *Spatial cognition: Brain bases and development* (pp. 423–432). Hillsdale, N.J.: Erlbaum.

Millar, S. (1988). Models of sensory deprivation: The nature/nurture dichotomy and spatial representation in the blind. *International Journal of Behavioral Development, 11,* 69–87.

Moore, R., & Young, D. (1978). Children outdoors: Toward a social ecology of the landscape. In I. Altman & J.F. Wohlwill (Eds.), *Children and the environment* (pp. 83–130). New York: Plenum.

Newcombe, N. (1985). Methods for the study of spatial cognition. In R. Cohen (Ed.), *The development of spatial cognition* (pp. 277–300). Hillsdale, N.J.: Erlbaum.

Newcombe, N., & Liben, L.S. (1982). Barrier effects in the cognitive maps of children and adults. *Journal of Experimental Child Psychology, 34,* 46–58.

Ohta, R.J., & Kirasic, K.C. (1983). The investigation of environmental learning in the elderly. In G.D. Rowles & R.J. Ohta (Eds.), *Aging and milieu: Environmental perspectives on growing old* (pp. 83–95). New York: Academic Press.

Overton, W.F. (1984). World views and their influence on psychological theory and research: Kuhn-Lakatos-Laudan. In H.W. Reese (Ed.), *Advances in child development and behavior* (Vol. 18, pp. 191–226). New York: Academic Press.

Overton, W.F., & Newman, J.L. (1982). Cognitive development: A competence-activation/utilization approach. In T.M. Field, A Huston, H. Quay, L. Troll, & G. Finley (Eds.), *Review of human development* (pp. 217–241). New York: Wiley.

Overton, W.F., & Reese, H.W. (1973). Models of development: Methodological implications. In J.R. Nesselroade & H.W. Reese (Eds.), *Life-span developmental psychology: Methodological issues* (pp. 65–86). New York: Academic Press.

Parr, J. (1980). The interaction of persons and living environments. In L.W. Poon (Ed.), *Aging in the 1980s.* Washington, D.C.: American Psychological Association.

Pascual-Leone, J. (1970). A mathematical model for the transition rule in Piaget's developmental stages. *Acta Psychologica, 32,* 301–345.

Pastalan, L.A. (1973). How the elderly negotiate their environment. *Housing and environment for the elderly.* Washington, D.C.: Gerontological Society.

Pepper, S. (1942). *World hypotheses.* Berkeley, Calif.: University of California Press.

Piaget, J. (1954). *The construction of reality in the child.* New York: Ballantine Books.

Piaget, J. (1970). Piaget's theory. In P. Mussen (Ed.), *Carmichael's manual of child psychology* (pp. 703–732). New York: Wiley.

Piaget, J. (1972). Intellectual evolution from adolescence to adulthood. *Human Development, 15,* 1–12.

Piaget, J., & Inhelder, B. (1956). *The child's conception of space.* New York: Norton.

Piaget, J., & Inhelder, B. (1969). *The psychology of the child.* New York: Basic Books.

Pick, H.L., Jr. (1988). Perceptual aspects of spatial cognitive development. In J. Stiles-Davis, M. Kritchevsky, & U. Bellugi (Eds.), *Spatial cognition: Brain bases and development* (pp. 145–156). Hillsdale, N.J.: Erlbaum.

Pick, H.L., Jr., & Lockman, J.J. (1981). From frames of reference to spatial representations. In L.S. Liben, A.H. Patterson, & N. Newcombe (Eds.), *Spatial representation and behavior across the life-span: Theory and application* (pp. 39–61). New York: Academic Press.

Poag, C.K., Cohen, R., & Weatherford, D.L. (1983). Spatial representations of young children: The role of self- versus adult-directed movement and viewing. *Journal of Experimental Child Psychology, 35,* 172–179.

Presson, C.C. (1982). The development of map-reading skills. *Child Development, 53,* 196–199.

Reese, H.W., & Overton, W.F. (1970). Models of development and theories of development. In L.R. Goulet & P.B. Baltes (Eds.), *Life-span developmental psychology: Research and theory* (pp. 116–145). New York: Academic Press.

Reiser, J.J., Guth, D., & Hill, E. (1982). Mental processes mediating independent travel: Implications for orientation and mobility. *Journal of Visual Impairment and Blindness, 76,* 213–218.

Reiser, J.J., Lockman, J.J., & Pick, H.L., Jr. (1980). The role of visual experience in knowledge of spatial layout. *Perception and Psychophysics, 28,* 185–190.

Regnier, V. (1983). Urban neighborhood cognition: Relationships between functional and symbolic community elements. In G.D. Rowles & R.J. Ohta (Eds.), *Aging and milieu: Environmental perspectives on growing old* (pp. 63–82). New York: Academic Press.

Rowles, G.D. (1983). Geographical dimensions of social support in rural Appalachia. In G.D. Rowles & R.J. Ohta (Eds.), *Aging and milieu: Environmental perspectives on growing old* (pp. 111–130). New York: Academic Press.

Schouela, D.A., Steinberg, L.M., Leveton, L.G., & Wapner, S. (1980). Development of the cognitive organization of an environment. *Canadian Journal of Behavioural Science, 12,* 1–16.

Siegel, A.W., Herman, J.F., Allen, G.L., & Kirasic, K.C. (1979). The development of cognitive maps of large- and small-scale spaces. *Child Development, 50,* 582–585.

Spencer, C., Harrison, N., & Darvizeh, Z. (1980). The development of iconic mapping ability in young children. *International Journal of Early Childhood, 12,* 57–64.

Uttal, D.H., & Wellman, A.M. (1987). *Young children's representation of information acquired from maps.* Paper presented at the meeting of the Society for Research in Child Development, Baltimore.

Wachs, T.D. (1978). The relationship of infants' physical environment to their Binet performance at $2\frac{1}{2}$ years. *International Journal of Behavioral Development, 1,* 51–65.

Wachs, T.D. (1979). Proximal experience and early cognitive-intellectual development: The physical environment. *Merrill-Palmer Quarterly, 25,* 3–41.

Wachs, T.D., & Gruen, G.E. (1982). *Early experience and human development.* New York: Plenum.

Walsh, D.A., Krauss, I.K., & Regnier, V.A. (1981). Spatial ability, environmental knowledge, and environmental use: The elderly. In L.S. Liben, A.H. Patterson, & N. Newcombe (Eds.), *Spatial representation and behavior across the life span* (pp. 321–357). New York: Academic Press.

Wellman, H.M. (Ed.). (1985). *Children's searching.* Hillsdale, N.J.: Erlbaum.

Wellman, H.M., Fabricius, W.V., & Sophian, C. (1985). The early development of planning. In H.M. Wellman (Ed.), *Children's searching* (pp. 123–149). Hillsdale, N.J.: Erlbaum.

Windley, P.G., & Scheidt, R.J. (1980). Person-environment dialects: Implications for competent functioning in old age. In L.W. Poon (Ed.), *Aging in the 1980s.* Washington, D.C.: American Psychological Association.

Wohlwill, J.F. (1973a). The environment is not in the head! In W. Preiser (Ed.), *Environmental Design Research Association* (IV, Vol. 2, pp. 166–181). Fourth International Conference.

Wohlwill, J.F. (1973b). *The study of behavioral development.* New York: Academic Press.

14

Developmental Perspectives on Decision Making and Action in Environments

ROGER A. HART AND MICHAEL K. CONN

The task we have been set is to review developmental theory concerning how individuals act in real-world environments. To simplify this difficult task we have emphasized the developmental span of childhood, the area of our professional expertise. Before proceeding with the review, a few comments regarding the framework of this book and, within it, the definition of our task will enable us to illuminate some of the assumptions inherent in the structure of this volume and to explain how this has affected our conceptualization of the problem.

The stated goal of this book is to look at the separate areas of human relatedness to the environment that are recognized by "most research in environmental psychology": environmental cognition, environmental appraisal and decision making, and action in environments (see Table 1.1 in Chapter 1 of this volume). We agree that although such a separation of cognition and evaluation from action is a reflection of the dominant tendency of research, it is true of only some theories. To accept this division and to discuss primarily action would prevent us from emphasizing those theorists who have argued that human relatedness to the environment must be thought of holistically and dynamically. Consequently, although we have tried to emphasize action, this chapter actually deals simultaneously with cognition and appraisal. The question of why more integrative and holistic theories have been largely ignored is itself important. We argue that the answer lies in a fear by psychologists of such research because it cannot easily meet the traditional tenets of what constitutes good theory—building through experimental research design.

A second problem in the task definition is the use of the word "space." We should not simply be addressing "spatial decisions and actions" but environmental decisions and actions. In the field of environmental psychology the terms "space" and "environment" are commonly used synonymously. We think of space as just one characteristic of objects in the environment. Unfortunately, space is the characteristic that most environmental cognition research has addressed. This is somewhat understandable, for environmental psychology finds its distinctiveness in the study of the large-scale environment in which space (spatial relatedness) is the most distinguishing variable. In such large-scale environments space is too readily thought of in the Kantian sense, as a container of things, rather than as one characteristic of things. We believe that in investigating "place cognition" rather than "spatial cognition," one is brought closer to meaning and action, for "place" is the focus of human intentions. Consequently, the study of place more readily leads us to the simultaneous investigation of thinking, feeling, and acting in the environment.

A common conception of "action" in social science is that it is all goal-directed behavior. This conception seems too sequential to us: movement in response to objective goals located within a "cognitive map" or "field." As Piaget has so thoroughly demonstrated with infants, action can come before representation. With infants representation emerges from nonintentional actions that develop into action schemas, the earliest representations (Piaget, 1952, 1960). In fact, as Piaget has also shown, our concept of actions is something each of us gradually constructed through experience in early childhood (Piaget, 1976). We believe that many of our actions as adults are rationalized afterward as goal-directed behavior when in fact they are often proceeding simultaneously with the process of representation and evaluation. We see more hope in finding meaning in human behavior by investigating action, representation, and appraisal or goal-setting simultaneously, allowing the issue of which comes first to emerge from the analysis.

A third way in which this chapter departs from the emphasis suggested in the conference outline is in the importance we place on the social environment in building a model of environmental action. When one investigates the development of children's environmental decision making and action the necessity of investigating social forces, which are so much a part of a child's relationship to the environment, is particularly clear. Again this is a strong argument for proceeding holistically and dynamically.

This chapter concludes with support for the development of a transactional perspective, which involves "the study of the changing relations among psychological and environmental aspects of holistic unities." The focus in such a perspective is on events and the fundamental unit of study is a person in the environment involved in an event over time (Altman & Rogoff, 1987, p. 9).

THE STATUS OF EMPIRICAL RESEARCH ON CHILDREN'S ACTIONS IN THE ENVIRONMENT

Most of the research on children's actions within the environment is atheoretical. There is, however, value to a review of this research literature: It reveals a wide range of reasons why the development of children's environmental decision making and action is an important domain of inquiry.

Environmental Planning and Design Research

Research related to the environmental planning and design of children's environments usually involves observations of *how* children use environments. Unfortunately these investigations rarely ask *why* children use these environments in particular ways (reviews by Hart, 1979, 1983). Consequently, the findings of such research are of limited value. For example, there is no way of knowing to what extent the patterns of children's use of an environment are a reflection of children's limited knowledge of environmental resources, their changing interests as they develop, their restricted freedom of access to environments, or other factors. The tendency, of course, is to interpret the data from such research simply in terms of the properties of the physical environment that appear to correlate with patterns of observed behavior. This not only ignores important organismic and developmental issues but also fails to recognize the varying social worlds that surround different children—pushing and pulling them in ways that may be more influential than the physical environment itself.

Spatial Behavior Research

Most accounts of human spatial behavior have been written by geographers and focus on adult populations. Remarkably few descriptive studies have been made of the behavior of children or of the elderly in the environment (see reviews by Hart, 1983; Rowles, 1984). There have not to our knowledge been any longitudinal studies of the development of people's spatial behavior over the life span. Neither have there been any formal attempts to compose and synthesize the accounts of spatial behavior to generate theory on the spatial range of human action across the entire life span (see Doxiadis, 1975, for an informal account by a city planner). An attempt to do so through longitudinal or autobiographical investigation might prove valuable both for its contribution to general theory on life-span development as well as to its more specific value to theory building in the environmental behavior, planning, and design fields. Carp (1987), for example, has pointed to the possible pitfalls of focusing on one age group, such as the elderly, when claiming to generalize about that group; to avoid misattribution of the distinctive behaviors of the group one must describe these behaviors for the entire life span.

Spatial Cognition Research

The largest area of environmental psychology research with children is concerned with "cognitive mapping." Most of the research in this area has been conducted by those trained in cognitive-developmental psychology. These studies usually have been designed to describe how people's mapping of the environment develops (reviewed in Evans, 1980; Hart & Moore, 1973; Moore, 1979; Siegel & White, 1975). We agree with Spencer and Darvizeh (1981) that this work, which commonly uses experimental research designs in laboratory-like settings, has generally underestimated the competence of children acting in environments. Although investigators have stressed the importance of action in their theories of how people learn to mentally represent the spatial properties of large-scale environments, they have not usually examined the relationship between action and representation empirically. Even fewer have considered people's appraisals or feelings for places as part of the research problem (a few instances in which this has been done are reviewed in the following section on Environmental Perception and Behavior). In spite of the lack of such integrated research, it is common for spatial cognition authors, when interpreting their cognitive data, to speculate about the relationship between people's spatial representations and their actions in, and appraisals of, environments.

The most commonly stated reason for investigating cognitive mapping is its relevance to understanding the development of people's navigation abilities. The assumption has been that people use "cognitive maps" to move through the environment, and that the extent and quality of their maps of the environment are directly related to their navigation ability in that environment. In fact, Spencer and Darvizeh (1981) present evidence to the contrary. They argue that children's competency in navigating the environment exceeds their ability to accurately represent it; a more integrated research program would have revealed this sooner.

There are some rare but interesting exceptions in which spatial cognition and action have been investigated together. In an extremely detailed case study of a child's knowledge of a route through a wayfinding task, Gale, Doherty, Pellegrino, & Golledge (1985) were able to test the hypothesis that knowledge of features and cues along a route is a systematic function of the actions and decisions that must be made at specific loci. By working with only one child for 5 successive days (5 hours per day) the investigators were able to test some important hypotheses regarding the relationship of action and decision making to the child's knowledge of the environment.

In this instance there were sufficient experimental controls through the use of standardized setting, predetermined decision points, and so on, that it would be possible to test the hypotheses with a larger sample. The time and expense of such a study of course would be enormous. A better suggestion might be to build on the strengths of their case study approach. As it is, the study is limited to children's knowledge in relation to action. We suggest that if this case study were to be opened up further to allow children to select their own routes and to talk about why they selected different paths and for what purposes, the authors could further expand their findings to the domain of environmental appraisal. This would move closer to the kind of integrative research we are calling for.

It is regrettable that so much research has been conducted on cognitive mapping and so little attention has been given to alternative knowledge structures that may vary in their importance for actions in different kinds of environments, for different tasks, and that may change in their utility with development (see Hart & Berzok, 1982). "Scripts," for example, may be a more useful structure for helping a young child adapt to their first school than a cognitive map of such an overwhelming environment. Later, however, the ability to represent the spatial properties of the school may be critical for the development of their ability to use its resources. On a playground, *strategies* for entry into social play and for negotiating conflict may be more valuable than the ability to cognitively map the layout of the playground. For building a sandcastle the ability to *plan* the sequence of construction may be more important than the ability to mentally map alternative spatial layouts of possible castle designs.

It has been empirically demonstrated that self-produced movement is an important variable influencing the ability of people of all ages to mentally represent the spatial properties of the environment (Acredolo, 1988; and edited volume by Liben, Patterson, & Newcombe, 1981). The importance of self-produced action varies throughout the life span, however. Acredolo (1988) has shown that for infants it is essential to their construals of the environment. Adults are capable of construing the environment without self-initiated movement but such movement remains an important variable, particularly when familiarizing themselves with a new environment. For elderly persons, their much reduced opportunities for movement in the environment have the important impact of making the local environment better known and much more important to them (Rowles, 1984).

Environmental Perception and Behavior Research by Environmental Psychologists and Geographers

Not all of the investigations of children's environmental cognition have focused exclusively on spatial aspects. Some research has recognized the functional nature of children's place knowledge; that is not knowledge of how to get somewhere but what resources places offer to children (Hart, 1979; Katz, 1986; Moore, 1986; Muchow & Muchow, 1980, originally 1935; Sell, 1985; Southworth, 1970; Wood, 1985).

Furthermore, some investigators have come closer to the integrative theme of this book by examining our three domains of interest simultaneously; spatial behavior, knowledge of the environment, and appraisal of the environment (Bjorklid, 1982; Hart, 1979; Katz, 1986; Lynch, 1977; Moore, 1986; Muchow & Muchow, 1980, originally 1935; Sell, 1985; Southworth, 1970). Unfortunately, although this descriptive research has included these three domains, it has rarely made formal, precise, statements between the data of these three domains. In fact, this research did not, in most cases, emerge from any deep conviction that there was theoretical merit in integrating them. It was rather the practical desire to be more relevant to planning or to environmental education for children that required the investigators to consider the whole child and consequently to investigate all three domains: cognition, appraisal, and action. The authors show little or no recognition of the writings of those few psychologists who have tried to integrate theory across these three domains and because of the lack of a shared conceptual framework, it is difficult to compare the data from these different studies. Consequently, they are best thought of as exploratory methodological studies, although often resulting in some intriguing insights. The greatest insights seem to emerge when the research resists the orthodox pull toward the study of large samples and proceeds instead with integrated descriptions of individual children or families in their environments.

The alternative to integration via case studies of individuals is to understand the relation of action to cognition and appraisal statistically, using large samples. A rare example of finding any convincing statistical relationship across our domains of interest has been the discovery of a relationship between children's direct experience of the environment and the organization of their maps of the environment (Hart, 1979; Moore, 1973).

Action Research

Knowledge, appraisal, and action come together in action research. The individual becomes the investigator and actor simultaneously. The goal of action research is for the individual to identify his or her own concerns for improving some life situation and to act to improve that situation. With no separation between investigator and investigated the whole person is never disaggregated. There are unfortunately few fully documented examples of environmental action research with children (review by Baldassari, Lehman, & Wolfe, 1987; Hart, 1987; Southworth, 1970). One study, though never published, serves as an excellent example of the potentials of this kind of research. Stephen Carr and Kevin Lynch worked with 20 adolescents in the city of Boston to investigate and to expand their knowledge of the city and its resources. With free passes from the city transit authority the youths discovered interesting places within easy reach of each subway station. They prepared a guidebook documenting these places and describing their locations. In the process, the investigators learned a great deal about how the city is differently known, used, and evaluated by its low-income inner city residents and its suburban middle-class youth. Simultaneously these youths were able to expand their knowledge of the city. Had a suitable publisher been found, the students' discoveries would have also been shared with a very large audience of teenagers. It would be valuable to see environmental psychologists engaged in more of this action research and developing improved qualitative methods for recording and communicating the changing environmental knowledge, appraisals, and actions of the participants. Denis Wood made a wonderful methodological contribution for such research with his "Environmental A": an open-ended map symbol system. This method enables students to simultaneously express their developing knowledge and appraisals of new places as they explore them (Wood, 1973).

It is important to note that each of the above examples of action research in environmental psychology has been educational (see also the Bulletin for Environmental Education). So much of the remainder of environmental psychology research is done, explicitly or implicitly, in service of environmental design and planning for people. The distinction is between research *with* people and research *for* people. Investigators who adopt an action research perspective do not simply do so because of a predilection for more integrative, inductive research but because of an ideological orientation toward research that is empowering. Kurt Lewin (1947) is credited with conceptualizing this kind of research and coining the term. He is better known, however, for his "field theory," which is reviewed in the following section.

CONTRIBUTIONS FROM IMPORTANT TRANSACTIONAL THEORIES

Kurt Lewin

Kurt Lewin's (1954) conceptualization of human behavior is fundamental to our argument that one must consider action, cognition, and appraisal of the environment simultaneously. Lewin believed that the way to establish scientific generalizations about behavior was to fully comprehend the dynamic organization and definition of particular cases. He developed a transactional theory that emphasizes that a person's behavior at any point in time is the result of the holistic organization of personal and environmental forces acting within the person's "life space." Life space is defined by Lewin as the sum total of all forces affecting behavior at any particular juncture. Understanding the holistic unity and organization of the "life space" was a key part of Lewin's theory. Personal and environmental factors were seen as dynamically enmeshed, not as separately definable. For Lewin, "environment," however, was usually understood as the perceived environment (Deutsch, 1968). Many who have followed Lewin's ideas lost the transactional nature of his theory and made it interactional, that is, they defined the environment and the person as independent of one another rather than as mutually defining.

Lewin (1954) conceived of development as the process of increasing differentiation and elaboration of a person's "life space." A key element of the life space was the capacity to represent the relationship of the psychological past and the psychological future to one's present state in a coordinated fashion. This capacity is intimately connected with a person's ability to organize environmental actions. This process involves something other than responding to immediate stimuli.

For example, Lewin (1954) described how two children—a 1 year old and a 5 year old—might respond differently to having their path toward a goal blocked by a U-shaped enclosure. The 5 year old, according to Lewin (1954), would see the situation in a more differentiated way. She would see the blocked path as the line of sight toward the goal, yet the direction around the barrier (and initially away from the goal) would be seen as the "direction toward the goal," consisting of a series of steps toward the goal. For the younger child, this path would exist neither psychologically nor behaviorally, because her conceptualization of the situation is not as differentiated or as extended as the older child's. For the younger child, an initial movement away from the goal would not be viewed as contributing toward reaching the goal. The younger child could not coordinate the series of steps necessary into a larger plan of action for reaching the goal (Lewin, 1954).

The key aspect of Lewin's theorizing, for the points we wish to develop later in this chapter, is its emphasis on describing psychological development in terms of holistic units and progressive differentiations throughout the life span. These characteristics of Lewin's theory were also shared, in varying degrees, by some of his contemporaries, particularly Werner (1957).

An important criticism of Lewin's theorizing is that he did not fully elaborate how the objective world (the "foreign hull" of the "life-space") was related to the "life-space" (Barker, 1963; Bronfenbrenner, 1977; see Brunswick's "lens model" for a solution to this problem, Brunswick, 1956). The description of the internal dynamics of the life space was the strength of Lewin's theory. But the lack of connection between the "life space" and the dynamics of the environment, as it exists and is defined independently of any one individual's perceptions, was a serious limitation of the theory. As Brunswick (1956) pointed out, psychological processes in Lewin's (1954) theory are overly "encapsulated." Thus, we believe that Lewin's theory, without modifications, has limitations that compromise its value for its direct application to geography, environmental psychology, environmental design, and other fields concerned with the environment. It was this deficiency of Lewin's theorizing that Barker (1968) and his colleagues and Bronfenbrenner (1979) sought to remedy.

Post-Lewinian Ecological Theory: Barker

The work of the ecological psychologists was an effort to articulate the "foreign hull" of the Lewinian "life space" (Barker, 1968). Barker and his colleagues were so determined to do this by recording only overt behavior that in most of their research they failed to investigate the "life space" from the child's perspective (however, see Wicker, 1987, for recent suggestions on incorporating personal–psychological factors into behavior setting theory). That is, they did not consider children's cognition and appraisal of the environment. Nevertheless, their research has resulted in some important conceptual contributions to the field.

Ecological psychology has been particularly significant for demonstrating how recurrent patterns of behavior have the effect of establishing "programs" for behavior within community settings. This demonstrates that it is inadequate to think of the problem as having only three dimensions: cognition of the physical environment, appraisal, and action. The ecological psychologists have revealed that past actions of people become an important part of the structure of environments, or of "settings," as they call them (Barker, 1968; Wicker, 1987). They also made some contributions specifically to the question of action within the environment as it develops in children. For instance, they demonstrated that "penetration," or the degree to which a child or adolescent influences or leads social interactions in a setting, increases with age (Barker & Wright, 1955). It is also interesting to note that Barker et al. devoted enormous effort to tracking individual children in their total situations over time—although a theoretical position for analyzing the empirical data was lacking in this work (Barker & Wright, 1951).

The research effort was too detailed and time consuming to give us any comprehensive picture of people's action in space in the town that they studied so closely. The portrait that emerged from the research was more one of the behavior of the town as a whole than of the behavior patterns of specific people. This portrait is consistent with an assumption within ecological psychology that the behavior patterns of settings would be internally consistent, whereas actors in the setting could be interchangeable without affecting the observed behavior patterns (but see Wicker, 1987, for modifications of this position). Nevertheless there are some valuable "nuggets" of findings relevant to the theme of this paper. For example, Barker and Barker (1961) found a "behavior regression" in the activity spaces of the elderly such that they had a mean occupancy time in all behavior settings that was equivalent to that of preschool children.

Post-Lewinian Ecological Theory: Bronfenbrenner

Urie Bronfenbrenner, another student of Lewin's, has tried to make his mentor's exciting concepts more useful. His central idea is that development—defined as the mutual and progressive accommodation of a person and his or her socioecological environment over time—occurs within a system of settings, ranging from the immediate "microsetting" (within the perceptual field) to the global, "macrosystem" level that represents the culture's assumptions about the structuring of institutions and social life (Bronfenbrenner, 1979). This system of settings provides the context within which development proceeds, and with which the developing person transacts, thus influencing the contents and course of development. Bronfenbrenner's (1977, 1979) work represented an attempt to describe the "foreign hull" of the "life space" and its relationship to psychological and behavioral phenomena. He offers a useful structure for generating an ecological developmental psychology: a system whereby we can conduct microinvestigations of the individual person's actions in the environment alongside other investigations of related people and settings. In this way the "foreign hull'' of the ''life space'' has been expanded to encompass all possible relationships, including indirect ones, between a person's behavior and the behavior of significant other persons and the functioning of institutions. Bronfenbrenner's (1977, 1979) work could be criticized for overemphasizing the social environment and underemphasizing the physical environment's role in development. Nonetheless, it provides an important extension of Lewinian theorizing.

Valsiner's Individual-Sociological Model of Children's Action

Recently, Jaan Valsiner constructed a model of the development of children's action that integrates several of the concepts we have identified in this chapter. The embracing nature of his model is the result of an integration of the work of some of the most ecologically minded theorists: Lewin, Vygotsky, Bason, and Piaget in psychology, and Waddington from evolutionary biology. Valsiner (1987) describes his theory as dynamic interactionism, but it meets the criteria of what we have been calling transactionalism in this chapter. One of the qualities of Valsiner's thinking most valuable to the field of environmental psychology is the way he incorporates the social world into his model of an individual's actions in the environment. For Valsiner, the context dependency of children's actions is the general rule rather than the exception. Understanding a child's actions therefore requires that the investigator go beyond the child's cognition and appraisal of environments to an understanding of the social constraints present in any particular context.

Valsiner's model inherits from the writings of Vygotsky (1978) an emphasis on the importance of culture in shaping development. The physical environment is meaningfully organized—made up of places, objects within places, and different actions that can be performed with objects. The result is an environment that carries culturally specific meanings, at least for adults and older children. The newborn, however, has to develop his/her own personal sense system under the guidance of other people, parents, relatives, and siblings. Each participant, including the child, is a coconstructor of those cultural meanings. The results are ''personal sense systems'' that are not direct copies of the parents' sense systems.

In Valsiner's model, both the developing child and the environment are organized structurally. These structures set up constraints within which the child acts. For example, the structural organization of a newborn child's anatomy and physiological functioning sets constraints on the range of behaviors that can be learned. At the same time, the physical environment is set up by the child's caregivers to constrain and direct certain behaviors through the arrangement of clothing, crib, and toys in certain configurations. Third, and of great importance in Valsiner's theory, the caregivers themselves work to constrain and promote the acquisition of certain behaviors. By actualizing some of their potentially learnable skills at any time, children participate actively in their own development. Valsiner describes this system as both deterministic and indeterministic; deterministic in that it is always guided by some set of constraints but indeterministic, or unpredictable in any exact way, because a child acts within a *system* of constraints that is connected in complex qualitative ways.

Valsiner introduces Waddington's (1970) notion of ''canalization'' to illustrate the bounded nature of developmental processes. In his modification of the concept for human development, guidance and direction along developmental pathways are achieved gradually by participants acting purposefully who, for example, set up constraints for the child. Furthermore, a child also participates actively by altering its own constraining structure. Valsiner uses the term constraint to mean control of action and not control against the actor's wishes or well-being, which the term often commonly implies. Constraint here refers to physically or behaviorally verifiable limitations placed on children's actions. The concept is also meant to refer to internalized constraints in middle childhood and beyond. Unfortunately, because his empirical research to date has been with infants and toddlers, he does not deal much with the internalized notion of constraint other than to admit that it promises methodological difficulties. Nevertheless the theory is relevant to other periods of the life span and we may anticipate an improved articulation of the theory as it begins to be more broadly applied. Lawton (1985), for example, has described how elderly adults proactively arrange their residences to maintain autonomous functioning when impairments increase. This suggests a fascinating research agenda of studying the ways in which individuals assess their own development and changing competencies and act on the environment to support themselves as they move through the different phases of their life.

Valsiner uses three zone concepts to describe the "canalization" of children's action within culture. They work only as a system, and so no direct causal properties should be attributed to any of the mechanisms described below.

The *Zone of Free Movement* (ZFM) derives from Lewin's concept of the region of freedom of movement. It refers not only to the space of children's free access but also to objects in that space and how the child should act with those available objects. With development the ZFMs are internalized, that is, the child learns to set them up within his or her personal thinking and feeling. These internalized ZFMs provide a structural framework for the child's cognitive activity and emotions in different social situations; they serve to regulate the person's relationship with the environment.

The Zone of Promoted Action (ZPA) is the complement of the ZFM. It is used to describe those activities, objects, or areas in the environment that are used to promote the development of new skills in the child. The ZFM represents the existing structure of a child's relationship to the environment and the ZPA represents the adults' desired direction for the child's development. Whether or not any part of the ZPA is actualized by a particular child is related to how well the adults in the child's life are able to assess his or her developing motor and cognitive abilities.

The Zone of Proximal Development (ZPD) was developed by Vygotsky (1978). It refers to those aspects of a child's development that have not yet moved from the sphere of the possible into that of the actual. It is the zone of behaviors that can be actualized, interdependently with the assistance of 'social others.' It provides a link between Valsiner's ZFM and ZPA. The more overlap there is between the ZPA and the ZPD, the more effective will adult instruction be on the child's learning of new skills. We believe this suggests an important new emphasis in developmental psychology on the investigation of parent's abilities to assess their child's ZPD.

Lewin's theory presented us with a snapshot approach to being developmental—of looking at the child's life space at different moments in time. It rarely specifies *how* the life space of a person changes over time, only that it does change. By contrast, Valsiner's notion of zones is contained within a developmental model of constraints that are manipulated by people, including the child, to canalize or direct development of the individual toward culturally desired achievements (Valsiner, 1987).

In summary, Valsiner's theory contains much of what we would recommend for a comprehensive developmental research program on children's action in the environment and is a refreshing addition to theoretical literature in developmental psychology. Although fundamentally ecological, it is, however, incomplete. This is partially because it seems to have grown out of research primarily with young children, which seems to overemphasize the power of social forces at the expense of the intentions of the child. Valsiner's theory would benefit for instance from the incorporation of Wapner's conception of the development of planning in older children. More generally we might observe that compared to Lewin's model Valsiner's zones seem to be the zones of adult intentions more than the child's. Perhaps we need a fourth zone to balance the model: the child's "Zone of Desired Action?" Second, in its emphasis on social forces in the system, Valsiner's work also pays too little attention to the physical structure of the environment. This is also a general weakness of theory in environmental psychology, probably because those theories have emerged primarily from psychology, which emphasizes intrapsychic processes. Third, Valsiner's work is currently limited to research concerning the context of individual children's development in particular settings; his "cultural historical" model could be improved by placing his microstudies within Bronfenbrenner's comprehensive model of the ecology of human development and its emphasis on the relationships between microsettings.

The Organismic-Developmental Perspective of Wapner and Colleagues

Seymour Wapner, a student of Heinz Werner, has for some time proposed the kind of research program that is now being called "transactionalism" (Wapner, 1987; Wapner, Kaplan, & Cohen, 1973). However, Wapner and colleagues adopt a distinctly teleological perspective that assumes that people–environment systems are developmentally orderable according to the "orthogenetic principle." The orthogenetic principle refers to the degree to which a system is organized: The more a system is differentiated and hierarchically organized the more developed it is said to be (Werner, 1948, 1957; Kaplan, 1967).

Recently, Wapner has emphasized the goals of individuals and how they plan their actions in the environment (Wapner, 1987; Wapner & Cirillo, 1973). A plan is a representation, verbal or otherwise, of a method of action being considered or adopted for the future (Wapner & Cirillo, 1973, p. 27.) Wapner and Cirillo have described how the orthogenetic principle can be applied to the issue of planning in people's actions in environments:

> Three distinct ideal forms of action constituting a developmental sequence delineate this differentiation: (1) Fusion of method and concrete action instrumental to a goal; (2) Differentiation of concrete preparatory actions from actions immediately instrumental to a goal; and (3) Differentiation of symbolic actions (planning) from other preparatory actions. There is a movement from merely acting in an attempt to achieve a goal, to getting ready for such actions concretely (motor set, finding an instrument etc.) to getting ready for such actions conceptually by formulating a method ahead of time.

This differentiation of method from action may be further specified as ways in which the growing distance of the person from his immediate milieu is evidenced: (1) Planning comes to have its own sub-goals, distinguishable from those of subsequent action—the plan should be formulated clearly and be communicable, planning itself should be carried out economically and efficiently, etc; (2) Instrumentalities different from those of the planned action are developed for planning—models, diagrams, pencil and paper, planning conferences, etc.; (3) The scene in which planning goes on becomes distinguished from the subsequent scene of action—the props of action are no longer necessary, the conditions for action need not be present to envisage the action, etc; and (4) The agents of planning become differentiated from the agents of action—the planning function may be carried out by people (planners) other than those realizing the plan. (Wapner & Cirillo, 1973, pp. 13–15, cited in Wapner, 1987, p. 1445)

The above sequence can be applied microgenetically, such as the growing ability one has to plan one's actions in a new environment or ontogenetically: the growing ability a person has throughout the lifespan to differentiate their plans for acting in environments.

There has in recent years been a burgeoning of interest in the field of developmental psychology in children's planning: first, with children's problem solving with computers and second with children's social development and their desire to participate in activities with other children. Many of our notions here are drawn from the work of Roy Pea, a Clark graduate who was influenced by the work of Wapner and colleagues in his conceptualization of planning and how it develops in children's activities with microcomputers (Pea, 1982). We will attempt to draw out the relevance of some of this literature for the question of children's planning for actions in environments. "Planning" may be defined as "an activity that goes on whenever an individual formulates a goal in advance of acting and then directs action in systematic pursuit of this goal" (Forbes & Greenberg, 1982, p. 1). It therefore has three central characteristics: formulation of some goal, formulation of strategies to achieve the goal, and continuous evaluation of how well the strategies are working, with alterations of the plan as required (Forbes & Greenberg, 1982, p. 1). How common such planning is in children's daily transactions in environments and how this activity develops have barely been addressed.

Pea complains that the existing models are top heavy; they are devoted to plan proposing, simulation, and refinement, when in fact most everyday planning is bottom heavy and plans are often not even self-consciously differentiated from actions— "people frequently spring into action" and only explicitly construct plans if their actions do not succeed. Furthermore, the popular conception of children is that their behavior is rarely planful in comparison to adults; theirs is the world of play, commonly defined as an entirely spontaneous affair. But in fact childhood involves more than play and even play is often planned. That planning is less common to children, however, seems likely when one considers the emphasis in the planning research literature on the principles of economy of action. One of us for example has observed that preadolescent children seem much less concerned with efficiency in route taking than adults (Hart, 1979).

Nevertheless, children do come to have to coordinate their schedules with those of their more planful elders and with a society that depends on this ability. It is rather surprising then that developmental psychology has paid so little attention to the development of some of the more important questions for investigation from a developmental perspective: knowing which settings and activities it is appropriate to plan for, knowing alternative methods and in which situations to apply them, the ability to "read" plans (i.e., shopping lists, diaries, school timetables, bus routes), and particularly knowing when it is appropriate to ask for help from others. Furthermore, if research is ultimately going to be useful in the education of children's environmental competence we need to trade the genetic route from plan construction to plan execution and use. Longitudinal case studies would be an informative research approach to this question.

"Metacognition" drives cognition in significant ways and so more highly developed planning may be facilitated when planners themselves have a perspective on planning. For this reason Roy Pea (1982) studied how children talk about planning through structured interviews. He interviewed 13 8–9 year olds and 13 11–12 year olds at Bank Street College of Education. He found that the children had a good idea of the meaning of planning and when it was and was not appropriate. It is noteworthy that in answer to the question "When do you or others plan?" more than half of the answers were environmental or spatial decisions such as "to go on a trip," "go somewhere after school," "move to a new house," and so on. The diversity of activities increased with age. The children also recognized that one can plan how to do something. How to build things constituted more than a third of the examples they gave of what kinds of problems they needed plans for. These interviews therefore suggest that if development psychology is to further investigate children's planning they would do well to move beyond children's social interactions and computer use into the larger domain of children's transactions with their everyday environment.

THE NEED FOR MULTIPLE RESEARCH STRATEGIES FOR A COMPREHENSIVE RESEARCH AGENDA

A Developmental Perspective on Case Studies

We have suggested that individual case studies are a valuable way of methodologically fulfilling the difficult demands of a transactional perspective that attempts to integrate environmental knowledge, appraisal and action. The question of how to do this developmentally remains. Using orthodox distinctions, one can either study the child–environment system at different times (a cross-sectional or single frame comparison) or one can study the child–environment system continuously (a longitudinal or frame sequence analysis). We wish to suggest a third possibility whereby critical transitions of the child–environment system are identified by both longitudinal and cross-sectional analyses and then subjected to more detailed longitudinal study of these systems at these critical periods. This approach might be thought of as the temporal or developmental version of Bronfenbrenner's spatial or ecological notion of needing to identify important interfaces. One such example might be the various transitions a child makes in increasing access to a potentially hazardous home environment such as learning to crawl, stand, walk, and climb (Hart & Iltus, 1988; Garling & Valsiner, 1985).

The Study of Different Actors
Within the Same System

Any system of people–environment transactions can be studied from the perspective of any one person in the system. This means that one person's cognition, appraisals, and actions will be the focus of the investigation. A more complete transactional approach than is common is to conduct separate studies of each of the actors in a system simultaneously. For example, we are currently attempting this in our study of families as safety management systems for children at home by investigating the cognitions, appraisals, and actions of both the caretakers and the children (Hart & Iltus, 1988). Furthermore, one can also study patterns of how a system of people's relationships changes over time without focusing on any individuals. Wicker (1987) is using this approach in a study of the history of behavior settings.

The Problem of Generalizability

We have suggested in this chapter that case studies are valuable for achieving a transactional approach to the study of people in environments. Like Lewin, we believe that general principles of behavior can be generated from fully understanding a case study. We agree with Valsiner that the connection between cognition, appraisal, and action is a system which "cannot be reduced to the sum of its parts" (Valsiner, 1987, p. 77). There is a very strong tendency in psychology to replace the unity of people–environment systems with samples of the case, which are then separated into domains of cognition, appraisal, and action and subjected individually to various independent quantitative measurement techniques. Such methodological orthodoxy often changes the object of the investigations; one might call this a kind of method-ological determinism. A common example is the tendency to compare different in-dividuals in context when one's question requires the comprehensive systemic study of an individual in context. The challenge remains to find ways to not only study individuals in context dynamically, but then to compare one such system with an-other. We are attempting this in our current study of the very different systems that are constructed within families to maintain children's safety as they develop (Hart & Iltus, 1988).

We believe that case studies can generate new principles that may be generaliza-ble. However, we still see a role for more orthodox experimental methods for vali-dating such principles. Lewin (1954) suggested that case studies and aggregate data could be complementary, with case studies revealing key principles and psychologi-cal dynamics, and aggregate data establishing the relative "locations" of cases and variables with one another in a statistical sense. For example, Hart (1979) found from a case study that a 7-year-old boy in a New England town was able to represent the spatial properties of much more of his world than would be suggested by existing theory, which stressed the importance of children's actions on (or locomotion through) the environment. The new principles suggested by this integrated case study were that verbal annotations by adults while a child is "passively" experiencing land-scapes from a car can be a valuable substitute for personal locomotion through the environment. It was also noted from this study that places visited by children walking alone were more likely to result in an ability to represent those places than when a child was accompanied by an adult in walking to these places. Both of these principles have since been subjected to experimental research and found to be important variables (Hazen, 1982).

If transactionalism stresses the study of psychological processes in context and these contexts cannot be assumed to be widely generalizable, but rather are often described as unique, how then does one develop research findings that are of general value for environmental design and for planning policy? We have already suggested the importance of locating transactional studies within a framework of more traditional large sample studies. Another answer is that one should not always pretend that one can provide generalizable design principles; rather one should engage in a participatory research and design process unique to each project that is informed, but not dictated, by past research. We should often be more concerned with developing and evaluating design *process* principles that can be applied to other settings and be less concerned with developing generalizations about people–environment relations as the *content* of design guidelines.

For the development of policy at a higher level, such as the establishment of principles or national guidelines for day-care planning, we suggest that our field look to the thinking of Bronfenbrenner. Bronfenbrenner's *Ecology of Human Development* (1979) argues that for the purpose of national policy we should develop a map of the settings through which children pass and design research with awareness of the much larger context of which they are a part. This contextual approach is advocated even for small-scale, and seemingly unique studies. In this way a transactional study of children's adaptation to a child care center, for example, can be related to other relevant "microsystems" such as the child's home or the parents' work place. Moreover, research can be designed that looks specifically at the relationship of these settings to one another and to national policy as a whole.

In conclusion, the important contexts of children's decision making and action need to be identified and studied representatively, and the ecological structures of particular cases need to be identified fully. Furthermore, we need to develop standards for comparing "patterns" of relationships among case, rather than insisting on strict comparability. In this way, the particularistic and embedded characteristics of case studies will not be lost to generalization.

REFERENCES

Acredolo, L. (1988). Infant mobility and spatial development. In J. Stiles-Davis, M. Kritchevsky, & U. Bellugi (Eds.), *Spatial cognition: Brain bases and development* (pp. 157–166). Hillsdale, N.J.: Erlbaum.

Altman, I., & Rogoff, B. (1987). World views in psychology: Trait, interactional, organismic, and transactional perspectives. In D. Stokols & I. Altman (Eds.), *Handbook of Environmental Psychology* (Vol. 1, pp. 7–40). New York: Wiley.

Baldassari, C., Lehman, S., & Wolfe, M. (1987). Imaging and creating alternative environments with children. In C.S. Weinstein & T.G. David (Eds.), *Spaces for children: The built environment and child development* (pp. 241–268). New York: Plenum.

Barker, R.G. (1963). On the nature of the environment. *Journal of Social Issues, 19*, 17–38.

Barker, R.G. (1968). *Ecological psychology*. Stanford, Calif.: Stanford University Press.

Barker, R.G., & Barker, L.S. (1961). The psychological ecology of old people in Midwest, Kansas and Yoredale, Yorkshire. *Journal of Gerontology, 61*, 231–239.

Barker, R.G., & Wright, H.F. (1951). *One boy's day*. New York: Harper & Row.

Barker, R.G., & Wright, H.F. (1955). *Midwest and its children*. New York: Harper & Row.

Bjorklid, P. (1982). *Children's outdoor environment: A study of children's outdoor activities on two housing estates from the perspective of environmental and developmental psychology*. Stockholm: Stockholm Institute of Education.

Bronfenbrenner, U. (1977). Lewinian space and ecological substance. *Journal of Social Issues, 33*, 199–213.

Bronfenbrenner, U. (1979). *The ecology of human development: experiments by nature and design*. Cambridge, Mass.: Harvard University Press.

Brunswick, E. (1956). *Perception and the representative design of psychology experiments* (2nd ed.). Berkeley, Calif.: University of California Press.

Bulletin of Environmental Education (now replaced by *Streetwise*. Index to back issues available from Streetwise, the National Association fro Urban Studies, Lewis Cohen Urban Studies Center, Brighton Polytechnic College, 68 Grad Parade, Brighton BN22JY, England).

Carp, F. (1987). Environment and aging. In D. Stokols & I. Altman (Eds.), *Handbook of environmental psychology* (Vol. 1, pp. 329–360). New York: Wiley.

Deutsch, M. (1968). Field theory in social psychology. In *Handbook of Social Psychology* (pp. 412–487). New York: Wiley.

Doxiadis, C. (1975). *Anthropopolis: A city for human development*. New York: Norton.

Evans, G.W. (1980). Environmental Cognition. *Psychological Bulletin, 88*, 250–281.

Forbes, D., & Greenberg, M. (Eds) (1982). *The development of planful behavior in children*. San Francisco: Jossey Bass.

Gale, N., Doherty, S., Pellegrino, J.W., & Golledge, R.G. (1985). Toward reassembling the image. *Children's Environments Quarterly, 2*(3), 10–18.

Gärling, T., & Valsiner, J. (Eds.) (1985). *Children within environments: Toward a psychology of accident prevention*. New York: Plenum.

Hart, R.A. (1979). *Children's experience of place*. New York: Irvington.

Hart, R.A. (1983). Children's geographies and the geography of children. In T. Saarinen, J. Sell & D. Seamon (Eds.) *Behavioral geography: Inventory and prospect*. Chicago: University of Chicago Monographs in Geography.

Hart, R.A. (1987). *The changing city of childhood*. The Annual Catherine Maloney Memorial Lecture, City College of New York.

Hart, R.A., & Berzok, M.A. (1982). A problem oriented perspective on children's representation of the geographic environment. In M. Potegal (Ed.) *The neural and developmental bases of spatial orientation*. New York: Academic Press.

Hart, R.A., & Iltus, S. (1988). *Families as safety management systems for children at home*. Paper presented at the Conference on Safety and the Built Environment, Portsmouth, England, July.

Hart, R.A., & Moore, G.T. (1973). The development of spatial cognition: A review. In R. Downs and D. Stea (Eds.), *Image and environment*. Chicago: Aldine-Atherton.

Hazen, N.L. (1982). Spatial exploration and spatial knowledge: Individual and developmental differences in very young children. *Child Development, 53*, 826–833.

Kaplan, B. (1967). Meditations on genesis. *Human Development, 10*, 65–87.

Katz, C. (1986). *'If there weren't kids there wouldn't be fields': Children's environmental learning, knowledge and interactions in a changing socio-economic context in rural Sudan*. Ph.D. dissertation, Clark University.

Lawton, M.P. (1985). The elderly in context: Perspectives from environmental psychology and gerontology. *Environment and Behavior, 17*, 501–519.

Lewin, K. (1947). Frontiers in group dynamics. Channel of group life: Social planning and action research. *Human Relations, 1*, 143–153.

Lewin, K. (1954). Behavior and development as a function of the total situation. In L. Carmichael (Ed.), *Manual of child psychology* (pp. 918–970). New York: Wiley.

Liben, L., Patterson, A., & Newcombe, N. (Eds.). (1981). *Spatial representation and behavior across the life span*. New York: Academic Press.

Lynch, K. (Ed.) (1977). *Growing up in cities: Studies of the spatial environment of adolescence in Cracow, Melbourne, Mexico City, Galta, Toluca, and Warszawa*. Cambridge, Mass.: MIT Press.

Moore, G.T. (1973). *Developmental variations between and within individuals in the cognitive representation of large-scale spatial environments*. M.A. thesis, Clark University.

Moore, G.T. (1979) Knowing about environmental knowing: the current state of theory and research on environmental cognition. *Environment and Behavior, 11*, 33–70.

Moore, R. (1986). *Childhood's domain*. London: Croom Helm.

Muchow, M., & Muchow, H. (1980). *Der Lebensraum des Grosstadtkindes*. Bensheim, Germany: pad. extra. (Original work published in 1935.)

Pea, R. (1982). What is planning development the development of? In D. Forbes and M. Greenberg (Eds.), *The development of planful behavior in children*. San Francisco: Jossey Bass.

Piaget, J. (1952). *The origins of intelligence in children*. New York: International Universities Press.

Piaget, J. (1960). *The psychology of intelligence*. Totowa, N.J.: Littlefield, Adams & Co.

Piaget, J. (1976). *The grasp of consciousness: Action and concept in the young child*. Cambridge, Mass.: Harvard University Press.

Rowles, G.D. (1981) Geographical perspectives on human development. *Human development, 24*, 67–76.

Rowles, G.D. (1984). Aging in rural environments. In I. Altman, M.P. Lawton, & J.F. Wohlwill (Eds.), *Elderly people and the environment*. New York: Plenum.

Sell, J. (1985). *Territoriality and children's experience of the neighborhood*. Ph.D. dissertation, University of Arizona.

Siegel, A.W., & White, S.H. (1975). The development of spatial representations of large-scale environments. In H.W. Reese (Ed.), *Advances in child development and Behavior* (Vol. 10). New York: Academic Press.

Southworth, M. (1970). *An urban service for children based on analysis of Cambridgeport boy's conception and use of the city*. Ph.D. dissertation, Massachusetts Institute of Technology.

Spencer, C., & Darvizeh, Z. (1981). The case for developing a cognitive environmental psychology that does not under-estimate the abilities of young children. *Journal of Environmental Psychology, 1,* 21–31.

Valsiner, J. (1987). *Culture and the development of children's action: A cultural-historical theory of developmental psychology*. Chichester: Wiley.

Vygotsky, L.S. (1978). *Mind in society*. Cambridge, Mass.: Harvard University Press.

Waddington, C.H. (1970). Concepts and theories of growth development, differentiation and morphogenesis. In C.H. Waddington (Ed.), *Towards theoretical biology* (Vol 7, pp. 1–41). Chicago: Aldine.

Wapner, S. (1987). A holistic, developmental, systems-oriented environmental psychology: Some beginnings. In D. Stokols & I. Altman (Eds.), *Handbook of environmental psychology* (Vol. 2, pp. 1433–1465). New York: Wiley.

Wapner, S., & Cirillo, L. (1973). *Development of planning* (Public Health Service Grant Application). Clark University, Worcester, Mass.

Wapner, S., Kaplan, B., & Cohen, S.B. (1973). An organismic-developmental perspective for understanding transactions of men in environments. *Environment and Behavior, 5,* 255–289.

Werner, H. (1948). *Comparative psychology of mental development*, revised edition (orig. 1940). New York: International Universities Press.

Werner, H. (1957). The concept of development from a comparative and organismic point of view. In D. Harris (Ed.), *The concept of development*. Minneapolis: University of Minnesota Press.

Wicker, A.W. (1987). Behavior settings reconsidered: Temporal stages, resources, internal dynamics, context. In D. Stokols & I. Altman (Eds.), *Handbook of Environmental Psychology* (pp. 613–653). New York: Wiley.

Wood, D. (1973) I don't want to but I will. The genesis of geographical knowledge: A real-time development study of adolescent images of novel environments (London, Paris and Rome). Worcester, Mass: Cartographic Laboratory, Graduate School of Geography, Clark University.

Wood, D. (1985). Nothing doing (extracts). *Children's Environments Quarterly, 2,*(2), 14–25.

15

Life-Span Changes in Activities, and Consequent Changes in the Cognition and Assessment of the Environment

CHRISTOPHER SPENCER

In this chapter, I sketch an integrated account of environmental assessment, cognition, and action throughout the individual's life span. Zimring and Gross (this volume) have already described how the schema is structured to include all three aspects; Canter (this volume) has extended this to stress the social context of meanings and actions in which these schema operate; and this chapter accepts and develops their positions.

What further can a life-span approach add to the arguments advanced in these earlier integrative chapters? Liben (this volume) has already stated the case most powerfully with respect to her topic, environmental cognition; and it can as easily be applied to evaluation and action. A life-span approach enables development to be put in context: what earlier stages have so far equipped the individual to do, what the demands of the current situation are on the individual, and how variations at the present stage can affect later development. Taking this developmental perspective throws the emphasis on *process* and on the *adaptive nature* of the environmental schema for the particular life stage reached by the individual. As such, the perspective provides a test bed for examining the range of theoretical relationships between affect, cognition, and action in the environment advanced in earlier chapters.

The life-span approach can also serve to reintroduce into the field a sense of the importance of *individual differences,* and *continuities of individuality* through life, which is conspicuously missing from many of the earlier chapters. The developmental tradition within psychology has not, as a whole, stressed individual differences as much as has done the life-span developmental. The life-span perspective has been much concerned with continuities and developments within the individual, as goals and tasks change over the life course.

Much mainstream "developmental" research lacks this sense of continuity, being often presented as a series of snapshots of the typical child at different ages or stages. In contrast, the life-span approach, as Liben's chapter reminds us, emphasizes the processes whereby developments occur, and conceptualizes this development as affected by biological changes, psychological development, changes in the individual's social role and context, cultural forces, and historical changes during the individual's life span.

DEVELOPMENT CONTINUES
THROUGHOUT THE LIFE-SPAN

As with much literature in developmental psychology as a whole, the preceding chapters have confined their discussion primarily to empirical research on children, although Liben has stressed that a properly developmental approach could be applied to any part of the life span.

We can ask whether the concentration on childhood is simply a matter of convenience, in that this is the focus of the majority of published papers? Or do the truly important conceptual changes occur during childhood, with the major schema and scripts being developed then; and that only minor modifications occur thereafter?

I would not accept this latter point, but would argue that development continues throughout the life span, and would consequently expect cognitive and affective changes to occur with relation to the environment just as they can be shown to, with relation to the individual's social relations, politics, religious beliefs, health behaviours, food preferences, and so on.

Clearly, major and rapid developments do take place in the first 5 years of life, with a decelerating curve of change until some point in later middle age, where the pace of change may accelerate into old age. Indeed, one might argue that the amount and type of change in old age accentuate individual differences. In our everyday understanding of the life span, we know that environmental preferences, activities, and (to some extent) cognitions continue to change throughout the life span. Why has this then not been the focus of much research in environmental psychology? As we shall see in the remainder of this chapter, there *are* the beginnings in the published literature of an integrated life-span account.

THE CHANGING OF ENVIRONMENTAL TASKS
THROUGH THE LIFE SPAN

Reading some of the earlier chapters (e.g., Golledge on wayfinding in outdoor spaces; Böök on angle and distance estimation) one might assume that the main life-span tasks faced by the individual in learning about the world had to do with learning its geometry. Central as this is, we suggest that environmental cognition covers the whole range of understanding of space—from close-body space, through immediate and social space, and directly experienced geographical space, to an understanding of distant, not directly experienced, places and areas (Spencer, Blades, & Morsley, 1989). The individual's developing understanding of the elements of the environments (how rivers and hills and clouds originate; and the relation of these features to others more closely related to human agency for their origins) supports this spatial awareness. Since Piaget's pioneering work on the child's understanding of the natural world (Piaget, 1929, 1930) this has received insufficient attention within developmental psychology.

To emphasize to the reader the range and development of environmental cognition over the life span, we have presented in Table 15.1 a preliminary attempt at a catalogue and agenda of the changing tasks the individual faces—in the left-hand column. On the right-hand side of the table we indicate the environmental activities and inputs driving the process. We have chosen the loose term "input" to cover the range of sources of information about the environment, from the direct exploratory interactions through to the formalized and symbolic sources such as maps and books. At each age, the nature of these inputs and their importance to the development of environmental cognition will differ. Thus, for example, in infancy, the visual monitoring of objects and one's own limbs as one moves is fundamental to the establishment of schema: schema of the body itself and its coordination, expectancies about objects, inferences from occlusion to estimates of relative distance of two objects away from oneself, and so on. Once these schema are firmly established, such visual monitoring inputs have altered functions. The conceptual framework that they helped to lay down now uses the visual inputs to monitor for changes in familiar environments, and to learn new ones, as well as providing continuous update on one's position in space.

Only when the normally competent individual has these fundamental schema challenged (e.g., by fever, alcohol, or fatigue) does he or she revert to a near-infant state of close monitoring of inputs.

The reader will note that a very approximate age band is used in the table: Liben, in her chapter, has already cautioned us about the use of age as a developmental marker, and the approximate ages give here are included in this spirit.

As one works down the table, individual variations, both personal/cognitive and experiential, become more and more marked. To date we have little research from developmental psychologists on the earliest expressions of such individual differences, though some (Little, 1987) have made strong claims for spatial specialisms.

Following this table, the next section of the chapter will attempt to clothe this skeleton of cognitive development with the affective/evaluative responses the individual makes as he or she assesses the environment; indicating what evidence we have and what we need for a full account of life-span changes in evaluation. This leads us inevitably into considering the relation of cognitions and evaluations for actions in the environment, in the following section of the chapter. The reader will, by then, already have been made aware of the importance, at each stage of cognitive development, of the individual's environmental activities (as the major set of "inputs" in the right-hand column of the table).

Superimposed on all the information in the table one could layer *secular, historical/cultural changes,* which include alterations in the awareness of space, and of geographical relations, brought about by, among other factors, changes in the immediacy of the media. We need to consider the effects on environmental cognition of universally shared television, and the coming of new forms of interactive media, linking individuals across space. Sociospatial relations may be profoundly altered by the availability of, for instance, computer/satellite conferencing facilities, videophones, as well as by rapid transportation facilities: we need research to monitor such changes.

At the more immediate level, there is preliminary evidence that the individual's spatial skills—and hence potentially their understanding of space—could be affected

Table 15.1 Changing Environmental Tasks across the Life Span

Age band	Task/topic	Input
Birth to 18 months	Development of early body awareness (Cratty & Sams, 1968, on body image)	Body exploration
	Location of objects in immediate space (Bower, 1975, on the development of object and spatial expectancies)	Cordination of eye and limb movements in grasping
	Relation of objects to self and to own movements (Piaget, 1930, on sensorimotor explorations)	Object manipulation
	Relating object permanence and position in space to number concepts (Harris, 1985)	Observation of object movements, occlusions, etc.
	Development of early frames of reference (Pick & Lockman, 1981; Presson & Ihrig, 1982)	Linkages of separate observations of landmark objects (Acredolo, 1988)
	Early understanding of social rules governing use of space (Hall, 1966; Valsiner, 1987)	Purposive input of caretakers; child's informal observation of social conventions (Argyle, Furnham, & Graham, 1981)
	Initial stages of place schemata development (Pick & Lockman, 1981)	Integration of many of the above inputs
1.5–6 years	Egocentrism overcome (NB controversial status of the concept—Acredolo, 1979); greater extension of spatial reference systems	Massively extended sensory input from wide-ranging locomotion: travel with adults and the beginnings of independence
	Explanatory systems for the natural and human-made world (Piaget, 1929)	Direct observations, and discussions with peers and adults on "how things come to be," stories, books
	Considerably diversified place schemata (Pick & Lockman, 1981)	Earlier schemata, developed by above inputs
6–10 years	Integration of spatial information into broad representations, capable of giving directional and distance estimates	Further extension of range of travel; fantasy games encouraging efficient use of space
	Emergence of idiosyncratic, personal structurings of areas (Lee, 1963)	Range and mode of travel (e.g., walking vs. bus to school)
	Early specialist knowledge of the locations of valued resources in the geographic environment (Hart, 1979; Moore, 1986)	Development of individual interests; school environment, home territory
	Beginnings of stable images of distant places not directly experienced	Media (especially TV, films), school inputs, formal representations (see Liben, this volume; McLuhan, 1964)

Age		
10 years–adolescence	Emergence of individual differences and preferences: early evidence of person/thing specialism (Little, 1987)	Personal projects: the selective channeling of activities, to reflect preferences and orientations (Little, 1983)
	Continuation of diversification of place schemata	Previous schemata and above inputs
	Greater detail and precision of cognitive maps, over a further extended geographic area; considerable individual variation (Anthony, 1985; Fisher, Murray, & Frazer, 1985; Fisher, Frazer, & Murray, 1986; Lynch, 1977)	Independent travel; range of membership groups, and of interests; formal representations (e.g., maps) used purposively (Evans, 1980)
	Greater detail of knowledge about distant places—with considerable individual variation (Spencer, Blades, & Morsley, 1989)	Media, formal education—e.g., geographical texts, language teaching background material; travel; television
	Detailed, "scientific-level" explanations of the origins and nature of natural and human-constructed world	Formal teaching, individual exploration
	Diversified, idiosyncratic place schemata	Childhood schemata modified and extended
		Individual variations related to
		Individual cognitive style
		Travel experiences and interests
		Particular space-related activities (e.g., orienteering, hiking—see Ottoson, 1987)
		Space-related professional activities (e.g., design; geology see Craik, 1970)
Adulthood	Further extension of both directly and indirectly known; considerable individual variation in basic and applied spatial cognition skills; and in resultant schemata	Range of previous environmental experience; amount of mobility (Murray & Spencer, 1979)
	Range in ability to rapidly structure and learn newly encountered environments (Devlin, 1976; Evans, Marrero, & Butler, 1981)	
Older adulthood	For some individuals, reduction in spatial awareness, confusion, possibility of informational overload (Walsh, Krauss, & Regnier, 1981)	Reduced cognitive capacity
	For other individuals, extended awareness of the world; appreciation of other cultures, other peoples	Retirement, increased leisure; travel and tourism (Pearce, 1988); increased use of media
	For many individuals, reduction in area directly experienced; change in self-initiated and self-controlled mobility; greater importance of previous environments via reminiscence (Carp & Carp, 1982); place schemata may show resultant changes	Reduced mobility; altered salience of environmental features as needs change; urban renewal, changing environment

by the informal spatial training afforded by computer games. Even the relatively trivial arcade games place demands on thinking and tracking, and may improve such skills (McClurg & Chaille, 1987).

The reader will be able to add to this list of possible cohort effects and changes over historical time. One could examine, for example, the effects of the amount and pace of change in the landscape. The degree of environmental modification can be shown to relate to sense of place or "placelessness" (Relph, 1976).

Similar changes in the individual's knowledge of and attachment to places could be studied with relation to two opposite trends: towards increased residential mobility and an increased use of home as a work base.

THE DEVELOPMENT OF ENVIRONMENTAL COGNITION

The critique of existing research on the development of environmental cognition has been well presented by Liben (this volume): too often it consists of cross-sectional snapshots, rather than giving an account of the *processes* of the development. How, for example, do the complex place schemata of adolescence and adulthood develop out of those of childhood? The literature most often is of the form: "at age X, children cannot . . .; but by age Y, some can; and by age Z, the majority have achieved adult understanding." What are the crucial inputs that bring about the transformation? How much are the changes dependent on the achievement of a general level of cognitive development (which would be reflected in parallel changes in other domains), and how much are they affected by particular environmental experiences? To study the interaction of these factors, one would need to assess both a range of cognitive skills—spatial, imagery, linguistic, reasoning, and so on—and a list of environmental experience factors, which would include extent of home range, variety of place experience, nature of travel through the environment, exposure to environmental experience surrogates and representations, and so on.

A second critique of some developmental research on environmental cognition is that, in demonstrating the difference in (spatial) understanding from that of adults, attention is deflected from what competencies the child has. We would suggest a reorientation, so that we can stress the *usefulness* of, for example, the room schema for the infant in locating prized resources with considerable efficiency (Acredolo, 1985), or the neighbourhood knowledge which enables 8 and 9 year olds to use play resources that adult inhabitants of their city do not even realize are there (Moore, 1987). We have written at length about the competence of the child and its underestimation within developmental psychology (Spencer & Blades, 1985; Spencer & Darvizeh, 1981). We endorse Liben's observation that young children are capable of shaping their understanding of space by the use of representations of that space in the form of maps and models. Spencer, Blades, and Morsley (1989) documented extensive empirical evidence that is more optimistic than that reported by Liben in her chapter. Children from the age of 3 can orient simple maps, and use them to locate objects in complex spaces (Blades & Spencer, 1987), and can understand and interpret map conventions and aerial photographs from about the age of 4. Similarly, we have demonstrated the usefulness of maps and models in giving young blind children a frame of reference into which to place otherwise isolated pieces of spatial information. Where the experimenter can devise tasks that are involving, exciting, and, in some cases, of considerable personal importance to the child, then a markedly better response is gained from the child.

As an additional limitation in developmental work in this area, there is not enough thought given to the integrative processes by which the individual comes to link up separate inputs of information, a criticism that is surprising given the early and continued emphasis of some developmental researchers on frames of reference and their construction and use (Pick & Lockman, 1981; Siegal & White, 1975). Maps and other such representations discussed by Liben in her chapter can be a rapid way of offering the individual an integrating frame that would otherwise have to be built up, as Siegal and White describe, around a network of landmarks and routes. They can, as Liben suggests, act as *amplifiers* of direct experience, providing in advance an organization for an environment yet to be encountered. They are also, as Downs (1985) reminds us, an offered *interpretation* of an environment—highly selective, and suggesting actual and metaphorical linkages that the individual may not have been previously aware. [Just before preparing this chapter, for example, my own awareness was extended by a map of England that overlaid the pattern of ancient trackways (long distance routes) of the country—the Fosse way, the Ickneild way, and so on—on a simplified surface geology, bringing home with startling clarity the extent to which these trackways followed the low limestone spines of England and avoided the clay country.]

A final criticism of much of the developmental work in this area is its failure to emphasize the *social* origins and shapings of much environmental information, a point strongly made by Valsiner (1987) and reemphasized by Hart and Conn in their chapter. It is curious to juxtapose the literature on the development of children's concepts (language based, and therefore almost by definition of social and cultural origin) with that on the development of environmental schemata. Axia and colleagues, in their chapter, have stressed the usefulness of verbal approaches for *extracting* environmental concepts from children, without stressing the point that verbal means were presumably central for their *inputting* in the first place. Parents, other adults, and media (TV, books) may as much influence the child's development of schema and scripts of *places* and *events* as they do the child's concepts of *objects,* by their verbal shaping and grouping of the child's experiences. And to anticipate the next section of our chapter, examination of such discourse shows how often it carries an evaluative label. This point can be closely paralleled by observations by social psychologists on the child's development of stereotypes of other groups and countries. Prior to gaining little if *any* factual content in the stereotype, the child has an evaluative response to the group or country, often incorporated into the socially given colloquial name that is the child's first indication of the existence of such a group or place (Tajfel, 1981).

THE DEVELOPMENT OF ENVIRONMENTAL ASSESSMENT

Using the cognitive development table, we could now hope to use a correspondingly large literature on life-span development of environmental assessment. But, as the chapter by Axia et al. has reminded us, this area is much less well researched. It is striking to reflect that in the *Handbook of Environmental Psychology*'s definitive chapter on environmental assessment (Craik & Feimer, 1987), there are virtually no developmental references. In this section of our chapter, we hope to show how existing research can be related to the life-span sequence, as outlined in the previous section.

Evaluation is a primitive, basic, and initial part of cognition of environments (just as has been long demonstrated in parallel fields—e.g., Warr & Knapper, 1968, showed evaluation to be the basic and structuring dimension of person perception). Indeed, the definition of "place schemata" offered by Axia and colleagues in their chapter includes "perception, cognitive evaluation, affective/emotional evaluation, and preference for places" as coequal components. What we lack is a truly developmental account, indicating the role of evaluation in the process of place-schemata formation. Axia et al. stress that one might expect this affective/emotional evaluation of processes to be more idiosyncratic than their cognitive evaluation—and indeed our table indicates how the individual's personal pattern of experiences, interests, and social meanings could shape the cognitive image at each and every stage of the life span—peaking in later childhood and through the adult years.

Axia and colleagues' review of the techniques often used in studying the evaluative response is useful, and reminds us how often developmental psychologists have relied on experimentation *away* from the environment referred to—by, for example, eliciting verbal accounts in the lab, or presenting the subject with sets of photographs for preference comparisons. Sometimes one suspects the results produced would not be reproduced in the real environment: thus, for example, Balling and Falk's (1982) study, which Axia et al. cite, presents scenes of habitats to 8 to 70 year olds, and derives comparative preferences for each age group. Yet surely this is a precarious basis from which to assert that 8 and 11 year olds actually *prefer* what Axia et al. call the "genetically primitive" savanna habitat, and are keener on deserts than are people at other ages. Might children not report "liking" deserts because of their Cowboy-and-Indian associations?

Our principal assertion in this section is that no account of environmental cognition is complete without examining its evaluative tone, nor could a simple study of the individual's environmental *knowledge* offer us a basis for predicting how the individual would act with relation to the range of alternative places available.

This must be as true of the neonate's evaluation of the range of known settings as it is of the adolescent's selection of places to "hang-out" (Wood, 1986), and the adult's choice of place to relocate when in search of employment.

In infancy, the evaluative response to objects and to the places they identify for him or her can be exemplified by studies of the young child's preferences for play objects (Herron & Sutton-Smith, 1971), and by the Presson and Ihrig's (1982) study, which indicates how the presence of the mother acts as a reassuring landmark from which to explore novel environments: portable evaluative tone, one could almost argue.

We have already noted that the adults shape the young child's understanding of what places are for, endowing them with meaning, and indicating the bounds of appropriate action (see Valsiner, 1987), all of which are essentially evaluative activities. Adults, too, continue for much of childhood to be gatekeepers on the child's range of place experiences—encouraging, and limiting. As Hart's 1979 natural history of middle childhood in New England shows, such gatekeeping may not be entirely successful in curbing the desire to explore the neighborhood.

In adolescence, the peer group and the individual's self-concept and new social role all become determinants of the individual's activity pattern in ways that were only emerging during later childhood: new areas of the environment become salient and positively evaluated. We have some studies on the resources that young people use in the city, for example, the catalogue of resources available in Toronto compiled by Hill and Michelson (1981); and several studies of particular venues that have come to be foci of adolescent social life, for example, urban shopping malls—see accounts given by Anthony (1985). A comparative and detailed cross-cultural study of the environmental settings and needs of adolescents was initiated for UNESCO by Lynch and colleagues (1977), but further natural histories are needed for both theoretical and applied reasons.

We have also the beginnings of a literature on the environmental needs and appraisal of old people: see for example, the review by Walsh, Krauss, and Regnier (1981). The study by Carp and Carp (1982) has shown the problems faced by less mobile older residents of major cities where access to facilities is predicated on high personal mobility. Where there is better fit between place and needs, then not only are preference ratings higher, but so are so measures of well-being, not surprisingly. The recent review by F.M. Carp (1987) indicates the availability of a small applied literature in this area, enabling future workers to identify preferred environments for the elderly at the level of the neighborhood, the housing project, and the home itself. But, as Carp warns, there is a danger in studies that concentrate upon the elderly: they may attribute to old age behaviors that also characterize younger adults. Would the same preference/well-being links be found if one adopted a life-span perspective? And would we find a life-span continuity of the clear individual differences one finds in the environmental preferences of the elderly? We must be just as aware of the dangers of inferences from snapshot studies of the elderly as, earlier, we were of those of the young.

For we do not have, labeled as such, a separate set of studies identified as "adult" or "mid-life" environmental preferences. There is, however, no shortage of studies in the area of environmental assessment, conducted with adults as subjects (Craik & Feimers' review, 1987, lists nearly 200 references); and it would take only a minor restructuring of this literature to reconceptualize it as part of the life-span account. There are then specialist reviews (such as Zimring, Carpman, & Michelson, 1987, on the needs of the mentally retarded, and hospital visitors) that could be used as type examples to illustrate the diversity of roles and settings subsumed within this mainstream literature. Such work also provides an avenue to explore underlying abilities and experiences that may account for differences demarcated by age. Similarly, a full life-span treatment of adulthood would draw on the extensive literature about individual differences in responses to hazardous environments (Fischoff, Svenson, & Slovic, 1987) and to the value placed on the natural world (Kaplan & Kaplan, 1989; Knopf, 1987).

IMPLICATIONS OF COGNITION AND ASSESSMENT FOR
ACTION ACROSS THE LIFE SPAN

Throughout this chapter, the individual's actions with relation to the environment have supplied the underlying theme, whether we were considering the infant's growing awareness of objects around him or her, experienced through the activity of reaching and manipulating, or discussing the adolescent's preferences for shopping atria as meeting places.

If one were to work through Table 15.1, the majority of "inputs" relate directly or indirectly to some form of action by the individual. Reverse the perspective, and examine the key role in determining action that is played by environmental knowledge and evaluation. In their chapter, Hart and Conn stressed the *functionality* of much of an individual's place knowledge. This is a point frequently asserted, but seldom researched, and we endorse Hart and Conn's call for case studies. We need to know from these studies how far the selective uptake and learning of information from the environment *is* specifically supportive of the individual's needs and interests. A snapshot or survey approach will not reveal the patterning over time of information gathering, against activity change. Hence, a number of longer term, individual-centered case studies will be needed to establish what has always seemed a plausible connection between knowledge and activity. Such connections may not always be borne out by the evidence: for example, Walsh, Krauss, and Regnier, 1981, have, in a small-scale study, shown that among a group of elderly residents, there is surprisingly *little* relationship between neighborhood knowledge and neighborhood use. We need a larger scale, longitudinal study here.

Similarly, the meaning and value attached to places, and the consequent effect on the patterns of behavior, would benefit considerably from a longitudinal perspective: the connection is plausible, but we need an account of the process at work. Too often, studies in environmental cognition use settings that are impoverished or lacking in long-term meaning for the individual. Contrast such experimenters' lack of sensitivity to this point with the care and attention to the meaning of settings that has characterized ecological psychology (Barker, 1987); and that is even coming to be true of those psychologists studying "social situations," such as Argyle, Furnham, and Graham (1981).

Canter (this volume) has already argued that the *socio*physical environment should be our topic of study; and Valsiner (1987) describes how, in the earliest years, the infant's world is socially constructed for him or her. The same point can be made for any point in the life span, especially where the individual is encountering a new setting. The new recruit, be it to school, to new work place, to nursing home, or to any other organization or setting, has not only to learn the place's physical dimensions and layout, but also the limits of appropriate actions. On occasions, the physical environment clarifies the rules of conduct: areas are divided according to function, signs instruct or suggest, furnishings prompts activities, and so on. Yet in many instances, the individual is offered no such physical cueing, and may make many false social moves across invisible "dividing lines." The setting and social generation of such rules and expectancies have been studied within the sociological tradition stemming from Goffman (1956, 1963).

How do these social constraints on behavior and place use come to be internalized? Valsiner's (1987) study of very young children, discussed by Hart and Conn in their chapter, shows how the process may begin. However, for a life-span account, we need to have studies of the way situation-specific scripts and schema are generalized. What are the limits? How are they available as structuring for the individual's encounter with newly encountered settings? How does the individual come to categorize settings as similar, and thus demanding similar sets of behavioral expectancies? Does flexibility in adapting previous scripts to new settings reduce with old age? "Renewal" of urban areas and changes in sociocultural norms may make such flexibility an important life skill, whose lack may isolate the elderly.

CONCLUSIONS

Life stages are, in themselves, construable as an extending and changing set of behavior settings, with (until old age for some) an expansion of the range of roles in which one encounters with the world. Social forces, and these developing social roles, mediate one's encounters with the world. A life-span account of the individual's environmental preferences, cognitions, and actions, in sum, becomes a developmental social psychology of the individual. Knowledge structures of the environment do not just arise through the individual's direct experience of the world, but as shaped by—among many other factors—Liben's representations, such as maps, Axia and colleagues' verbal accounts, and Hart and Conn's parental structurings of the possible.

In this chapter we have stressed the range of individual experiences throughout the life span, as precursors of differences in environmental knowledge and assessment. Case studies and longitudinal designs are therefore major candidates for support, although material of value can be obtained from the more traditional cross-sectional studies.

The role of such studies in a life-span account can be seen in filling in the gaps in the preliminary Table 15.1, which was designed to illustrate the range of environmental tasks and inputs across the life span. The table is clearly incomplete: it is offered as an incentive to the readers to shape the research agenda and to suggest that we can best think of the development of environmental cognition and assessment as functionally related to life-span changes in activities.

REFERENCES

Acredolo, L.P. (1979). Laboratory versus home: The effect of the 9-month-old infant's choice of spatial reference system: *Developmental Psychology, 15,* 666–667.

Acredolo, L.P. (1985). Co-ordinating perspectives in infant spatial orientation. In R. Cohen (Ed.), *The development of spatial cognition.* Hillsdale, N.J.: Erlbaum.

Acredolo, L.P. (1988). From signal to 'symbol': The development of landmark knowledge from 9–13 months. *British Journal of Developmental Psychology, 6,* 269–272.

Anthony, K.H. (1985). The shopping mall: a teenage hangout. *Adolescence, 20,* 307–312.

Argyle, M., Furnham, A., & Graham, J.A. (1981). *Social Situations.* Cambridge: Cambridge University Press.

Balling, J.D., & Falk, J.H. (1982). Development of visual preference for natural environments. *Environment and Behavior, 14,* 5–28.

Barker, R.G. (1987). Prespecting in environmental psychology: Oskaloosa revisited. In D. Stokols & I. Altman (Eds.), *Handbook of environmental psychology.* New York: Wiley.

Blades, M., and Spencer, C. (1987). Young children's strategies when using maps with landmarks. *Journal of Environmental Psychology, 7,* 201–218.

Bower, T.G.R. (1975). Infant perception of the third dimension and object concept development. In L.B. Cohen & P. Salapatek (Eds.), *Infant perception: From sensation to cognition.* New York: Academic Press.

Carp, F.M. (1987). Environment and Aging. In D. Stokols & I. Altman (Eds.), *Handbook of environmental psychology.* New York: Wiley.

Carp, F.M., & Carp, A. (1982). Perceived environmental quality of neighbourhoods: Development of assessment scales and their relation to age and gender. *Journal of Environmental Psychology, 2,* 295–312.

Craik, K.H. (1970). Environmental psychology. In K.H. Craik (Ed.), *New directions in psychology.* New York: Holt, Rinehart & Winston.

Craik, K., & Feimer, N. (1987). Environmental assessment. In D. Stokols & I. Altman (Eds.), *Handbook of environmental psychology.* New York: Wiley.

Cratty, B.J., & Sams, T.A. (1968). *The body-image of blind children.* New York: American Foundation for the Blind.

Devlin, A. (1976). The ''small town'' cognitive maps: Adjusting to a new environment. In G.T. Moore & R.G. Golledge (Eds.), *Environmental knowing.* Stroudsburg, Penn.: Dowden, Hutchinson & Ross.

Downs, R.M. (1985). The representation of space: Its development in children and in cartography. In R. Cohen (Ed.), *The development of spatial cognition.* Hillsdale: N.J.: Erlbaum.

Evans, G.W. (1980). Environmental cognition. *Psychological Bulletin, 88,* 259–287.

Evans, G.W., Marrero, D.G., & Butler, P.A. (1981). Environmental learning and cognitive mapping. *Environment and Behavior, 13,* 83–104.

Fischoff, B., Svenson, O., & Slovic, P. (1987). Active responses to environmental hazards: perceptions and decision making. In D. Stokols & I. Altman (Eds.), *Handbook of environmental psychology.* New York: Wiley.

Fisher, S., Murray, K.J., & Frazer, N.A. (1985). Homesickness, health and efficiency in first year students. *Journal of Environmental Psychology, 5,* 181–195.

Fisher, S., Frazer, N., & Murray, K. (1986). Homesickness and health in boarding school children. *Journal of Environmental Psychology, 6,* 35–47.

Goffman, E. (1956). *The presentation of self in everyday life.* Edinburgh: Edinburgh University Press.

Goffman, E. (1963). *Behavior in public places.* Glencoe, Ill.: Free Press.

Hall, G.T. (1966). *The hidden dimension.* New York: Doubleday.

Harris, P.L. (1985). The origins of search and number skills. In H.M. Wellman (Ed.), *Children's searching: The development of search skills and spatial representation*. Hillsdale, N.J.: Erlbaum.

Hart, R. (1979). *Children's experience of place: A developmental study*. New York: Irvington Press.

Herron, R., & Sutton-Smith, B. (1971). *Child's play*. New York: Wiley.

Hill, F., & Michelson, W. (1981). Towards a geography of urban children and youth. In D.T. Herbert & R.J. Johnston (Eds.), *Geography and the urban environment: Progress in research and applications* (Vol. 4). Chichester: Wiley.

Kaplan, R., & Kaplan, S. (1989). *The nature book*. Cambridge: Cambridge University Press.

Knopf, R. (1987). Human behavior, cognition and affect in the natural environment. In D. Stokols & I. Altman (Eds.), *Handbook of environmental psychology*. New York: Wiley.

Lee, T.R. (1963). On the relation between the school journey and social and emotional adjustment in rural infant children. *British Journal of Educational Psychology, 27*, 100–114.

Little, B.R. (1983). Personal projects: A ratonale and method for investigation. *Environment and Behavior, 15*, 273–309.

Little, B.R. (1987). Personality and the environment. In D. Stokols & I. Altman (Eds.), *Handbook of Environmental Psychology*. New York: Wiley.

Lynch, K. (1977). *Growing up in cities: Studies of the spatial environment of adolescence in Cracow, Melbourne, Mexico City, Salta, Toluca and Warszawa*. Cambridge, Mass.: M.I.T. Press.

McClurg, P.A., & Chaille, C. (1987). Computer games: Environments for developing spatial cognition? *Journal of Educational Computing Research, 3*, 95–111.

McLuhan, M. (1964). *Understanding media*. London: Routledge & Kegan Paul.

Moore, R. (1986). *Childhood's domain*. London: Croom Helm.

Murray, D., & Spencer, C.P. (1979). Individual differences in the drawing of cognitive maps: The effects of geographical mobility, strength of mental imagery, and basic graphic ability. *Transactions, Institute of British Geographers, 4*, 385–391.

Ottosson, T. (1987). Map reading and wayfinding. *Göteborg Studies in Educational Sciences, 65* (whole).

Pearce, P.L. (1988). *The Ulysses factor: Educating visitors in tourist settings*. New York: Springer-Verlag.

Piaget, J. (1929). *The child's conception of the world:* London: Kegan Paul.

Piaget, J. (1930). *The child's conception of physical causality*. London: Kegan Paul.

Pick, H.L., & Lockman, J.J. (1981). From frames of reference to spatial representations. In L.S. Liben, A.H. Patterson, & N. Newcombe (Eds.), *Spatial representation and behavior across the life span*. New York: Academic Press.

Presson, C.C., & Ihrig, L.H. (1982). Using mother as a spatial landmark: Evidence against egocentric coding in infancy. *Developmental Psychology, 18*, 699–702.

Relph, E.E. (1976). *Places and placelessness*. London: Pion Press.

Siegel, A.W , & White, S. (1975). The development of spatial representations of large-scale environments. In H.W. Reese (Ed.), *Advances in child development and behavior* (Vol. 10). New York: Academic Press.

Spencer, C.P., & Blades, M. (1985). Children at risk: Are we underestimating their general competence whilst overestimating their performance? In T. Gärling & J. Valsiner (Eds.), *Children within environments: Toward a psychology of accident prevention*. New York: Plenum.

Spencer, C.P., Blades, M., & Morsley, K. (1989). *The child in the physical environment*. Chichester: Wiley.

Tajfel, H. (1981). *Human groups and social categories*. Cambridge: Cambridge University Press.

Valsiner, J. (1987). *Culture and the development of children's action: A cultural-historical theory of developmental psychology*. Chichester: Wiley.

Walsh, D.A., Krauss, I.K., & Regnier, V.A. (1981). Spatial ability, environmental knowledge and environmental use: the elderly. In L.S. Liben, A.H. Patterson, & N. Newcombe (Eds.), *Spatial representation and behavior across the life span*. New York: Academic Press.

Warr, P.B., & Knapper, C. (1968). *The perception of people and events*. London: Wiley.

Wood, D. (1986). *Doing nothing*. Raleigh, N.C.: North Carolina State University School of Design.

Zimring, C., Carpman, J.R., & Michelson, W. (1987). Design for special populations: Mentally retarded persons, children, hospital visitors. In D. Stokols & I. Altman (Eds.), *Handbook of environmental psychology*. New York: Wiley.

16

Life-Span Developmental Issues in Environmental Assessment, Cognition, and Action: Applications to Environmental Policy, Planning, and Design

GARY T. MOORE

This chapter addresses the question of how research on environmental assessment, cognition, and action can be utilized in the professional arenas of public policy, urban planning, and architectural design. Initially a discussion on three papers (Chapters 12, 13, and 14), the chapter attempts to extrapolate policy and design implications for the built environment from current knowledge on life-span developmental issues as represented by these three chapters. Suggestions of other research questions, issues, and strategies that might better inform policy and design are then discussed. In conclusion, the chapter briefly explores six general issues about the interaction of environmental cognition and research utilization.

The contributions to this volume by Giovanna Axia, Erminielda Mainardi Peron, and Maria Rosa Baroni, by Lynn Liben, and by Roger Hart and Michael Conn have dealt heavily with *child development* and very little with aging or life-span development. Little evidence is presented from the gerontological and geriatric literatures, and less from the life-span literature. Liben presents a clear conceptualization of life-span developmental approaches to environmental cognition, but to date there have been few studies and thus no data specifically on life-span developmental changes in environmental cognition. My chapter, therefore, will be weighted most heavily on the earlier phases of human development though, where feasible, it will comment on implications for the environment of elderly adults and on the environmental context of life-span developmental changes.

Despite their titles and intentions, the three chapters focus most heavily on *environmental cognition* and much less on assessment and action. For example, after discussing the wide variety of possible definitions of assessment, including appraisal, evaluation, preferences, and attachment. Axia et al. focus most heavily on the cognitive aspects of schemata, representation, and organization of knowledge. Similarly, Hart and Conn valiantly take on the challenge of reporting on children's decision making and environmental behavior, but their empirical examples are also limited to

309

cognitive and metacognitive issues. My chapter will thus also focus on environmental knowing.

There are many interesting points of a theoretical and conceptual nature to raise about environmental assessment, cognition, and action from these three chapters, but this task is left to the other commentary chapter by Christopher Spencer. This chapter will concentrate on how the information in these chapters has been—or could be— applied to better inform *environmental policy and practice*.

There will be three parts to the chapter:

1. Policy and design implications from current knowledge as represented by these three chapters.
2. Suggestions of other research questions, issues, and strategies that might better inform policy and design.
3. Exploration of more general issues for consideration in the integration of environmental cognition and research utilization.

THE UTILIZATION OF RESEARCH IN POLICY, PLANNING, AND DESIGN

One- and Two-Community Approaches to Research Utilization

To organize the chapter, I will refer to a framework that might help us think about the gamut of research utilization. In exploring the nature of research utilization in environment and behavior, we have come to the realization that there are two main approaches to resolving the research utilization question—a ''two community model'' and a ''one-community model'' (Min, 1988; Moore, 1988).

The *two-community model* is based on the assumption that research and practice are separate. It is quite familiar, even if not under this title, to most academic researchers and professional practitioners. The two-community perspective assumes that:

> Research and practice are inherently separate and independent with few ideas shared between each other. Research, as the major way of creating knowledge, should be free from practical concerns and intended use. Any teleological interference in the process of inquiry is thus considered to cause an error in knowledge creation. Difficulties of research utilization are thus accounted for by the conceptual and vocational gap between research and practical activities. (Min, 1987, p. 4)

We hear and read, for example, of ''information transfer,'' of ''communication,'' of developing ''primers for professional application,'' of the ''use of knowledge in environmental design and planning,'' of ''channels of influence,'' of ''informing design,'' and of ''facility programming,'' ''post-occupancy evaluation,'' and ''design guides'' (Caplan, 1980; Moore, 1988; Moore, Cohen, Van Ryzin, & Oertel, 1979; Sanoff, 1989; Weisman, 1983; Wener, 1989).

There are two variations on the two-community model: conceptual applications and instrumental applications (Seidel, 1982; Weiss, 1977, 1980). *Conceptual applications* involve the application of ideas, concepts, and images usually through an informal process of implementation. It is akin to what Weisman (this volume) has referred to as the process of deepening, broadening, and extending policy makers' capacities for judgment. *Instrumental applications,* on the other hand, are straightforward, direct applications of a research finding in a project, program, policy, or administrative context, usually in the form of rules, codes, or standards, and most often through a one-to-one correspondence between research information and policy or design implication.

On the other hand, the *one-community model* is based on a quite different assumption, that research and practice can be integrated in one holistic process without seams. It is not the same as research application (cf. Weisman's chapter, this volume) in that in this view research and practice are integrated, not separated, in a linear sequence. Although not a new approach (Lewin, 1946; cf. Wisner, Stea, & Kruks, 1991), it is of more recent interest in the environment and behavior field.

> A keenly contrasting argument is observed in the one-community perspective, that in order to create knowledge, the integration of research and practice is inevitable. In this perspective, acting and knowing simultaneously occur in an integrated process, in which action leads to knowledge and the knowledge guides the direction of action. (Min, 1987, pp. 4–5)

On this other side of the fence, we hear and read of "participation," "social negotiation," developing a "common basis for agreeing," of developing procedures to "share experiences and negotiate priorities," of "direct involvement of the public," and of an "organized participatory approach" (Farbstein & Kantrowitz, 1991; Moore, 1988; Schneekloth, 1987; Susman & Evered, 1978; Wisner et al., 1991).

The one-community perspective is sometimes called "action research" (Sommer, 1977, 1984) or "reflective practice" (Schon, 1983), though we see these as particular forms or examples of the more general one-community model (Min, 1988; Moore, 1988).

Research can and does have an impact on the quality of the built and natural environment. Avenues of impact include public policy making at both legislative and administrative levels (Ventre, 1989), resource management, planning in its various forms, the several design professions including architecture, landscape architecture, and urban design, and environmental education.

I will not try to elaborate on all of these, only to explore where the current chapters draw policy, planning, and design conclusions and to show how they fit this typology. I will also try to suggest where we might *extrapolate* implications for policy, planning, and design from their findings and from the research results they reference, and will suggest some future research priorities to aid in the integration of research and practice.

Logic and Cohesion: Conceptual Utilization

At the most general level of conceptual utilization, all the chapters, and even the existence of this book, argue for the **logic and cohesion** of the physical form of the environment. [The design ideas derived from these chapters, called "design patterns" or "design principles" (Cohen & Moore, 1977), are indicated by boldface type.] From the accumulated empirical evidence, there is no doubt that environmental cognition is aided and abetted by a cohesive logic to and organization of the physical environment. This general notion of the logic and cohesion of the environment may be decomposed into several more specific design principles.

Evidence in all three chapters and in their references shows the importance of **cohesion balanced by complexity** (S. Kaplan, 1975; Rapoport & Hawkes, 1970; Wohlwill, 1976; see also Küller, this volume). Based on the empirical evidence to that time, Rapoport and Hawkes (1970) were the first to point out the importance of urban complexity for environmental perception and cognition. On the other hand, research by Wohlwill (1976) underscored that stimulus overload can lead to confusion and breakdown of perceptual and cognitive functions, and affirmed the inverted ''U''-shaped relationship between stimulus complexity and exploration and preference. These two sets of findings lead to the conclusion that environmental complexity needs to be balanced by coherence if the environment is to be explored, enjoyed, and comprehended.

The chapters also all suggest the cognitive value of making the environment more **legible** or conceptually clearer (Lynch, 1960) which may imply also making it more **accessible and usable** (Figure 16.1). Legibility is the degree to which different cities and different parts of cities stand out and can be recognized and organized into a coherent pattern in people's minds. The connection between legibility and accessibility, or more generally between environmental cognition and use, has been explored in great detail in social and behavior geography. [My thanks to Harry Timmermans who brought this literature to my attention. The reader is referred to a review article by Timmermans and Golledge (1990) that gives many typical references to studies on the relation between spatial awareness and actual behavior.] Considerable evidence has now been accumulated on the causal relations between environmental clarity and subsequent accessibility and use (Hanson, 1978, 1984; Horton & Reynolds,

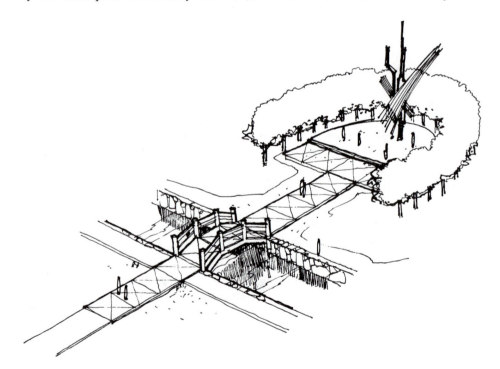

Figure 16.1. An illustration of accessible and usable space.

1969; Potter, 1979, 1984; Timmermans, Van der Heijden, & Westerveld, 1982). These causal links imply that making the environment more knowable leads to increased accessibility to resources and greater life-style alternatives. The logic can be pushed further, suggesting that lack of knowledge leads to inaccessibility, which might in turn lead to increased stress or poor life quality and ultimately to ill health (see Zimring, 1982). Some of the preliminary evidence for these latter links between lack of knowledge and ill health are analyzed in the introductory chapter to this volume by Evans and Gärling.

Axia, Mainardi Peron, and Baroni's chapter presents an interesting discussion of Mandler's (1979, 1984) four types of mental organization of knowledge: *categorical* (taxonomic class-inclusion hierarchy), *matrix* (two-dimensional organization), *serial* (unidirectional series), and *schematic* (sets of expectations). Further research could indicate in what ways these four *types* are interrelated in the specific context of environmental cognition. For example, it appears that the serial type is akin to the well-known findings about nodes, paths, anchor points, and the sequential organization of environmental knowledge (Appleyard, 1970; Evans & Pezdek, 1980; Garling, Book, Lindberg, & Nilsson, 1981; Golledge, 1975; Hart & Moore, 1973). It also appears that the two-dimensional matrix type is akin to the earlier discovery of the aerial, survey, or cluster structure of higher-order environmental representations (Appleyard, 1970; Moore, 1976; Shemyakin, 1962). Further research could also indicate in what way these four types are hierarchical ordered, and whether they undergo a developmental progression (as would be predicted from earlier work, eg., Moore, 1976).

But in addition, each of these principles of cognitive organization has strong implications for design. To draw their implications, we need to assume a possible isomorphism between mind and environment (Koffka, 1922), or at least an increased ability to perceive and comprehend environments if they are in accordance with existing structures of mind, that is, akin to the Piagetian assumption of the equilibration of assimilation and accommodation (Piaget, 1950, 1970).

Assuming for the moment the equilibrated processes of assimilation and accommodation, for which there is tremendous support in the literature, Mandler's categorical type of mental organization, which is really a class-inclusion hierarchy, supports the design concept of a **nested hierarchy** to the city (Alexander, 1965). A nested hierarchy is the notion that a well-functioning city is comprised of small neighborhoods that are embedded in larger communities, which in turn are embedded in larger urban geographic areas. Alexander (1965) pointed out that cities function best and are healthiest when these different scales overlap with each other rather than being separate and discrete. It is true that the larger scale spaces are typically the province of resource managers, urban planners, landscape architects, urban designers, and civil engineers. The intermediate scale is typically the province of architects, building designers, consulting engineers, and construction managers. The very smallest scale— that of interiors, product design, and materials—falls within the province of interior designers, product and industrial designers, and graphic designers dealing with building subsystems and furnishings. Although distinct linguistically and in terms of organized professions, these scales of the environment are actually nested one within the other. Rather than separate places with firm boundaries, Mandler's notion that an important part of the cognitive organization of knowledge (including, therefore, knowledge of the city) is organized in terms of a *class-inclusion hierarchy* seems to me to call for and support the value of a nested hierarchy at the largest scale of a building's location within a neighborhood and city and its proximity of facilities and services, to, at the smallest scale, individual room sizes, layout and doors, windows, furniture, and other physical attributes. Not only is cognition hierarchically organized across scales, but overall satisfaction with the environment is a function of factors at all three scales—large, intermediate, and small; when viewing these issues holistically, rather in terms of professional allegiances, the relation between scales and the nested hierarchy among scales are critical to human satisfaction (cf. review in Moore, Tuttle, & Howell, 1985).

The *matrix* structure of cognition supports a simpler two-dimensional organization to the city in terms of **routes, landmarks, and nodes** as has been discovered earlier in a variety of studies (Appleyard, 1970; Hart & Moore, 1973; Lynch, 1960; Moore, 1976; Siegel & White, 1975).

Mandler's *serial* mental organization, a unidirectional series, suggests strengthening **mnemonic sequences** in the city, as Halprin (1965, 1969) suggested many years ago. This can be done, in interaction with the matrix structure of cognition, by emphasizing the terminuses of routes by landmarks, statues, and sculpture, and by vistas to even slightly distant significant viewpoints (see Bacon, 1967).

Finally, Mandler's category of the *schematic* organization of mind—defined as sets of expectations—implies something parallel to that of Appleyard's (1969) findings that people recall buildings first in terms of use significance, then location, and then architectural style or character. Both Mandler's and Appleyard's work suggest the environment may be rendered more knowable, and perhaps more accessible and used, by increasing the **clarity of use significance and environmental expectation.** (Figure 16.2).

Mandler's five *effects* of place schemata, also summarized in the chapter by Axia

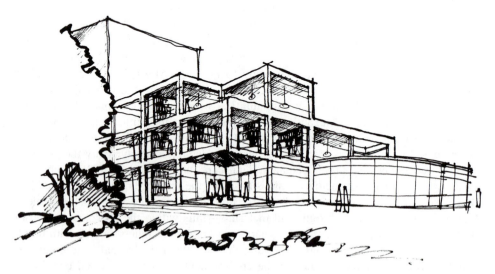

Figure 16.2. The design concept of clarity of use significance and environmental expectation.

Figure 16.3.   An example of a well-organized environment.

et al., are even more pregnant for environmental design and planning. Objects are coded more quickly (Mandler, 1979, 1984): when they are in a **familiar scene,** when the are in a **well-organized environment** [parallel to Küller's notion of unity (this volume)], when they are **anomalous objects** and/or **violate physical laws** (e.g., as shown in Figure 16.4, the buildings by the Texas firm, Site, which seem to fall down around you because they are missing a corner, tilt walls up and away from you in an improbable angle, or include a planned rubble of bricks left in a very visible location), and when they possess scheme-relevant information (the least physical of the

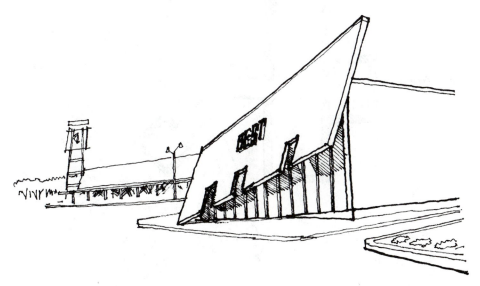

Figure 16.4.   An illustration of the design concept of violation of physical law. (Tilt showroom, Eudowood Shopping Mall, Towson, Maryland, 1976–78, designed by Site.)

four). But although pregnant, each of these is very general and immediately leads to more specific research questions that need to be answered before utilization in the design professions can proceed on a sound, empirical basis.

Research in Action: Instrumental Utilization

So far, these suggestions are in a realm of conceptual utilization. However, there are also parts of the rich chapters by Axia et al., Liben, and Hart and Conn that imply *instrumental* applications. There are more than can be presented here. A few examples will suffice to illustrate the practical and professional utility of current research on environmental assessment, cognition, and action.

The Appleton (1975) results as reported in the chapter by Axia et al. suggest that adults in the middle of the life span prefer environments offering both **prospect and refuge** (e.g., a hill from which a large portion of the landscape can be seen and a place surrounded by trees). Similarly, we know that developmentally appropriate cognitive and social behavior is more pronounced in what have been called **modified open space** in schools and child care centers, that is, where there is both visual access to a variety of activity areas, yet privacy and quiet nooks as places of refuge (Cohen, Moore, McGinty, & Armstrong, 1982; Moore, 1987b). These are very direct, one-to-one instrumental applications of research findings in the realm of assessment and preference. They parallel the design principle for children called **breakaway and retreat** (Figure 16.5) (Moore, Cohen, Van Ryzin, & Oertel, 1979). The notion of "prospect" (Figure 16.6) also parallels the findings of Howell (1980) that elderly people use spaces for social interaction more, and feel more comfortable,

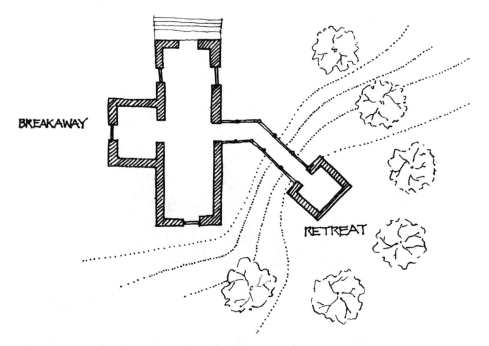

Figure 16.5.   The design principle of breakaway and retreat.

Figure 16.6. An environment that offers prospect and refuge.

when there is the possibility of **viewing and** (more precisely) **previewing** an activity and a space before entering.

There are a range of other design implications suggested in Axia and colleagues' chapter: Kaplan and Kaplan's (1982) work on **mystery** and **legibility** (Figure 16.7) related to exploration and making sense of environments, Hart's (1979) work together with R. Moore's (1986) and Axia and Nicolini's (1989) showing that children prefer **open space**, and Nicolini's (1985) work finding that toddlers prefer corners and narrow **closed spaces** in day-care centers. The latter parallels other findings on the greater social and cognitive development potentials in **well-defined, resource-rich activity pockets** in child-care centers (G.T. Moore, 1986).

From Liben's chapter (this volume), we are reminded of some other important instrumental environmental implications. Liben notes the importance of clear **landmarks** (based on Acredolo, 1976; Acredolo & Evans, 1980; Berenthal, Campos, & Barrett, 1984) for infants, toddlers, and early school-age children before the devel-

Figure 16.7. Illustration of mystery, a component of contradiction and complexity.

opment of concrete operations and survey-type coordinated representations, and also for orthopedically handicapped children. The importance of stable landmarks has also been demonstrated for facilitating knowledge and orientation among the elderly (Evans, Smith, & Pezdek, 1982).

We can also refer to Acredolo's (1988) notion of visual tracking, the importance of visual attention that accompanies infants' movement through environments, which supports what is called **modified open space** (Cohen, et al., 1982).

Ainsworth, Bell, and Stayton's (1973) work and Hazen and Durrett's (1982) study showing greater exploration with attachment is rich with possibilities. These two studies imply that *environments* affording attachment may be more conducive to exploration and therefore to the active development of environmental cognition than environments not encouraging attachment. The analysis of **resource-rich activity pockets** and of **circulation that overlooks** (Cohen et al., 1982) as well as the findings that caregivers spend more time in active engagement with children in child care centers designed in terms of **modified open space** than they do in other types of arrangements (like open and closed space; Moore, 1987b) may be relevant here.

Other instrumental implications from Liben's chapter include the fact that cognitive maps are affected by **barriers within rooms** that define subspaces (Kosslyn, Pick, & Fariello, 1974), by **subdivisions along a route** (Allen, 1981, 1982), and by **conceptual divisions of large environments** (Acredolo, 1988). To achieve this, one might install 90- to 120-cm partitions in rooms to give some spatial definition and possibilities for legibility to otherwise open space, or might ensure alcoves and changes in ceiling heights or lighting in otherwise long corridors, and might ensure the spatial identification of neighborhoods of different visual character in an otherwise undifferentiated urban landscape.

In a different line, the findings reported by Liben about preschoolers' performance on layout reproduction tasks (Liben, Moore, & Goldbeck, 1982) suggest that opportunities for **viewing and previewing** in the environment may significantly improve cognitive maps.

On an instrumental policy level, it is also interesting to consider recent work suggesting that **orientation programs** that enable older adults to learn about the function and location of new facilities to which they will be moved appear to ameliorate the negative effects often associated with relocation among the elderly (Hunt, 1984).

As a last example of instrumental research utilization, R. Kaplan's work (1976) showing that junior high school students exposed to hard copy representations of natural environments perform better and report more positive affect implies **the role of advanced organizers of the environment.** Work on the design of environmental orientation systems for people at different stages of the life cycle including maps of areas, schematic plans of complex buildings, and tactile route maps is progressing well (Golledge, this volume; Hunt, 1984; Hunt & Pastalan, 1987; Passini, 1984; Schulz & Krantz, 1980).

CRITICAL RESEARCH ISSUES TO INFORM POLICY AND DESIGN

The chapters in this section of the book, and the findings they review, are rich with implications for change and improvement in the physical environment to enhance environmental knowing, to make environmental decision making and action easier and experientially richer, and to raise people's assessment of their everyday environment. But the question may be asked, are there other kinds of questions or research strategies not included in these chapters that might also inform policy and practice, or that might better lead to design directives and policy considerations? I have argued elsewhere that the best research can simultaneously inform theory and inform practice, and wondered if it might be possible to create a symbiosis of theoretical research and environmental design (Moore, 1975). The three chapters suggest, albeit between the lines, several ways in which we might take a step in the direction of conducting research that can simultaneously inform theory and aid in the solution of environmental problems. The next sections of this chapter offers two examples of what seem to me to be important research directions if we are simultaneously to advance our understanding of environmental assessment, cognition, and action and our impact on the quality of the environment.

Place Types, Environmental Variables, and the Structure of the Environment

The first issue concerns *what* we study—the structure of mind, or the structure of the environment.

Axia, Mainardi Peron, and Baroni's characterization of environmental assessment is focused on appraisal and evaluation, including preferences, and on the notion of supportive environments seen as an interactional concept. They caution against reductionism to too simple a concept of assessment. Rather than treat assessment as a simple concept of pragmatic evaluation or superficial preference, Axia et al. suggest that environmental assessment be seen in terms of the concepts of *place evaluation/goals* (Canter, 1983; Kaplan & Kaplan, 1982), *supportive environments and events* (Kaplan & Kaplan, 1982), *attachment to place* (Fried & Gleicher, 1961), *attractiveness* (Zube & Pitt, 1981), and *environmental quality standards and indexes* (Craik, 1981). This focus on qualitative concepts is a clear advance over earlier work.

But the question can be focused more sharply (and can be asked of all three chapters and the empirical research they review): What *qualities and characteristics of different physical environments* give them a positive valence for various sets of goals, for different events or situations, and for distinct groups and cultures? In other words, it is a partial and important step to identify concepts like "attractiveness," "supportive environments," "attachment," and so on, but what are the *actual environmental variables* that make up these constructs? This is the question that must be asked in order to move smoothly to the realm of policy, planning, and design.

In their chapter, Axia et al. remind us about Kaplan's (1975) and Wohlwill's (1976) findings that preference for complexity is limited by the need for coherence. This raises two related research questions: What creates "coherence" and "complexity"? What are the environmental cues related to coherence? What environmental variables make up the construct "complexity." These concepts are shorthand notations, constructs for where we lack knowledge about environmental cues.

A similar comment can be made about Axia et al.'s discussion of "the place that makes me feel shy" or "the place that is depressing for me." How might we operationalize "shy place" or "depressing place" for different groups in different settings?

Liben raises a related research question. She suggests it would be useful to consider the extent to which environmental exploration and cognition are affected by what Hart (1981) earlier called "different affective potentials" of place. Again, as in all the chapters in this section, I would suggest we might focus more on the *environmental cues* that relate to the effective potential of space, and for different groups at different stages of the life cycle. My call for explicit research on environmental cues might be able to be related to, and aided and abetted by, Gibson's (1979) concept of *affordances* (see Krampen, 1991).

The same comment can be made about Roger Hart and Michael Conn's chapter, in which they devote considerable attention to Valsiner's (1987) individual-sociological theory of children's actions. Whereas considerable emphasis is given to the role of culture, of the structural organization of the child's anatomy and physiology, and of the social environment in, as Hart says, "shaping development," very little discussion pertains to the role of the physical environment. Is this a theory that holds that the physical environment, the designed and natural environment, does not affect or influence development? Might we be better to choose theories that include the role of the physical environment? Might we then be able to expand further on the role of the physical environment—not only physical environmental variables but also the *structure* of the environment—to understand children's environmental decision making and action?

We see the same question lurking behind the work of Mandler as discussed by Axia et al. Mandler's (1979, 1984) four types of schemata, or four types of mental organization of knowledge (categorical, matrix, serial, and schematic), advance earlier, more global conceptualizations of mental schemata. I have tried above to draw out a few implications for the design of the everyday environment from this taxonomy. But as in the above comment about the chapter by Axia et al., the question again is: Are there more implications for the organization of the environment, and especially for how we organize the structure of the environment, from these four organizational structures of knowledge?

It is useful to conceptualize schemata not only quantitatively but qualitatively. We need to know more about people's judgments not only of location, but also of the appearance of a place, what items are expected in different places, whether all things and all qualities considered, a particular place is or is not a prototypical instance of that archetypal place. This way of thinking about schema can lead to fruitful research questions that can inform applications. For example, we may ask the following questions: What are the major place types that make up the environment? How "close" does a particular place have to come to the place type to be recognized and assessed as an example of the place type? Further, what are the salient environmental variables that inform this decision-making process; said differently, in what ways does a place have to resemble the template to be recognized? In addition to examining the categories of mind, this way of thinking might move us also to exploring the categories of the known *environment*.

From Mandler's analysis of the effects of schemata, we may ask what environmental cues lead to places being assessed as "familiar" or "well organized," or for the schema to have "expected information," "compatible information," "irrelevant information," or "discrepant or opposed information"? What I am suggesting here has been suggested in my earlier commentaries on environmental cognitive representations and implications for design (Moore, 1977, 1980). Much of the work of the field of environmental psychology continues to focus on the "environment" in a very global way, as the backdrop for behavior, often without specifying the particular environmental variables under consideration. Without articulating specific *physical* environmental variables, and without developing a typology of environments and environmental variables, environmental psychology can do little to advance. It can do little to inform policy, planning, or design. How can practitioners change the environment if we do not articulate and study particular environmental variables? How can practitioners know what portions of the built and natural environments around us to preserve by evasive action (e.g., historic preservation) if we have no data relating particular environmental variables to significant outcome variables? Some policy makers, planners, and especially architects have become tired and disenchanted with environment–behavior research. Perhaps this is because many researchers continue to explore the categories of mind, without giving equal attention to the categories of environment—place types, the structure of the environment, and environmental cues (Wohlwill, 1976).

If we conceive of environmental schemata as idiosyncratic, application is difficult if not impossible. If we consider them as generalizable, and research and discover the breadth of their generality, research utilization becomes possible. The question then is, how general, and to what populations, settings, and times are each of the major categories of environmental schemata generalizable?

Character, Meaning, and Symbolism in the Environment

A second major issue concerns the content of mind but in a way that integrates mind with the sociophysical environment—namely, research on the character, meaning, and symbolism of the environment, not just on its geometric, spatial qualities.

Axia summarized part of her own work (Axia, 1986, 1988) on a three-phase descriptive model of the development of children's representations of the *non*spatial components of environments. Her model is parallel to an earlier three-stage theory of the development of environmental cognition (Hart & Moore, 1973). Research on the nonspatial components of peoples' images of the environment was of course first suggested by Lynch (1960). In my view, questions about the nonspatial components of environments continues to deserve considerably more attention. Environmental experience, and certainly assessment, decision making, and action, are influenced by the holistic quality of the sociophysical environment, not just the spatial environment, yet the vast majority of work to date has been on cognition of the spatial qualities of environments.

In her chapter, Liben made two important conclusions related to this theme: "Although controversial, the weight of evidence seems to support the position that environmental cognition rests heavily on a foundation established through visual experience" (p. 260). Second, Liben showed that environmental representations may be at least as important as direct environmental experience as a source of environmental knowing. Although most of the subsequent discussion in Liben's chapter deals with wayfinding and directions in the environment, is it possible to extend the discussion to a broader set of qualities of the environment? Can we examine not only the role of environmental barriers and divisions on environmental cognition, but also environments differentiated in terms of nonvisual qualities such as friendly and "dangerous," community and privacy, sacred and profane?

Hart and Conn suggest that when one investigates "place cognition" instead of "spatial cognition," one is brought closer to meaning and to action. The difference may seem just linguistic, but I would maintain that when the focus of research is on "spatial cognition," the researchers tends to focus on the geometric–perceptual qualities of space, whereas when we try to understand what it is that makes for place, and for the knowledge and identification with place, we tend to focus on the more holistic sociopolitical–economic–spatial qualities of the environment.

We continue to know far more about the spatial than the nonspatial qualities of the environment, and about how the children, adults, and older people conceptualize space more than how they conceptualize the other social, political, economic, and cultural aspects of the everyday environments around them. We know more about the environmental cognition of spatial relations, like cognitive maps, than we do about the meanings and symbols that people ascribed to different parts of the environment over the life span (see also Appleyard, 1969; Krampen, 1991; Moore, 1979; Rapoport, 1977). I challenge these three groups of researchers to expand on this point by suggesting new research that looks at the development of the appreciation of the *character* of the environment, including its meaning and symbolism at different stages over the life span.

THE INTERACTION OF ENVIRONMENTAL COGNITION AND RESEARCH UTILIZATION

In conclusion, I would like to raise six general issues about the utilization of research on environmental cognition, assessment, and action in the environmental professions.

Strategies: Choice of Underlying Theory and Philosophical Assumptions

First I would like to raise the question of the role of theory explicitly or implicitly lying behind one's research and the role of the underlying and often unstated ontological and epistemological assumptions in that theory. In Liben's chapter, we see theories and assumptions that stress the role of psychological processes, in Axia et al.'s the role of schemata, in Hart and Conn's the role of the intellectual construction of the environment. These are largely psychological models, or psychological approaches. By starting with rather strictly psychological models connecting heavily with theory in mainline cognitive psychology, might we focus rather narrowly on strictly psychological phenomena and traditional psychological variables?

Conversely, Hart and Conn ask about the possibility of starting inquiry from the base of a cognitive anthropological emphasis on environmental classification (see also Rapoport, 1977). We could also ask about the impact of taking a semiotic focus on environmental meaning (as Krampen, 1991, recently has) or about the possibility of studying environmental metaphor and symbolism from the tradition of the humanities. Rapoport (1977) has gone so far as to say that in his view there are two fundamental approaches to environmental cognition—the psychological and the anthropological—and tries to show that the psychological approach is a special case of a more general anthropological approach. The psychological, he argues, tends to stress *knowledge* of the environment, whereas the anthropological takes the position that cognitive processes are concerned with making the environmental *meaningful.*

The point here is not to argue the relative merits of one approach or another, but to point out that the choice of epistemology is critical in determining the type of questions asked and the mode of asking them. The issue is much more fine-grained than taking an approach that might be labeled psychological or that of some other social science or environmental profession. The issue also involves particular sets of assumptions underlying one's implicit or explicit theory (e.g., phenomenological, empiricist, ecological, structural; cf. Altman & Rogoff, 1987; Moore, 1987a; Zube & Moore, 1987–present). A phenomenological orientation, for instance, might suggest asking questions about the interaction or integration of environmental knowing and environmental experience, whereas a structural orientation might direct one to ask questions about the underlying or deep structure behind more manifest images of the environment. Being grounded in one framework or another, being brought up in it, trained in it, highly experienced in it, will strongly influence a researcher to see only questions that can be seen from that perspective and to inquire about them only in the methods more preferred from the point of view of that theory or perspective. Being grounded in a general psychological framework seems to orient researchers to ask questions about the processes of environmental cognition much more than about the content of them, about their meaning, and about their connection with other environmental phenomena such as decision making and action.

An interactional–constructivist model that explicitly looks at the developmental construction of environmental knowledge through the reciprocal interaction of environmental and organismic variables and that intentionally crosses physical environmental with psychological and social independent variables may open new avenues to theory development and to utilization (see Moore, 1987a, 1989, for a fuller treatment of this issue).

Environmental Cues

There have been a continuous set of concerns raised about the neglect of the physical environment in environmental cognition research (Evans, 1980; Evans, Smith, & Pezdek, 1982; Evans, Skorpanich, Garling, Bryant, & Bresolin, 1984; Heft, 1981; Moore, 1977, 1979; Wohlwill, 1976). Much of the environmental cognition research of the late 1970s did not include physical environmental variables as independent variables, making the derivation of implications for design extremely difficult. Notable exceptions were the work of Appleyard (1969) on why buildings are known, Cooper (1975) on recall for parts of row housing, Acredolo (1976) on landmarks in children's cognition, and Weisman (1977) on orientation and wayfinding in complex buildings. We have made great strides since then, not only in finding the environment again, but also conceptually and methodologically (cf. Evans, 1980).

The point is, as mentioned earlier, if we are to apply environmental assessment, cognition, and action research to the design of real environments, we need to move out of the black box of basic cognitive processes to ask what *place types,* what *structures of the environment,* and what *environmental cues* are related to these processes and mechanisms.

Levels of Analysis

A related issue (discussed also elsewhere in this volume) concerns the appropriate *level of analysis* for research investigations. The decision about what level of analysis at which to ask particular questions must be made in reference to (1) predictability of relevant outcome variables and/or (2) language of choice of decision makers. The more predictable the level of analysis, the less generalizable; the more reliable, often times the less valid. If one chooses a level of analysis so as to try to optimize these two functions, how do we correlate these two without confusing level of analysis (which in some situations may need to be very particular) with rules (which often are, but maybe should not be) deterministic?

Integration of Theory and Application

The fourth issue is very general—just a question really. Summarizing our earlier discussion, we can ask again the question about the possible integration of science and action. We can even posit the existence of a third dimension to the currently two-dimensional cell structure that organized this book. The third dimension would be the integration of conceptual advances and applications. Is it possible to do research in the domain of environmental assessment, cognition, and action that simultaneously informs and integrates theory and practice (see Schon's, 1983, *Reflective Practitioner*)?

Lest we assume, uncritically, that "application" is necessarily good, let me raise two final questions without any attempt to resolve them.

One- and Two-Community Models of Research Utilization

Is the approach called "application" misguided? Earlier in this chapter I differentiated between what we have been calling "two-community" versus "one-community" approaches to the utilization/integration of research and practice. As Hart and Conn alluded to in their chapter, it may be that the approach to "application" of supposedly generalizable findings to specific field situations is misguided. Might one-community approaches of action-oriented case studies research be the better way to proceed? What are the advantages and limitations in the realm of environmental assessment, cognition, and action?

Environmental Cognition as a Basic or Applied Field

Is it even possible, going one step further, to say that the research domain of environmental assessment, cognition, and action is basic not applied research? Might it be that the most interesting and important questions are of theory and of conceptual integration across the two-dimensional front plane of the Evans/Gärling matrix (as developed in this volume)? Should we be happy with that, get on with it, and not worry about the utility of our research?

ACKNOWLEDGMENTS

My thanks to the U.S. National Science Foundation, the Swedish Building Research Council and the Office of International Studies and Programs at the University of Wisconsin-Milwaukee for support to present the paper, to Gary Evans and Tommy Gärling for organizing the Umeå Symposium and for valuable comments on an earlier version of this chapter. All illustrations in this chapter were done for the author by Raymond Shireal and Andy Siswanto.

REFERENCES

Acredolo, L.P. (1976). Frames of reference used by children for orientation in unfamiliar spaces. In G.T. Moore & R.G. Golledge (Eds.), *Environmental knowing: Theories, research, and methods* (pp. 165–172). New York: Van Nostrand Reinhold.

Acredolo, L.P. (1988). Infant mobility and spatial development. In J. Stiles-Davis, M. Kritchevsky, & U. Bellugi (Eds.), *Spatial cognition: Brain bases and development* (pp. 157–186). Hillsdale, N.J.: Erlbaum.

Acredolo, L.P., & Evans, D. (1980). Developmental changes in the effects of landmarks on infant spatial behavior. *Developmental Psychology, 16,* 312–318.

Ainsworth, M.S., Bell, S.M.V., & Stayton, D.J. (1973). Individual differences in the strange-situation behavior of one-year olds. In L.S. Stone, H.T. Smith, & L.B. Murphy (Eds.), *The competent infant* (pp. 1–10). New York: Basic Books.

Alexander, C. (1965). The city is not a tree. *Architectural Forum, 122* (April), 58–62, and (May), 58–61.

Allen, G.L. (1981). A developmental perspective on the effects of ''subdividing'' macrospatial experience. *Journal of Experimental Psychology: Human Learning and Memory, 7,* 120–132.

Allen, G.L. (1982). The organization of route knowledge. In R. Cohen (Ed.), *New directions in child development: Children's conceptions of spatial relationships* (pp. 31–39). San Francisco: Jossey-Bass.

Altman, I., & Rogoff, B. (1987). World views in psychology: Trait, interactional, organismic, and transactional. In D. Stokols & I. Altman (Eds.), *Handbook of environmental psychology* (pp. 7–40). New York: Wiley.

Appleton, J. (1975). *The experience of landscape.* London: Wiley.

Appleyard, D. (1969). Why buildings are known. *Environment and Behavior, 1,* 131–156.

Appleyard, D. (1970). Styles and methods of structuring a city. *Environment and Behavior, 2,* 100–117.

Axia, G. (1986). *La mente ecologica: La conoscenza dell'ambiente nel bambino.* Firenze, Italy: Giunti.

Axia, G. (1988). Language and orientation: Memory for route elements in verbal descriptions by children and adults. In H. van Hogdalen, N.L. Prak, T.J.M van der Voordt, & H.B.R. van Wegen (Eds.), *Looking back to the future* (Vol. 2, pp. 513–522). Delft, The Netherlands: Delft University Press.

Axia, G., & Nicolini, C. (1989). *Image and description of home, school and town in Venetian children.* Unpublished manuscript.

Bacon, E.G. (1967). *The design of cities.* New York: Viking.

Berenthal, B.I., Campos, J.J., & Barrett, K.C. (1984). Self-produced locomotion: An organizer of emotional, cognitive, and social development in infancy. In R. Emde & R. Harmon (Eds.), *Continuities and discontinuities in development* pp. 175–210. New York and London: Plenum.

Canter, D. (1983). The purposive evaluation of places: A facet approach. *Environment and Behavior, 15,* 659–698.

Caplan, N. (1980). The use of social science knowledge in policy decisions at the national level. In N. Caplan, *The utilization of the social sciences in policymaking in the U.S.* (pp. 161–217). Paris: Organization for Economic Cooperation and Development.

Cohen, U., & Moore, G.T. (1977). The organization and communication of behaviorally based research information. In L. Van Ryzin (Ed.), *Behavior-environment research methods* (pp. 77–93). Madison: University of Wisconsin-Madison, Institute for Environmental Studies.

Cohen, U., Moore, G.T., McGinty, T., & Armstrong, B.T. (1982). The spatial organization of an early childhood development center: Open space, zoning, and circulation. *Day Care Journal, 1,* 35–38.

Cooper, C.C. (1975). *Easter Hill Village: Some social implications for design.* New York: Free Press.

Craik, K.W. (1981). Environmental assessment and situational analysis. In D. Magnusson (Ed.), *Toward a psychology of situations: An interactional approach* (pp. 37–48). Hillsdale, N.J.: Erlbaum.

Evans, G.W. (1980). Environmental cognition. *Psychological Bulletin, 88,* 259–267.

Evans, G.W., Brennan, P.L., Skorpanich, M.A., & Held, D. (1984). Cognitive mapping and elderly adults: Verbal and location memory for urban landmarks. *Journal of Gerontology, 39,* 452–457.

Evans, G.W., & Pezdek, K. (1980). Cognitive mapping: Knowledge of real world distance and location information. *Journal of Experimental Psychology: Human Learning and Memory, 6,* 13–24.

Evans, G.W., Skorpanich, M.A., Gärling, T., Bryant, K., & Bresolin, B. (1984). The effects of pathway configuration, landmarks, and stress on environmental cognition. *Journal of Environmental Psychology, 4,* 323–335.

Evans, G.W., Smith, C., & Pezdek, K. (1982). Cognitive maps and urban form. *Journal of the American Planning Association, 48,* 232–244.

Farbstein, J., & Kantrowitz, M. (1991). Design research in the swamp: Toward a new paradigm. In E.H. Zube & G.T. Moore (Eds.), *Advances in environment, behavior, and design* (Vol. 3). New York and London: Plenum.

Fried, M., & Gleicher, P. (1961). Some sources of residential satisfaction in an urban slum. *Journal of the American Institute of Planners, 27,* 305–315.

Gärling, T., Böök, A., Lindberg, E., & Nilsson, T. (1981). Memory for the spatial layout of the everyday physical environment: Factors affecting the rate of acquisition. *Journal of Experimental Psychology: Human Learning and Memory, 1,* 263–277.

Gibson, J.J. (1979). *An ecological approach to visual perception.* Boston: Houghton Mifflin.

Golledge, R.G. (1975). *On determining cognitive configurations of a city.* Columbus, Ohio: Ohio State University Research Foundation, Department of Geography, Report #6S-37969.

Halprin, L. (1965). Motations. *Progressive Architecture, 46,* 126–133.

Halprin, L. (1969). Scores and notations. *The RSVP cycles: Creative process in the environment.* New York: Braziller.

Hanson, S. (1978). Measuring the cognitive levels of urban residents. *Geografiska Annaler B, 59,* 67–81.

Hanson, S. (1984). Environmental cognition and travel behavior. In D. Herbert & R. Johnston (Eds.), *Geography in the urban environment: Progress and research in applications* (pp. 95–126). London: Wiley.

Hart, R.A. (1979). *Children's experience of place.* New York: Irvington.

Hart, R.A. (1981). Children's spatial representation of the landscape: Lessons and questions from a field study. In L.S. Liben, A.H. Patterson, and N. Newcombe (Eds.), *Spatial representation and behavior across the life span* (pp. 195–233). New York: Academic Press.

Hart, R.A., & Moore, G.T. (1973). The development of spatial cognition: A review. In R.M. Downs & D. Stea (Eds.), *Image and environment: Cognitive mapping and spatial behavior* (pp. 246–288). Chicago: Aldine.

Hazen, N.L., & Durrett, M.E. (1982). Relationship of security of attachment to exploration and cognitive mapping abilities in 2-year olds. *Developmental Psychology, 18,* 751–759.

Heft, H. (1981). An examination of constructivist and Gibsonian approaches to environmental psychology. *Population and Environment, 4,* 227–245.

Horton, F., & Reynolds, D. (1969). An investigation of individual action spaces: A progress report. *Proceedings of the Association of American Geographers, 1,* 70–75.

Howell, S.C. (1980). *Designing for aging: Patterns of use.* Cambridge, Mass: MIT Press.

Hunt, M.E. (1984). Environmental learning without being there. *Environment and Behavior, 16,* 257–258.

Hunt, M.E., & Pastalan, L.A. (1987). Easing relocation: An environmental learning process. In V. Regnier & J. Pynoos (Eds.), *Housing the aged: Design directives and policy considerations* (pp. 421–440). New York: Elsevier.

Kaplan, R. (1976). Way-finding in the natural environment. In G.T. Moore & R.G. Golledge (Eds.), *Environmental knowing: Theories, research, and methods* (pp. 46–57). New York: Van Nostrand Reinhold.

Kaplan, S. (1975). An informal model for the prediction of preference. In E.H.

Zube, R.O. Brush, & J.G. Fabos (Eds.), *Landscape assessment* (pp. 92–101). New York: Van Nostrand Reinhold.

Kaplan, S., & Kaplan, R. (1982). *Cognition and environment.* New York: Praeger.

Koffka, K. (1922). Perception: An introduction to Gestalt Theorie. *Psychological Bulletin, 19,* 551–585.

Kosslyn, S.M., Pick, H.L., & Fariello, G.R. (1974). Cognitive maps in children and men. *Child Development, 45,* 707–716.

Krampen, M. (1991). Environmental meaning. In E.H. Zube & G.T. Moore (Eds.), *Advances in environment, behavior, and design* (Vol. 3). New York and London: Plenum.

Krantz, D.S., & Schulz, R. (1980). A model of life crisis, control, and health outcomes: Cardiac rehabilitation and relocation of the elderly. In A. Baum & J.E. Singer (Eds.), *Advances in environmental psychology* (Vol. 2, pp. 23–52). Hillsdale, N.J.: Erlbaum.

Lewin, K. (1946). Action research and minority problems. *Journal of Social Issues, 1–2,* 34–36.

Liben, L.S., Moore, M.L., & Goldbeck, S.L. (1982). Preschoolers' knowledge of their classroom environment: Evidence from small-scale and large-size spatial tasks. *Child Development, 53,* 1275–1284.

Lynch, K. (1960) *Image of the city.* Cambridge, Mass.: M.I.T. Press.

Mandler, J.M. (1979). Categorical and schematic organization in memory. In C.R. Puff (Ed.), *Memory organization and structure* (pp. 304–306). New York: Academic Press.

Mandler, J.M. (1984). *Stories, scripts, and scenes: Aspects of schema theories.* Hillsdale, N.J.: Erlbaum.

Mandler, J.M. (1988). The development of spatial cognition: On topological and Euclidian representation. In J. Stiles-Davis, M. Kritchevsky, & U. Bellugi (Eds.), *Spatial cognition: Brain bases and development* (pp. 423–432). Hillsdale, N.J.: Erlbaum.

Min, B.-H. (1987) *Relationship of strategic models and contexts to success of research utilization.* Unpublished dissertation proposal, Department of Architecture, University of Wisconsin-Milwaukee.

Min, B.-H. (1988). *The relationship of strategic models and contexts to success of research utilization: Analyses of selected case studies* (Unpublished doctoral dissertation, Department of Architecture, University of Wisconsin-Milwaukee). Ann Arbor, Mich: University Microfilms.

Moore, G.T. (1975). Research and design for persons-in-environments: An example from environmental cognition theory, research, and application. Paper presented at the College of Architecture and Urban Planning, University of Washington. Unpublished manuscript, School of Architecture and Urban Planning, University of Wisconsin-Milwaukee.

Moore, G.T. (1976). Theory and research on the development of environmental cognition. In G.T. Moore & R.G. Golledge (Eds.), *Knowing about environmental knowing: Theories, research, and methods* (pp. 138–164). New York: Van Nostrand Reinhold.

Moore, G.T. (1977). Cognitive representations: Research and implications for design. In P. Suedfeld & J.A. Russell (Eds.), *The behavioural basis of design*, Vol. 2 (pp. 61–63). Stroudsburg, Pa: Dowden, Hutchinson & Ross.

Moore, G.T. (1979). Knowing about environmental knowing: The current state of theory and research on environmental cognition. *Environment and Behavior, 11*, 33–70.

Moore, G.T. (1980). Holism, environmentalism, and the systems approach. *Man-Environment Systems, 10*, 11–21.

Moore, G.T. (1986). Effects of the spatial definition of behavior settings on children's behavior: A quasi-experimental field study. *Journal of Environmental Psychology, 6*, 205–231.

Moore, G.T. (1987). Environment-behavior research in North America: History, developments, and unresolved issues. In D. Stokols & I. Altman (Eds.), *Handbook of environmental psychology* (pp. 1359–1410). New York: Wiley.

Moore, G.T. (1987). The physical environment and cognitive development in child care centers. In C.S. Weinstein & T.G. David (Eds.), *Spaces for children: The built environment and child development* (pp. 41–72). New York and London: Plenum.

Moore, G.T. (1988, July). Two-community and one-community theories as means of thinking about research utilization. Paper presented at the 10th biennial conference of the Association for the Study of People and their Physical Surroundings, Delft, The Netherlands.

Moore, G.T. (1989). Theoretical perspectives on development and the environment: A paper in memory of Joachim Wohlwill. In S. Apner (Ed.), *Children in their environments*. Special issue of *Children's Environments Quarterly, 5*, 5–12.

Moore, G.T., Cohen, U., Van Ryzin, L., & Oertel, J. (1979). *Designing environments for handicapped children*. New York: Educational Facilities Laboratories.

Moore, G.T., Tuttle, D.P., & Howell, S.C. (1985). *Environmental design research directions: Process and prospects*. New York: Praeger.

Moore, R.C. (1986). *Childhood's domain: Play and place in child development*. London: Croom Helm.

Nicolini, C. (1985, December). *Il comportamento spaziale nei bambini da zero a tre anni*. Paper presented at the International Symposium "Rischio Psichico e Rischio Sociale en Eta' Evolutiva," Trento, Italy.

Passini, R. (1984). *Wayfinding in architecture*. New York: Van Nostrand Reinhold.

Piaget, J. (1950). *The psychology of intelligence*. London: Routledge and Kegan Paul.

Piaget, J. (1970). Piaget's theory. In P. Mussen (Ed.), *Carmichael's manual of child psychology* (Vol. 1, pp. 703–732). New York: Wiley.

Potter, R. (1979). Perception of urban retailing facilities: An analysis of consumer information fields. *Geografiska Annaler B, 61*, 19–29.

Potter, R. (1984). Consumer behavior and spatial cognition in relation to extraversion/introversion: Dimensions of personality. *Journal of Social Psychology, 123*, 29–34.

Rapoport, A. (1977). *Human aspects of urban form: Toward a man-environment approach to urban form and design*. London: Pergamon.

Rapoport, A., & Hawkes, R. (1970). The perception of urban complexity. *Journal of the American Institute of Planners, 36,* 106–111.

Sanoff, H. (1989). Advances in facility programming. In E.H. Zube & G.T. Moore (Eds.), *Advances in environment, behavior, and design* (Vol. 2). New York and London: Plenum.

Schneekloth, L. (1987). Advances in practice in environment, behavior, and design. In E.H. Zube & G.T. Moore (Eds.), *Advances in environment, behavior, and design* (Vol. 1, pp. 307–334). New York and London: Plenum.

Schon, D. (1983). *The reflective practitioner: How professionals think in action.* New York: Basic Books.

Seidel, A. (1982). Usable EBR: What can we learn from other fields? In P. Bart, A. Chen, & G. Francescato (Eds.), *Knowledge for design* (pp. 16–25). Washington, D.C.: Environmental Design Research Association.

Shemyakin, F.N. (1962). Orientation in space. In G.G. Anan'yev et al. (Eds.), *Psychological science in the USSR* (Vol. 1, pp. 184–255). Washington, D.C.: Office of Technical Services.

Siegel, A.H., & White, S.W. (1975). The development of spatial representations of large-scale environments. In H.W. Reese (Eds.), *Advances in child development and Behavior* (Vol. 1, pp. 37–45). New York: Academic Press.

Sommer, R. (1977). Action research. In D. Stokols (Ed.), *Perspectives on environment and behavior* (pp. 195–204). New York and London: Plenum.

Sommer, R. (1984). Action research is not business as usual. In D. Duerk & D. Campbell (Eds.), *The challenge of diversity* (pp. 3–8). Washington, D.C.: Environmental Design Research Association.

Susman, G.I., & Evered, R.D. (1978). An assessment of the scientific merits of action research. *Administrative Science Quarterly, 23,* 582–603.

Timmermans, H., & Golledge, R.G. (1988). *The relation between awareness spaces in information fields and actual behaviour.* Unpublished manuscript, Department of Economic Geography, Technical University, Eindhoven, The Netherlands.

Timmermans, H., Van der Heijden, R., & Westerveld, H. (1982). Decision-making between multiattribute choice alternatives: A model of spatial shopping behaviour using conjoint measurements. *Environment and Planning A, 16,* 377–387.

Valsiner, J. (1987). *Culture and the development of children's action: A cultural-historical theory of developmental psychology.* Chicester, England: Wiley.

Ventre, F.T. (1989). The policy environment for environment-behavior research. In E.H. Zube & G.T. Moore (Eds.), *Advances in environment, behavior, and design* (Vol. 2, pp. 317–342). New York and London: Plenum.

Weiss, C.H. (1977). *Using social research in public policymaking.* Lexington, Mass.: Heath.

Weiss, C.H. (1980). *Social science research and decision-making.* New York: Columbia University Press.

Weisman, G.D. (1983). Environmental programming and action research. *Environment and Behavior, 15,* 381–408.

Wener, R. (1989). Advances in evaluation of the built environment. In E.H. Zube

& G.T. Moore (Eds.), *Advances in environment, behavior, and design* (Vol. 2). New York and London: Plenum.

Wisner, B., Stea, D., & Kruks, S. (1991). Participatory and action research methods. In E.H. Zube & G.T. Moore (Eds.), *Advances in environment, behavior, and design* (Vol. 3). New York and London: Plenum.

IV

SUMMARY AND CONCLUSION

17

From Environmental
To Ecological Cognition

TOMMY GÄRLING, ERIK LINDBERG,
GUNILLA TORELL, AND GARY W. EVANS

In this book we have discussed how two subfields of environmental psychology—environmental cognition and assessment—are linked to each other as well as to research in related fields on decision making and action in real-world environments. We hope this discussion will stimulate integration of these heretofore unrelated fields of research. By integration we mean the establishment of a framework that shows how research in the different subfields fits together into some overall view of environmental psychology. Initially a framework of this kind must be established through analyses of existing research. The chapters in this book include such analyses. However, an integrative framework should eventually develop into a theory subject to empirical tests.

This final chapter analyzes what bearings the preceding chapters have on the possibility of integration across environmental cognition, assessment, and action. We will do this by discussing a number of obstacles to integration. In doing so, a tentative, integrative framework and an agenda for future research directions are proposed.

The basic motivation behind this book is that integration should lead to future, more promising research directions than currently available for understanding human–environment relationships. However, there are other benefits of integration as well. One additional such benefit is its potential value for applications through policy formation, planning, and design. Because applications have been and continue to be important to environmental psychology, a final section of the present chapter comments on this issue.

OBSTACLES TO INTEGRATION AND
HOW THEY CAN BE OVERCOME

The preceding chapters have revealed a number of potentially significant obstacles to the integration of research on cognition, assessment, and action in real-world environments. The most critical ones are that different researchers prefer different theoretical perspectives, that they, partly as a consequence of that, emphasize different aspects of their respective problems, and that they often prefer research paradigms that may make integration more difficult.

Integration of Theoretical Perspectives

A serious obstacle to integration across the different subfields of environmental cognition, assessment, and action is created by the low level of integration even within the subfields. Particularly striking are differences in theoretical perspectives. Such differences have far-reaching consequences because they determine how problems are framed, how hypotheses are formulated, and what research methods are chosen (Gärling & Golledge, 1989; Moore, 1987; Saegert & Winkel, 1990). In research on environmental assessment, a neuropsychological perspective is represented in the chapter by Küller (Chapter 7), a cognitive-motivational perspective in the chapter by R. Kaplan (Chapter 2), and a cognitive, information-processing perspective in the chapter by Axia, Mainardi Peron, and Baroni (Chapter 12). Exemplifying with chapters addressing life-span development there are, in addition to the chapter by Axia and colleagues, chapters by Liben (Chapter 13) and by Hart and Conn (Chapter 14). Liben represents a Piagetian developmental perspective and Hart and Conn a transactional perspective. The remaining four chapters by Golledge (Chapter 3), Timmermans (Chapter 4), Böök (Chapter 8), and S. Kaplan (Chapter 9) represent the information-processing perspective. The dominance of the latter perspective in the different chapters reflects its strong influence on research.

Despite the noted differences in theoretical perspectives both within and between subfields, these differences may be less than apparent at first glance. The cognitive-motivational theoretical perspective is not so different from the cognitive, information-processing perspective that they cannot be integrated. Attempts to extend the study of so-called "cold cognition" to motivational factors is recognized as an important, emerging area within psychological research (Bower, 1981; Hamilton & Warburton, 1979; Mandler, 1975). Arousal is a central concept in the neuropsychological approach discussed by Küller, as well as certainly being a topic that has been of great interest in cognitive psychology (Broadbent, 1971; Kahneman, 1973). Another important direction of current cognitive psychology appears to be the study of the neurological basis of cognitive processes (Rumelhart, Hinton, & McClelland, 1986).

The Piagetian developmental perspective is often treated as if it were very different from the information-processing perspective. However, at least one authorative source (Flavell, 1963) sees Piaget's theory as a good proponent of the information-processing approach in cognitive psychology. From the chapters by Axia and colleagues and Liben one can see that the use of a Piagetian developmental perspective in research on spatial cognition is, partly, dependent on the fact that Piaget did research on spatial cognition, whereas those representing the information-processing perspective have focused more, or exclusively, on language processing. Another important reason for adopting the Piagetian rather than the information-processing perspective is perhaps that the latter does not focus extensively on developmental issues.

The most serious difference in theoretical perspectives may be between the transactional perspective and the others. However, it is not easy to pinpoint the difference (Altman & Rogoff, 1987), except that a transactional perspective explicitly attempts to avoid fragmentation. A problem arises, however, if it thereby defies analysis. It can, on the other hand, become a fruitful perspective for our purpose if it fosters a new, more integrative kind of analysis.

Underlying the bulk of research on environmental cognition, assessment, and action, as well as our choice of sections for this volume, is a conceptual framework that defines the physical environment as one entity that affects another entity, the individual (or, possibly, aggregation of individuals), through mediating processes within the individual (or group). The broad questions asked in research coincide with our sections. As noted in the introductory chapter, research has thus in varying degrees investigated (1) how observable responses made by individuals relate to factors in the physical environment, (2) what psychological processes mediate between these observables, and (3) how the relationships between observables change due to changes in the mediating psychological processes, the specific process change we focus on being individuals' growth across the life span.

This central conceptual framework has been criticized because it does not encompass mutual effects of the social and physical environment and because it does not include the individual's influence on the environment (Cohen, Evans, Stokols, & Krantz, 1986). Even if it were not too difficult to counter such criticisms with modifications of the proposed framework, there are other reasons why it should be abandoned. One presently important reason is that it tends to preserve fragmentation.

Pressure on environmental psychology to contribute knowledge about how the physical environment affects people has led to an analysis of human–environment systems that takes as its starting point factors in the physical environment. If environmental psychology is to have a more profound impact on psychology (and its applications), then it needs to focus primarily on knowledge about the ecology of psychological processes such as cognition, assessment, and action. A related suggestion is made by Canter (Chapter 10). Taking his point of departure in action rather than in cognition, Canter views the concept of purpose as a possible integrator of cognition, assessment, and action. The link between action and purpose is perhaps the most obvious one. The very term action implies deliberation and goal orientation. Cognitions are seen as being shaped by the individual's purpose or plans for his or her actions in the environment. Assessment may then be best understood in terms of the purposes that different places are perceived to support or counteract. These points are further elaborated in the model proposed by Canter as a paradigm for research in environmental psychology, which he labels as cognitive ecology. In a discussion of place rules, environmental roles, and physical forms, he stresses the need to incorporate the social as well as the physical dimension in the study of environmental assessment, cognition, and action.

We would like to broaden Canter's notion of cognitive ecology to what may be termed ecological rather than environmental cognition, highlighting the need to study not only the ecological prerequisites for cognition but also the ecology of the cognitive processes themselves. This will bring environmental psychology closer to ecological psychology (Kaminski, 1989) with its roots in the pioneering work of Barker (1968), Brunswik (1956), and Gibson (1979). The unique contribution of environmental psychology should be to emphasize (but not to treat exclusively) physical aspects of the environment. An appropriate focus is individuals' overall functioning or adjustment in their environments and the role the physical aspects of these environments play in that functioning. Adjustment processes would then be a better term than cognitive processes. These processes include cognition, assessment, and action. It is also important to extend the time dimension. This requires a control-theory perspective in which actions are viewed as controlled by negative feedback loops (Carver & Scheier, 1981, 1990; Powers, 1973). As Figure 17.1 illustrates, an individual (or a group of individuals) has certain purposes or goals that he or she tries to attain over time. He or she perceives, judges, assesses, and acts in the interest of attaining these goals. Acting may change the environment so that it facilitates goal attainment. The adjustment processes may furthermore change the individual to make him or her more able to adjust in the future. If the individual is unsuccessful in adjusting, he or she may change his or her goals.

Our emphasis on individuals' overall functioning in the environment has a clear counterpart in research on life-span development. As Spencer (Chapter 15) stresses, this perspective can enrich our attempts at integration by emphasizing the importance of individual differences and the continuity of the individual throughout life. He further gives an account of how environmental tasks and inputs change across the life span, and of how, as a consequence, cognition, assessment, and action may be expected to change. The life-span-development perspective provides a testing ground for examining many of the theoretical relationships between cognition, assessment, and action in the environment proposed in several other chapters in this volume.

If research is to be conducted on adjustment processes, then cognition, assessment, and action should be viewed as integrated. Thus an important question becomes exactly how? Do we have another concept that covers these processes when they work together? Zimring and Gross (Chapter 5) suggest the concept of schema. Although it is difficult to give an exact definition of schema, the term is commonly used to refer to the general knowledge a person possesses about a particular domain (Alba & Hasher, 1983). In the present context, relevant domains could be different types of places or behavioral settings. A knowledge-based definition of schema, however, is not particularly useful for our present purpose since it focuses exclusively on cognition. Zimring and Gross try to overcome this limitation by showing how assessment and action may be seen as components of schemata. For instance, moderately atypical instances of a schema may be experienced as pleasing. Although the role of schemata as the basis for action is less clearly spelled out, it nevertheless seems reasonable to think of many schemata as involving action components. Other similar terms which have been used more often to refer to actions are scripts or plans (Anderson, 1983).

In our opinion plan may be a better concept than schema (Brand, 1984; Gärling, Böök, & Lindberg, 1984; Miller, Galanter, & Pribram, 1960; Russell & Ward, 1982) for integrating cognition, assessment, and action because of its focus on action. A

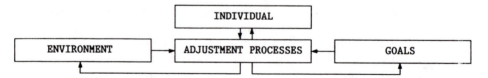

Figure 17.1. Schematic illustration of how the processes of cognition, assessment, and action accomplish an individual's (or group's of individuals) adjustment to his or her (sociophysical) environment.

plan is thus a broader concept that entails the current goals, means to attain those goals, and procedures for assessing how successful the means are in attaining the goals. Different schemata and scripts may play a crucial role in the execution of plans. Thus much could possibly be learned about individuals' adjustments to their environments through investigations of the plans they are executing.

Integration of Concepts, Principles, and Facts

Another avenue to integration would be to find communalities between concepts, principles, and facts across environmental cognition, assessment, and action. It may be presumed that different theoretical perspectives imply different views. There is therefore a possibility that relevant concepts, principles, and facts in a neighboring subfield (or, for that matter, in the same subfield) are overlooked. Taking as a point of departure the integrative theoretical perspective we have advocated, such omissions may stand out more clearly. Three examples that we find particularly striking will be given below.

As is evident from the chapters by R. Kaplan (Chapter 2) and Küller (Chapter 7), research on environmental assessment includes what may be termed descriptive (and predictive), not only evaluative, responses. Descriptive responses are also investigated in environmental cognition (see Golledge, Chapter 3). The reason why these research traditions are disconnected is perhaps that in the former spatial aspects tend to be deemphasized. It may be significant that when Axia and colleagues (Chapter 12) discuss scene schemata, they mention only in passing that such schema are, in fact, presumed to also contain spatial information. As discussed in the introductory chapter, a linkage can perhaps be made here with the concept of a cognitive map. However, there are also differences that would be of interest to disentangle. Spatial extension is such an important aspect of the real-world environment that it is surprising it is often overlooked in research on environmental assessment. Several issues suggest themselves. For instance, what differences in place experiences are conveyed by different spatial arrangements and how are these perceived and evaluated? In answering such questions knowledge about how spatial information is perceived and remembered, which has been accumulated in environmental cognition research (Gärling & Golledge, 1989), should be directly relevant.

The other side of the coin represents our second example: In research on environmental cognition knowledge of places has largely been ignored. Furthermore, memory (for spatial information) as opposed to perception and assessment has been stressed too much. Böök (Chapter 8), in trying a fresh start, analyzes environmental cognition as spatiotemporal events with the aim of finding out how different subprocesses are integrated in such real-life events that represent individuals' adjustments. Even though Böök's approach could very well serve as a model, it has shortcomings in the context we are discussing. It is true that Böök notes the fallacy of treating places as points in space, but he does not go far enough in his analysis of place knowledge. One way of doing this would be to evoke processes of selective attention, recognition, classification, and assessment or appraisal (S. Kaplan & R. Kaplan, 1982). Such processes are discussed in the literature on environmental assessment (see R. Kaplan in Chapter 2 and Küller in Chapter 7), thus there should be ample opportunities to apply theories and facts from that subfield.

Our final example is taken from research on decisions and choices as conceptualized by Timmermans in Chapter 4 of this volume. In the usual research paradigm actions are conceived of as the implementation of choices between action alternatives. The actual research has predominantly focused on the rule the decision maker uses when choosing between the alternatives. Drawing on the convincing criticisms by S. Kaplan (Chapter 9) of the psychologically narrow theoretical underpinnings of the research, we feel it is justified to argue that both research on memory for spatial information (environmental cognition research) and on how places are assessed (environmental assessment research) should have much to contribute. In fact, as reviewed in Golledge and Timmermans (1990) and Timmermans and Golledge (1990), there are several examples of recent research projects focusing on how decision alternatives (e.g., different locations) are assessed. For instance, studies have used methods for research on environmental assessment to find out how people perceive and assess shopping locations which they choose among. However, how spatial information is remembered appears to remain largely neglected (Gärling & Golledge, 1989).

With these three examples we hope to demonstrate the value of a common integrative framework for future attempts at integration of concepts, principles, and facts. It is this kind of integration that ultimately must take place.

An Integrative Research Paradigm

An obviously important question to discuss here is whether there are paradigms that foster integrative research more than others. It has been argued that case studies (Hart & Conn, Chapter 14; Küller, Chapter 7) may constitute a research strategy that facilitates integration. Spencer (Chapter 15) also seems to think that research on life-span development may have this property. Zube (Chapter 6) mentions postoccupancy evaluation research as a possible integrative research paradigm.

Our general view on this matter is that an integrative framework has to be established first. The availability of such a framework then leads to the search for research paradigms that make possible empirical evaluation. Is a research paradigm of this kind available? The closest example we can find is that employed in research on decision making (see Timmermans, Chapter 4). As mentioned briefly above, in this research paradigm actions are conceived of as the implementation of choices between action alternatives that are assessed by the decision maker, relative to some objectives, on the basis of his or her knowledge of these alternatives. Thus both environmental cognition and assessment are investigated as related to each other and to actions. The same may be accomplished in case studies, in studies of life-span development, or in postoccupancy evaluations. However, in these cases the integrative feature is not an indispensable part of the paradigm.

If the paradigm for research on decision making is taken as a first approximation to what we are looking for, it may be fruitful to constructively criticize it, taking the proposed integrative framework as our point of departure. As illustrated in Chapter 4 by Timmermans, the decision-making paradigm can be used for detailed analyses of how cognitive and affective factors contribute to specific decisions, for instance, of where to carry out daily shopping. However, as pointed out by Gärling (1989), a serious criticism from our point of view is that an analysis of a particular action or decision that an individual undertakes, even though integrating it with cognition and assessment, gives a fragmented picture of the individual's adjustment, which is accomplished through many actions executed over time. In the example above concerning shopping, we would, for instance, also like to know what other decisions and choices are related to the decision of where to do the shopping, and what utility for the individual's psychological adjustment this set of decisions has. As alluded to earlier, a complementary analysis of individuals' plans may be a possibility.

The paradigm may furthermore be too individualistic. Canter (Chapter 10), Spencer (Chapter 15), and Zimring and Gross (Chapter 5) all seem to agree that integration will entail greater emphasize on the role of the social environment. However, there are many ways of doing this. For instance, without basically changing the paradigm, the study of decisions could be and has been extended to groups. Other social factors influencing decision making, such as shared cognitions and assessments, norms, and role prescriptions, may be conceptualized as being taken into account by an individual decision maker, either as constraints on the set of decision alternatives or as heuristic rules used by him or her in making decisions (Fischhoff, Svenson, & Slovic, 1987).

Still another feature of the decision-making paradigm that can be criticized is the assumption that actions are invariably preceded by deliberate decisions. Furthermore, the process of assessing or evaluating action alternatives may neither be as serial (Neisser, 1976; Rumelhart, et al., 1986) nor as deliberate as seems to be implied (Küller, Chapter 7; Ulrich, 1983; Zajonc, 1980). Rather than using an explicit decision rule people may choose on the basis of their affective reactions to action alternatives. The repeated execution of plans already formed (habit or routine) is furthermore an obvious reason why a particular observed choice sometimes is made without deliberation.

It should be clear then that the decision-making research paradigm has shortcomings. One of its virtues is in fact that it makes these shortcomings obvious. At the same time a discussion of them raises several interesting research questions. We feel that research addressing these questions will contribute not only to an improved integrative framework but eventually to a theory that makes important statements about the role of physical factors for individuals' adjustments to their environments.

INTEGRATION AND APPLICATION

Solving practical problems is not in general an immediate goal of science. On the other hand, one important reason why environmental psychology came into existence was its concern with deteriorating environmental quality (Evans, 1982; Proshansky & O'Hanlon, 1977; Stokols, 1977). It is natural then to ask how the research findings in this area can be used. The preceding chapters by Zube (Chapter 6), Weissman (Chapter 11), and Moore (Chapter 16) have dealt in a general way with this question.

It is important to note the distinction between conceptual and instrumental applications (Seidel, 1985; Weiss, 1980). The latter is described as a direct utilization of research findings to solve specific practical problems. Conceptual applications are, in contrast, seen as indirect, involving an increased understanding, which is implemented in a less formal way. It is tempting to think of the latter as being most affected by integration.

As Zube (Chapter 6) and Moore (Chapter 16) point out and exemplify, there are many findings from research on environmental assessment and cognition that have clear, specific implications for the design of physical environments for people. In what way would such specific applications be improved if the mentioned subfields were better integrated? Taking again our suggested integrative framework as a point of departure, we feel that a greater concern with individuals' overall functioning or adjustment should result. Thus rather than asking narrow questions, for instance, about how people would assess as certain way of designing an environment, it should lead to raising broader issues, such as if a certain way of designing an environment facilitates different people's goals. Furthermore, how the physical environment affects the social environment, which in turn affects people, as well as how people change the physical and social environments are other issues that may be raised. Whether more specific suggestions, at the instrumental level, will also result is highly dependent on whether viable, integrative research emerges.

SUMMARY AND CONCLUSIONS

On the basis of discussions in preceding chapters of this work, this final chapter proposes a framework that goes some way to provide an integrated picture of cognition, assessment, and action in real-world environments. The term ecological cognition is preferred to environmental cognition to emphasize that the focus is on individuals' (or groups' of individuals) overall functioning or adjustment in their everyday environments. Cognition, assessment, and action are viewed as integrated means by which individuals strive to attain the goals they have. The task of environmental psychology is to disentangle the role of the physical environment in this process of adjustment or goal attainment. An accompanying goal is to provide guidelines for how the physical environment can be changed to facilitate individual (or group) adjustment.

Whereas the framework defines an integrated theoretical perspective, further work is needed to integrate concepts, principles, and facts across each of the separate subfields. Examples of directions in which such integration seems feasible are given. It should, however, be emphasized that integration at this level requires research. A paradigm for such integrative research is found in the subfield of decision-making research but a critical analysis, within the proposed integrative framework, yields many potential shortcomings. The decision-making research paradigm may still be instrumental in the attainment of the goal of eventually replacing the proposed integrative framework with an integrative theory.

The concern of environmental psychology with using established research findings to improve or maintain the quality of environments may also be addressed more adequately by further integration of the subfields of environmental cognition, assessment, and action. We believe that a greater concern with different individuals' overall adjustment in different environments would result.

REFERENCES

Alba, J.W., & Hasher, L. (1983). Is memory schematic? *Psychological Bulletin, 93*, 203–231.

Altman, I., & Rogoff, B. (1987). World views in psychology: Trait, interactional, organismic, and transactional perspectives. In D. Stokols & I. Altman (Eds.), *Handbook of environmental psychology* (Vol. 1, pp. 7–40). New York: Wiley.

Anderson, J.R. (1983). *The architecture of cognition.* Cambridge, Mass.: Harvard University Press.

Barker, R.G. (1968). *Ecological psychology.* Stanford, Calif.: Stanford University Press.

Bower, G.H. (1981). Mood and memory. *American Psychologist, 17*, 911–926.

Brand, M. (1984). *Intending and acting: Towards a naturalized action theory.* Cambridge, Mass.: MIT Press.

Broadbent, D. (1971). *Decision and stress.* New York: Academic Press.

Brunswik, E. (1956). *Perception and the representative design of psychological experiments.* Berkeley: University of California Press.

Carver, C.S., & Scheier, M.F. (1981). *Attention and self-regulation: A control theory approach to human behavior.* New York: Springer.

Carver, C.S., & Scheier, M.F. (1990). Origins and functions of positive and negative affect: A control-process view. *Psychological Review, 97*, 19–35.

Cohen, S., Evans, G.W., Stokols, D., & Krantz, D.J. (1986). *Behavior, health, and environmental stress.* New York: Plenum.

Evans, G.W. (Ed.) (1982). *Environmental stress.* New York: Cambridge University Press.

Fischhoff, B., Svenson, O., & Slovic, P. (1987). Active response to environmental hazards: Perceptions and decision making. In D. Stokols & I. Altman (Eds.), *Handbook of environmental psychology* (Vol. 2, pp. 1089–1133). New York: Wiley.

Flavell, J.H. (1963). *The developmental psychology of Jean Piaget.* New York: Van Nostrand Reinhold.

Gärling, T. (1989, March). *Attempts at integration within environmental psychology.* Paper presented at a conference of environmental psychology, Universitat de les Illes Balears, Palma De Mallorca, Spain.

Gärling, T., Böök, A., & Lindberg, E. (1984). Cognitive mapping of large-scale environments: The interrelationships of action plans, acquisition, and orientation. *Environment and Behavior, 16*, 3–34.

Gärling, T., & Golledge, R.G. (1989). Environmental perception and cognition. In E.H. Zube & G.T. Moore (Eds.), *Advances in environment, behavior, and design* (Vol. 2, pp. 203–236). New York: Plenum.

Gibson, J.J. (1979). *The ecological approach to visual perception.* Boston: Houghton Mifflin.

Golledge, R.G., & Timmermans, H. (1990). Applications of behavioral research on spatial problems. I. Cognition, *Progress in Human Geography, 19*, 57–99.

Hamilton, V., & Warburton, D.M. (Eds.) (1979). *Human stress and cognition.* Chicester: Wiley.

Kahneman, D. (1973). *Attention and effort*. Englewood Cliffs, N.J.: Prentice-Hall.

Kaminski, G. (1989). The relevance of ecologically oriented conceptualizations to theory building in environment and behavior research. In E.H. Zube & G.T. Moore (Eds.), *Advances in environment, behavior, and design* (Vol. 2, pp. 3–36). New York: Plenum.

Kaplan, S., & Kaplan, R. (1982). *Cognition and environment*. New York: Praeger.

Mandler, G. (1975). *Mind and emotion*. New York: Wiley.

Moore, G.T. (1987). Environment and behavior research in North America: History, developments, and unresolved issues. In D. Stokols & I. Altman (Eds.), *Handbook of environmental psychology* (Vol. 2, pp. 1359–1410). New York: Wiley.

Miller, G.A., Galanter, E., & Pribram, K.H. (1960). *Plans and the structure of behavior*. New York: Holt, Rinehart & Winston.

Neisser, U. (1976). *Cognition and reality*. San Francisco: Freeman.

Powers, W.T. (1973). *Behavior: The control of perception*. Chicago: Aldine.

Proshansky, H.M., & O'Hanlon, T. (1977). Environmental psychology: Origins and development. In D. Stokols (Ed.), *Perspectives on environment and behavior* (pp. 101–129). New York: Plenum.

Rumelhart, D.E., Hinton, G.E., & McClelland, J.L. (1986). A general framework for parallell distributed processing. In D.E. Rumelhart, J.L. McClelland, & the PDP Research Group (Eds.), *Parallel distributed processing: Explorations in the microstructure of cognition* (Vol. 1, pp. 45–76). Cambridge, Mass.: MIT Press.

Russell, J.A., & Ward, L.M. (1982). Environmental psychology. *Annual Review of Psychology, 33,* 651–688.

Saegert, S., & Winkel, G. (1990). Environmental psychology. *Annual Review of Psychology, 41,* 441–477.

Seidel, A.D. (1985). What is success in E&B research utilization? *Environment and Behavior, 17,* 47–70.

Stokols, D. (1977). Origins and directions of environment-behavior research. In D. Stokols (Ed.), *Perspectives on environment and behavior* (pp. 5–36). New York: Plenum.

Timmermans, H., & Golledge, R.G. (1990). Applications of behavioural research on spatial problems. II. Preference and choice. *Progress in Human Geography, 14,* 311–354.

Ulrich, R.S. (1983). Aesthetic and affective response to natural environment. In I. Altman & J.F. Wohlwill (Eds.), *Human behavior and environment* (Vol. 6, pp. 85–125). New York: Plenum Press.

Weiss, C.H. (1980). *Social science research and decision making*. New York: Columbia University Press.

Zajonc, R.B. (1980). Feeling and thinking: Preferences need no inferences. *American Psychologist, 35,* 151–175.

Name Index

Subject Index